Writing
Research
Papers

Why Do You Need This New Edition?

Five good reasons why you should buy this new edition of *Writing Research Papers*!

1. **Updated MLA and APA coverage** brings you up to speed with the latest revisions to the two most commonly assigned documentation styles. Both MLA and APA now handle electronic sources differently than in the past, and this new edition provides all the details.

2. **New advice on plagiarism** to help you better understand what is and is not plagiarism. New strategies and advice help you avoid the traps of "unintentional plagiarism."

3. **New visual checklist on using databases** in Chapter 5 shows you exactly how to use database searches to go beyond Google and find credible sources your teachers will love.

4. **New sample research proposals and research papers** show you what the final product should look like, whether you are using MLA or APA style.

5. **Updated coverage of online research strategies** to help you decide if and when to use Google, Wikipedia, or other search engines, including detailed advice on where to find respected scholarly sources.

PEARSON

Writing Research Papers

A Complete Guide

Thirteenth Edition

James D. Lester

James D. Lester, Jr.
Austin Peay State University

Longman

New York San Francisco Boston
London Toronto Sydney Tokyo Singapore Madrid
Mexico City Munich Paris Cape Town Hong Kong Montreal

Senior Vice President and Publisher: Joseph Opiela
Senior Development Editor: Michael Greer
Senior Supplements Editor: Donna Campion
Senior Media Producer: Stefanie Liebman
Senior Marketing Manager: Susan Stoudt
Production Manager: Bob Ginsberg
Project Coordination, Text Design, and Electronic Page Makeup:
    Electronic Publishing Services, Inc.
Senior Cover Design Manager/Designer: Nancy Danahy
Cover Photos: *(left)* © Chris Schmidt/iStockphoto, *(upper right)* © Bart Coenders/iStockphoto, *(lower right)* © Willie B. Thomas/iStockphoto
Visual Researcher: Rona Tuccillo
Senior Manufacturing Buyer: Dennis J. Para
Printer and Binder: Quebecor World/Taunton
Cover Printer: The Lehigh Press, Inc.

For permission to use copyrighted material, grateful acknowledgment is made to the copyright holders on page 384, which are hereby made part of this copyright page.

Library of Congress Cataloging-in-Publication Data

Lester, James D., [date].
    Writing research papers: a complete guide / James D. Lester; James D. Lester, Jr. — 13th ed.
        p.   cm.
    Includes bibliographical references and index.
    ISBN-13: 978-0-205-65192-4 (pbk.)
    ISBN-10: 0-205-65192-5 (pbk.)
    ISBN-13: 978-0-205-65191-7 (spiral)
    ISBN-10: 0-205-65191-7 (spiral)
1. Report writing—Handbooks, manuals, etc.   2. Research—Handbooks,
manuals, etc.   I. Lester, James D., 1959-   II. Title.
    LB2369.L4 2009
    808′.02–dc22   2008031895

www.pearsonhighered.com

Longman
is an imprint of

12345678910—QWT—12 11 10 09

(paperbound edition) ISBN 13: 978-0-205-65192-4
                      ISBN 10:   0-205-65192-5
(tabbed edition) ISBN 13: 978-0-205-65191-7
                 ISBN 10:   0-205-65191-7

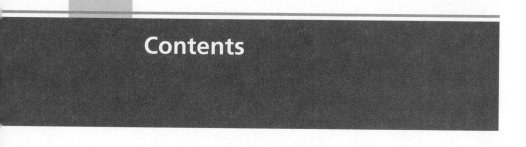

Contents

CHAPTER 7   Understanding and Avoiding Plagiarism   94

CHAPTER 8   Reading and Evaluating Sources   107

CHAPTER 9   Writing Effective Notes and Creating Outlines   132

CHAPTER 12 Writing the Introduction, Body, and Conclusion   194

CHAPTER 13 Revising, Proofreading, and Formatting the Rough Draft   213

Preface

Since 1967 this text has kept students and instructors current with academic styles of writing and documentation. Now, the new thirteenth edition brings even more updates to assist the student researcher in keeping pace with electronic publishing.

What's New to This Edition?

To stay current with rapid changes in the nature and practices of academic research, the increasing diversity of electronic sources, as well as recent, substantive changes in the major documentation styles, this edition includes the following new and updated coverage:

- Updated MLA documentation coverage: The Modern Language Association published the third edition of its *MLA Style Manual and Guide to Scholarly Publishing* in 2008, significantly revising its documentation style for both print and electronic sources. An updated edition of the MLA student research handbook is expected in 2009. All sample citations and student papers in Chapters 1 through 14 reflect the new MLA style guidelines.
- Updated APA documentation coverage: The American Psychological Association supplemented the fifth edition of its style guide in 2007 with the publication of the *APA Style Guide to Electronic References,* which revises and updates the information in the fifth edition of the APA *Publication Manual*. All sample citations and student papers in Chapter 15 reflect these changes.
- New and expanded coverage of plagiarism: Beginning with a new section in Chapter 1, "Understanding and Avoiding Plagiarism," this edition clearly explains what plagiarism is and presents strategies students can use to avoid unintentional plagiarism, with a special focus on how to use and document Internet sources.
- New material on using databases: Highlighted by a new visual checklist in Chapter 5, with sample screenshots illustrating the steps in database searches, this edition devotes more attention than ever before to library databases and search strategies to use in finding and evaluating database sources.
- New sample student papers: New, fully annotated sample research papers in both MLA and APA style present current models of proper presentation and format in each major documentation style.

Help with Electronic Research and Presentation

Computers and the electronic revolution are so pervasive in research writing today that a single chapter cannot properly encompass such work. Instead, every chapter of the text touches on various aspects of the Internet's effect on topic searches, discovery of source material, gathering notes and drafting the paper, plagiarism and academic integrity, and, of course, documentation of the sources.

Compounding the problem is that the style guides each advance a different method for documenting electronic sources, making a guide of this sort vital to students who move from class to class and thus from one discipline to another.

Nevertheless, *Writing Research Papers: A Complete Guide* takes the students step by step through the various documentation forms of Internet sources. It also spends considerable space in helping students blend electronic citations into their writing. A checklist, "Evaluating Online Sources," helps students gauge the quality of Internet articles.

Student Papers

Student writing examples show how young writers researched and drafted papers on a wide range of topics. With seven annotated sample papers, more than any other text of this nature, this text demonstrates format, documentation, and the different academic styles.

Anthony Murphy "Wilfred Owen – Battlefront Poet" (MLA Style)

Kaci Holz "Gender Communication" (MLA style)

Caitlin Kelley "More Academics for the Cost of Less Engaged Children" (APA style)

Jamie Johnston "Prehistoric Wars: We've Always Hated Each Other" (CMS style)

Sarah Bemis "Diabetes Management: A Delicate Balance" (CSE style)

"Annotated Bibliography: Gender Communication" (MLA style)

Kaci Holz "Gender Communication: A Review of the Literature" (MLA style)

Sample abstracts in MLA and APA style are also displayed. Additional sample research papers are available in the *Instructor's Manual, Model Research Papers from across the Curriculum*, and on the MyCompLab.

Reference Works by Topic

The list of references in Appendix B, "Finding Reference Works for Your General Topic," provides a user-friendly list of sources for launching your research project. Arranged into ten general categories, as listed on page 377, Appendix B allows a student who is examining an issue in health, fitness, or athletics to have quick access to relevant library books, library databases, and Internet sites.

Additional Resources

The NEW MyCompLab Website. The new MyCompLab integrates the market-leading instruction, multimedia tutorials, and exercises for writing, grammar and research that users have come to identify with the program with a new online composing space and new assessment tools. The result is a revolutionary application that offers a seamless and flexible teaching and learning environment built specifically for writers. Created after years of extensive research and in partnership with composition faculty and students across the country, the new MyCompLab provides help for writers in the context of their writing, with instructor and peer commenting functionality, proven tutorials and exercises for writing, grammar and research, an e-portfolio, an assignment-builder, a bibliography tool, tutoring services, and a gradebook and course management organization created specifically for writing classes. Visit www.mycomplab.com com for more information.

Interactive E-book. An e-book version of *Writing Research Papers* is also available in MyCompLab. This online version integrates the many resoures of MyCompLab into the text to create an enriched, interactive learning experience for writing students.

Instructor's Manual. This handy guide contains chapter-by-chapter classroom exercises, research assignmens, quizzes, and handouts. Available to instructors upon request.

Acknowledgments

The preface would not be complete without the recognition of many key people who served in the development of *Writing Research Papers: A Complete Guide*, Thirteenth Edition.

As you will see in the text and the ancillary material, thanks is extended to several students: Anthony Murphy, Sarah Bemis, Jamie Johnston, Kaci Holz, and Caitlin Kelly.

For editorial assistance that kept us focused, special thanks are extended to the Longman group headed by Joe Opiela, Senior Vice President and Publisher. Sincere appreciation must go to Michael Greer, Senior Development Editor; and Lake Lloyd, Production Editor. Finally we want to recognize a great group of reviewers who offered penetrating and perceptive suggestions for this new edition: Emory Reginald Abbot, Georgia Perimeter College; Lauren Bishop-Weidner, Ball State University; Michelle Buchberger, Franklin University; Cheryl Clark, Miami-Dade College; Richard Hunt, Delaware Valley College; Marshall Myers, Eastern Kentucky University; Michael Pennell, University of Long Island; Christy Rieger, Mercyhurst College; Melanie Thomas, Three Rivers Community College; Katrina Parker Williams, Wilson Community College.

Heartfelt appreciation is also extended to the members of our family: Martha, Mark, Caleb, and Sarah. Their love and patience made this project possible.

JAMES D. LESTER, JR.
JAMES.LESTER@CMCSS.NET

1 Writing from Research

Communication begins when we make an initial choice to speak or to record our ideas in writing. When we speak, our words disappear quickly, so we are often lax about our grammar because no record of what we say remains. The written word, however, creates a public record of our knowledge, our opinions, and our skill with language, so we try to make our writing accurate, forceful, and honest.

Regardless of the writer's experience or the instructor's expert direction, writing is a demanding process that requires commitment. Discovering a well-focused topic, and more importantly a reason for writing about it, begins the process. Choosing a format, exploring sources through critical reading, and then completing the writing task with grace and style are daunting tasks.

Despite this, writing is an outlet for the inquisitive and creative nature in each of us. Our writing is affected by the richness of our language, by our background and experiences, by our targeted audience, and by the form of expression that we choose. With perceptive enthusiasm for relating detailed concepts and honest insights, we discover the power of our own words. The satisfaction of writing well and relating our understanding to others provides intellectual stimulation and insight into our own beliefs and values.

As a college student, you will find that your writing assignments will extend past personal thoughts and ideas to explore more complex topics. Writing will make you confident in your ability to find information and present it effectively in all kinds of ways and for all sorts of projects, such as:

- A theme in a first-year composition course on the value of Web logs, online journals, and other online discussion groups.
- A paper in history on Herbert Hoover's ineffectual policies for coping with the Great Depression of the early 1930s.
- A report for a physical fitness class on the benefits of ballroom dancing as exercise.
- A sociological field report on free and reduced-cost lunches for school-aged children.
- A brief biographical study of a famous person, such as labor leader César Chávez.

All of these papers require some type of "researched writing." Papers similar to these will appear on your schedule during your first two years of college and increase in frequency in upper-division courses. This book takes off the pressure—it shows you how to research "online discussion groups" or "the Great Depression," and it demonstrates the correct methods for documenting the sources.

We conduct informal research all the time. We examine various models and their options before buying a car, and we check out another person informally before proposing or accepting a first date. We sometimes search the classified ads to find a summer job, or we roam the mall to find a new tennis racket, the right pair of sports shoes, or the latest CD. Research, then, is not foreign to us. It has become commonplace to use a search engine to explore the Internet for information on any subject—from personal concerns, such as the likely side effects of a prescribed drug, to complex issues, such as robotics or acupuncture.

In the classroom, we begin thinking about a serious and systematic activity, one that involves the library, the Internet, or field research. A research paper, like a personal essay, requires you to choose a topic you care about and are willing to invest many hours in thinking about. However, unlike a personal essay, a research paper requires you to develop your ideas by gathering an array of information, reading sources critically, and collecting notes. As you pull your project together, you will continue to express personal ideas, but now they are supported by and based on the collective evidence and opinions of experts on the topic.

Each classroom and each instructor will make different demands on your talents, yet all stipulate *researched writing*. Your research project will advance your theme and provide convincing proof for your inquiry.

- *Researched writing* grows from investigation.
- *Researched writing* establishes a clear purpose.
- *Researched writing* develops analysis for a variety of topics.

Writing Research Papers introduces research as an engaging, sometimes exciting pursuit on several fronts—your personal knowledge, ideas gleamed from printed and electronic sources, and research in the field.

1a   Why Do Research?

Instructors ask you to write a research paper for several reasons:

Research teaches methods of discovery. Explanation on a topic prompts you to discover what you know on a topic and what others can teach you. Beyond reading, it often expects you to venture into the field for interviews, observation, and experimentation. The process tests your curiosity as you probe a complex subject. You may not arrive at any final answers or solutions, but you will come to understand the different views on a subject. In your final paper, you will synthesize your ideas and discoveries with the knowledge and opinions of others.

Research teaches investigative skills. A research project requires you to investigate a subject, gain a grasp of its essentials, and disclose your findings. Your success will depend on your negotiating the various sources of information, from reference books in the library to computer databases and from special archival collections to the most recent articles in printed periodicals. The Internet, with its vast quantity of information, will challenge you to find reliable sources. If you conduct research by observation, interviews, surveys, and laboratory experiments, you will discover additional methods of investigation.

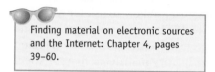

Finding material on electronic sources and the Internet: Chapter 4, pages 39–60.

Research develops inquiry-based techniques. With the guidance of your instructor, you are making inquiry to advance your own knowledge as well as increase the data available for future research by others.

Research teaches critical thinking. As you wade through the evidence on your subject, you will learn to discriminate between useful information and unfounded or ill-conceived comments. Some sources, such as the Internet, will provide timely, reliable material but may also entice you with worthless and undocumented opinions.

Research teaches logic. Like a judge in the courtroom, you must make perceptive judgments about the issues surrounding a specific topic. Your decisions, in effect, will be based on the wisdom gained from research of the subject. Your paper and your readers will rely on your logical response to your reading, observation, interviews, and testing.

Research teaches the basic ingredients of argument. In most cases, a research paper requires you to make a claim and support it with reasons and evidence. For example, if you argue that "urban sprawl has invited wild animals into our backyards," you will learn to anticipate challenges to your theory and to defend your assertion with evidence.

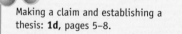

Making a claim and establishing a thesis: **1d**, pages 5–8.

1b Learning the Conventions of Academic Writing

Researched writing in each discipline follows certain conventions—that is, special forms are required for citing sources and designing pages. These rules make uniform the numerous articles written internationally by millions of scholars. The society of language and literature scholars, the Modern Language Association, has a set of guidelines generally known as MLA style. Similarly, the American Psychological Association has its own APA style. Other groups of scholars prefer a footnote system, while still others use a numbering system. These variations are not meant to confuse; they have evolved within disciplines as the preferred style.

What is important for you, right now, is to determine which documentation style to use. Many composition instructors will ask you to use MLA style, as explained in Chapters 11–14, but they are just as likely to ask for APA style (Chapter 15) if your topic concerns one of the social sciences. In a like manner, your art history instructor might expect the footnote style but could just as easily request the APA style. Ask your instructor early which style to use and organize accordingly.

MLA Style, pages 239–281
APA Style, pages 282–309
Chicago (CMS) Style, pages 310–337
CSE Style, pages 338–357

1c   Understanding and Avoiding Plagiarism

The most important convention of academic writing is the principle of giving proper credit to the work of others. **Plagiarism is defined as the act of claiming the words or ideas of another person as your own.** Plagiarism is a serious violation of the ethical standards of academic writing and most colleges and universities have strict penalties, including academic probation or expulsion, for students who are guilty of plagiarism. Most schools publish an official code of student conduct (sometimes called an academic

---

CHECKLIST

Avoiding Unintentional Plagiarism

The following guidelines will help you avoid unintentional plagiarism.

- **Citation.** Let readers know when you borrow from a source by introducing a quotation or paraphrase with the name of its author.
- **Quotation marks.** Enclose within quotation marks all quoted words, phrases, and sentences.
- **Paraphrase.** Provide a citation to indicate the source of a paraphrase just as you do for quotations.
- **Parenthetical citations and notes.** Use one of the academic documentation styles (MLA, APA, CMS, or CSE) to provide specific in-text citations for each source according to the conventions of the discipline in which you are writing.
- **Works cited or references pages.** Provide a complete bibliography entry at the end of your paper for every source you use, conforming to the standards of the documentation style you are using.

integrity policy), and you should be familiar with this document as it applies to your research and writing.

Some students will knowingly copy whole passages from outside sources into their work without documentation. Others will buy research papers from online sources or friends. These intentional acts of academic dishonesty are the most blatant forms of plagiarism. **Unintentional plagiarism,** however, is still a violation of academic integrity. Unacknowledged use of another person's sentences, phrases, or terminology is plagiarism, so provide a citation and use quotation marks to show exactly where you are drawing on others' work. Similarly, unacknowledged use of another person's ideas, research, or approach is also plagiarism, so write careful paraphrases.

1d Understanding a Research Assignment

Beyond selecting an effective subject, you will need a reason for writing the paper. Literature instructors might expect you to make judgements about the structure and poetic techniques of Walt Whitman. Education instructors might ask you to examine the merits of a balanced curriculum for secondary students. History instructors might want you to explore an event—perhaps the tactics and strategies of the abolitionist movement leading up to the American Civil War.

Understanding the Terminology

Assignments in literature, history, and the fine arts will often require you to *interpret, evaluate*, and *perform causal analysis*. Assignments in education, psychology, political science, and other social science disciplines will usually require *analysis, definition, comparison*, or a search for *precedents* leading to a *proposal*. In the sciences, your experiments and testing will usually require a discussion of the *implications* of your findings. The next few pages explain these assignments.

Evaluation

To evaluate, you first need to establish clear criteria of judgment and then explain how the subject meets these criteria. For example, student evaluations of faculty members are based on a set of expressed criteria—an interest in student progress, a thorough knowledge of the subject, and so forth. Similarly, you may be asked to judge the merits of a poem, an art show, or a new MP3 player. Your first step should be to create your criteria. What makes a good movie? How important is a poem's form and structure? Is space a special factor in architecture? You cannot expect the sources to provide the final answers; you need to experience the work and make your final judgments on it.

Let's see how evaluation develops with one student, Sarah Bemis, who was asked to examine diabetes. At first, Sarah worked to define the disease and its basic attack on the human system. However, as she read the literature she shifted her focus from a basic definition to evaluate and examine the methods for controlling diabetes. Her paper, "Diabetes Management: A Delicate Balance," appears on pages 347–357.

In many ways, every research paper is an evaluation.

Interpretation

To interpret, you must usually answer, "What does it mean?" You may be asked to explain the symbolism in a piece of literature, examine a point of law, or make sense of test results. Questions often point toward interpretation:

What does this passage mean?
What are the implications of these results?
What does this data tell us?
Can you explain your reading of the problem to others?

For example, your instructor might ask you to interpret the 1954 Supreme Court ruling in *Brown v. Board of Education*; interpret results on pond water testing at site A, in a secluded country setting, and site B, near a petrochemical plant; or interpret a scene from Henrik Ibsen's *An Enemy of the People*.

In a paper on Internet dating, Valerie Nesbitt-Hall found herself asking two interpretive questions: What are the social implications of computer dating? and What are the psychological implications?

Definition

Sometimes you will need to provide an extended definition to show that your subject fits into a selected and well-defined category. Note these examples:

1. A low-fat diet reduces the risk of coronary disease.

   You will need to define "low-fat" by describing foods that make up a low-fat diet and naming the benefits from this type of diet.

2. Title IX has brought positive changes to college athletic programs.

   You will need to define the law in detail and specify the changes.

3. The root cause of breakups in relationships is selfishness.

   This topic will require a definition of selfishness and examples of how it weakens relationships.

A good definition usually includes three elements: the subject (low-fat diet); the class to which the subject belongs (diets in general); and the differences between others in this class (low-carb or Atkins). Definition will almost always become a part of your work when some of the terminology is subjective. If you argue, for example, that medical experiments on animals are cruel and inhumane, you may need to define what you mean by *cruel* and explain why *humane* standards should be applied to animals that are not human. Thus, definition might serve as your major thesis.

Definition is also necessary with technical and scientific terminology, as shown by Sarah Bemis in her paper on diabetes. The paper needed a careful, detailed definition of the medical disorder in addition to the methods for managing it. By her inquiry, she reached her conclusion that medication in harmony with diet and exercise were necessary for victims of the disease.

Proposal

A proposal says to the reader, "We should do something." It often has practical applications, as shown by these examples:

- To maintain academic integrity, college administrators must enact stringent policies and punishments for cheating and plagiarism.
- A chipping mill should not be allowed in our town because its insatiable demand for timber will strip our local forests and ruin the environment.

A proposal calls for action—a change in policy, a change in the law, and, sometimes, an alteration of accepted procedures. Again, the writer must advance the thesis and support it with reasons and evidence.

In addition, a proposal demands special considerations. First, writers should convince readers that a problem exists and is serious enough to merit action. In the previous example about chipping mills, the writer will need to establish that, indeed, chipping mills have been proposed and perhaps even approved for the area. Then the writer will need to argue that they endanger the environment: They grind vast amounts of timber of any size and shave it into chips that are reprocessed in various ways. As a result, lumberjacks cut even the immature trees, stripping forests into barren wastelands. The writer presumes that clear-cutting damages the land.

Second, the writer must explain the consequences to convince the reader that the proposal has validity. The paper must defend the principle that clear-cutting damages the land, and it should show, if possible, how chipping mills in other parts of the country have damaged the environment.

Third, the writer will need to address any opposing positions, competing proposals, and alternative solutions. For example, chipping mills produce chip board for decking the floors of houses, thus saving trees that might be required for making expensive plywood boards. Without chipping mills, we might run short on paper and homebuilding products. The writer will need to note opposing views and consider them in the paper.

Causal Argument

Unlike proposals, which predict consequences, causal arguments show that a condition exists because of specific circumstances—that is, something has caused or created this situation, and we need to know why. For example, a student's investigation uncovered reasons why schools in one state benefit greatly from a lottery but do not in another.

Let's look at another student who asked the question, "Why do numerous students, like me, who otherwise score well on the ACT test, score poorly in the math section of the test and, consequently, enroll in developmental courses that offer no college credit?" This question merited his investigation, so he gathered evidence from his personal experience as well as data drawn from interviews, surveys, critical reading, and accumulated test results.

Ultimately, he explored and wrote on a combination of related issues—students' poor study skills, bias in the testing program, and inadequate instruction in grade school and high school. He discovered something about himself and many things about the testing program.

Comparison, Including Analogy

An argument often compares and likens a subject to something else. You might be asked to compare a pair of poems or to compare stock markets—NASDAQ with the New York Stock Exchange. Comparison is seldom the focus of an entire paper, but it can be useful in a paragraph about the banking policy of Andrew Jackson and that of his congressional opponents.

An analogy is a figurative comparison that allows the writer to draw several parallels of similarity. For example, the human circulatory system is like a transportation system with a hub, a highway system, and a fleet of trucks to carry the cargo.

Precedence

Precedence refers to conventions or customs, usually well established. In judicial decisions, it is a standard set by previous cases, a *legal precedent*. Therefore, a thesis statement built on precedence requires a past event that establishes a rule of law or a point of procedure. As an example, let's return to the argument against the chipping mill. If the researcher can prove that another mill in another part of the country ruined the environment, then the researcher has a precedent for how damaging such an operation can be.

Implications

If you conduct any kind of test or observation, you will probably make field notes in a research journal and tabulate your results at regular intervals. At some point, however, you will be expected to explain your findings, arrive at conclusions, and discuss the implications of your scientific inquiry. Lab reports are elementary forms of this task. What did you discover, and what does it mean?

For example, one student explored the world of drug testing before companies place the products on the market. His discussions had chilling implications for consumers. Another student examined the role of mice as carriers of Lyme disease. This work required reading as well as field research and testing to arrive at final judgments. In literature, a student examined the recurring images of birds in the poetry of Thomas Hardy to discuss the implications of the birds in terms of his basic themes.

1e   Establishing a Schedule

Setting a schedule at the beginning of a research project helps you stay on track and reminds you to follow the basic steps in the process. This book is organized to help you follow along with each step in the process. Write dates in the spaces below next to each step and keep yourself on schedule.

___ *Finding and narrowing a topic.* Your topic must have a built-in question or argument so you can interpret an issue and cite the opinions found in your source materials.

___ *Drafting a thesis and research proposal.* Even if you are not required to create a formal research proposal, you need to draft some kind of plan to help direct and organize your research before you start reading in depth. See sections 2f and 2g and Chapter 3.

___ *Reading and creating a working bibliography.* Preliminary reading establishes the basis for your research, helping you discover the quantity and quality of available sources. If you can't find much, your topic is too narrow. If you find too many sources, your topic is too broad and needs narrowing. Chapters 4 and 5 explain the processes for finding reliable sources online and in the library.

___ *Creating notes.* Begin entering notes in a digital or printed research journal. Some notes will be summaries, others will be carefully selected quotations from the sources, and some will be paraphrases written in your own voice. Chapter 9 details the techniques for effective notetaking.

___ *Organizing and outlining.* You may be required to create a formal outline; formal outlines and additional ideas for organizing your ideas are presented in sections 9h and 9i.

___ *Drafting the paper.* During your writing, let your instructor scan the draft to give you feedback and guidance. He or she might see further complications for your exploration and also steer you clear of any simplistic conclusions. Drafting is also a stage for peer review, in which a classmate or two looks at your work. Section 13a, pages 218–220, gives more details on peer review. The instructor may also have classroom workshops that offer in-class review of your work in progress. Chapters 10, 11, and 12 explain matters of drafting the paper.

___ *Formatting the paper.* Proper document design places your paper within the required format for your discipline, such as the number system for a scientific project or the APA style for an education paper. Chapters 14–17 provide the guidelines for the various disciplines.

___ *Writing a list of your references.* You will need to list in the proper format the various sources used in your study. Chapters 14–17 provide documentation guidelines.

___ *Revising and proofreading.* At the end of the project, you should be conscientious about examining the manuscript and making all necessary corrections. With the aid of computers, you can check spelling and some aspects of style. Chapter 13 gives tips on revision and editing. Appendix A is a glossary of terms to explain aspects of form and style.

___ *Submitting the manuscript.* Like all writers, you will need at some point to "publish" the paper and release it to the audience, which might be your instructor, your classmates, or perhaps a larger group. Plan well in advance to meet this final deadline. You may publish the paper in a variety of ways—on paper, on a disk, on a CD-ROM, or on your own Web site.

Instructors usually allow students to find their own topics for a major writing assignment; thus, choose something of interest so you won't get bored after a few days. At the same time, your chosen topic will need a scholarly perspective. To clarify what we mean, let's take a look at how two students launched their projects.

- Valerie Nesbitt-Hall saw a cartoon about a young woman saying to a man, "Sorry—I only have relationships over the Internet. I'm cyber-sexual." Although laughing, Valerie knew she had discovered her topic—online romance. Upon investigation, she found her scholarly angle: Matching services and chat rooms are like the arranged marriages from years gone by.
- Norman Berkowitz, while watching news reports of the Iraq War, noticed dry and barren land, yet history had taught him that this land between the Tigris and the Euphrates rivers was formerly a land of fruit and honey, perhaps even the Garden of Eden. What happened to it? His interest focused, thereafter, on the world's water supply, and his scholarly focus centered on the ethics of distribution of water.

As these examples show, an informed choice of subject is crucial for fulfilling the research assignment. You might be tempted to write from a personal interest, such as "Fishing at Lake Cumberland"; however, the content and the context of your course and the assignment itself should drive you toward a serious, scholarly perspective: "The Effects of Toxic Chemicals on the Fish of Lake Cumberland." This topic would probably send you into the field for hands-on investigation (see Chapter 6 for more on field research).

In another example, you might be tempted by the topic "Computer Games," but the research assignment requires an evaluation of issues, not a description. It also requires detailed definition. A better topic might be "Learned Dexterity with Video and Computer Games," which requires the definition of learned dexterity and how some video games promote it. Even in a first-year composition class, your instructor may expect discipline-specific topics, such as:

Education	Differentiated Instruction: Options for Classroom Participation
Political Science	Conservative Republicans and the Religious Right

---

CHECKLIST

Narrowing a General Subject into a Scholarly Topic

Unlike a general subject, a scholarly topic should:

- Examine one narrowed issue, not a broad subject.
- Address knowledgeable readers and carry them to another plateau of knowledge.
- Have a serious purpose—one that demands analysis of the issues, argues from a position, and explains complex details.
- Meet the expectations of the instructor and conform to the course requirements.

Literature	Kate Chopin's *The Awakening* and the Women's Movement
Health	The Effects of Smoking during Pregnancy
Sociology	Parents Who Lie to Their Children

A scholarly topic requires inquiry, like those above, and it sometimes requires problem solving. For example, Sarah Bemis has a problem—she has diabetes—and she went in search of ways to manage it. Her solution—a balance of medication, monitoring, diet, and exercise—gave her the heart and soul of a good research paper. (See pages 347–357 for "Diabetes Management: A Delicate Balance.")

Thus, your inquiry into the issues or your effort to solve a problem will empower the research and the paper you produce. When your topic addresses such issues, you have a reason to:

- Examine with intellectual curiosity the evidence found in the library, on the Internet, and in the field.
- Share your investigation of the issues with readers, bringing them special perspectives and enlightening details.
- Write a meaningful conclusion that discusses the implications of your study rather than merely presenting a summary of what you said in the body.

2a   Relating Your Personal Ideas to a Scholarly Problem

Try to make a connection between your interests and the inherent issues of the subject. For instance, a student whose mother became seriously addicted to the Internet developed a paper from the personal experiences of her dysfunctional family. She worked within the discipline of sociology and consulted journals of that field. Another student, who worked at Wal-Mart, developed a research project on discount pricing and its effect on small-town shop owners. She worked within the discipline of marketing and business management, reading appropriate literature in those areas. Begin with two activities:

1. Relate your experiences to scholarly problems and academic disciplines.
2. Speculate about the subject by listing issues, asking questions, engaging in free writing, and using other idea-generating techniques.

Connecting Personal Experience to Scholarly Topics

You can't write a personal essay and call it a research paper, yet you can choose topics close to your life. Use one of the techniques described in the following list:

1. Combine personal interests with an aspect of academic studies:

Personal interest:	Skiing
Academic subject:	Sports medicine
Possible topics:	"Protecting the Knees"
	"Therapy for Strained Muscles"
	"Skin Treatments"

2. Consider social issues that affect you and your family:

Personal interest:	The education of my child
Social issue:	The behavior of my child in school
Possible topics:	"Children Who Are Hyperactive"
	"Should Schoolchildren Take Medicine to Calm Their Hyperactivity?"

3. Consider scientific subjects, if appropriate:

Personal interest:	The ponds and well water on the family farm
Scientific subject:	Chemical toxins in the water
Possible topic:	"The Poisoning of Underground Water Tables"

4. Let your cultural background prompt you toward detailed research into your heritage, your culture, or the mythology of your ethnic background:

Ethnic background:	Native American
Personal interest:	History of the Apache tribes
Possible topic:	"The Indian Wars from the Native American's Point of View"

Ethnic background:	Hispanic
Personal interest:	Struggles of the Mexican child in an American classroom
Possible topic:	"Bicultural Experiences of Hispanic Students: The Failures and Triumphs"

> **HINT:** Learn the special language of the academic discipline and use it. Every field of study, whether sociology, geology, or literature, has words to describe its analytical approach to topics, such as the *demographics* of a target audience (marketing), the *function* of loops and arrays (computer science), the *symbolism* of Maya Angelou's poetry (literature), and *observation* of human subjects (psychology). Part of your task is learning the terminology and using it appropriately.

Speculating about Your Subject to Discover Ideas and to Focus on the Issues

At some point you may need to sit back, relax, and use your imagination to contemplate the issues and problems worthy of investigation. Ideas can be generated in the following ways:

Free Writing

To free write, merely focus on a topic and write whatever comes to mind. Do not worry about grammar, style, or penmanship, but keep writing nonstop for a page or so to develop valuable phrases, comparisons, personal anecdotes, and specific thoughts that help focus issues of concern. Below, Jamie Johnston comments on violence and, perhaps, finds his topic.

> The savagery of the recent hazing incident at Glenbrook North High School demonstrates that humans, men and women, love a good fight. People want power over others, even in infancy. Just look at how siblings fight. And I read one time that twins inside the womb actually fight for supremacy, and one fetus might even devour or absorb the other one. Weird, but I guess it's true. And we fight vicariously, too, watching boxing and wrestling, cheering at fights during a hockey game, and on and on. So personally, I think human beings have always been blood thirsty and power hungry. The French philosopher Rousseau might claim a "noble savage" once existed, but personally I think we've always hated others.

This free writing set the path for this writer's investigation into the role of war in human history. He found a topic for exploration. (To see the completed paper, go to pages 325–337.)

Listing Keywords

Keep a list of words, the fundamental terms, that you see in the literature. These can help focus the direction of your research. Jamie Johnston built this list of terms:

prehistoric wars	early weapons	noble savages
remains of early victims	early massacres	slaves
sacrificial victims	human nature	power
limited resources	religious sacrifices	honor

These key words can help in writing the rough outline, as explained in the following section.

Arranging Keywords into a Preliminary Outline

Writing a rough outline early in the project might help you see if the topic has substance so you can sustain it for the length required. At this point, the researcher needs to recognize the hierarchy of major and minor issues.

Prehistoric wars
    Evidence of early brutality
        Mutilated skeletons
    Evidence of early weapons
        Clubs, bows, slings, maces, etc.
        Walled fortresses for defense
    Speculations on reasons for war
        Resources
        Slaves
        Revenge
        Religion
    Human nature and war
        Quest for power
        Biological urge to conquer

This initial ranking of ideas would grow in length and mature in depth during Johnston's research (see pages 325–337 for his paper).

Clustering

Another method for discovering the hierarchy of your primary topics and subtopics is to cluster ideas around a central subject. The cluster of related topics can generate a multitude of interconnected ideas. Here's an example by Jamie Johnston:

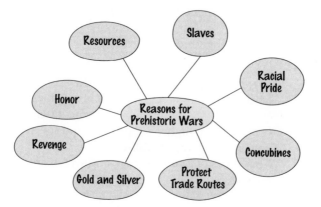

Narrowing by Comparison

Comparison limits a discussion to specific differences. Any two works, any two persons, any two groups may serve as the basis for a comparative study. Historians compare Civil War commanders Robert E. Lee and Ulysses S. Grant. Political scientists compare conservatives and liberals. Literary scholars compare the merits of free verse and those of formal verse. Jamie Johnston discovered a comparative study in his work, as expressed in this way:

> Ultimately, the key questions about the cause of war, whether ancient or current, centers on one's choice between biology and culture. One the one side, society as a whole wants to preserve its culture, in peace if possible. Yet the biological history of men and women suggests that we love a good fight.

That comparative choice became the capstone of Johnston's conclusion (see pages 333–335).

Asking Questions

Research is a process of seeking answers to questions. Hence, the most effective researchers are those who learn to ask questions and seek answers. Raising questions about the subject can provide clear boundaries for the paper. Stretch your imagination with questions to develop a clear theme.

1. General questions examine terminology, issues, causes, and so on. For example, having read Henry Thoreau's essay "Civil Disobedience," one writer asked:

   What is civil disobedience?
   Is dissent legal? Is it moral? Is it patriotic?
   Is dissent a liberal activity? Conservative?

Should the government encourage or stifle dissent?

Is passive resistance effective?

Answering the questions can lead the writer to a central issue or argument, such as "Civil Disobedience: Shaping Our Nation by Confronting Unjust Laws."

2. Rhetorical questions use the modes of writing as a basis. One student framed these questions:

Comparison:	How does a state lottery compare with horse racing?
Definition:	What is a lottery in legal terms? in religious terms?
Cause/Effect:	What are the consequences of a state lottery on funding for education, highways, prisons, and social programs?
Process:	How are winnings distributed?
Classification:	What types of lotteries exist, and which are available in this state?
Evaluation:	What is the value of a lottery to the average citizen? What are the disadvantages?

3. Academic disciplines across the curriculum provide questions, as framed by one student on the topic of sports gambling.

Economics:	Does sports gambling benefit a college's athletic budget? Does it benefit the national economy?
Psychology:	What is the effect of gambling on the mental attitude of the college athlete who knows huge sums hang in the balance on his or her performance?
History:	Does gambling on sporting events have an identifiable tradition?
Sociology:	What compulsion in human nature prompts people to gamble on the prowess of an athlete or team?

4. Journalism questions explore the basic elements of a subject: Who? What? Where? When? Why? and How? For example:

Who?	Athletes
What?	Illegal drugs
When?	During off-season training and also on game day
Where?	Training rooms and elsewhere
Why?	To enhance performance
How?	By pills and injections

The journalist's questions direct you toward the issues, such as "win at all costs" or "damaging the body for immediate gratification."

5. Kenneth Burke's *pentad* questions five aspects of a topic: act, agent, scene, agency, purpose.

What happened (the act)?	Crucifixion scene in *The Old Man and the Sea*.
Who did it (agent)?	Santiago, the old fisherman.
Where and when (scene)?	At the novel's end.
How did it occur (the agency)?	Santiago carries the mast of his boat up the hill.

| What is a possible motive for this event (purpose)? | Hemingway wanted to make a martyr of the old man. |

This researcher can now search the novel with a purpose—to find other Christian images, rank and classify them, and determine if, indeed, the study has merit.

2b   Talking with Others to Refine the Topic

Personal Interviews

Like some researchers, you may need to consult formally with an expert on the topic or explore a subject informally while having coffee or a soda with a colleague, relative, or work associate. Ask people in your community for ideas and for their reactions to your general subject. For example, Valerie Nesbitt-Hall knew about a couple who married after having met initially in a chat room on the Internet. She requested an interview and got it.

Nesbitt-Hall's interview can be found on pages 84–87.

Casual conversations that contribute to your understanding of the subject need not be documented. However, the conscientious writer will credit a formal interview if the person approves. The interviewed subjects on pages 84–87 preferred anonymity.

Online Discussion Groups

What are other people saying about your subject? You might share ideas and messages with other scholars interested in your subject. Somebody may answer a question or point to an interesting aspect that has not occurred to you. With discussion groups, you have a choice:

- Classroom e-mail groups that participate in online discussions of various issues.

CHECKLIST

Exploring Ideas with Others

- Consult with your instructor.
- Discuss your topic with three or four classmates.
- Listen to the concerns of others.
- Conduct a formal interview (see pages 84–86).
- Join a computer discussion group.
- Take careful notes.
- Adjust your research accordingly.

- Online courses that feature a discussion room.
- Discussion groups on the Internet.
- Real-time chatting with participants online—even with audio and video, in some cases.

More on discussion groups on the Internet, 4h, page 55.

For example, your instructor may set up an informal classroom discussion list and expect you to participate online with her and your fellow students. In other cases, the instructor might suggest that you investigate a specific site, such as

alt.religion

for a religious subject. You can find many discussion groups, but the manner in which you use them is vital to your academic success. Rather than chat, solicit ideas and get responses to your questions about your research.

2c   Using Online Searches to Refine Your Topic

The Internet provides a quick and easy way to find a topic and refine it to academic standards. Chapter 4 discusses these matters in greater detail. For now, use the subject directories and keyword searches.

Internet searches, Chapter 4, pages 39–60.

Using an Online Subject Directory

Many search engines have a subject directory that organizes sources by topic. Google Directory, for example, organizes online sources in broad categories like arts, business, computers, health, and so forth. If you started out with a topic such as "alternative medicine," you would quickly realize that your topic was too broad: Google Directory lists about 50 subtopics under "Health>Alternative." The directory might help you identify a narrower topic such as aromatherapy or meditation that you might be able to research more effectively.

However, the Internet has made it difficult to apply traditional evaluations to an electronic article: Is it accurate, authoritative, objective, current, timely, and thorough in coverage? Some Internet sites are advocates to special interests, some sites market products or sprinkle the site with banners to commercial sites and sales items, some sites are personal home pages, and then many sites offer objective news and scholarly information. The answers:

1. Go to the reliable databases available through your library, such as Info-Trac, PsychInfo, UMI ProQuest, Electric Library, and EBSCOhost. These are monitored sites that give information filtered by editorial boards and peer review. You can reach them from remote locations at home or the dorm by connecting electronically to your library.

2. Look for articles on the Internet that first appeared in a printed version. These will have been, in most cases, examined by an editorial board.
3. Look for a reputable sponsor, especially a university, museum, or professional organization.
4. Go to Chapter 4, which discusses the pros and cons of Internet searching.

Using an Internet Keyword Search

Using Google or a similar search engine allows you to search for keywords related to your topic. A keyword search for "American history manuscripts," for example, leads to the Library of Congress page shown in Figure 2.1. This page allows users to search the Library's manuscript collection by keyword, name and subject, date, or by topic. Topic headings include military history, diplomacy and foreign policy, and women's history, all of which would help find sources leading to a more focused topic.

Help with keyword searches, 4c, pages 46–50.

Internet search engines will force you to narrow your general subject. For example, one student entered "Internet + addiction," and the computer brought up thousands of sources. By tightening the request to the phrase "Internet addiction," enclosed within quotation marks, she cut the list considerably and discovered other keywords: cyber-wellness, weboholics, and netaddiction. She realized she had a workable topic.

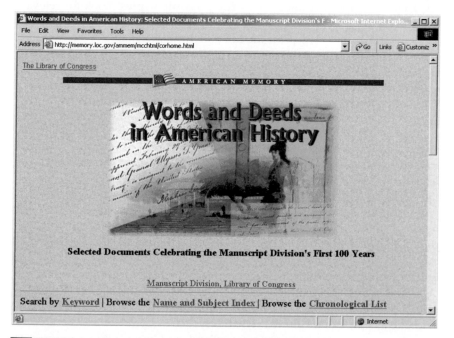

FIGURE 2.1 A Library of Congress site "Words and Deeds in American History," found by using a keyword search for American history manuscripts.

2d   Using the Library's Electronic Databases to Find and Narrow a Topic

College libraries have academic databases not found on general search engines, such as InfoTrac, Silverplatter, and UMI-ProQuest. These database files are reliable because they refer you to thousands of articles that have been peer reviewed by experts or filtered through editorial processes. For now,

Evaluating Internet Sources, pages 42–43.

examine various titles as you search for your own topic. If you see one of interest, click on it for more information. Follow these steps:

1. **Select a database.** Some databases, such as InfoTrac and UMI-ProQuest, are general; use them to find a subject. Other databases focus on one discipline; for example, PsycINFO searches psychological sources, ERIC indexes educational sources, and Health & Wellness describes itself. These databases will move you quickly to a list of articles on your topic.
2. **List keywords or a phrase to describe your topic, enclosed within quotation marks.** Avoid using just one general word. For example, the word *forestry* on the EBSCOhost database produced 6,000 possible sites. The two-word phrase *forest conservation* produced a more manageable number of sites. Here is one of the entries: "Treading Water." By: Tuhus, Melinda. E—The Environmental Magazine, Jan/Feb2008, Vol. 19, Issue 1, p20–22, 2p; *(AN 28052797)*.
3. **Examine the various entries for possible topics.** Look for relevant articles, browse the descriptions, read the abstracts, and—when you find something valuable—print the full text, if it's available.

2e   Using the Library's Electronic Book Catalog to Find a Topic

Instructors expect you to cite information from a few books, and the library's book index will suggest topics and confirm that your subject has been treated with in-depth studies in book form, not just on the Internet or in magazines. Called by different names at each library (e.g., Acorn, Felix, Access), the electronic index lists all books housed in the library, plus film strips, videotapes, and similar items. It does not index articles in magazines and journals, but it will tell you which periodicals are housed in the library and whether they are in printed form or on microforms. Like the electronic databases described in 2d, the index will help you find a workable topic by guiding you quickly from general subjects to subtopics and, finally, to specific books.

Pages 64–65 describe the process in great detail with examples. For now, enter your subject, such as *food, nutrition, allergies*, to see what titles are available in the library. The titles, such as *Children and Food Allergies, Environmental Poisons in Our Food*, or *Living with Something in the Air*, will suggest a possible topic, perhaps "Special Diets to Control

Allergic Reactions to Food." If you go into the stacks to find a book, take the time to examine nearby books on the same shelf, for they will likely treat the same subject.

With your working topic in hand, do some exploratory reading in books to enhance your understanding of the topic. Carefully read the **titles** of books and chapter titles, noting any key terms:

The Lessons of the French Revolution
Napoleon's Ambition and the Quest for Domination
"Perspectives: Napoleon's Relations with the Catholic Church"

These titles provide several keywords and possible topics for a research paper: *Napoleon's ambition, Napoleon and the church, the French Revolution.*

Inspect a book's **table of contents** to find topics of interest. A typical history book might display these headings in the table of contents:

The French Revolution
The Era of Napoleon
Reaction to Napoleon and More Revolutions
The Second Empire of France

If any of these headings look interesting, go to the book's **index** for additional headings, such as this sample:

Napoleon
        becomes Emperor, 174–176
        becomes First Consul, 173
        becomes Life Consul, 174
        and the Catholic Church, 176–178
        character of, 168–176
        and codes of law, 178–179
        defeated by enemies, 192–197
        defeats Austrians, 170
        encounters opposition, 190–191
        extends empire in Europe, 180–189
        seizes power for "One Hundred Days," 198
        sent to Elba, 197
        sent to St. Helena, 199

If you see something that looks interesting, read the designated pages to consider the topic further.

> **HINT:** Topic selection goes beyond choosing a general category (e.g., "single mothers"). It includes finding a research-provoking issue or question, such as "The foster parent program seems to have replaced the orphanage system. Has it been effective?" That is, you need to take a stand, adopt a belief, or begin asking questions.

2f Developing a Thesis Statement, Enthymeme, or Hypothesis

One central statement will usually control an essay's direction and content, so as early as possible, begin thinking in terms of a controlling idea. Each has a separate mission:

- A **thesis statement** advances a conclusion the writer will defend: *Contrary to what some philosophers have advanced, human beings have always participated in wars.*
- An **enthymeme** uses a *because* clause to make a claim the writer will defend: *There has never been a "noble savage," as such, because even prehistoric human beings fought frequent wars for numerous reasons.*
- A **hypothesis** is a theory that must be tested in the lab, in the literature, and/or by field research to prove its validity: *Human beings are motivated by biological instincts toward the physical overthrow of perceived enemies.*

Let us look at each type in more detail.

Thesis

A thesis statement expands your topic into a scholarly proposal, one that you will try to prove and defend in your paper. It does not state the obvious, such as "Langston Hughes was a great poet from Harlem." That sentence will not provoke an academic discussion because your readers know that any published poet has talent. The writer must narrow and isolate one issue by finding a critical focus, such as this one that a student considered for her essay:

> Langston Hughes used a controversial vernacular language that paved the way for later artists, even today's rap musicians.

This thesis statement advances an idea the writer can develop fully and defend with evidence. The writer has made a connection between the subject, *Langston Hughes*, and the focusing agent, *vernacular language*. Look at two other writers' preliminary thesis statements:

THESIS: Chat rooms and online matching services enable people to meet only after a prearranged engagement by e-mail.

THESIS: Hamlet's character is shaped, in part, by Shakespeare's manipulation of the stage setting for Hamlet's soliloquies.

In the first, the writer will defend online romance as similar to prearranged marriages of the past. In the second, the writer will discuss how various shifts in dramatic setting can affect the message of the primary character.

Depending on the critical approach, one topic might produce several issues from which the writer might pick:

Biological approach: Functional foods may be a promising addition to the diet of those who wish to avoid certain diseases.

Economic approach: Functional foods can become an economic weapon in the battle against rising health care costs.

Historic approach: Other civilizations, including primitive tribes, have known about food's healing properties for centuries. Why did we let modern chemistry blind us to its benefits?

Each of the previous statements will provoke a response from the reader, who will demand a carefully structured defense in the body of the paper.

Your thesis anticipates your conclusion by setting in motion the examination of facts and pointing the reader toward the special idea of your paper. Note in the following examples how three writers developed different thesis statements even though they had the same topic, "Santiago in Hemingway's *The Old Man and the Sea.*" (This novel narrates the toils of an old Cuban fisherman named Santiago, who desperately needs the money to be gained by returning with a good catch of fish. On this day he catches a marlin. After a long struggle, Santiago ties the huge marlin to the side of his small boat. However, during the return in the darkness, sharks attack the marlin so that he arrives home with only a skeleton of the fish. He removes his mast and carries it, like a cross, up the hill to his home.)

THESIS: Poverty forced Santiago to venture too far and struggle beyond reason in his attempt to land the marlin.

This writer will examine the economic conditions of Santiago's trade.

THESIS: The giant marlin is a symbol for all of life's obstacles and hurdles, and Santiago is a symbol for all suffering humans.

This writer will examine the religious and social symbolism of the novel.

THESIS: Hemingway's portrayal of Santiago demonstrates the author's deep respect for Cuba and its stoic heroes.

This writer takes a social approach in order to examine the Cuban culture and its influence on Hemingway.

Enthymeme

Your instructor might want the research paper to develop an argument expressed as an enthymeme, which is a claim supported with a *because* clause. Examples:

ENTHYMEME: Hyperactive children need medication because ADHD is a medical disorder, not a behavioral problem.

The claim that children need medication is supported by the stated reason that the condition is a medical problem, not one of behavior. This writer will need to address any unstated assumptions—for example, that medication alone will solve the problem.

ENTHYMEME: Because people are dying all around the globe from water shortages, the countries with an abundance of water have an ethical obligation to share it.

The claim that countries with water have an ethical obligation to share is, of course, the point of contention.

Hypothesis

A hypothesis proposes a theory or suggests an explanation for something. Here are the various types of hypotheses.

The Theoretical Hypothesis:

Discrimination against young women in the classroom, known as "shortchanging," harms the women academically, socially, and psychologically.

Here the student will produce a theoretical study by citing literature on "shortchanging."

The Conditional Hypothesis:

Diabetes can be controlled by medication, monitoring, diet, and exercise.

Certain conditions must be met. The control will depend on the patient's ability to perform the four tasks adequately to prove the hypothesis valid.

The Relational Hypothesis:

Class size affects the number of written assignments by writing instructors.

This type of hypothesis claims that as one variable changes, so does another, or it claims that something is more or less than another. It could be tested by examining and correlating class size and assignments, a type of field research (see pages 91–92).

The Causal Hypothesis:

A child's toy is determined by television commercials.

This causal hypothesis assumes the mutual occurrence of two factors and asserts that one factor is responsible for the other. The student who is a parent could conduct research to prove or disprove the supposition. A review of the literature might also serve the writer.

2g Drafting a Research Proposal

A research proposal is presented in one of two forms: (1) a short paragraph to identify the project for yourself and your instructor, or (2) a formal, multipage report that provides background information, your rationale for conducting the study, a review of the literature, your methods, and the conclusions you hope to prove.

The Short Proposal

A short proposal identifies five essential ingredients of your work:

- The specific topic.
- The purpose of the paper (to explain, analyze, or argue).
- The intended audience (general or specialized).
- Your voice as the writer (informer or advocate).
- The preliminary thesis statement or opening hypothesis.

For example, here is the proposal of Norman Berkowitz:

> The world is running out of fresh water while we sip our Evian. However, the bottled water craze signals something—we do not trust our fresh tap water. We have an emerging crisis on our hands, and some authorities forecast world wars over water rights. The issue of water touches almost every facet of our lives, from religious rituals and food supply to disease and political stability. We might frame this hypothesis: Water will soon replace oil as the economic resource most treasured by nations of the world. However, that assertion would prove difficult to defend and may not be true at all. Rather, we need to look elsewhere, at human behavior, and at human responsibility for preserving the environment for our children. Accordingly, this paper will examine (1) the issues with regard to supply and demand, (2) the political power struggles that may emerge, and (3) the ethical implications for those who control the world's scattered supply of fresh water.

This writer has identified the basic nature of his project and can now go in search of evidence that will defend the argument.

CHECKLIST

Addressing the Reader

Identify your audience. Have you visualized your audience, its expertise, and its expectations? Your perception of the reader will affect your voice, style, and choice of words.

Identify your discipline. Readers in each discipline will bring differing expectations to your paper with regard to content, language, design, and documentation format.

Meet the needs of your readers. Are you saying something worthwhile? Something new? Do not bore the reader with known facts from an encyclopedia. (This latter danger is the reason many instructors discourage the use of an encyclopedia as a source.)

Engage and even challenge your readers. Find an interesting or different point of view. For example, a report on farm life can become a challenging examination of chemical contamination because of industrial sprawl into rural areas, and an interpretation of a novel can become an examination of the prison system rather than a routine discourse on theme or characterization.

The Long Proposal

Some instructors may assign the long proposal, which includes some or all of the following elements:

1. A *cover page* with the title of the project, your name, and the person or agency to whom you are submitting the proposal.

More Academics for the Cost of Less Engaged Children

Caitlin Kelley

Submitted to

Dr. Maxine Girdner

In fulfillment of course requirements for English 4010

2. An *abstract* that summarizes your project in 50 to 100 words (see pages 301–303 for additional information).

The elimination of elementary school recess periods was investigated to examine the theoretical implications of depriving learners of these important mental and physical stimuli. The goal was to determine the effect of the modern trend to use recess time for longer academic periods. The social and psychological implications

were determined by an examination of the literature, including
comments from educational leaders. Results are mixed, as the end
result of an increased emphasis on standardized testing will not be
realized for several years. The social implications affect the
mental and physical lives of school-aged children who are
learning less about cooperation with their peers and more about
remaining stagnant with little activity for lengthy periods of time.

3. A *purpose statement* with your *rationale* for the project. In essence, this
   is your thesis statement or hypothesis, along with your identification of
   the audience that your work will address and the role you will play as
   investigator and advocate.

   This project was suggested by Dr. Maxine Girdner to fulfill the
   writing project for English 4010 and also to serve the University
   Committee on Strategies and Needs in Elementary Education, which has
   launched a project on Contemporary Student Needs, Grades K–12. This
   paper, if approved, would become part of the committee's findings and
   contribute to the final report booklet.

4. A *statement of qualification* that explains your experience and, perhaps,
   the special qualities you bring to the project. Caitlin Kelley included this
   comment in her proposal:

   I bring firsthand experience to this study. I have completed my
   methods courses for my degree in elementary education. Moreover,
   I am nearing the end of my practicum for my student teaching
   requirement. Entering a classroom of third graders was exciting at
   first, but then I realized that teaching is truly a lot of work. It is work
   for me, but also requires a great attention to detail by my students.
   I was surprised to find that my learners were only allowed thirty
   minutes of recess three times during the week and a structured
   physical education class on only two days. This caused me to ponder
   whether the education that these children are receiving is
   developing the physical as well as the academic abilities of each
   learner.

5. A *review of the literature*, which surveys the articles and books that you
   have examined in your preliminary work (see pages 124–130 for an explanation and another example).

Limited research is being done concerning the role of recess in the development of elementary-aged children. My search of the literature produced several informative articles. According to Poynter (2008), "40 percent of schools in the United States have cut recess or are considering dropping it." The question is why are nearly half of the elementary schools around the country dropping free play and expression from the daily lives of young children? Svensen (2008) outlines that the two prevailing reasons for the reduction and elimination of free play are to reduce the risk of accidents and to provide students more time in their day for academics, "mostly reading and math." Contradicting these arguments are parents and doctors who feel that "recess provides children with the opportunity to develop friendships, negotiate relationships and build positive connections" (DeGregory, 2005). The research of Greg Toppo has revealed that the process of eliminating or limiting recess is the decision of the principal of the elementary school. "The principal of each school respectively decides whether his or her children need that extra time for play, or whether it would be better spent on academics" (Toppo, 2007, p. 1-A). In the typical classroom, children sit in their seats for up to six hours each day. One source stated, "shortening recess by five minutes daily provides 25 minutes of additional instruction time each week" (Matthews, 2004, p. B1). This lack of a break often proves to be a problem because the students are restless and fidgety (Adelman & Taylor, 2008). In some schools, however, "with the principal's permission, a teacher can take his or her class outside for 15 minutes. For the kids, it's like a jailbreak" (DeGregory, 2005).

6. A *description of your research methods*, which is the design of the *materials* you will need, your *timetable*, and, where applicable, your *budget*. These elements are often a part of a scientific study, so see Chapters 15 and 17 for work in the social, physical, and biological sciences. Here is Kelley's description:

This paper will examine the problems associated with eliminating recess and the effect of an over-emphasis on academics in elementary schools. Cutting out play time for young children affects their social skills and their physical skills. Students need to learn to make up their own rules and play their own games. With recess, students can experience uninstructed play in contrast to being constantly directed all day. On the playground, with adults serving only as supervisors, children learn to work through altercations, to make decisions, and also how to make friends. Because of the stagnant environment of school, too many children would rather play inside with electronics than go outside. It is essential to have physical contact with other children in a world of technology where students often play by themselves while staring at the video screen; additionally, children who are glued to their computers interact less with other children, become passive learners, and read less. Recess is a physical activity for most children, which is constructive toward their health and well-being. If children have recess as an outlet to run around and play, the rates of childhood obesity would be cut because the children would be

---

CHECKLIST

Explaining Your Purpose in the Research Proposal

Research papers accomplish several tasks:

- They explain and define the topic.
- They analyze the specific issues.
- They persuade the reader with the weight of the evidence.

1. Use *explanation* to review and itemize factual data. Sarah Bemis explains how diabetes can be managed (see pages 347–357), and Jamie Johnston explains the nature of prehistoric wars (see pages 325–337).
2. Use *analysis* to classify various parts of the subject and to investigate each one in depth. Anthony Murphy examines the emotions in poetry that is generated by a historical event (pages 222–225), and Caitlin Kelley analyzes the importance of recess for elementary students (pages 302–309).
3. Use *persuasion* to question the general attitudes about a problem and then affirm new theories, advance a solution, recommend a course of action, or—at least—invite the reader into an intellectual dialog. Norman Berkowitz argues for ethical distribution of the world's water supply.

burning calories. However, when children are taken outside for recess after lunch, they are exposed to and become used to playing outdoors, an activity that can be repeated in the home environment.

YOUR RESEARCH PROJECT

1. Make a list of your personal interests and items that affect your mental and physical activities, such as homework, hiking, or relations with your family. Examine each item on the list see if you can find an academic angle that will make the topic fit the context of your research assignment. See section 2a, pages 11–17, for more help.

2. Ask questions about a possible subject, using the list on pages 15–17.

3. Look around your campus or community for subjects. Talk with your classmates and even your instructor about campus issues. Focus on your hometown community in search of a problem, such as the demise of the Main Street merchants. Investigate any environmental concerns in your area, from urban sprawl to beach erosion to waste disposal. Think seriously about a piece of literature you have read, perhaps Fitzgerald's *The Great Gatsby*. If you are a parent, consider issues related to children, such as finding adequate child care. Once you have a subject of interest, apply to it some of the narrowing techniques described on pages 11–17, such as clustering, free writing, or listing keywords.

4. To determine if sufficient sources will be available and to narrow the subject even further, visit the Internet, investigate the library's databases (e.g., InfoTrac), and dip into the electronic book catalog at your library. Keep printouts of any interesting articles or book titles.

For more resources in research, writing, and documentation, go to MyCompLab.com

3 Organizing Ideas and Setting Goals

Instead of plunging too quickly into research, first decide *what* to look for and *why* you need it. One or more of these exercises will help your organization:

- Chart the course of your work with a basic order.
- Revisit your research proposal, if you developed one, for essential issues.
- List key terms, ideas, and issues that you must explore in the paper.
- Rough out an initial outline.
- Ask a thorough set of questions.
- Use modes of development (e.g., definition or cause/effect) to identify key issues.
- Search issues across the curriculum (e.g., economics, psychology, biology).
- Let your thesis statement point you toward the basic issues.

Each of these techniques is explored on the following pages.

3a Using a Basic Order to Chart the Course of Your Work

Your finished paper should trace the issues, defend and support a thesis, and provide dynamic progression of issues and concepts that point forward to the conclusion. The paper should provide these elements:

Identification of the problem or issue.
A review of the literature on the topic.
Your thesis or hypothesis.
Analysis of the issues.
Presentation of evidence.
Interpretation and discussion of the findings.

In every case, you must generate the dynamics of the paper by (1) building anticipation in the introduction, (2) investigating the issues in the body, and (3) providing a final judgment. In this way, you will satisfy the demands of the academic reader, who will expect you to:

- Examine a problem.
- Cite pertinent literature on it.
- Offer your ideas and interpretation of it.

All three are necessary in almost every instance. Consequently, your early organization will determine, in part, the success of your research paper.

3b   Using Your Research Proposal to Direct Your Notetaking

Your research proposal, if you developed one, introduces issues worthy of research. For example, the last sentence of this research proposal names four topics:

> Everybody thinks water is plentiful and will always be here. I'm afraid that water might soon replace oil as an economic resource most treasured by nations. We already have legal battles about the sharing of water, and we may one day have wars over it. Preliminary reading has shown that a growing world population faces a global water supply that is shrinking. Accordingly, this paper will examine some of the issues with regard to supply and demand, the political power struggles that are emerging, and the ethical and perhaps even moral implications engulfing the world's scattered supply of fresh water.

This writer will search the literature and write notes to build an environmental examination on those who have good supplies of water and those who do not.

Note: For a discussion of and directions for completing the research proposal, see Chapter 2, pages 25–30.

Another writer sketched the following research proposal, which lists the types of evidence necessary to accomplish her project:

> Organ and tissue donation is a constant concern in our society. This paper will expose the myths that prevail in the public's imagination and, hopefully, dispel them. It will explore the serious need of and benefits derived from donated organs and tissue. It will also itemize the organs and their use to rehabilitate the diseased and wounded. It will evaluate, but it will also be a proposal: Sign the donor card!

3c   Listing Key Terms and Phrases to Set Directions for Notetaking

Follow two fairly simple steps: (1) Jot down ideas or words in a rough list, and (2) expand the list to show a hierarchy of major and minor ideas. Student

Norman Berkowitz started listing items that are affected by and depend on the world's water supply:

> wildlife survival
>
> sanitation and hygiene
>
> irrigation of farms and the food supply
>
> bioscience issues
>
> water distribution
>
> global warming
>
> the Ogallala aquifer

Berkowitz could begin notetaking with this list and label each note with one of the phrases.

HINT: What you are looking for at this point are terms that will speed your search on the Internet and in the library's indexes.

3d Writing a Rough Outline

As early as possible, organize your key terminology in a brief outline, arranging the words and phrases in an ordered sequence, as shown in this next example. Jamie Johnston began research in the matter of prehistoric wars. He soon jotted down this rough outline:

> Prehistoric wars
>> Evidence of weapons
>>
>> Evidence from skeletal remains
>>
>> Evidence of soldiers and fortresses
>
> Reasons for early fighting
>> Resources
>>
>> Slaves, concubines, and sacrificial victims
>>
>> Gold, silver, bronze, copper
>>
>> Revenge
>>
>> Defend honor
>
> Cause for human compulsion to fight
>> Biology
>>
>> Culture

This outline, although sketchy, provides the terminology needed for keyword searches on the Internet and in your library's databases. Also, it's not too early to begin initial reading and writing notes for the items on the list.

3e   Using Questions to Identify Issues

Questions can invite you to develop answers in your notes. (See also section 2a, "Asking Questions," pages 15–17.) Early in her work, one student made this list of questions:

> What is a functional food?
>
> How does it serve the body in fighting disease?
>
> Can healthy eating actually lower health care costs?
>
> Can healthy eating truly prolong one's life?
>
> Can we identify the components of nutritional foods that make
>
>   them work effectively?
>
> What is an antioxidant? a carcinogen? a free radical? a
>
>   triglyceride?

She then went in search of answers and built a body of notes. One question might lead to others, and an answer to a question, "Are nutritional foods new?" might produce a topic statement for a paragraph:

> Although medical professionals are just beginning to open their
> minds and eyes to the medicinal power of food, others have known
> about food's healthful properties for centuries.

3f   Setting Goals by Using Organizational Patterns

Try to anticipate the kinds of development, or organizational patterns, you will need to build effective paragraphs and to explore your topic fully. Then base your notes on the modes of development: *definition, comparison and contrast, process, illustration, cause and effect, classification, analysis,* and *description.* Here's a list by one student who studied the issues of organ and tissue donation.

> <u>Define</u> tissue donation.
>
> <u>Contrast</u> myths, religious views, and ethical considerations.
>
> <u>Illustrate</u> organ and tissue donation with several examples.
>
> Use <u>statistics</u> and <u>scientific data</u>.
>
> Search out <u>causes</u> for a person's reluctance to sign a donor card.
>
> Determine the <u>consequences</u> of donation with a focus on saving the
>
>   lives of children.
>
> Read and use a <u>case study</u> on a child's death and organ donation by
>
>   the public.

Explore the step-by-step stages of the <u>process</u> of organ donation.

<u>Classify</u> the types and <u>analyze</u> the problem.

Give <u>narrative</u> examples of several people whose lives were saved.

With this list in hand, a writer can search for material to develop as *contrast, process, definition*, and so forth.

> **HINT:** Try developing each important item on your list into a full paragraph. Write a definition paragraph. Write a paragraph to compare and contrast the attitudes expressed by people about organ donation. Then write another paragraph that gives four or five examples. By doing so, you will be well on your way to developing the paper.

One student recorded this note that describes the subject:

> Organ and tissue donation is the gift of life. Each year, many people confront health problems due to diseases or congenital birth defects. Organ transplants give these people the chance to live a somewhat normal life. Organs that can be successfully transplanted include the heart, lungs, liver, kidneys, and pancreas (Barnill 1). Tissues that can be transplanted successfully include bone, corneas, skin, heart valves, veins, cartilage, and other connective tissues (Taddonio 1).

3g   Using Approaches across the Curriculum to Chart Your Ideas

Each scholarly field gives a special insight into any given topic. Suppose, for example, that you wish to examine an event from U.S. history, such as the Battle of Little Big Horn. Different academic disciplines will help you approach the topic in different ways.

Political science:	Was Custer too hasty in his quest for political glory?
Economics:	Did the government want to open the western lands for development that would enrich the nation?
Military science:	Was Custer's military strategy flawed?
Psychology:	Did General Custer's ego precipitate the massacre?
Geography:	Why did Custer stage a battle at this site?

These approaches can also produce valuable notes as the student searches out answers in the literature, as shown in this example:

> The year 1876 stands as a monument to the western policies of Congress and the President, but Sitting Bull and Custer seized their share of glory. Custer's egotism and political ambitions overpowered his military savvy (Lemming 6). Also, Sitting Bull's military tactics (he told his braves to kill rather than show off their bravery) proved devastating for Custer and his troops, who no longer had easy shots at "prancing, dancing Indians" (Potter 65).

3h   Using Your Thesis to Chart the Direction of Your Research

Often, the thesis statement sets the direction of the paper's development.

Arrangement by Issues

The thesis statement might force the writer to address various issues and positions.

THESIS: Misunderstandings about organ donation distort reality and set serious limits on the availability of those persons who need an eye, a liver, or a healthy heart.

ISSUE 1.   Many myths mislead people into believing that donation is unethical.

ISSUE 2.   Some fear that as a patient they might be terminated early for their body parts.

ISSUE 3.   Religious views sometimes get in the way of donation.

The outline above, though brief, gives this writer three categories that require detailed research in support of the thesis. The notetaking can be focused on these three issues.

Arrangement by Cause/Effect

In other cases, the thesis statement suggests development by cause/effect issues. Notice that the next writer's thesis on television's educational values points the way to four very different areas worthy of investigation.

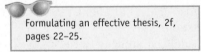

Formulating an effective thesis, 2f, pages 22–25.

THESIS: Television can have positive effects on a child's language development.

CONSEQUENCE 1.   Television introduces new words.

CONSEQUENCE 2.   Television reinforces word usage and proper syntax.

CONSEQUENCE 3.   Literary classics come alive verbally on television.

CONSEQUENCE 4.   Television provides the subtle rhythms and musical effects of accomplished speakers.

This outline can help the writer produce a full discussion on television viewing.

Arrangement by Interpretation and Evaluation

Evaluation will evolve from thesis statements that judge a subject by a set of criteria, such as your analysis of a poem, movie, or museum display. Notice how the next student's thesis statement requires an interpretation of Hamlet's character.

THESIS: Shakespeare manipulates the stage settings for Hamlet's soliloquies to uncover his unstable nature and forecast his failure.

1. His soul is dark because of his mother's incest.

2. He appears impotent in comparison with the actor.

3. He is drawn by the magnetism of death.

4. He realizes he cannot perform cruel, unnatural acts.

5. He stands ashamed by his inactivity in comparison.

Arrangement by Comparison

Sometimes a thesis statement stipulates a comparison on the value of two sides of an issue, as shown in one student's preliminary outline:

THESIS: Discipline often involves punishment, but child abuse adds another element: the gratification of the adult.

COMPARISON 1:   A spanking has the interest of the child at heart but a beating or a caning has no redeeming value.

COMPARISON 2:   Time-outs remind the child that relationships are important and to be cherished, but lockouts in a closet only promote hysteria and fear.

COMPARISON 3:   The parent's ego and selfish interests often take precedence over the welfare of the child or children.

CHECKLIST

Evaluating Your Overall Plan

1. What is my thesis? Will my notes and records defend and illustrate my proposition? Is the evidence convincing?
2. Have I found the best plan for developing the thesis with elements of argument, evaluation, cause/effect, or comparison?
3. Should I use a combination of elements—that is, do I need to evaluate the subject, examine the causes and consequences, and then set out the argument?

YOUR RESEARCH PROJECT

1. Make a list of key terms related to your topic (see section 3c for examples). When you have a list, try to group the terms into main ideas and subtopics. You can use this list as a rough working outline to guide your reading and notetaking.
2. Develop a list of questions about your topic. Try to generate a list of questions yourself and then follow up by asking some of your friends or classmates to suggest questions that they would like to know more about based on your initial topic. See section 3e.
3. Revisit your thesis statement to think about what kind of direction it sets for your paper's development. Consider some of the development patterns described in section 3h and experiment with applying one or more of these patterns to your topic and thesis statement.

For more resources in research, writing, and documentation, go to MyCompLab.com

4   Gathering Sources Online

Electronic sources are now a major source of research information, and we know that many students start their research on the Web. That's okay. You may start your research on the Web, but do not stop there! Let's review immediately the good, the bad, and the ugly on matters of using electronic sources and the Internet. First, the ugly: You can buy a canned research paper and submit it as your own. This is considered plagiarism and can result in your failing the course or even being expelled. Also ugly, and also considered **plagiarism**, is downloading Internet material into your paper without citation and documentation, thereby making it appear to be your own work. (See Chapter 7 for ways to avoid plagiarism.)

More about plagiarism, pages 94–106.

Second, the bad: You will find articles that are not worthy of citation in your research paper. You must filter personal opinion pieces that are unsubstantiated in any way. You must also filter commercial sites that disguise their sales pitch with informative articles. In other cases, you will encounter advocacy pages with a predetermined bias that dismisses objective analysis of an issue in favor of the group's position on the environment, gun control, immigration, and so forth. This chapter will help you identify these sites. (See also the Checklist, pages 42–43, "Evaluating Online Sources.")

Third, the good: The Internet, if you know where to look, is loaded with absolutely marvelous material that was unattainable just a few years ago. It offers instant access to millions of computer files relating to almost every subject, including articles, illustrations, audio and video clips, and raw data. Much of it meets basic academic standards, yet you should keep in mind that the best academic material is available only through databases at your college library, such as InfoTrac and PsycINFO. That is, you can rest assured that scholarly articles found through the library's databases are far more reliable than those you might find through Google or Yahoo!

Therefore, this chapter will help you with two tasks: (1) to become an efficient searcher for academic information on the Web, and (2) to become accomplished at evaluating and filtering online sources.

CHECKLIST

Using Online Rather Than Print Versions

Online versions of articles offer advantages, but they also present problems. On the plus side, you can view them almost instantly on the computer monitor. You can save or print an abstract or article without the hassle of photocopying, and you can even download material to your flash drive and, where appropriate, insert it into your paper. However, keep these issues in mind:

- The text may differ from the original printed version and may even be a digest. Therefore, cite the Internet source to avoid giving the appearance of citing from the printed version. There are often major differences between the same article in *USA Today* and the one found at www.usatoday.com. Cite the correct one in your Works Cited.

- Online abstracts may not accurately represent the full article. In fact, some abstracts are not written by the author at all but by an editorial staff. Therefore, resist the desire to quote from the abstract and, instead, write a paraphrase of it—or, better, find the full text and cite from it (see also pages 69-70).

- You may need to subscribe (at a modest cost) to some sites. A company has the right to make demands before giving you access. However, your school library can often provide you with access to the sites most suitable for your research.

4a   Beginning an Online Search

To trace the good and the bad, let's follow the trail of one student, Sherri James, who has decided, because she is a competitive swimmer, to investigate the use of drugs for enhancing one's performance in the pool—not that she wants to try drugs but rather to educate herself and produce a research paper at the same time.

Probably the first thing most of you do, like Sherri James, is visit your favorite search engine, such as one of these:

About.com	http://www.about.com
AltaVista	http://www.altavista.com
Excite	http://www.excite.com
Go.com	http://go.com
Google	http://www.google.com
Hotbot	http://www.hotbot.com
Dogpile	http://www.dogpile.com

| Webcrawler | http://webcrawler.com |
| Yahoo! | http://www.yahoo.com |

At the search window, Sherri James typed "fitness and drugs." Immediately, she was directed to Beachbody.com, healthandfitness.com, and trulyhuge.com. Notice that all three sites are commercial sites (*.com*). Also, they each want to sell something—Power 90 supplements, a carb-electrolyte drink, and cyber-genics nutritional products and instructional videos. One site advertised steroids for sale, such as Epogen and Erythropoietin. For Sherri James, these Internet locations offered no information, except to suggest this note that she jotted into her research journal:

> With supplements, drugs, and even steroids readily available on Web sites, it's no wonder so many athletes get caught in the "quick-fix" bodybuilding trap.

Next, Sherri James found two articles about swimming: "Three Steps to Swimming Success" and "Beat Fatigue in Long Meets." These were written by Rick Curl, a noted swim coach who has trained Olympic champions. For nutrition, Curl encourages swimmers to "refuel their muscles with a sports drink containing plenty of carbohydrates." And guess what? The articles are promoting and selling two sports drinks. Sherri James noticed that the site, Powering Muscles, is sponsored by PacificHealth Laboratories, the makers of ACCELERADE sports drink and Eudurox Recovery drink. Thus, Sherri James wrote a note to position the good instruction from the swim coach within the commercial context of the site:

> Despite promoting two commercial supplements for swimmers, successful swim coach Rick Curl goes beyond pitching the nutritional products to offer valuable advice on in-pool techniques as well as out-of-pool aerobic training, stretching, and calisthenics.

At this point, Sherri James decided to try a subject directory. In Yahoo! she found hyperlinks to:

Business and Economy
Computer and Internet
News and Media
Entertainment
Recreation and Sports

She clicked on the last one and found another list, which contained what she was looking for: a hyperlink to **Drugs in Sports**. At this site she found thirteen links, among them:

Doping and Sports—collective expert assessment on doping by bicyclists
Drugs in Sport—provides information on performance-enhancing drugs in sport, the latest articles on the subject, reports, resources, and useful Web sites

Findlaw: Drug Use in Sports—includes a story archive and background information on testing, prevention, policies, and commonly used drugs

NCAA Drug Testing—information on the association's drug testing policy

PlayClean—promotes anti-doping policies and preventing youth drug use through sports; from the Office of National Drug Control Policy

Sherri had now found site domains other than commercial ones, such as *.org*, *.gov*, *.net*, and *.edu*. At NCAA.org she was able to print out the NCAA (National Collegiate Athletic Association) Drug-Testing Program and use portions of the rules in her paper. Here is one of her notes:

> *The NCAA clearly forbids blood doping. It says, "The practice of blood doping (the intravenous injection of whole blood, packed red blood cells or blood substitutes) is prohibited and any evidence confirming use will be cause for action consistent with that taken for a positive drug test" (Bylaw 31.1.3.1.1).*

At playclean.org, Sherri found a link to **www.whitehousedrugpolicy .gov** and an article entitled "Women and Drugs" by the Office of National Drug Control Policy. She was now finding material worthy of notetaking:

> *A study by scientists at Columbia University has found the signals and situations of risk are different for girls and that "girls and young women are more vulnerable to abuse and addiction: they get hooked faster and suffer the consequences sooner than boys and young men" ("Women and Drugs").*

Sherri James has begun to find her way to better sources on the Internet, but she will still need to examine the academic databases by logging on at her college library (see pages 61–83, where we will again watch Sherri search for sources). She will also need to consider doing field research, such as interviewing fellow athletes or developing a questionnaire (see pages 84–86 and 90).

CHECKLIST

Evaluating Online Sources

The Internet and other online sources supply huge amounts of material, some of it excellent and some not so good. You must make judgments about the validity and veracity of these materials. In addition to your commonsense judgment, here are a few guidelines:

1. Prefer the *.edu* and *.org* sites. Usually, these are domains developed by an educational institution, such as Ohio State University, or by a professional organization, such as the American Psychological Association. Of course, *.edu* sites also include many student papers, which can include unreliable information.

2. The *.gov* (government) and *.mil* (military) sites are generally considered to be reliable, but look closely at any information that involves politically sensitive materials.

3. The *.com* (commercial) sites are generally developed by for-profit organizations. Keep in mind that (a) they are selling advertising space, (b) they often charge you for access to their files, (c) they can be ISP sites (Internet Service Provider) that people pay to use and to post their "material." Although some .com sites contain good information (for example, reputable newspaper and magazine sites), use these sites with caution unless you can verify their reliability.

4. Look for the *professional* affiliation of the writer, which you will find in the opening credits or an e-mail address. Search for the writer's home page: Type the writer's name into a search engine to see how many results are listed. Also, type the writer's name into Amazon.com for a list of his or her books. If you find no information on the writer, you will need to rely on a sponsored Web site. That is, if the site is not sponsored by an organization or institution, you should probably abandon the source and look elsewhere.

5. Look for a bibliography that accompanies the article, which will indicate the scholarly nature of this writer's work.

6. Usenet discussion groups offer valuable information at times, but some articles lack sound, fundamental reasoning or evidence to support the opinions.

7. Look for the timeliness of the information on the site. Check dates of publication and how often the information is updated.

8. Treat e-mail messages as "mail," not scholarly articles. A similar rule applies to "chat."

9. Does the site contain hypertext links to other professional sites or to commercial sites? Links to other educational sites serve as a modern bibliography to more reliable sources. Links to commercial sites are often attempts to sell you something.

10. Learn to distinguish from among the different types of Web sites, such as advocacy pages, personal home pages, informational pages, and business and marketing pages. One site provides evaluation techniques: **http://www.widener.edu/Tools_Resources/Libraries/ Wolfgram_Memorial_Library/Evaluate_Web_Pages/659/**.

11. Your skills in critical thinking can usually determine the validity of a site. For more help in critical thinking and Internet evaluation, visit **http://www.virtualsalt.com**.

4b Reading an Online Address

Following is some information to help you understand online addresses. In the library, you must employ a book's call number to find it. On the Internet, you employ a Uniform Resource Locator (URL), like this one: **http://www.georgetown.edu/home/libraries.html.**

- The *protocol* (http://) transmits data.
- The *server* (www, for World Wide Web) is the global Internet service that connects the multitude of computers and the Internet files.
- The *domain* (georgetown.edu) names the organization feeding information into the server with a *suffix* to label the type of organization: *.com* (commercial), *.edu* (educational), *.gov* (government), *.mil* (military), *.net* (network organization), and *.org* (organization).
- The *directory/file* (library_catalogues) finds one of the server's directories and then a specific file.
- The *hypertext markup language* (html) names the computer language used to write the file.

FIGURE 4.1 The home page for the Library of Congress.

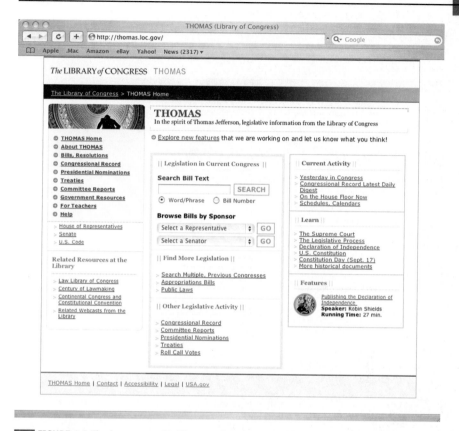

FIGURE 4.2 The home page for Thomas, the congressional site for the Library of Congress.

Often, knowing just the protocol and the server.domain will get you to a home site from which you can search deeper for files. The URL **http://loc.gov/homepage/** will take you to the Library of Congress (see Figure 4.1), where you can examine a specific directory, such as **Thomas: Congress at Work** (see Figure 4.2). In Thomas, you have access to legislation of both the House and Senate, with links to many other sites and a search engine for finding specific information.

You can search the current Congress for the text of bills. At the Thomas search engine, enter a word or phrase, such as "student financial aid," and the site will take you to a list of resolutions, bills, and acts, like the five listed here:

1. College Affordability and Transparency Act of 2007 (Introduced in House) [H.R.472.IH]
2. Securing Success for Veterans on Campus Act of 2008 (Introduced in House) [H.R.5143.IH]
3. New Savers Act (Introduced in Senate) [S.1967.IS]

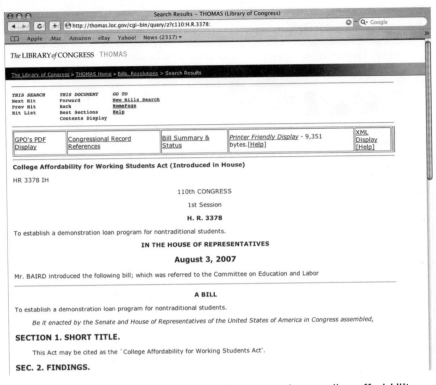

4. Nontraditional Student Success Act (Introduced in Senate) [S.301.IS]
5. Higher Education Amendments of 2007 (Reported in Senate) [S.1642.RS]

At this point, you have the option of reading the House bills, the resolution, or the Senate bill by clicking on the colored links. The House bill on college affordability for working students is shown in Figure 4.3. In effect, you will have moved rather quickly from the home page of the Library of Congress to a specific piece of legislation you might wish to use in your paper.

4c Using a Search Engine

You probably have a favorite search engine and know how to use it. So this section merely lists the types and the way they perform. Keep in mind that search engines change often, and more are added each year while others disappear. We cannot stress enough the importance of using the educational search engines as listed on pages 49–50; with those, you can have confidence that the articles have a scholarly basis, not a commercial one.

Subject Directory Search Engines

These search engines are human compiled and indexed to guide you to general areas that are then subdivided to specific categories. Your choices control the list.

About.com	http://www.about.com
Go.com	http://go.com
Lycos	http://www.lycos.com
Yahoo!	http://www.yahoo.com

Yahoo.com is an edited site with directories arranged by topic. Figure 4.4 shows the opening page from Yahoo.com with numbered annotations keyed to important features of the screen shot. You can use a keyword search or click on one of the topic categories, such as **African History**, to go deeper into the Web directories.

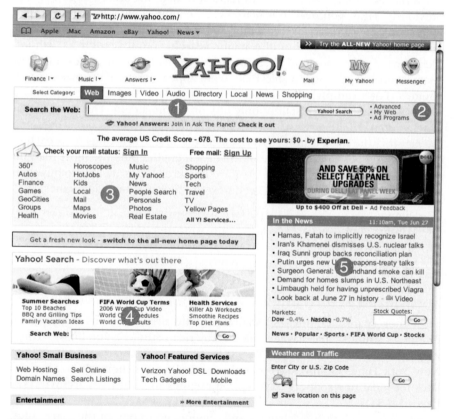

FIGURE 4.4 Opening home page of Yahoo.com, an edited Web directory.

1. Type a keyword into the search field. 2. Use Advanced Search to refine date, language, or number of results. 3. Click on hyperlinks for specific types of information—auctions, maps, movies, and so forth 4. Use the subject directory to move quickly from a general subject to specific categories and specific articles 5. For current events, click on hyperlinks to news, sports, and events.

Robot-Driven Search Engines

Another set of engines responds to a keyword by electronically scanning millions of Web pages. Your keywords will control the size of the list.

AltaVista	http://www.altavista.com
Ask	http://www.ask.com
Excite	http://www.excite.com
Google	http://www.google.com
Go.com	http://go.com
Hotbot	http://www.hotbot.com
Webcrawler	http://www.webcrawler.com

Metasearch Engines

A metasearch examines your topic in several of the search engines listed previously. Thus, you need not search each engine separately. For example, when you enter a query at the Mamma.com Web site, the engine simultaneously queries about ten of the major search engines, such as Yahoo!, Webcrawler, and Google. It then provides you with a short, relevant set of results. You will get fewer results than might appear at one of the major search engines. For example, the request for "chocolate + children" produced 342,718 results on AltaVista but only fifty on Mamma.com. The claim is that a metasearch engine gives you the more relevant sites. This claim is based on the fact that the metasearch engine selects the first few listings from each of the other engines under the theory that each engine puts the most relevant sites at the top of its list; however, some commercial sites are able to buy their way to the top of various lists. Listed next are four metasearch engines:

Dogpile	http://www.dogpile.com
Mamma.com	http://www.mamma.com
Metacrawler.com	http://www.metacrawler.com
Surfwax.com	http://www.surfwax.com

Specialized Search Engines

Other search engines specialize in one area, such as WWWomen (women's studies), TribalVoice (Native American Studies), and Bizweb (business studies). In addition, many Web sites, such as the Library of Congress and New York Times Online, have search engines just for themselves. Even the sites for local newspapers have search engines to their own archives (see pages 52–54).

To discover any specialized search engine, go to one of the major sites, such as AltaVista, and ask, "Where can I find a search engine on journalism?" or "Where can I find a search engine on the environment?" The computer will name specialized search engines, such as these two:

www.journalism.net
www.cbd.int/ (Convention on Biological Diversity)

Educational Search Engines

Educational search engines provide subject indexes to the various disciplines (humanities, sciences) and to subtopics under those headings (history, literature, biochemistry, and so on). Try several, because they will take you to academic material, not commercial sites with advertising banners popping up all over the screen.

English Server	http://eserver.org
Internet Public Library	http://ipl.org/
ProQuest K–12	http://www.proquestk12.com/
Library of Congress	http://www.loc.gov/index.html
Discovery Channel	http://dsc.discovery.com/
SearchEDU	http://www.searchedu.com
SearchGOV	http://www.searchgov.com
SearcheBOOKS	http://www.searchebooks.com
SearchMIL	http://www.searchmil.com
Voice of the Shuttle	http://vos.ucsb.edu/

Returning once again to Sherri James and her investigations, we find her entering the phrase "blood doping" at the SearchEDU engine, which directed her to the United States Olympic Committee at **http://www.usoc.org/**, where she found the following source:

What Is Doping?

Currently national anti-doping agencies around the world are working to harmonize the definition of doping. For USADA testing, each athlete is responsible for his/her International Federation's (IF) definition of doping since USADA looks to IF definitions. The Olympic Movement Anti-Doping Code (OMADC), revised by the International Olympic Committee (IOC) in late 2005, set forth one definition of doping as follows:

> "The presence of a substance, defined as a prohibited substance under the Olympic Movement Anti-Doping Code (OMADC), in a competitor's sample or the use of a prohibited method under OMADC."

Doping does not necessarily mean that performance is enhanced. The ethics of both sport and medical science are breached when someone dopes. It is important to remember that a doping violation can happen regardless of whether an athlete deliberately uses a prohibited substance, or unknowingly uses a product containing a prohibited substance. The presence of a prohibited substance or evidence of the use of prohibited method in your sample constitutes a doping violation, irrespective of how it got there.

The bottom line is that you are responsible for any substance that you ingest—it is your responsibility to ensure that any product you take does not contain a prohibited substance.

Why Is Doping Prohibited?

Doping is prohibited to protect your rights to compete on a level playing field without the use of prohibited substances or prohibited methods. There are other reasons to prohibit doping, including the fact that doping can cause:

- **Harm to athletes who dope.** Most sports carry a certain amount of risk. Many prohibited substances and methods may add serious risks of harm to those that use them. Clean and ethical sport does not require that athletes take unnecessary risks.
- **Harm to athletes who do not dope.** Athletes who dope ruin fair sport for all athletes who do not dope. Clean athletes may perceive the need to dope in order to compete with other athletes they suspect are doping. This senseless cycle of doping can bring about personal devastation through health and safety risks, and the destruction of sport.

Sherrie James can draw several ideas from this source.

Educational Search Engines Maintained by Libraries

Here's a list of excellent sites that provide valuable academic information.

BUBL Link	**http://bubl.ac.uk/**
Internet Public Library	**http://www.ipl.org/ref**
Librarians Index to the Internet	**http://lii.org**
Scout Select	**http://scout.wisc.edu/ Projects/PastProjects/ toolkit/bookmarks/**

HINT: Most Web programs include a Bookmark or Favorites tool to save addresses for quick access. When you find a file you want to access later, create a bookmark so you can revisit it with just a click of the mouse. In Microsoft Internet Explorer, use the button bar marked Favorites to make your bookmarks. *Note*: If you are working at a university computer laboratory, do not add bookmarks to the hard drive. Instead, save the bookmarks to your flash drive by using Save As in the File menu.

4d Searching for Articles in Journals and Magazines

The Internet helps you find articles in online journals and magazines. *Note*: The *best* source for academic journals is your library's database collection. (See section 5d.)

Online Journals

You can find online journals in one of three ways:

- First access your favorite search engine and use a keyword search for "journals" plus the name of your subject. For example, one student accessed AltaVista and used a keyword search for "journals + fitness." The search produced links to twenty online journals devoted to fitness, such as *Health Page, Excite Health*, and *Physical Education*. Another student's search for "women's studies + journals" produced a list of relevant journals, such as *Feminist Collections, Resources for Feminist Research*, and *Differences*. By accessing one of these links, the student can examine abstracts and articles.
- Second access a search engine's subject directory. In Yahoo!, for example, one student selected Social Science from the key directory, clicked on Sociology, clicked on Journals, and accessed links to several online journals, such as *Edge: The E-Journal of Intercultural Relations* and *Sociological Research Online*.
- Third, if you already know the name of a journal, go to your favorite search engine to make a keyword query, such as "Psycholoquy," which will link you to the social science journal of that name.

Online Magazines

Several directories exist for discovering articles in magazines.

NewsDirectory.Com   http://www.newsdirectory.com/new/

This search engine directs you to magazine home pages where you can begin your free search in that magazine's archives. Under "current events," for example, it will send you to *Atlantic Monthly* at <theatlantic.com>, *Harper's* at <Harpers.org>, and *Newsweek* at <Newsweek.com>.

Highbeam Research   http://www.highbeam.com/

This site has a good search engine, but it requires membership (which is free for one month). Remember to cancel your membership after you finish research, or charges will accrue.

Pathfinder   http://pathfinder.com/

This site gives you free access to *Time* magazine; it has a good search engine with links to thousands of archival articles.

ZD Net   http://www.zdnet.com/

This search engine provides excellent access to industry-oriented articles in banking, electronics, computers, management, and so on. It offers two weeks of free access before charges begin to accrue.

4e Searching for Articles in Newspapers and Media Sources

First, to find almost any newspaper in the United States, even the local weeklies, consult:

www.newspapers.com

This site takes you to the *Aspen Times* or the *Carbondale Valley Journal* or one of 800-plus newspapers. In most cases, the online newspaper has its own internal search engine that enables you to examine articles from its archives. Figure 4.5 shows the opening page of the online site for a local newspaper in Los Angeles, California. Notice especially the hyperlink at the upper left, **Archives**, a feature that enables you to find articles from past issues.

Most major news organizations maintain Internet sites. Consult one of these:

The Chronicle of Higher Education   http://chronicle.com

This site requires a paid subscription, so access it through your library at no cost.

CNN Interactive   http://www.cnn.com

CNN maintains a good search engine that takes you quickly, without cost, to transcripts of its broadcasts. It's a good source for research in current events.

C-SPAN Online   http://www.c-span.org

This site focuses on public affairs and offers both a directory and a search engine for research in public affairs, government, and political science.

Fox News   http://www.foxnews.com

This site provides articles from its own network and also from news services such as Reuters and the Associated Press.

London Times   http://www.timesonline.co.uk/tol/news/

The *Times* provides directories and indexes, but not a search engine, so improve your search for articles in the *Times* with **searchuk.com**.

National Public Radio Online   http://www.npr.org

NPR provides audio articles via RealPlayer or some other audio engine. Be prepared to take careful notes.

The *New York Times* on the Web   http://www.nytimes.com

You can read recent articles for free. However, if you search the 365-day archive, be prepared with your credit card. Articles cost $2.50. After purchase, they appear on the monitor for printing or downloading.

USA Today   http://www.usatoday.com

FIGURE 4.5 Los Angeles's *Larchmont Chronicle*.

This site has a fast search engine that provides information about current events.

U.S. News Online   http://www.usnews.com

This magazine site has a fast search engine and provides free, in-depth articles on current political and social issues.

Wall Street Journal   http://online.wsj.com/public/us

This business-oriented site has excellent information, but it requires a subscription.

The *Washington Times*   http://www.washingtontimes.com/

Look here for up-to-the-minute political news.

To find other newspapers and online media, search for "newspapers" on Yahoo! or AltaVista. Your college library may also provide Lexis-Nexis, which searches news sources for you.

4f   Searching for Photographs and Other Visual Sources

For some topics, you may want to find photographs or other visual sources as part of your research. A paper on representations of women in World War II propaganda posters, for example, would require visual evidence to support its thesis. In disciplines like history and art, visual sources might be central to your paper. Because of their persuasive power, images need to be selected and used carefully in any research paper.

The best place to begin searching for photographs and other visual sources is one of three search engines tailored to finding images.

Google Image Search   http://images.google.com/
Yahoo! Image Search   http://images.search.yahoo.com/
Picsearch   http://www.picsearch.com/

For topics in U.S. history and culture, the Library of Congress has a comprehensive archive of visual and multimedia sources in its American Memory collection, which you can access and search at http://memory.loc.gov/ammem/index.html.

Remember that visual sources, like all other sources, need to be carefully incorporated into your paper and properly documented. See section 10e for more advice about using visuals effectively in your paper. Photographs and other visual sources are copyrighted works like any other published source, and need to be cited to give proper credit to their creators. See pages 164–166 for examples showing proper citation format for photographs, graphs, and other visual sources.

4g   Accessing E-books

One of the best sources of full-text online books is the Online Books Page at the University of Pennsylvania: **http://digital.library.upenn.edu/books/**. This site indexes books by author, title, and subject. It has a search engine that will take you quickly, for example, to the full text of Thomas Hardy's *A Pair of Blue Eyes* or to Linnea Hendrickson's *Children's Literature: A Guide to the Criticism*. This site adds new textual material almost every day, so consult it first. Understand, however, that contemporary books, still under copyright protection, are not included. That is, you can freely download an Oscar Wilde novel but not one by Alice Walker. JSTOR is another site for accessing books in a photocopied format (see pages 63–64). *Caution:* Other sites offer e-books, but they are commercial and require a subscription.

4h Using Listserv, Usenet, and Chat Groups

E-mail discussion groups have legitimacy for the exchange of academic ideas when everybody in the group has the same purpose, project, or course of study. Chat rooms seldom have academic value. Let's look at each briefly.

E-mail News Groups

The word **listserv** is used to describe discussion groups that correspond via e-mail about a specific educational or technical subject. For example, your literature professor might ask everybody in the class to join a listserv group on Victorian literature. To participate, you must have an e-mail address and subscribe to the list as arranged by your instructor.

In like manner, online courses, which have grown in popularity, usually have a discussion area where students are expected to participate by responding to general questions for the group or corresponding with each other about assignments, issues, and other topics. On the Blackboard system, for example, online students have a Discussion Board with any number of Forums where they may participate or where they are required to participate.

Usenet.com   http://www.usenet.com
Search the main directory of Usenet.com for more than 2 million articles and 120,000 mailing lists.

Tile.Net   http://www.tile.net/
This site provides access to lists, usenet newsgroups, and other sites.

At some point you may wish to join a list, and each site will explain the procedure for subscribing and participating via e-mail in a discussion.

Real-Time Chatting

Usenet and chat groups use Internet sites with immediate messaging rather than e-mail. To access usenet, go to <dogpile.com> or <metacrawler.com> and click the People & Chat button before launching the search. Typing "fitness" might take you, under a fictional name, to a reasonable discussion, but probably not. Another way to find discussion groups is through a keyword search for "List of online chat groups" at one of the search engines. If you want a commercial site that requires a monthly fee, try Usenet.com. However, *you cannot cite from these anonymous sources*, so they are best avoided for your academic work.

4i Examining Library Holdings via Online Access

Most major libraries now offer online access to their library catalog. This allows you to search their collections for books, videos, dissertations, audio tapes, special collections, and other items. However, you must open an account and use your identification to log in, just as you do with your college library. You may sometimes order books online through interlibrary loan. Additionally, some libraries now post full-text documents, downloadable bibliographies, databases, and links to other sites.

If you need identification of all books on a topic, as copyrighted and housed in Washington, DC, consult:

Library of Congress   http://www.loc.gov/index.html
This site allows you to search by word, phrase, name, title, series, and
    number. It provides special features, such as an American Memory
    Home Page, full-text legislative information, and exhibitions, such as
    the various drafts of Lincoln's "Gettysburg Address."

For an Internet overview of online libraries, their holdings, and addresses, consult:

LIBCAT   http://www.librarysites.info
This site gives you easy access to almost 3,000 online library catalogs.

LIBWEB   http://lists.webjunction.org/libweb
This site takes you to home pages of academic, public, and state libraries.
    You will be prompted for a public-access login name, so follow the
    directions for entering and exiting the programs.

Another kind of online library is:

IngentaConnect   http://www.ingentaconnect.com
This site provides a keyword search of 17,000 journals by author, title, or
    subject. Copies of the articles can be faxed to you, usually within the
    hour, for a small fee.

4j   Finding an Internet Bibliography

You can quickly build a bibliography on the Internet in two ways: by using a search engine or by visiting an online book store.

Search Engine

At a search engine on the Internet, such as AltaVista, enter a descriptive phrase, such as "Child Abuse Bibliographies." You will get a list of bibliographies, and you can click on one of them, such as:

Child Abuse
Child Abuse. Child Abuse Articles. Child Abuse Reports.
http://www.childwelfare.com

Clicking on the hypertext address will carry you to a list:

Child Abuse Articles
Child Abuse Reports

Child Sexual Abuse

Substance Abuse

Clicking on the first item will produce a set of hypertext links to articles you might find helpful, such as this one:

Lombard, Antoinette. "The Impact of Social Transformation on the

Non-Government Welfare Sector and the Social Work Profession."

International Journal of Social Welfare 17.2 (Apr. 2008): 124–31.

Online Bookstore

Use the search engines of Amazon.com and BarnesandNoble.com to gain a list of books currently available. In most cases, the books on the list will be available in your library. For example, one student searched BarnesandNoble.com for books on "fad dieting." She received the list as shown in Figure 4.6, which gave her the beginnings of a complete bibliography.

FIGURE 4.6 A page from the Barnes & Noble Web site listing books on the topic "fad dieting."

4k   Conducting Archival Research on the Internet

The Internet has made possible all kinds of research in library and museum archives. You may have an interest in this type of work. If so, consider several ways to approach the study.

Go to the Library

Go into a library and ask about the archival material housed there, or use the library's electronic catalog. Most libraries have special collections. The Stanford University Library, for example, offers links to antiquarian books, old manuscripts, and other archives. It also provides ways to find material by subject, by title, and by collection number. It carries the researcher to a link, such as the London (Jack) Papers, 1897–1916 at the Online Archive of California. These can be accessed by Internet if the researcher has the proper credentials for entering and using the Stanford collection.

Go to an Edited Search Engine

An edited search engine, such as Yahoo!, may give you results quickly. For example, requesting "Native American literature + archives" produced such links as:

American Native Press Archives
Native American History Archive
Native Americans and the Environment
Indigenous Peoples' Literature
Sayings of Chief Joseph

One or more of these collections might open the door to an interesting topic and enlightening research.

Go to a Metasearch Engine

A metasearch engine such as Dogpile.com offers a way to reach archival material. Make a keyword request, such as "Native American literature + archives." Dogpile will list such sites as Reference Works and Research Material for Native American Studies, which is located at **www.stanford.edu**. There, the Native American Studies Collections offers several valuable lists:

Native American Studies Encyclopedias and Handbooks
Native American Studies Bibliographies
Native American Studies Periodical Indexes
Native American Biography Resources
Native American Studies Statistical Resources
Links to other Native American sites on the Internet
Links to usenet discussion groups related to Native Americans

Thus, the researcher would have a wealth of archival information to examine.

FIGURE 4.7 The home page of the Red Earth Museum, where a student might find archival information on Native Americans.

Use Search Engine Directories

Use the directory and subdirectories of a search engine and let them take you deeper and deeper into the files. Remember, this tracing goes quickly. Here are examples of links at several engines:

Excite Guide	Lifestyle: Cultures and Groups: Native Americans: Literature
Lycos	Entertainment: Books: Literature: Native American Literature
AltaVista	Society: History: Indigenous People: Native Americans: Art

The latter site, for example, carried one researcher to the National Museum of the American Indian (see Figure 4.7).

Go to a Listserv or Usenet Group

Using a search engine, simply join your topic with the word listserv: "Native American literature + listserv." The search engine will produce such links as **Native-L: Native Literature listserv and archives**. By following the proper procedures, you can log on and begin corresponding. Participants might quickly point you in the direction of good topics and sources for developing the paper.

Go to Newspaper Archives

Use **www.newspapers.com** to locate a newspaper of interest, and then use the newspaper's search engine to explore its archives of articles. See page 52 for more information on this valuable resource.

YOUR RESEARCH PROJECT

1. To look for an online discussion group on your topic, go to a metasearch engine (see page 48); however, before entering your subject, select the button for searching newsgroups rather than the Web. Explore the choices. You may also search the lists described in 4h, page 55.

2. Voice of the Shuttle is a large and powerful search engine for educational information. Enter this URL, **http://vos.ucsb.edu/**, and search for your topic. If unsuccessful, try one of the other educational search engines listed on pages 49–50.

3. When you have found an Internet article directly devoted to your subject, apply to it an evaluation as described on pages 42–43. Ask yourself, "Does this site have merit?" Apply that same test to other Internet articles as you find them.

4. Practice using the Bookmark feature of your browser. That is, rather than print an article from the Internet, bookmark it instead for future reference (see page 50).

5. As you would with library sources, begin making bibliography entries and writing notes about promising Internet sources. Begin building a computer file of promising sources, develop a folder of printouts from the Internet, and save pertinent information you will need for your bibliography entries later on (see pages 62–63 for more information on a working bibliography, and see pages 266–271 for examples of the bibliography for Internet sources).

For more resources in research, writing, and documentation, go to MyCompLab.com

5 Gathering Sources in the Library

The library should be the center of your research, whether you access it electronically from your laptop or go there in person. As the repository of the best books and periodicals, it is the highest quality resource you can access. You cannot ignore it.

Why is the library a better source than the Internet? Scholarship, that's why! The articles you access through the library are written by scholars and published in journals only after careful review by a board of like-minded scholars.

Also, in today's libraries, sources can be accessed just as easily as online. In fact, many of the library's databases are part of the Web. Logged in at the library, you can download articles to your computer, print files, and read some books online. But you also need to visit the library in person to soak up the atmosphere of academia as well as consult books in the reference room and visit the stacks to find and check out books.

5a Launching the Search

Your research strategy in the library should include four steps, with adjustments for your individual needs.

1. **Conduct a preliminary search for relevant sources.** Scan the reference section of your library for its electronic sources as well as the abundance of printed indexes, abstracts, bibliographies, and reference books. Search the library's electronic book catalog and dip into the electronic databases, such as Academic Search Premier or InfoTrac. This preliminary work will serve several purposes:
   - It shows the availability of source materials with diverse opinions.
   - It provides a beginning set of reference citations, abstracts, and full-text articles.
   - It defines and restricts your subject.
   - It gives you an overview of the subject by showing how others have researched it.

2. **Refine the topic and evaluate the sources.** As soon as you refine the topic, you can spend valuable time reading abstracts, articles, and pertinent sections of books. Most instructors will expect you to cite from the library's scholarly sources, so a mix of journal articles and books should accompany your online articles and field research.

61

3. **Take shortcuts.** First, consult Appendix B of this book, "Finding Reference Works for Your General Topic" (pages 377–383), which lists appropriate electronic and printed sources. It sends you to key sources in psychology, art, literature, and most other disciplines. For example, if your work is on an education topic, it sends you to ERIC (online), *Current Index to Journals in Education*, and Edweb (online), but it sends computer science students to INSPEC (online) or to *Computer Literature Index*.

   In addition, you will need to access a variety of computer sources in the library, such as the electronic book catalog (see pages 64–65) and the electronic services like InfoTrac (see pages 69–70). Without leaving the computer workstation in the reference room of the library, you can develop a working bibliography, read a few abstracts and full-text articles, and, in general, make substantive advances before you ever enter the library stacks.

4. **Read and take notes.** Examine books, articles, essays, reviews, computer printouts, and government documents. Whenever possible, write complete notes as you read so you can transcribe them or paste them into your text.

5. **Consult with a reference librarian.** If your topic does not initially generate a number of sources, confer with a reference librarian. A reference librarian may suggest more appropriate words or phrases for the subject; this can be a critical step when you feel that you might be stuck.

HINT: Just as we learn proper Internet behavior, we learn basic library etiquette, such as talking softly out of respect for others and not bringing in food or drinks. Also, the best researchers do not reshelve books and periodicals; they leave them at the reshelving bins so librarians can return them to the correct place. They rewind microfilm and leave it in the reshelving bin. They avoid breaking down the spines of books in attempts to copy the pages. At the computer station, they analyze sources and then print; they do not randomly print everything. (See pages 42–43 for methods of analyzing a source.)

5b Developing a Working Bibliography

Because the research paper is a major project involving many papers and notes, organization is crucial. That means keeping a copy of every abstract, article, and downloaded file with full publication information and the URLs of Internet materials. Your final manuscript will require a bibliography page listing all your sources, so now is the time to start developing a working bibliography. A working bibliography serves three purposes:

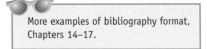
More examples of bibliography format, Chapters 14–17.

1. It locates articles and books for notetaking purposes.

2. It provides information for the in-text citations, as in this example in MLA style:

> The healing properties of certain foods have been noted by Milner
> (682–88) and Hasler (6–10).

3. It provides information for the final reference page (see Chapters 14–17). If you keep your entries current in a computer file, you can easily insert them into your Works Cited page at the end of your manuscript.

Whether you keyboard your sources or make handwritten notes for easy access, each working bibliography entry should contain the following information—with variations, of course, for books, periodicals, and government documents:

1. Author's name
2. Title of the work
3. Publication information
4. Library call number
5. (Optional) A personal note about the location or contents of the source
6. The URL for online sources

Works Cited Entry for a Book (MLA style):

> Kennedy, D. James, and Jerry Newcombe. *How Would Jesus Vote?* New
> York: Doubleday, 2008. Print.

Works Cited Entry for a Journal Article (MLA style):

> Hill, Marc Lamont, Biany Perez, and Decoteau J. Irby. "Street Fiction:
> What Is It and What Does It Mean for English Teachers?" *English*
> *Journal* 97 (Jan. 2008): 76–81. Print.

Works Cited Entry for an Article Found on an Academic Database (MLA style):

> Box, Richard C. "Redescribing the Public Interest." *Social Science*
> *Journal* 38 (2007): 585–98. *EBSCOHost.* Web. 3 Nov. 2008.

Works Cited Entry for a Magazine Article (MLA style):

> Rios, Alberto. "Refugio's Hair." *Read.* 8 Feb. 2008: 18–19. Print.

Bibliography Entry for an Internet Article (MLA style):

> Pankratz, Howard. "Teachers Turn Tables on Disinterested Students."
> *Denver Post Online.* 7 Mar. 2008. Web. 14 Mar. 2008.

5c Finding Books on Your Topic

Much of your research will be conducted on the library's electronic network with call numbers to its own books and with links to sources around the world.

Using Your Library's Electronic Book Catalog

Your library's computerized catalog to its holdings probably has a special name, such as LIBNET, FELIX, ACORN, UTSEARCH, and so forth. In theory, it will include every book in the library filed by subject, author, and title. Begin your research at the catalog by using a *keyword search* to a subject, such as "Health." You will get a list of books on the monitor, and you can click on each one to gather more information. The list will look something like this:

Search Results

Women's Qigong for Health and Longevity: A Practical Guide for Women.
Deborah Davis. 2008.

Healthiest Meals on Earth: The Surprising Unbiased Truth about What Meals
You Should Eat and Why. Jonny Bowden and Jeannette Bessinger. 2008.

The Cure: Heal Your Body, Save Your Life. Timothy Brantley. 2007.

The electronic card catalog, in effect, has provided a bibliography that lists a variety of available books on a particular subject.

The next procedure is to click on one, such as *The Cure: Heal Your Body, Save Your Life*, to get the full details with call number and availability, as shown in the following example. You can print the information and use it to find the book in the stacks and to write your working bibliography. The entry at your library will be similar to this example:

The Success Principles: How to Get from Where You Are to
   Where You Want to Be / Jack Canfield and Janet Switzer.
By Jack Canfield and Janet Switzer.
New York: Harper Collins, 2004
Subjects: Self-improvements—Self-help—Success—Relationships
Description: 473 p,; ill,; 34 cm.
Series: Self-help and improvement
COPY / HOLDING INFORMATION

Location	Collection	Call No.	Status
Woodward Library	General Book Collection, Level 3	TE331.A8 D75 2004	Available

---

The card catalog will also help you find subject-specific bibliographies. For instance, one student entered *bibliographies + women's studies*. The catalog provided a large list of sites, each appearing as a hypertext link to full data on the source. Here's an example of four items from a list of 30 or more:

- **Bibliographies on Native American Women's Theatre** (2006)
- **Bibliography: Gender and Technology** (2008)
- **Women Immigrants 1945 to the Present: A Bibliography** (2007)
- **Black American Feminism: A Multidisciplinary Bibliography** (2006)

HINT: Many college libraries as well as public libraries are now part of library networks. The network expands the holdings of every library because one library will loan books to another. Therefore, if a book you need is unavailable in your library, ask a librarian about an interlibrary loan. Understand, however, that you may have to wait several days for its delivery. Periodical articles usually come quickly by fax.

Using the Library's Printed Bibliographies

You may need to supplement your computer printouts by searching printed reference guides, bibliographies, and indexes.

Searching the General Bibliographies

When ordering its research databases, the library subscribes to electronic versions or print versions. You will need to determine which are available. Three general works provide page numbers to many books and journals that contain bibliographies on numerous subjects.

> *Bibliographic Index: A Cumulative Bibliography of Bibliographies.* New York: Wilson, 1938–date. Available both in print and online within your library's network.
> Hillard, James, and Bethany J. Easter. *Where to Find What: A Handbook to Reference Service.* 4th ed. Metuchen, NJ: Scarecrow, 2000.
> Balay, Robert, et al. *Guide to Reference Books.* 11th ed. Chicago: ALA, 1996.

These guides will also give you a list of books relating to your subject. Figure 5.1 shows how *Bibliographic Index* will send you to bibliographic lists that are hidden inside books; these are sources you might not find otherwise. Entries will look something like this to show that a bibliography will be found in LeBlanc's book on pages 247–64. Such a list could be a valuable resource in the early stages of research.

Prehistoric War

LeBlanc, Steven A. *Constant Battles: The Myth of the Peaceful, Noble Savage.* New York: St. Martin's, 2003 p 247–64.

FIGURE 5.1 Example from *Bibliographic Index*, 2003.

If the book fits your research, you will probably want to write a bibliography entry for this source. Then you can examine the text as well as the bibliography on pages 247–64 of LeBlanc's book, where you might find additional articles on this topic. Here is a student's bibliography notation:

LeBlanc, Steven A. <u>Constant Battles: The Myth of the Peaceful, Noble Savage</u>.

    New York: St. Martin's, 2003. Bibliography on pages 247–64. Print.

Using the Trade Bibliographies

Trade bibliographies, intended primarily for use by booksellers and librarians, can help you in three ways:

1. Discover sources not listed in other bibliographies or in the card catalog.
2. Locate facts of publication, such as place and date.
3. Determine if a book is in print.

Search this work for your topic:

Subject Guide to Books in Print (New York: Bowker, 1957–date).

Note: Online, this source may appear as **Books in Print**.

Use this work for its subject classifications, any one of which will provide a ready-made bibliography to books. Figure 5.2 shows a sample found with the keyword "education."

The following trade bibliographies may also lead you to valuable sources available online or in printed versions:

Books in Print lists by author and title all books currently in print.

Publishers' Weekly offers the current publication data on new books and new editions.

Paperbound Books in Print locates all paperback books on one topic; these are usually books available at local bookstores.

Cumulative Book Index provides complete publication data on one book but will also locate *all* material in English on a particular subject.

Library of Congress Catalog: Books, Subject provides a ready-made bibliography to books on hundreds of subjects.

Ulrich's International Periodicals Directory helps you locate current periodicals, both domestic and foreign, and to order photocopies of articles.

Using the Bibliographies in Appendix B

Go to Appendix B of this book, pages 377–383. It furnishes a guide to important reference works—some in print at the library, some online in the

1 —— Foster, Charles R., et al. Educating Clergy:

2 —— Teaching Practices and the Pastoral Imagination.

3 —— LC 2005-024316. xx, 435p. 2005. —— 4 / 5

6 —— 40.00 (0787977446) Wiley Pub. —— 7 / 8

FIGURE 5.2 From *Subject Guide to Books in Print*, 2005.
1. Author 2. Title 3. Library of Congress number 4. Number of pages 5. Date of publication 6. Price
7. International Standard Book Number (used when ordering) 8. Publisher

library's electronic network, and others available on the Internet. Reference sources are listed for nine major categories (see page 377–383). Here are three examples of titles to reference works that you will find under the heading "Issues in the Arts, Literature, Music, and Language." The first is a printed source in the library, the second is available on the library's electronic network, and the third is available on the Internet.

> *MLA International Bibliography of Books and Articles on the Modern Languages and Literatures.* New York: MLA, 1921–present. The best overall index to major literary figures, literary issues, and language topics. Online and in print.

> *MLA International Bibliography of Books and Articles on the Modern Languages and Literatures.* New York: MLA, 1921–date. This reference work indexes major literary figures, literary issues, and language topics; may be listed on the library's network as *MLA Bibliography*.

> *Netlibrary* **http://www.netlibrary.com**. This site provides a vast collection of full-text stories, poems, novels, and dramas; search by title or author and then read the text online or print it out; must create a membership account.

Searching for Bibliographies in Encyclopedias

Search for specialized encyclopedias in your field at the electronic book catalog. Entering "encyclopedia of psychology" might give you a list that looks like this:

BF31.E52 2000
> **Encyclopedia of psychology**

BF31.E52 2001
> **The Corsini encyclopedia of psychology and behavioral science**

BF31.B25 1999
> **Baker encyclopedia of psychology and counseling**

Click on one, scan an article, and look especially at the end of the article for a bibliography. It might point you to additional sources, like the one shown in Figure 5.3.

Examining the Bibliography at the End of a Book

When you get into the stacks, look for bibliographies at the end of books. Jot down titles on cards or photocopy the list for further reference. An example is shown in Figure 5.4.

Searching for Bibliographies at the End of Journal Articles

See also 8a, "Finding Reliable Sources."

Look for bibliographies at the end of articles in scholarly journals. For example, students of history depend on the bibliographies in various issues of *English Historical Review*, and students of literature find bibliographies in

---

FURTHER REFERENCES

Clarke, E., & Dewhurst, K. *An illustrated history of brain function.*
Clarke, E., & O'Malley, C.D. *The human brain and spinal cord.*
Ferrier, D. *The functions of the brain.*
Finger, S., & Stein, D.G. *Brain damage and recovery: Research and clinical perspectives.*
McHenry, L.C., Jr. *Garrison's history of neurology.*

FIGURE 5.3 Sample bibliography from the end of an article in *Encyclopedia of Psychology*.

SECONDARY SOURCES

Abbott, Edith. "The Civil War and the Crime Wave of 1865–70." *Social Service Review,* 1977.
Amis, Moses N. *Historical Raleigh,* 1913.
Andrews, Marietta M. *Scraps of Paper.* 1929.
Badeau, Adam. *Military History of U.S. Grant.* 1885.
Bailey, Mrs. Hugh. "Mobile's Tragedy: The Great Magazine Explosion of 1865."*Alabama Review,* 1968.
Bakeless, John. "The Mystery of Appomattox." *Civil War Times Illustrated,* 1970.

FIGURE 5.4 A portion of a bibliography list at the end of N. A. Trudeau's book, *Out of the Storm*.

Studies in Short Fiction. In addition, the journals themselves provide subject indexes to their own contents. If your subject is "Adoption," you will discover that a majority of your sources are located in a few key journals. In that instance, going straight to the annual index of one of those journals will be a shortcut.

5d Finding Articles in Magazines and Journals

An index furnishes the exact page number(s) of specific sections of books and of individual articles in magazines, journals, and newspapers. The library's online index of databases not only directs you to articles in magazines, it also gives an abstract of the article, and more and more often, it provides the full text. Thus, at the library's computer terminals, you might download several articles without going into the stacks at all.

Searching the General Indexes to Periodicals

The library network gives you access to electronic databases. Here are just a few of the many that will be available to you:

AGRICOLA	Agriculture, animal and plant sciences
America: History and Life	U.S. history
American Chemical Society Publications	Chemistry
BioOne	Biological, ecological, and environmental sciences
CINAHL	Nursing, public health, and allied health fields
ERIC	Education and mass communication
GPO	Government publications on all subjects
HighWire	Science, technology, and medicine

The Journal of Nutrition, January 2006, 136:277S-280S

Amino Acids and Muscle Loss with Aging.

Full Text: COPYRIGHT 2006 American Society for Nutrition

Byline: Satoshi Fujita and Elena Volpi

Aging is associated with a progressive loss of muscle mass (sarcoopenia), which increases the risks of injury and disability. Although the mechanisms of sarcopenia are not clearly elucidated, age-associated alterations in the muscle anabolic response to nutritional stimuli and a decline in protein intake may be significant contributing factors. The most recent findings regarding the role of nutritional intake on protein metabolism in the elderly will be reviewed. Specifically, aging is associated with changes in the muscle protein metabolism response to a meal, likely due to alterations in the response to endogenous hormones. Nonetheless, the older muscle is still able to respond to amino acids, mainly the essential and BCAAs, which have been shown to acutely stimulate muscle protein synthesis in older individuals. It is likely that this stimulatory effect of essential and BCAA is due to the direct effect of leucine on the initiation of mrna translation, which is still present in older age, although it appears to be attenuated in aged animals. Recent data suffest that excess leucine may be able to overcome this age-related resistance of muscle proteins to leucine. For this reason, long-term essential amino acid supplementation may be a useful tool for the prevention and treatment of sarcopenia, particularly if excess leucine is provided in the supplement.

▮▮▮ **FIGURE 5.5 InfoTrac printout with abstract.**

InfoTrac	All subjects
JSTOR	Social sciences
Lexis-Nexis Academic	News, business, law, medicine, reference
MLA Bibliography	Literature, linguistics, and folklore
Music Index	Music
ProjectMUSE	Social sciences, arts, humanities
PsycINFO	Psychology, medicine, education, social work
Westlaw	Legal subjects, including laws and cases

One of these databases will usually guide you to several sources, provide an abstract, and often provide a full-text version of the article, as shown in Figure 5.5.

CHECKLIST

Using Databases

Library databases are the most effective way to locate and access scholarly journal articles. If you can, visit your library for a tutorial on using databases. Use the following steps to find articles in databases.

1. **Go to your library home page and find the links to the databases.**

Bakersfield College

Calendar · Webmail · My BanWeb · A-Z Index Faculty Sites Departments Search

Search the BC Site

Home Admissions & Records Student Services Programs & Classes Community Resources Employee Services About BC

Student Services
Assessment Center
Athletics
Bookstore
Career Center
Child Care
Counseling
Disabled Students
Programs & Services
EOPS
ESL Tutoring
Financial Aid
Fitness Center
Health Center
International Students
Library

Home > Student Services
Grace Van Dyke Bird Library

Find a Book...
   BC Library Catalog
   BC eBooks Collection
   Other Libraries

Search the Internet ...
   Useful Internet Resources
   Quick Reference Links
   Search Engines
   Websites for Classes

Research Guides...

Find an Article ...
   EBSCOhost
   Gale Expanded Academic
   Gale Literature Resource Center
   Gale Biography Resource Center
   LexisNexis
   Free Online Periodical Databases
   Trial Periodical Databases

   Is this Journal Available Full-Text Online?
   Serials Solutions
   Off-Campus Connections Problems?

Every library's home page is different, but you can usually find a section that will link you to the database collections.

2. **Select a database and search by keyword for articles on your topic.** A keyword search for "gender and communication" results in a list of articles like this one. From your results list, you can preview article titles and publication information to select articles that look promising for your topic.

3. Locate the full text of the articles you need.

By clicking on the "PDF Full Text" link on the search results page, you can download the full text of this article. If the full text is not available online, you will need to copy the title and publication information and find the printed article in your library stacks.

Be sure to record the author, title, and publication information for your source, as well as the database you used to retrieve it. You'll need that information later for your works cited page. See pages 172-174 for information about citing sources retrieved from databases.

Finding Indexes by Topic in Appendix B

Appendix B in this textbook, pages 377-383, lists many indexes to periodical articles. The list is organized by topic, so you can find the best references for your field. Shown below are a few of the entries for Music:

Bibliographic Guide to Music. Boston: Hall, 1976-present. Annually. This reference work provides an excellent subject index to almost every topic in the field of music. It will give you the bibliographic data to several articles on most topics in the field.

Music Article Guide. Philadelphia: Information Services, 1966-present. This reference work indexes music education and instrumentation in such journals as *Brass and Wind News, Keyboard, Flute Journal*, and *Piano Quarterly*.

Music Index. Warren, MI: Information Coordinators, 1949-date. This reference work indexes music journals such as *American Music Teacher, Choral Journal, Journal of Band Research, Journal of Music Therapy*.

The New Grove Dictionary of Music and Musicians. Ed. Stanley Sadie and John Tyrrell. 29 vols. New York: Grove, 2001. This mammoth work will provide you with information on almost every topic related to music. A good place to find technical definitions.

RILM Abstracts of Music Literature. Online and in print. This massive collection provides you with brief descriptions to help you in selecting appropriate works for you bibliography.

Using the H. W. Wilson Indexes

For many years, the Wilson Company in Minneapolis has provided excellent indexes to periodical literature. The tradition continues, and the indexing firm has kept its lists current by making its indexes available online as well as in printed versions. The index topics will send you to articles in a wide variety of periodicals in many disciplines.

Readers' Guide to Periodical Literature

The *Readers' Guide to Periodical Literature* (online and in print) indexes important reading for the early stages of research in magazines such as:

Aging	*Foreign Affairs*	*Psychology Today*
American Scholar	*Foreign Policy*	*Scientific Review*

Astronomy	*Health*	*Science Digest*
Bioscience	*Negro History*	*Science*
Business Week	*Oceans*	*SciQuest*
Earth Science	*Physics Today*	*Technology Review*

An entry from *Readers' Guide to Periodical Literature* will look something like this:

> My whole soul is in it. (Smithsonian Bookshelf).
> *Smithsonian* January 2006 v36 i10 p48(8)
> <u>Text with graphics</u> / <u>Library holdings</u>

This entry identifies the title, the magazine, the publication information, and provides a hyperlink to the full text and to any library holdings of *Smithsonian*. Make a bibliographic entry to the source if it looks promising:

> "My Whole Soul Is in It." *Smithsonian* Jan. 2006: 48+. Print.

Note: Writing the pages as "48+." means page 48 and discontinuous pages thereafter.

Social Sciences Index

The *Social Sciences Index* (online and in print) indexes journal articles for 263 periodicals in these fields:

anthropology	geography	political science
economics	law and criminology	psychology
environmental science	medical science	sociology

Humanities Index

The *Humanities Index* (online and in print) catalogs 260 publications in several fields:

archeology	folklore	performing arts
classical studies	history	philosophy
language and literature	literary	religion
area studies	political criticism	theology

Other Indexes

Other indexes of importance include:

Applied Science and Technology Index for articles in chemistry, engineering, computer science, electronics, geology, mathematics, photography, physics, and related fields.

Biological and Agricultural Index for articles in biology, zoology, botany, agriculture, and related fields.

Education Index for articles in education, physical education, and related fields.

Business Periodicals Index for articles in business, marketing, accounting, advertising, and related fields.

Recently Published Articles for articles in history and related fields.

In addition to these major indexes, you should examine the reference work for your topic as listed in Appendix B of this book, pages 377–383.

Searching for an Index to Abstracts

An abstract is a brief description of an article, usually written by the author. An index to abstracts can accelerate your work by allowing you to read the abstract before you assume the task of locating and reading the entire work. You may find them at the electronic book catalog by entering the keyword "abstracts," which will produce a list with great variety. It will look something like this:

show detail	Abstracts of current studies
show detail	Dissertation abstracts international
show detail	Social work abstracts
show detail	Women studies abstracts

1 — AN: 29972501

2 — DT: Article

3 — TI: Vehicles of desistance? The impact of electronically monitored curfew orders

4 — AU: Hucklesby, Anthea

5 — SO: Criminology & Criminal Justice: An International Journal; Feb2008, Vol. 8 Issue 1, p51-71, 21p, 1 graph

6 — IS: 1748-8958

7 — AB: Electronic monitoring has become as integral part of the criminal justice process in England and Wales. Since the first trials in the 1980s the range of applications of electronic monitoring and the number of offenders subject to it have increased. Knowledge about the impact of electronic monitoring on offenders is limited and crucial questions about its effect on offending and desistance remain unanswered. This article addresses these questions by reviewing evidence from a study that interviewed offenders subject to electronically monitored curfew orders. It suggests that for some offenders curfew orders reduce offending and contribute to desistance by addressing levels of social capital in two ways. First, by decreasing levels of anti-social capital by reducing offenders' links with situations, people, places and network correlated with their offending. Second, by improving levels of pro-social capital by encouraging offenders to connect or re-connect with influences linked with desistance such as family and employment. Curfew orders can also have negative impacts on pro-social capital particularly by disrupting employment and family ties and responsibilities. This article concludes that curfew orders have the potential to play a positive and distinctive role in supporting desistance and complement work undertaken as part of the new community order.

FIGURE 5.6 Sample entry from Academic Search Complete.
(1) AN = accession number; (2) DT = document type; (3) TI = title of the article; (4) AU = author; (5) SO = source; (6) IS = ISSN number; (7) AB = abstract of the article.

A more specific keyword search will include your discipline, such as "psychology abstracts." This will produce a reference, most likely, to PsycINFO, the searchable database produced by the American Psychological Association. It will give you the type of entry shown in Figure 5.6.

Searching for Abstracts of Dissertations

You may also wish to examine the abstracts to the dissertations of graduate students in *Dissertation Abstracts International,* which you can access from the Internet via the ProQuest software platform under *ProQuest Dissertations & Theses* or find in a printed version in the library's reference room. In the printed versions, you will need to look for issue no. 12, Part 11, of each volume, for it contains the cumulated subject and author indexes for Issues 1–12 of the volume's two sections—A: *Humanities and Social Sciences,* and B: *Sciences and Engineering.* For example, an online search of *ProQuest Dissertations & Theses* for 2005–2006 listed the three entries shown in Figure 5.7 under the heading "Novels."

The abstract of Charles Eaton Baraw's dissertation is shown in Figure 5.8.

You may cite the abstract in your paper, but inform your readers you are citing from the abstract, not the actual dissertation.

5e Searching for a Biography

When you wish to examine the life of a person, you will find biographies in both books and articles and in print versions as well electronic versions. The electronic card catalog will usually provide multiple sources if you enter the keywords "biography + index."

Novels

1 —— Hawthorne and the traveling eye: Nineteenth-century tourism and American literary culture (Nathaniel Hawthorne). By Baraw,
2 —— Charles Eaton, PhD
3 —— YALE UNIVERSITY, 2005, 265 pages —— 4
5 —— AAT 3168856

American regionalist modernism: Willa Cather, William Faulkner, Oscar Zeta Acosta, and Sandrea Cisneros. By Alumbaugh, Heather Anne, PhD
NEW YORK UNIVERSITY, 2005, 269 pages
AAT 3157808

Native domesticity: Eighteenth-century representations of the multiracial family in the Americas. By Bush, Shannon Alms, PhD
UNIVERSITY OF CALIFORNIA, REVERSIDE, 2005, 245 pages
AAT 3179365

FIGURE 5.7 Findings for an online search of *ProQuest Dissertations & Theses.*
(1) Title of dissertation, (2) author, (3) affiliation, (4) number of pages, (5) publication number.
Image published wih the permission of ProQuest LLC. Further reproduction is prohibited without permission.

1 — AAT 3157808

2 — Hawthorne and the travelling eye: Nineteenth-century tourism and American literary culture (Nathaniel Hawthorne).

3 — By Baraw, Charles Eaton, PhD
YALE UNIVERSITY, 2005, 265 pages — 4

5 — This dissertation presents a new account of nineteenth-century American literary culture by elucidating the crucial and unacknowledged role aesthetic tourism played throughout the paradigmatic career of Nathaniel Hawthorne. The theoretical basis for this study is the assumption that nineteenth-century tourism, as a hybrid social form that combines the pictorialism and perspectivism of the visual arts, the textuality and narrativity of literature, and the performativity of ritual and drama, becomes a new epistemology that I call "the traveling eye," a portable subject position applicable to both literary practice and tourism itself. Using this new conceptual frame, I suggest how Hawthorne's professional travels, following those of Irving, Cooper, and Hale and anticipating those of James, Howells, and Jewett, illustrate the intimate connection between the structures of tourism and the basis of literary authorship in the United States. Throughout the century, aesthetic tourism animated the invention of authorial personae, the construction of the reader, and the creation of literary form. Chapter One outlines this process, taking Washington Irving's invention of Geoffrey Crayon as a central model, and then reading Hawthorne's abandoned book, The Itinerant Story-teller, as his own sophisticated revision of his predecessors. Chapter Two reads all of Hawthorne's professional utterances—letters, prefaces, first-person fictions and sketches—as performances of a fictive (and in Hawthorne's case, a touristic) character and demonstrates how Hawthorne transposes the structure of his epistolary relations with the critic Evert Duyckinck to the imagined relation between the Author as tour-guide and the reader as tourist. Chapter Three, an extended reading of The Blithedale Romance, looks at the narrative errancy, disturbances of memory, and verbal repetition that characterize the narrator's touristic representation of both the utopian community and the new urban sensorium. My interpretations of Hawthorne's later novels demonstrate how the "traveling eye" shapes their form on the levels of verbal style, figuration, and narrative structure. Chapter Four integrates the methodological strategies of previous chapters in a study of the conception, composition, and reception of The Marble Faun, a novel that is experimental in its approach to narrative, description, and characterization and a celebrated attraction on the Anglo-American tour of Rome. Together these chapters introduce both a new version of Hawthorne's work and a new conceptual model for understanding the links between the aesthetics of social practice and the transatlantic production of American literature.

FIGURE 5.8 From *ProQuest Dissertations & Theses*, 2005–2006.
(1) Publication number; (2) title of dissertation; (3) author, degree earned, school, and date; (4) total number of pages of the dissertation; (5) the abstract.
Image published wih the permission of ProQuest LLC. Further reproduction is prohibited without permission.

Show detail	Black biography, 1790–1950
Show detail	Index to literary biography
Show detail	Index to artistic biography
Show detail	Biography index

Several electronic indexes, like InfoTrac and ProQuest, will provide you with abstracts to some biographies and even full-text biographies, such as these:

Biography Reference Bank
Current Biography: 1940–Present
Current Biography Illustrated
Marquis Who's Who Online
Wilson Biographies Plus Illustrated

Other indexes, in print and online, also have value for finding biographies.

Biography Index

The *Biography Index*, in its printed form, has long been a starting point for studies of famous persons. It will lead you to biographical information for people of all lands. See Figure 5.9 for the type of information it provides.

Current Biography Yearbook

Current Biography Yearbook provides a biographical sketch of important people. Most articles are three to four pages in length, and they include references to other sources at the end. It is current, thorough, and has international scope.

Contemporary Authors

Contemporary Authors provides a biographical guide for current writers in fiction, nonfiction, poetry, journalism, drama, motion pictures, television, and a few other fields. It provides a thorough overview of most contemporary writers, giving a list of writings, biographical facts (including a current

---

1 — **Clinton, Hillary Rodham,** **1947-,** **senator** — 3   2
4 — **Bernstein, Carl.** *A Woman in Charge: The Life of Hillary* — 5
   Rodham Clinton. New York: Knopf. 2008. — 7
6
   Wilenze, Sean. Competing Visions of the Presidency?. por
      The Washington Monthly Jan./Feb. 2008.
   Williams, Krissah. Clinton Criticizes Obama Aides Comments
      on Iraq. por *Washington Post* pA01 7 Mar 2008.

FIGURE 5.9 From *Biography Index*, 2008.
(1) Subject, (2) dates of subject's birth and death, (3) subject's profession, (4) author of the biography, (5) title of the biography, (6) publisher, (7) date of publication.

address and agent), a list of writings, sidelights, and, in many cases, an interview by the editors of the guide with the author. Most entries include a bibliography of additional sources about the writer. It has good coverage of major writers and stays current with updates on the important authors.

Dictionary of Literary Biography

Dictionary of Literary Biography provides profiles of thousands of writers in over 100 volumes under such titles as these:

American Humorists, 1800–1950
Victorian Novelists after 1885
American Newspaper Journalists, 1926–1950

5f   Searching for Articles in the Newspaper Indexes

For many years, searching for newspaper articles was difficult, if not impossible. There were no indexes capable of doing the task. Now the electronic networks enable you to find newspaper articles from across the nation. Your library may have a newspaper search engine on its network, or you may need

More on newspapers on the Internet, 4e, pages 52–54.

to go to the World Wide Web and access **newspapers.com**. It will take you quickly to over 800 newspapers, from the *Aspen Times* to the *Carbondale Valley Journal*. In most cases, online newspapers have their own internal search engine that enables you to examine articles from the archives. See pages 52–54 for a full discussion and image of a hometown newspaper. In addition, several indexes are helpful:

Bell and Howell's Index to the Christian Science Monitor
The New York Times Index
Official Index [to *The London Times*]
Wall Street Journal Index

5g   Searching the Indexes to Pamphlet Files

Librarians routinely clip items of interest from newspapers, bulletins, pamphlets, and miscellaneous materials and file them alphabetically by subject in loose-leaf folders.

Vertical File Index

Make the pamphlet file a regular stop during preliminary investigation. Sometimes called the *vertical file*, it will have clippings on many topics, such as:

"Asbestos in the Home"
"Carpel Tunnel Syndrome"

"Everything Doesn't Cause Cancer"

"Medicare and Coordinated Care Plans"

The *Vertical File Index* gives a description of each entry, the price, and how to order the pamphlet. Check at your library's electronic card catalog to see if your librarians have created an online index to local pamphlets.

Social Issues Resources Series (SIRS)

Also important to you are published pamphlets that feature articles on a common topic. *Social Issues Resources Series* (SIRS), online or in print, collects articles on special topics and reprints them as one unit on a special subject, such as abortion, AIDS, prayer in schools, or pollution. With *SIRS* you will have ten or twelve articles readily available in one booklet. Figure 5.10 shows one of numerous sources on this topic as listed in *SIRS Researcher* bibliography.

The CQ Researcher

The CQ Researcher, online and in print, will have one pamphlet, like *SIRS*, devoted to one topic, such as "Energy and the Environment." It will examine central issues on the topic, give background information, show a chronology of important events or processes, express an outlook, and provide an annotated bibliography. In one place you have material worthy of quotation and paraphrase as well as a list of additional sources.

HINT: For the correct citation forms to articles found in *SIRS* or *The CQ Researcher*, section 14c, pages 258–263.

The Irony of Climate, *World Watch Vol. 18, No. 2*

March/April 2005; Lexile Score: 1480; 22K, SIRS Researcher

Summary: "Archaeologists believe that the shift to a warmer, wetter, and more stable climate at the end of the last ice age was key for humanity's successful foray into food production. Yet, from the American breadbasket to the North China Plain to the fields of southern Africa, farmers and climate scientists are finding that generations-old patterns of rainfall and temperature are shifting. Farming may be the human endeavor most dependent on a stable climate—and the industry that will struggle the most to cope with more erratic weather, severe storms, and shifts in growing season lengths." (**World Watch**) This article examines how climate change may affect farming practices in the future.

FIGURE 5.10 An annotated bibliography from *The SIRS Researcher*.

5h   Searching for Government Documents

All branches of the government publish massive amounts of material. Many of these documents have great value for researchers, so investigate the following source if your topic is one that government agencies might have investigated.

GPO on Silverplatter on your library's network or
GPOAccess on the Internet

Either of these sites will take you to the files of the Government Printing Office. The database list includes *Congressional Bills, Congressional Record, Economic Indicators, Public Laws*, the *U.S. Constitution*, and much more. Figure 5.11 shows a record from *GPO Access*, a catalog of U.S. government publication. Following is a works cited entry for the report.

> United States. Congress. Senate. Committee on the Judiciary.
>
> "Comprehensive Immigration Reform: Hearing Before the
>
> Committee on the Judiciary." *Hearing*. 110th Cong., 2nd sess. S
>
> Hearing 110–110, part 2. Washington: GPO, 2007. Print.

Other works that provide valuable information on matters of the government are:

Monthly Catalog of the United State Government Publications. The printed version of GPO.

Public Affairs Information Service Bulletin (PAIS), online and in print. This work indexes articles and documents published by miscellaneous organizations. It's a good place to start because of its excellent index.

Congressional Record, online and in print. This daily publication features Senate and House bills, documents, and committee reports.

1	PB: Washington : U.S. G.P.O. : For sale by the Supt. of Docs., U.S. G.P.O., 2007
2	TI: Comprehensive Immigration reform: hearing before the
3	Committee on the Judiciary, United States Tenth Cogresss, first session, February 28,2007.
4	AU: United States. Congress. Senate. Committee on the Judiciary.
5	LC: KF26 .J8 2007n
6	IS: 9780160792366

FIGURE 5.11 From GPO Access.
(1) PB = Publication Information, (2) TI = Title, (3) CN = Committee Name, (4) AU = Author, (5) LC = Library of Congress Number, (6) IS = GPO Item.

Public Papers of the Presidents of the United States, online and in print. This work is a publication of the Executive Branch, which includes not only the president but also all members of the cabinet and various agencies.

The U.S. Code, online and in print. The Supreme Court regularly publishes decisions, codes, and other rulings, as do appellate and district courts. State courts also publish rulings and court results on a regular basis.

Works Cited entries for government documents, pages 264–266.

5i   Searching for Essays within Books

Some essays get lost in collections and anthologies. You can find essays listed by subject on this database at your library:

Essay and General Literature Index on Silverplatter

The print version is:

Essay and General Literature Index, 1900-1933. New York: H. W. Wilson, 1934. Supplements, 1934–date.

This reference work helps you find essays hidden in anthologies. It indexes material of both a biographical and a critical nature. The essay listed in the following example might easily have been overlooked by any researcher.

King, Martin Luther, 1929–1968
Raboteau, A. J. Martin Luther King and the tradition of black religious protest. (*In* Religion and the life of the nation; ed. by R. A. Sherrill, p. 46–65).

Your electronic book catalog will give you the call number to Sherrill's book.

5j   Using the Microforms

Online sources are gradually replacing microforms, but your library may have magazines and newspapers converted to a small, single sheet of film called *microfiche* (flat sheet of film) or *microfilm* (roll). Your library will specify in the cardex files (the list of periodicals) how journals and magazines are housed—whether they are in bound printed volumes or microforms.

Your library may also house guides to special microform holdings with titles such as *American Culture 1493-1806: A Guide to the Microfilm Collection* or perhaps *American Periodicals 1800-1850: A Guide to the Microfilm Collection*. Every library has its own peculiar holdings of microfilm and microfiche materials; if you need assistance, the librarian can help you.

YOUR RESEARCH PROJECT

1. If you have not already done so with an orientation group, take the time to stroll through your library. Identify its various sections and the types of information available there. Especially learn about the reference room, the stacks, and the printed periodical articles. Pick up a bound volume of a journal, open it, and notice how it contains 12 issues (or 6) of one year's publications.

2. At the library, sit down at one of the computer terminals and investigate its options. Make up a topic for the moment and search for books or articles at the terminal. Try to find an abstract or a full-text article and then print it.

3. Go to the reference desk and ask the librarian for a specialized bibliography on your topic—that is, say something like this: "Do you have a specialized bibliography on global warming?"

4. Locate the library's holdings of *The CQ Researcher* and *Social Issues Resources Series*. Page through the various booklets to note how they provide several penetrating articles on a common topic. In the indexes, search to see if your favorite topic has been treated in a special issue.

5. To test the resources of the library, go in search of information about the day you were born. Don't limit yourself to major events of the day; go also in search of hometown news. Look at the advertisements to see what people were wearing and what things cost back then.

CHECKLIST

The Library Search

When you start your research on a topic, you will need to switch between the computer terminals, the library stacks of books and periodicals, and the printed bibliographies and indexes, according to the resources in your library. Start, perhaps, with the sources on this list.

   To find books:
      electronic book catalog with keyword
      online with keywords "bibliographies + [your discipline]"

   To find periodical articles:
      an electronic database with a keyword
      online with keywords "indexes + [your discipline]"
      the Wilson indexes

To find an abstract:
online with keywords "abstracts + [your discipline]"

To find biographies in books and periodicals:
online with keywords "biography + indexes"
Biography Index, online or in print

To find newspaper articles:
Internet at **http://www.newspapers.com**
electronic database under keyword "newspapers"

To find pamphlet files:
online with the library's network to *SIRS* and *The CQ Researcher*
Ask your librarian for local files

To find government documents:
online with the library network to **GPO on Silverplatter**
Internet access to **GPOAccess**

To find essays within books:
Essay and General Literature Index, online or in print

To find microforms:
online with the library network to **ERIC**

For more resources in research,
writing, and documentation, go to
MyCompLab.com

6 Conducting Field Research

Field research refers, in general, to any studies conducted outside the library, such as digging at an archeology site, measuring a sinkhole fault, observing student behavior at a parking lot, or surveying a selected group with a questionnaire. This type of work is not beyond the realm of first-year students, and you should consider it an important ingredient in your research plans. Therefore, converse with people by letter or e-mail, and if time permits it, conduct personal one-on-one interviews or use a questionnaire. Watch television specials, visit the courthouse archives, and conduct research by observation under the guidance of an instructor (see pages 90–92).

Set up your field research in an objective manner in order to control subjective feelings. Student Odette Ogburn (see her letter on pages 86–87) had strong personal feelings about her own daughter's condition as she researched attention deficit hyperactivity disorder, so she had to force herself to look objectively for viable evidence. All writers get deeply involved in their subject, but they must couple that involvement with the skill of detachment. What are the facts? What conclusions do they support? Conduct the test, get results, and then discuss their implications.

6a Investigating Local Sources

Interviewing Knowledgeable People

Talk to people who have experience with your subject. Personal interviews can elicit valuable in-depth information. Interviews provide information that few others will have. Look to organizations for knowledgeable experts. For example, if writing on folklore, you might contact the county historian, a senior citizens' organization, or the local historical society. If necessary, post a notice soliciting help: "I am writing a study of local folklore. Wanted: People who have a knowledge of regional tales." Another way to accomplish this task is to join an e-mail discussion group to invite commentary from a group interested in the same topic (see pages 17–18 for more details). Try using the discussion board if yours is an online class. For accuracy, save files or record the interview (with permission of the person interviewed, of course). When finished, make a bibliography entry just as you would for a book:

Thornbright, Mattie Sue. Message to the author. 15 Sept. 2008. E-mail.

Note: For a paper written in APA style, you should document an e-mail interview in the text only, not in the references. To maintain the anonymity of the source, write this in-text citation: (Anonymous interview, April 6, 2008). The APA style requires that you omit from the References items that are not retrievable, such as e-mail messages, interviews, personal letters, memos, or private papers.

In addition to the checklist of guidelines listed on page 89 you need to remember several vital matters. First, be prepared for interviews, which means that you know your interviewee's professional background and that you have a set of pertinent questions, with followups. Second, keep your focus on the principal issue. Subjects may wish to wander toward tangential ideas, so you need to bring them back to the central subject with an appropriate question. Third, maintain an ethical demeanor that honors with accuracy the statements of the subject.

Student Valerie Nesbitt-Hall researched the role of matching services and chat rooms in promoting online romance. Because she was acquainted with a couple that had met online and eventually married, she decided to request an interview—online, of course. These were her questions and, in brief form, the responses of the subjects, Stephen of Scotland and Jennifer of the United States.

1. When did you first meet online? Answer: *September of 1996*
2. What prompted you to try an online matching service? Answer: *We didn't really try online matching services. We chatted in a chat room, became friends there, and met in person later.*
3. Who initiated the first contact? Answer: *Stephen initiated the first online chat.*
4. How long into the relationship did you correspond by e-mail before one of you gave an address and/or phone number? Who did it first, Steve or Jennifer? Answer: *We chatted and corresponded by e-mail for nine months before Jennifer shared her phone number.*
5. How long into the relationship did you go before sharing photographs? Answer: *At nine months we began to share written correspondence and photographs.*
6. Who initiated the first meeting in person? Where did you meet? How long were you into the relationship before you met in person? Answer: *Stephen first requested the meeting, and Jennifer flew from the States to Glasgow, Scotland. This was about a year into the relationship.*
7. How much time elapsed between your first online meeting and your marriage? Answer: *One and a half years after our first chat, we were married.*
8. Did you feel that online romance enabled you to prearrange things and protect your privacy before meeting in person? Answer: *Yes. We were cautious and at times reluctant to continue, but we kept coming back to each other, online, until we knew the other well enough to trust in the relationship. Once we got offline into what we might call real-time dating, the love blossomed quickly.*

9. Did you feel, when you finally met in person, that you really knew the other person—Spiritually? Emotionally? Intellectually? Answer: *Yes*.

10. Not to put you on the spot, but do you feel as a couple that the relationship has been excellent to this point? Answer: *Yes, super*.

11. Has the difference in nationalities been a problem? Answer: *Yes, but only in relation to sorting out immigration matters. Also, Jennifer's parents were concerned that she was going to another country to see someone she had never met.*

12. Finally, would you recommend online matching services or chat rooms to others who are seeking mates? Answer: *Yes, in the right circumstances. We were lucky; others might not be.*

Writing Letters and Corresponding by E-mail

Correspondence provides a written record of research. As you would in an interview, ask pointed questions so correspondents respond directly to your central issues. Tell the person who you are, what you are attempting to do, and why you have chosen to write to this particular person or set of persons. If germane, explain why you have chosen this topic and what qualifies you to write about it.

Odette Ogburn

1551 Grayside Road

Topeka, KS 66612

Ms. Evelyn Casasola, Principal

Parkview Elementary School

Topeka, KS 66612

Dear Ms. Casasola:

I am a college student conducting research into methods for handling

hyperactive children in the public school setting. I am surveying

each elementary school principal in Shawnee County. I have contacted

the central office also, but I wished to have perspectives from

those of you on the front lines. I have a child with ADHD, so I have a

personal as well as a scholarly reason for this research. I could ask

specific questions on policy, but I have gotten that from the central

office. What I would like from you is a brief paragraph that describes

your policy and procedure when one of your teachers reports a

hyperactive child. In particular, do you endorse the use of medication

for calming the child? May I quote you in my report? I will honor your

request to withhold your name. I have enclosed a self-addressed, stamped envelope for your convenience. You may e-mail me at

oogburn@washburn.edu.

Sincerely,

Odette Ogburn

> If Ogburn decided to build a table or graph from the nine replies of the various principals, she would need to document the survey in a Works Cited entry as shown on page 90.

This letter makes a fairly specific request for a minimum amount of information. It does not require an expansive reply. Should Ogburn use a quotation from the reply, she should provide a bibliography entry on her Works Cited page.

Casasola, Evelyn. Principal of Parkview Elementary School, Topeka, KS.

Message to the author. 5 Apr. 2008. E-mail.

Reading Personal Papers

Search out letters, diaries, manuscripts, family histories, and other personal materials that might contribute to your study. The city library may house private collections, and the city librarian can usually help you contact the county historian and other private citizens who have important documents. Obviously, handling private papers must be done with the utmost decorum and care. Again, make a bibliography entry for such materials:

Joplin, Lester. "Notes on my visits to the Robert Penn Warren family

home and museum in Guthrie, Kentucky." Nashville. October 13,

2007. MS.

Attending Lectures and Public Addresses

Watch bulletin boards and the newspaper for featured speakers who might visit your campus. When you attend a lecture, take careful notes and, if it is available, request a copy of the lecture or speech. Remember, too, that many lectures, reproduced on video, will be available in the library or in departmental files. Always make a bibliography entry for any words or ideas you use.

Petty-Rathbone, Virginia. "Edgar Allan Poe and the Image of Ulalume."

Heard Library, Vanderbilt U., Nashville. 25 Jan. 2009. Address.

6b   Investigating Government Documents

Local Government

Visit the courthouse or county clerk's office, where you can find facts on elections, censuses, marriages, births, and deaths. These archives include wills, tax rolls, military assignments, deeds to property, and much more.

State Government

Contact by phone or online a state office that relates to your research, such as Consumer Affairs (general information), Public Service Commission (which regulates public utilities such as the telephone company), and the Department of Human Services (which administers social and welfare services). The agencies may vary by name in your state. Remember, too, that the state will have an archival storehouse whose records are available for public review. Figure 6.1 shows the type of information readily available to a student conducting research on a city's population and demographics.

Federal Government

The Government Printing Office (GPO) provides free access to a wealth of information produced by the federal government. Begin searching these resources at http://www.gpo.gov/. In addition, you can gain access to the National Archives Building in Washington, DC, or to one of the regional branches in Atlanta, Boston, Chicago, Denver, Fort Worth, Kansas City, Los Angeles, New York, Philadelphia, and Seattle. Their archives contain court records and government documents, which you can review in two books: *Guide to the National Archives of the United States* and *Select List of Publications of the National Archives and Record Service* (see http:/ /www. archives. gov.) You can borrow some documents on microfilm if you consult the *Catalog of National Archives Microfilm Publications*. One researcher, for example, found the table shown in Figure 6.1 while looking for information on shifts in population.

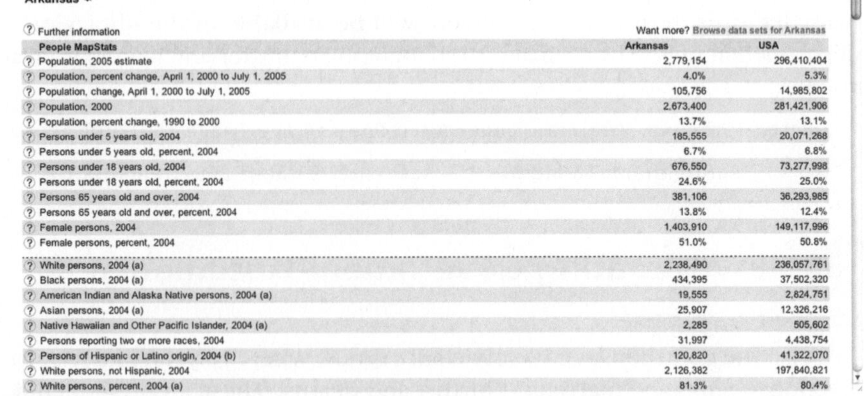

Arkansas MapStats from FedStats
http://www.fedstats.gov/qf/states/05000.html

MapStats FEDSTATS
USA MapStats | Select a State | What's New

Arkansas

Arkansas counties - selection map | Arkansas cities - place search
State Court Districts
Federal Judicial Districts
Congressional Districts

Arkansas

Further information — Want more? Browse data sets for Arkansas

People MapStats	Arkansas	USA
Population, 2005 estimate	2,779,154	296,410,404
Population, percent change, April 1, 2000 to July 1, 2005	4.0%	5.3%
Population, change, April 1, 2000 to July 1, 2005	105,756	14,985,802
Population, 2000	2,673,400	281,421,906
Population, percent change, 1990 to 2000	13.7%	13.1%
Persons under 5 years old, 2004	185,555	20,071,268
Persons under 5 years old, percent, 2004	6.7%	6.8%
Persons under 18 years old, 2004	676,550	73,277,998
Persons under 18 years old, percent, 2004	24.6%	25.0%
Persons 65 years old and over, 2004	381,106	36,293,985
Persons 65 years old and over, percent, 2004	13.8%	12.4%
Female persons, 2004	1,403,910	149,117,996
Female persons, percent, 2004	51.0%	50.8%
White persons, 2004 (a)	2,238,490	236,057,761
Black persons, 2004 (a)	434,395	37,502,320
American Indian and Alaska Native persons, 2004 (a)	19,555	2,824,751
Asian persons, 2004 (a)	25,907	12,326,216
Native Hawaiian and Other Pacific Islander, 2004 (a)	2,285	505,602
Persons reporting two or more races, 2004	31,997	4,438,754
Persons of Hispanic or Latino origin, 2004 (b)	120,820	41,322,070
White persons, not Hispanic, 2004	2,126,382	197,840,821
White persons, percent, 2004 (a)	81.3%	80.4%

FIGURE 6.1 Population and demographics: Fort Smith, Arkansas.

The researcher also made a bibliography entry to record the source of this table.

FedStats. "MapStats: Arkansas." 31 July 2007. Web. 8 Aug. 2008.

6c Examining Audiovisual Materials, Television, and Radio

Important data can be found in audiovisual materials: films, filmstrips, music, CDs, slides, audio cassettes, video cassettes, and DVDs. You will find these sources both on and off campus. Consult such guides as *Educators Guide* (film, filmstrips, and tapes), *Media Review Digest* (nonprint materials), *Video Source Book* (video catalog), *The Film File*, and *International Index to Recorded Poetry*. Television, with its many educational channels, such as *The History Channel*, offers invaluable data. With a DVR or VCR, you can record a program for detailed examination. Again, write bibliography entries for any materials that contribute to your paper.

Willis, Gerri. "Candidates and Your Cash." Interview. CNN.

7 Mar. 2008. Television.

CHECKLIST

Interviews, Letters, Private Papers, Courthouse Documents

- Set up appointments in advance.
- Consult with experienced persons. If possible, talk to several people in order to weigh their different opinions. Telephone and e-mail interviews are acceptable.
- Be courteous and on time for interviews.
- Be prepared in advance with a set of focused, pertinent questions for initiating and conducting the interview.
- Handle private and public papers with great care.
- For accuracy, record the interview with a tape recorder (with permission of the person interviewed, of course).
- Double-check direct quotations with the interviewee or the tape.
- Get permission before citing a person by name or quoting his or her exact words.
- Send helpful people a copy of your report, along with a thank-you note.

6d Conducting a Survey with a Questionnaire

Questionnaires can produce current, firsthand data you can tabulate and analyze. Of course, to achieve meaningful results, you must survey a random sample—that is, each one must represent the whole population in terms of age, sex, race, education, income, residence, and other factors. Various degrees of bias can creep into the questionnaire unless you remain objective. Thus, use the formal survey only when you are experienced with tests and measurements as well as with statistical analysis or when you have an instructor who will help you with the instrument. Be advised that most schools have a Human Subjects Committee that sets guidelines, draws up consent forms, and requires anonymity of participants for information gathering that might be intrusive. An informal survey gathered in the hallways of campus buildings lacks credibility in the research paper. If you build a table or graph from the results, see "Using Visuals," pages 164–166, for examples and instructions. Label your survey in the bibliography entry:

Castor, Diego, and Carmen Aramide. "Child Care Arrangements of

Parents Who Attend College." Questionnaire. Coeur d'Alene, Idaho:

North Idaho College, 2008.

Unlike interview questions (see pages 84–86), which are meant to elicit a response from one person or a couple, questionnaires are designed for multiple responses from many people, from twenty-five to thirty up to several thousand. Design them for ease of tabulation with results you can arrange in graphs and charts.

CHECKLIST

Using Media Sources

- Watch closely the opening and closing credits to capture the necessary data for your Works Cited entry. The format is explained on pages 274–281.
- Your citations may refer to a performer, director, or narrator, depending on the focus of your study.
- As with live interviews, be scrupulously accurate in taking notes. Try to write with direct quotations because paraphrases of television commentary can unintentionally be distorted and colored by bias.
- Plan carefully the review of a media presentation, even to the point of preparing a list of questions or a set of criteria to help with your judgment.

6e Conducting Experiments, Tests, and Observation

Empirical research, usually performed in a laboratory, can determine why and how things exist, function, or interact. Your paper will explain your methods and findings in pursuit of a hypothesis (your thesis). An experiment thereby becomes primary evidence for your paper.

Observation is field research that occurs outside the lab—"in the field"— which might be a child care center, a movie theater, a parking lot, or the counter of a fast food restaurant. The field is anywhere you can observe, count, and record behavior, patterns, or systems. It might also include observing and testing the water in a stream, the growth of certain wildflowers, or the nesting patterns of deer.

Most experiments and observations begin with a *hypothesis*, which is similar to a thesis statement (see pages 22–23). The hypothesis is a statement assumed to be true for the purpose of investigation. *Hummingbirds live as extended families governed by a patriarch* is a hypothesis needing data to prove its validity. *The majority of people will not correct the poor grammar of a speaker* is a hypothesis that needs testing and observation to prove its validity.

However, you can begin observation without a hypothesis and let the results lead you to conclusions. Assignment 1, page 93, asks you to conduct a double-entry observation for one week and to write a short reflection about what you learned by keeping the field notes. This could be your introduction to field research.

CHECKLIST

Conducting a Survey

- Keep the questionnaire short, clear, and focused on your topic.
- Write unbiased questions. Let your professor review the instrument before using it.
- Design a quick response to a scale (Choose A, B, or C), to a ranking (first choice, second choice, and so on), or to fill the blanks.
- Arrange for an easy return of the questionnaire, even to the point of providing a self-addressed, stamped envelope.
- Retain e-mail responses until the project is complete.
- Provide a sample questionnaire and your tabulations in an appendix.
- Tabulate the results objectively. Even negative results that deny your hypothesis have value.

Generally, a report on an experiment or observation follows an expected format featuring four distinct parts: introduction, method, results, discussion. Understanding these elements will help you design your survey:

Introduction to explain the design of your experiment:
- Present the point of the study.
- State the hypothesis and how it relates to the problem.
- Provide the theoretical implications of the study.
- Explain the manner in which this study relates to previously published work.

Method to describe what you did and how you conducted the study:
- Describe the subjects who participated, whether human or animal.
- Describe the apparatus to explain your equipment and how you used it.
- Summarize the procedure in execution of each stage of your work.

Results to report your findings:
- Summarize the data you collected.
- Provide the necessary statistical treatment of the findings with tables, graphs, and charts.
- Include findings that conflict with your hypothesis.

Discussion that explains the implications of your work:
- Evaluate the data and its relevance to the hypothesis.
- Interpret the findings as necessary.
- Discuss the implications of the findings.
- Qualify the results and limit them to your specific study.
- Make inferences from the results.

CHECKLIST

Conducting an Experiment or Observation

- Express a clear hypothesis.
- Select the proper design for the study—lab experiment, observation, or the collection of raw data in the field.
- Include a review of the literature, if appropriate.
- Keep careful records and accurate data.
- Don't let your expectations influence the results.
- Maintain respect for human and animal subjects. In that regard, you may find it necessary to get approval for your research from a governing board. Read your college's rules and regulations on research that requires the use of humans and animals.

YOUR RESEARCH PROJECT

1. Select an event or object from nature to observe daily for one week. Record field notes in a double-entry format by using the left side of the page to record and the right side of the page to comment and reflect on what you have observed. Afterwards, write a brief paragraph discussing your findings.

Record:	*Response:*
Day 1	
10-minute session at window, three hummingbirds fighting over the feeder	Is the male chasing away the female, or is the female the aggressor?
Day 2	
10-minute session at window, saw eight single hummingbirds and one guarding feeder by chasing others away	I did some research, and the red-throated male is the one that's aggressive.

2. Look carefully at your subject to determine if research outside the library will be helpful for your project. If so, what kind of research: correspondence? local records? the news media? a questionnaire? an observation or experiment?

3. Work closely with your instructor to design an instrument that will affect your research and your findings. In fact, most instructors will want to examine any questionnaire that you will submit to others and will want to approve the design of your experiment or observation.

4. Follow university guidelines on testing with humans and animals.

> For more resources in research, writing, and documentation, go to MyCompLab.com

7 Understanding and Avoiding Plagiarism

You probably know that buying a research paper online and turning it in as your own work is plagiarism of the worst kind. But do you really understand what plagiarism is and what it is not? Are you comfortable that you understand when you need to document (cite) a source and when you do not? Do you know what criteria to apply when you need to decide if a particular piece of information needs to be documented in your paper? Most students who encounter plagiarism problems in college do so because they lack a clear understanding of the ethical and community standards in an academic environment.

Plagiarism is defined as the act of claiming the words or ideas of another person as your own. Plagiarism is a serious violation of the ethical standards of academic writing, and most colleges and universities have strict penalties, including academic probation or expulsion, for students who are guilty of plagiarism. Most schools publish an official code of student conduct (sometimes called an academic integrity policy), and you should be familiar with this document as it applies to your research and writing.

Some students will knowingly copy whole passages from outside sources into their work without documentation. Such intentional academic dishonesty is the most blatant form of plagiarism. **Unintentional plagiarism**, however, is still a violation of academic integrity. Unacknowledged use of another person's sentences, phrases, or terminology is plagiarism, so provide a citation and use quotation marks to show exactly where you are drawing on others' work. Similarly, unacknowledged use of another person's ideas, research, or approach is also plagiarism, so write careful paraphrases. Review the checklist in Chapter 1 (page 4) for guidelines to help avoid unintentional plagiarism.

This chapter is intended to provide additional information and strategies to help you become knowledgeable about how to document sources and avoid plagiarism when writing research-based papers and projects. The proper use of source material can enhance your credibility as a researcher at the same time it ensures that you will not be guilty of unintentional plagiarism.

7a Using Sources to Enhance Your Credibility

What some students fail to realize is that citing a source in their papers, even the short ones, signals something special and positive to your readers—that you have researched the topic, explored the literature about it, and have the talent to share it. Research is something you need to share, not hide. Research writing exercises your critical thinking and your ability to collect ideas. You will discuss not only the subject matter, such as water pollution in the Delaware River, but also the *literature* of the topic, such as articles from the Internet and current periodicals found at your library's databases. By announcing clearly the name of a source, you reveal the scope of your reading and thus your credibility, as in this student's notes:

> Americans consume an average of 300 plus liters of water per day per capita while the average person needs only 20 to 40 liters, according to O'Malley and Bowman.
>
> Sandra Postel says water is "a living system that drives the workings of a natural world we depend on" (19).
>
> Postel declares: "A new water era has begun" (24). She indicates that the great prairies of the world will dry up, including America's. Hey, when folks in America notice the drought, then maybe something will happen.

These notes, if transferred into the paper, will enable readers to identify the sources used. The notes give clear evidence of the writer's investigation into the subject, and they enhance the student's image as a researcher. You will get credit for displaying the sources properly. The opposite, plagiarism, presents the information as though it were your own:

> The great prairies of the world will soon dry up, and that includes America's, so a new water era has begun.

That sentence borrows too much. If in doubt, cite the source and place it within its proper context.

7b Placing Your Work in Its Proper Context

Your sources will reflect all kinds of special interests, even biases, so you need to position them within your paper as reliable sources. If you must use a biased or questionable source, tell your readers up front. For example, if you are writing about the dangers of cigarette smoke, you will find different opinions in a farmer's magazine, a health and fitness magazine, and a trade journal sponsored by R.J. Reynolds. You owe it to your readers to scrutinize Internet sites closely and examine printed articles for:

- Special interests that might color the report.
- Lack of credentials.
- An unsponsored Web site.
- Opinionated speculation, especially that found in chat rooms.
- Trade magazines that promote special interests.
- Extremely liberal or extremely conservative positions.

Here's an example: Norman Berkowitz, in researching articles on the world's water supply, found an article of interest but positioned it with a description of the source, as shown in this note.

Earth First, which describes itself as a radical environmental journal, features articles by an editorial staff that uses pseudonyms, such as Sky, Jade, Wedge, and Sprig. In his article "The End of Lake Powell," Sprig says, "The Colorado River may soon be unable to provide for the 25 million people plumbed into its system" (25). The danger, however, is not limited to Lake Powell. Sprig adds, "This overconsumption of water, compounded with a regional drought cycle of 25 years, could mean that Lake Powell and every other reservoir in the upper Colorado River area will be without water" (24-25).

Not only does Berkowitz recognize the source with name, quotation marks, and page numbers, he identifies the nature of the magazine for his readers.

7c   Understanding Copyright

The principle behind copyright law is relatively simple. Copyright begins at the time a creative work is recorded in some tangible form—a written document, a drawing, a tape recording. It does not depend on a legal registration with the copyright office in Washington, DC, although published works *are* usually registered. Thus, the moment you express yourself creatively on paper, in song, on a canvas, that expression is your intellectual property. You have a vested interest in any profits made from the distribution of the work. For that reason, songwriters, cartoonists, fiction writers, and other artists guard their work and do not want it disseminated without compensation. Recent attempts to prevent the downloading of music onto private computers is a demonstration of this concern.

Scholarly writing is not a profitmaking profession, but the writers certainly deserve recognition. We can give that recognition by providing in-text citations and bibliography entries. As a student, you may use copyrighted material in your research paper under a doctrine of *fair use* as described in the U.S. Code, which says:

> The fair use of a copyrighted work . . . for purposes such as criticism, comment, news reporting, teaching (including multiple copies for classroom use), scholarship, or research is not an infringement of copyright.

Thus, as long as you borrow for educational purposes, such as a paper to be read by your instructor, you should not be concerned. Just give the source the proper recognition and documentation, as explained next in section 7d. However, if you decide to *publish* your research paper on a Web site, then new considerations come into play (see 7g, "Seeking Permission to Publish Material on Your Web Site").

7d   Avoiding Plagiarism

There are a number of steps you can take to avoid plagiarizing. First, develop personal notes full of your own ideas on a topic. Discover how you feel about the issue. Then, rather than copy sources one after another onto your pages of text, try to express your own ideas while synthesizing the ideas of the authorities by using summary, paraphrase, or direct quotation, which are explained fully on pages 133–142. Rethink and reconsider ideas gathered during your reading, make meaningful connections, and, when you refer to the ideas or exact words of a source—as you inevitably will—give the other writer full credit.

To repeat, *plagiarism* is offering the words or ideas of another person as one's own. Major violations, which can bring failure in the course or expulsion from school, are:

- The use of another student's work.
- The purchase of a "canned" research paper.
- Copying whole passages into a paper without documentation.
- Copying a key, well-worded phrase into a paper without documentation.
- Putting specific ideas of others into your own words without documentation.
- Inadequate or missing citation.
- Missing quotation marks.
- Incomplete or missing Works Cited entry.

Whether deliberate or not, these instances all constitute forms of plagiarism. Unintentional plagiarism is often a result of carelessness. For example:

- The writer fails to enclose quoted material within quotation marks, yet he or she provides an in-text citation with name and page number.
- The writer's paraphrase never quite becomes paraphrase—too much of the original is left intact—but he or she provides a full citation to name and page.

In these situations, instructors must step in and help the beginning researcher, for although these cases are not flagrant instances of plagiarism, they can mar an otherwise fine piece of research.

As an academic writer, you must document fully any borrowed ideas and words. The academic citation—author, page number, and bibliography entry—establishes two things beyond your reliability and credibility:

1. A clear trail for other researchers to follow if they also want to consult the source.
2. Information for other researchers who might need to replicate (reproduce) the project.

When you provide an academic citation, you've made it clear *who* you've read, *how* you used it in your paper, and *where* others can find it.

Common Knowledge

You do not need to document information that is considered "common knowledge." But how do you know what is or is not common knowledge? Use the following criteria to determine whether or not a particular piece of information can be considered common knowledge.

CHECKLIST

Documenting Your Sources

- Let the reader know when you begin borrowing from a source by introducing the quotation or paraphrase with the name of the authority.
- Enclose within quotation marks all quoted materials—both key phrases and sentences.
- Use an indented block for quotations of four lines or more.
- Make certain that paraphrased material has been rewritten in your own style and language. The simple rearrangement of sentence patterns is unacceptable.
- Provide specific in-text documentation for each borrowed item, but keep in mind that styles differ for MLA, APA, CSE, and CMS standards.
- Provide a bibliography entry in the Works Cited for every source cited in the paper, including sources that appear only in content footnotes or an appendix.

1. **Local knowledge.** You and your reader might share local or regional knowledge on a subject. For example, if you attend Northern Illinois University, you need not cite the fact that Illinois is known as the Land of Lincoln, that Chicago is its largest city, or that Springfield is the capital city. Information of this sort requires *no* in-text citation, as shown in the following example.

> The flat rolling hills of Illinois form part of the great Midwestern Corn Belt. It stretches from its border with Wisconsin in the north to the Kentucky border in the south. Its political center is Springfield in the center of the state, but its industrial and commercial center is Chicago, that great boisterous city camped on the shores of Lake Michigan.

However, a writer in another place and time might need to cite the source of this information. Most writers would probably want to document this next passage.

> Early Indian tribes on the plains called themselves *Illiniwek* (which meant strong men), and French settlers pronounced the name *Illinois* (Angle 44).

2. **Shared experiences.** Coursework and lectures will give you and members of your class a similar perspective on the subject. For example,

students in a literary class studying African American writers would share common information, so the student might write, without documentation, something like this:

> Langston Hughes, an important poet in the 1920s and 1930s, became a leader of the Harlem Renaissance, and like so many writers, he took great pride in his African American heritage. He was not afraid to use the vernacular black dialect, and I would say that he is one of the fathers of today's rap music.

If the student shifts to nongeneral information, then a citation is in order:

> Hughes has been described by Gerald Early as the major artistic link between the revolutionary poet Paul Lawrence Dunbar and the radical poet Amiri Baraka (246).

3. **Common facts.** Common factual information that one might find in an almanac, fact book, or dictionary need not be cited. Here is an example:

> President George Herbert Walker Bush launched the Desert Storm attack in 1991 against Iraq and its leader, Saddam Hussein, with the support of allies and their troops from several nations. His son, President George W. Bush, launched a similar attack in 2003 against the same dictator and his army.

CHECKLIST

Common Knowledge That Does Not Need to Be Documented

- Do not document the source if an intelligent person would and should know the information, given the context of both writer and audience.
- Do not document terminology and information from a classroom environment that have become common knowledge to all members of the class.
- Do not document the source if you knew the information without reading it in an article or book.
- Do not document almanac-type information, such as date, place of birth, occupation, and so on.
- Do not document information that has become general knowledge by being reported repeatedly in many different sources (i.e., Michael Jordan holds several National Basketball Association [NBA] scoring records).

The passage needs no documentation, but the farther we move in history from that time and place, the more likely will be the need for documentation. Of course, provide a citation for analysis that goes beyond common facts.

The elder Bush demonstrated great mastery in his diplomatic unification of a politically diverse group of allies (Wolford 37).

Correctly Borrowing from a Source

The next examples in MLA style demonstrate the differences between the accurate use of a source and plagiarism. First is the original reference material that discusses methods for solving the world's water shortage; it is followed by the student versions that use the passage, along with discussions of their failures and merits.

Original Material:

> The impulse to memorialize the Civil War dead does not stop with southerners. In 1964, roughly a century after Gettysburg, when the Civil Rights movement had brought new battles and more bloodshed to the southern countryside, the quintessential Yankee poet Robert Lowell celebrated the Confederacy's ancient opponents in his own elegy, "For the Union Dead." Instead of a confederate graveyard, Lowell contemplates the famed monument to Col. Robert Gould Shaw and the 54th Massachusetts Volunteers that stands on the Boston Common. Shaw was a Boston Brahmin, Lowell's relative by marriage, who led a regiment of African American soldiers in the assault on Fort Wagner in South Carolina and was buried with them in a common grave when their attack failed. Like Tate, Lowell admires his subject's courage and contrasts it to his own feckless complicity in modern urban society, choked with automobiles and parking garages, where warfare has been degraded to the mass horror of the mushroom cloud, and even Hiroshima has become and advertising image. Harry L. Watson, "Front Porch," *Southern Cultures* (Summer 2005): 3.

STUDENT VERSION A (A case of deliberate plagiarism that is ethically and morally wrong)

> The impulse to memorialize the Civil War dead does not stop with southerners. In 1964, roughly a century after Gettysburg, when the Civil Rights movement had brought new battles and more bloodshed to the southern countryside, the quintessential Yankee poet Robert Lowell celebrated the Confederacy's ancient opponents in his own elegy, "For the Union Dead." Instead of a confederate graveyard, Lowell contemplates the famed monument to Col. Robert Gould Shaw and the 54th Massachusetts Volunteers that stands on the Boston Common.

This passage reads well, and the unsuspecting reader will probably think so as well. However, the writer has borrowed the entire passage from Watson, so it is plagiarism of the first order. The writer implies to the reader that these sentences are an original creation when, actually, the sentences are stolen.

STUDENT VERSION B (Plagiarism that steals the ideas of another)

> Proper respect and ardor is needed in our modern society for remembering the dead of the American Civil War. Poet Robert Lowell's elegy, "For the Union Dead" commemorates the brave accomplishments of the 54th Massachusetts Volunteers, a regiment of African American soldiers who were led by the white commander Colonel Robert Gould Shaw. Their blood was shed together in a futile attempt to take Fort Wagner in South Carolina, and their burial is in a common grave.

This version borrows extensively from the original with paraphrasing. The writer has stolen the key ideas of the original without credit of any sort. The words might belong to the student writer, but the ideas belong to Watson.

STUDENT VERSION C (Plagiarism that paraphrases improperly and offers a vague citation)

> Memorializing the fallen dead of the American Civil War is sadly a thing of the past. The celebrations of the first few generations after the end of the Civil war have been replaced by modernization and the fickleness of American society; we live in a world that is more consumed by individual consumption and driving a fancy automobile than remembering the bloodshed that preserved the rights and privileges we now possess (Watson 3).

This version is somewhat better. It provides a reference to Watson, but readers cannot know that the paraphrase contains far too much of Watson's language—words that should be enclosed within quotation marks. Also, the citation to Watson is ambiguous; when does the borrowing begin? The next version handles these matters in a better fashion.

STUDENT VERSION D (An acceptable version with a proper citation to a block quotation)

> The commemoration of the fallen dead of the American Civil War has diminished with our modern generation. While the parades, poetry, and memorials do not hold the same significance as they once did, the heroes are still held in reverence by many in the South. According to

> Harry L. Watson, Director of the Center for the Study of the American
> South, the desire to honor the Civil War dead is not unique to
> southerners only:
>
> > Yankee poet Robert Lowell celebrated the Confederacy's
> > ancient opponents in his own elegy, "For the Union Dead."
> > Instead of a confederate graveyard, Lowell contemplates the
> > famed monument to Col. Robert Gould Shaw and the 54th
> > Massachusetts Volunteers that stands on the Boston
> > Common. (3)

This version represents a satisfactory handling of the source material. The
source is acknowledged at the outset of the borrowing, the passage has been
quoted as a block of material, and a page citation closes the material. Let's
suppose, however, that the writer does not wish to quote an entire passage.
The following example shows a paraphrased version.

STUDENT VERSION E (An acceptable version with a citation to the
source)

> Once honored with parades, poetry, and memorials, the heroic
> deeds of the fallen dead of the American Civil War have been
> forgotten. Our current generation is consumed with self-gratification
> and individualism that has no time for moldy monuments under the
> leaves of mighty oaks. According to Harry L. Watson, Director of the
> Center for the Study of the American South, the previous generation's
> remembrance of the past has been replaced by a "feckless complicity in
> modern urban society, choked with automobiles and parking garages,
> where warfare has been degraded to the mass horror of the mushroom
> cloud, and even Hiroshima has become and advertising image" (3).

This version also represents a satisfactory handling of the source material. In
this case, a direct quotation is employed, the author and the authority are
acknowledged and credited, and an introduction presented in the student's
own language precedes Watson's ideas.

7e   Sharing Credit in Collaborative Projects

Joint authorship is seldom a problem in collaborative writing, especially
if each member of the project understands his or her role. Normally, all members of the team receive equal billing and credit. However, it might serve you
well to predetermine certain issues with your peer group and the instructor:

- How will the project be judged and grades awarded?
- Will all members receive the same grade?
- Can a nonperformer be dismissed from the group?
- Should each member write a section of the work and everybody edit the whole?
- Should certain members write the draft and other members edit and load it onto a CD or onto the Web?
- Can the group work together via e-mail rather than meeting frequently for group sessions?

Resolving such issues at the beginning of a project can go a long way toward eliminating entanglements and disagreements later on. *Note*: Electronic publishing of your collaborative project on the Web raises other legal and ethical questions (see section 7g, pages 104–105).

CHECKLIST

Information That Must Be Documented

1. An original idea derived from a source, whether quoted or paraphrased. This next sentence requires an in-text citation and quotation marks around a key phrase:

    Genetic engineering, by which a child's body shape and intellectual ability is predetermined, raises for one source "memories of Nazi attempts in eugenics" (Riddell 19).

2. Your summary of original ideas by a source:

    Genetic engineering has been described as the rearrangement of the genetic structure in animals or in plants, which is a technique that takes a section of DNA and reattaches it to another section (Rosenthal 19–20).

3. Factual information that is not common knowledge within the context of the course:

    Genetic engineering has its risks: A nonpathogenic organism might be converted into a pathogenic one or an undesirable trait might develop as a result of a mistake (Madigan 51).

4. Any exact wording copied from a source:

    Kenneth Woodward asserts that genetic engineering is "a high-stakes moral rumble that involves billions of dollars and affects the future" (68).

7f   Honoring and Crediting Sources in Online Classrooms

A rapidly growing trend in education is the Web-based course or online course via e-mail. In general, you should follow the fair use doctrine of printed sources (see page 96)—that is, give proper credit and reproduce only limited portions of the original.

The rules are still emerging, and even faculty members are often in a quandary about how to transmit information. For educational purposes, the rules are pretty slack, and most publishers have made their texts or portions thereof available on the Web. Plus, the copyrights of many works have expired, are now in the public domain, and are therefore free. In addition, many magazines and newspapers have made online versions of their articles available for free.

What you send back and forth with classmates and the instructor(s) has little privacy and even less protection. Rules are gradually emerging for electronic communication. In the meantime, abide by a few commonsense principles:

1. Credit sources in your online communications just as you would in a printed research paper, with some variations:
   - The author, creator, or Webmaster of the site.
   - The title of the electronic article.
   - The title of the Web site.
   - The date of publication on the Web.
   - The medium of publication (Web).
   - The date you accessed the site.
2. Download to your file only graphic images and text from sites that have specifically offered users the right to download them.
3. Non-free graphic images and text, especially an entire Web site, should be mentioned in your text, even paraphrased and quoted in a limited manner, but not downloaded into your file. Instead, link to them or point to them with URL addresses. In that way, your reader can go find the material and count it as a supplement to your text.
4. Seek permission if you download substantive blocks of material. See section 7g if you wish to publish your work on the Web.
5. If in doubt, consult by e-mail with your instructor, the moderator of a listserv, or the author of an Internet site.

7g   Seeking Permission to Publish Material on Your Web Site

If you have your own home page and Web site, you might wish to publish your papers on the Web. However, the moment you do so, you are *publishing* the work and putting it into the public domain. That act carries responsibilities. In particular, the *fair use* doctrine of the U.S. Code refers to the personal educational purposes of your usage. When you load onto the Internet borrowed images, text, music, or artwork, you are making that intellectual property available to everybody all over the world.

Short quotations, a few graphics, and a small quantity of illustrations to support your argument are examples of fair use. Permission is needed, however, if the amount you borrow is substantial. The borrowing cannot affect the market for the original work, and you cannot misrepresent it in any way. The courts are still refining the law. For example, would your use of three Doonesbury comic strips be substantial? Yes, if you reproduce them in full. Would it affect the market for the comic strip? Perhaps. Follow these guidelines:

- Seek permission for copyrighted material you publish within your Web article. Most authors will grant you free permission. The problem is tracking down the copyright holder.
- If you make the attempt to get permission and if your motive for using the material is *not for profit*, it's unlikely you will have any problem with the copyright owner. The owner would have to prove that your use of the image or text caused him or her financial harm.
- You may publish without permission works that are in the public domain, such as a section of Hawthorne's *The Scarlet Letter* or a speech by the president from the White House.
- Document any and all sources that you feature on your Web site.
- If you provide hypertext links to other sites, you may need permission to do so. Some sites do not want their address clogged by inquiring students. However, right now the Internet rules on access are being freely interpreted.
- Be prepared for people to visit your Web site and even borrow from it. Decide beforehand how you will handle requests for use of your work, especially if it includes your creative efforts in poetry, art, music, or graphic design.

YOUR RESEARCH PROJECT

1. Begin now to maintain a systematic scrutiny of what you borrow from your sources. Remember that direct quotation reflects the voice of your source and that paraphrase reflects your voice. Just be certain, with paraphrase, that you don't borrow the exact wording of the original.

2. Look at your college bulletin and the student handbook. Do they say anything about plagiarism? Do they address the matter of copyright protection?

3. Consult your writing instructor whenever you have a question about your use of a source. Writing instructors at the freshman level are

there to serve you and help you avoid plagiarising (among other responsibilities).

4. If you think you might publish your paper on the Web and if it contains substantial borrowing from a source, such as five or six cartoons from the *New Yorker* magazine, begin now to seek permission for reproducing the material. In your letter or e-mail, give your name, school, the subject of your research paper, the material you want to borrow, and how you will use it. You might copy or attach the page(s) of your paper in which the material appears.

For more resources in research, writing, and documentation, go to MyCompLab.com

8 Reading and Evaluating Sources

With your research and writing, you will enter the intellectual discussions found in numerous places, but questions will arise quickly during your reading:

- How do I find and evaluate the best, most appropriate sources?
- How can I evaluate a source by analyzing its parts?
- How do I respond to it?

One answer to all three questions is this: Be skeptical and cautious. Don't accept every printed word as the truth. Constantly review and verify to your own satisfaction the words of your sources, especially in this age of electronic publication. It is wise to consider every article on the Internet as suspect until you verify its sponsoring organization and scholarly intent (see especially pages 42–43 for guidelines on judging the value of Internet articles).

Your task is twofold: (1) You must read and personally evaluate the sources for your own benefit as a writer, and (2) you must present them to your reader in your text as validated and authentic sources. This chapter offers a few tips on those two responsibilities.

8a Finding Reliable Sources

Several resources are readily at hand to guide you in finding reliable sources.

Your instructors. Do not hesitate to ask your instructor for help in finding sources. Instructors know the field, know the best writers, and can provide a brief list to get you started. Sometimes instructors will even pull books from their office shelves to give you a starting point.

Librarians. Nobody knows the resources of the library like the professionals. They are evaluated on how well they meet your needs. If you ask for help, they will often walk into the stacks with you to find the appropriate reference books or relevant journal articles.

The library. The college library provides the scholarly sources—the best books, certainly, but also the appropriate databases and the important journals—in your field of study. As we discussed in Chapter 4, the library databases are grounded in scholarship and, in general, they are not available to the general public on the Web. Your access is by your student identification.

A public library may have, but seldom does have, the scholarly resources of an academic library.

The date. Try to use recent sources. A book may appear germane to your work, but if its copyright date is 1975, the content has probably been replaced by recent research and current developments. Scientific and technical topics *always* require up-to-date research. Learn to depend on monthly and quarterly journals as well as books.

Choices. An inverted pyramid shows you a progression from excellent sources to less reliable sources. The pyramid chart does not ask you to dismiss items at the bottom, but it indicates that sources at the top are generally more reliable and therefore preferred.

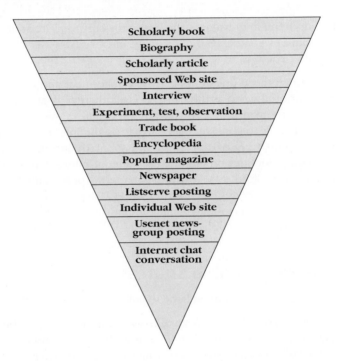

Scholarly Book

A college library is a repository for scholarly books—technical and scientific works, doctoral dissertations, publications of university presses, and textbooks. These sources offer in-depth discussions and careful documentation of the evidence. Two works will help you evaluate a book:

> *Book Review Digest* provides an evaluation of several thousand books each year. Arranged alphabetically, it features summaries and brief quotations from the reviews to uncover the critical reception of the work.
> *The Booklist*, a monthly magazine that reviews new books for librarians, includes brief summaries and recommendations.

Book reviews hidden within magazines and journals can be found by using these sources:

Book Review Index will send you to reviews in 225 magazines and journals.

Index to Book Reviews in the Humanities indexes book reviews in history, philosophy, literature, art, and similar fields.

Index to Book Reviews in the Social Sciences provides book reviews in education, psychology, political science, and similar fields.

Current Book Review Citations gives an author-title index to book reviews in more than 1,000 periodicals.

Another quick source of the review is the computer. One student in Environmental Studies used her library access to *Project Muse* to find a review on the topic of ecological stress. Using the site's search mechanism, she found this listing:

Swidler, Eva-Maria.
The Recurring Dark Ages: Ecological Stress, Climate Changes, and System Transformation (review)
Journal of World History—Volume 18, Number 4, December 2007, pp. 523–525—Review
[View HTML] [View PDF]

Subject Headings:
Chew, Sing C.—Recurring Dark Ages: ecological stress, climate changes, and system transformation.
Environmental degradation.

Clicking on the access link took the student to the book review by Eva-Maria Swindler on Sing C. Chew's book *Recurring Dark Ages: Ecological*

Swidler, Eva-Maria.
The Recurring Dark Ages: Ecological Stress, Climate Changes, and System Transformation (review)
Journal of World History—Volume 18, Number 4, December 2007, pp. 523–525
University of Hawai'i Press

Eva-Maria Swidler—*The Recurring Dark Ages: Ecological Stress, –Climate Changes, and System Transformation* (review)—Journal of World History 18:4 Journal of World History 18.4 (2007) 523–525 Muse Search Journals This Journal Contents Reviewed by Eva-Maria Swidler Villanova University The Recurring Dark Ages: Ecological Stress, Climate Changes, and System Transformation. By Sing C. Chew. Lanham, Md.: AltaMira Press: 2006. 314 pp. $80.00 (cloth); $34.95 (paper).

The Recurring Dark Ages emerges squarely from the world-systems discourse of sociology, and in these origins lie many of its flaws as well as its strengths.

The thesis of this social scientist's book is admirably clear, concisely stated, and reiterated at relevant points in the text; no reading between the lines or coppering of bets here, as in so many writings from the humanities. First, Chew proposes that rather than the explanatory model of society which he calls "economy-in-command," readers should instead consider a model of "ecology-in-command." He is quite frank in his conviction that environmental determinism explains the course of the world, and in particular in his conviction that climate changes are the driver of the meta-trends of history. (No option other than these two explanatory paradigms is given press by him here; the text as well as the footnotes indicate that he assumes that his audience is pretty well limited to world-systems sociologists and Annales-style historians who are presumably weighing these as their only two theoretical options.)

According to Chew, world history is characterized by periods of expansion and progress, each of which has been followed by a crisis and a "Dark Age." There have been three of these Dark Ages so far, each one fundamentally precipitated by climatic shifts that caused drought, famine, disease, population collapse, environmentally instigated migrations and invasions, and then finally a resulting political and economic collapse. The human contribution to historical crises lies mostly in intensifying and straining a straightforward exploitative relationship between society and nature sufficiently that a vulnerability to natural events is created. During the Dark Ages that always ensue after these crises, and which are taken to be in fact quite dark times for humans, nature is finally relieved of the unrelenting exploitation of humans and is able to heal.

Stress, Climate Changes, and System Transformation. A portion of the review is reproduced here to show you that book reviews can provide penetration into the essence of a text.

Biography

The librarian can help you find an appropriate printed biography from among the thousands available. Short biographies appear in such works as *Contemporary Authors, Dictionary of American Negro Biography*, and *Who's Who in Philosophy*. Longer critical biographies are devoted to the life of one person, such as Richard Ellmann's *Oscar Wilde*, a study of the British poet and playwright, and Alf Mapp's *Thomas Jefferson: A Strange Case of Mistaken Identity*, which interprets the life and times of the former president. To find a critical biography, use the electronic

Reference works by topics and issues, Appendix B, pages 377–383.

card catalog at the library. You can also find biographies on the Internet. Most notable figures have several Web sites devoted to them that include articles by and about them.

Refer to biography for these reasons:

1. To verify the standing and reputation of somebody you want to para-phrase or quote in your paper.
2. To provide biographical details in your introduction. For example, the pri-mary topic may be Carl Jung's psychological theories of the unconscious, but information about Jung's career might be appropriate in the paper.
3. To discuss a creative writer's life in relation to his or her work. That is, Jamaica Kincaid's personal life may shed some light on your reading of her stories or novels.

Scholarly Article

A scholarly article usually appears in a journal you access through the library's databases. With a journal article, you may feel confident in its authen-ticity because the authors of journal articles write for academic honor, they document all sources, and they publish through university presses and academic organizations that use a jury to judge an article before its publica-tion. Thus, a journal article about child abuse found in *Child Development* or in *Journal of Marriage and the Family* should be reliable, but an article about child abuse in a popular magazine may be less reliable in its facts and opinions. Usually, but not in every case, you can identify a journal in these ways:

1. The journal does not have a colorful cover; in fact, the table of contents is often displayed on the cover.
2. No colorful drawings or photography introduce each journal article, just a title and the name of the author(s).
3. The word *journal* often appears in the title (e.g., *The Journal of Sociology*).
4. The yearly issues of a journal are bound into a book.
5. Usually, the pages of a journal are numbered continuously through all issues for a year (unlike magazines, which are paged anew with each issue).

Sometimes you may face a bewildering array of articles, and you will won-der which pieces are the best. One way to evaluate a set of articles is with *citation searching*, which will search for authors who have been cited repeat-edly in the literature. For example, while researching for sources on the world's water supply, one student saw repeated references to Mark J. Hammer in these three citations:

Hammer, Mark J. *Wastewater Treatment in Dry Climates*. Alexandria, VA: Water Environment Federation, 2001.

Hammer, Mark J. *Water and Wastewater Technology*. 6th ed. New York: Prentice Hall, 2007.

Viessman, Warren, Jr., Mark J. Hammer, Elizabeth Perez, and Paul Chadick. *Water Supply and Pollution Control*. 8th ed. New York: Prentice Hall, 2008.

Common sense told the student to search out something by Hammer; that he is respected in this field is evident from these numerous citations in the literature.

Three reference books provide citation indexes:

Arts and Humanities Citation Index (AHCI) 1977–date
Science Citation Index (SCI) 1961–date
Social Sciences Citation Index (SSCI) 1966–date

Sponsored Web Site

> Online article, annotated by a student, page 117.

The Internet supplies both excellent information and some that is questionable in value. You must make judgments about the validity of these materials. On that note, see section 4b for a set of guidelines. Ask yourself a few questions about any article from a Web site:

Is it appropriate to my work?
Is it reliable and authoritative?
Is it sponsored by an institution or organization?

Usually, just the name of a Web site offers clues about its validity. For example, how would you rank the following sites as most reliable for information?

Spank! Youth Culture Online: An Ezine for Youth and Teens
Project Muse: Scholarly Journals Online
www.factmonster.com
CBC News: Canada's Online Information Service
Thomas: Legislative Information on the Internet, sponsored by the Library of Congress

Probably you picked Project Muse and Thomas first, with CBC News third— all good choices.

Interview

Interviews with knowledgeable people provide excellent information for a research paper. Whether conducted in person, by telephone, or by e-mail, the interview brings a personal, expert perspective to your work. The key element, of course, is the expertise of the person.

Experiment, Test, or Observation

Gathering your own data for research is a staple in many fields, especially the sciences. An experiment will bring primary evidence to your paper as you explain your hypothesis, give the test results, and discuss the implications of your findings. For a full discussion on conducting scientific investigation, with guidelines and details on format, see section 6e, pages 91–92.

Trade Book

CNC Robotics: Build Your Own Workshop Bot and *A Field Guide to Industrial Landscapes* are typical titles of nonfiction trade books found in bookstores and some public libraries, but not usually in a college library. Designed for commercial consumption, trade books seldom treat with depth a scholarly subject. Trade books have specific targets—the cook, the gardener, the antique dealer. In addition, trade books, in general, receive no rigorous prepublication scrutiny like that of scholarly books and textbooks. For example, if your topic is "dieting" with a focus on "fad diets," you will find plenty of diet books at the local bookstore and on commercial Web sites. However, pass them by in favor of serious discussions backed by careful research that you will find by searching your library's databases.

Encyclopedia

By design, encyclopedias contain brief surveys of well-known persons, events, places, and accomplishments. They will serve you well during preliminary investigation, but most instructors prefer that you go beyond encyclopedias in order to cite from scholarly books and journal articles. Encyclopedias seldom have the critical perspective you can gain from books and journal articles. There are some exceptions, of course, because specialized encyclopedias (see page 67) often have in-depth articles by noted scholars.

Popular Magazine

Like trade books, magazines have a targeted audience—young women, wrestling fans, computer connoisseurs, travelers. The articles are written rather quickly and seldom face critical review by a panel of experts. Therefore, exercise caution when reading a popular commercial magazine. However, some magazines target an intellectual audience and thereby have a superior quality with academic merit; these include *Atlantic Monthly, Scientific Review, Astronomy, Smithsonian, Discover, Harper's*, and the *New Yorker*. In general, college libraries house the intellectual magazines, but they can also be found at most chain bookstores, such as Borders and Barnes & Noble.

Newspaper

Some newspaper articles are not carefully researched or peer reviewed, but major newspapers such as the *New York Times*, the *Los Angeles Times*, and the *Wall Street Journal* offer carefully fact-checked information and rigorously researched stories. Generally, newspapers offer an excellent source of information, especially of local information that may not be found elsewhere.

Listserv

E-mail information via listserv deserves consideration when it focuses on an academic issue, such as British Romantic literature or, more specifically, Shelley's poetry. In many cases, listservs originate from a college or scholarly organization. In fact, many instructors establish their own listserv sites for individual classes. Online courses usually feature a listserv site for exchange of ideas and peer review. These listservs can be a great way to seek out possible topics and learn what literature teachers or sociologists are talking about these days. *Caution:* Use the listserv to generate ideas, not as a source for facts to use in quotations.

Individual Web Site

A person's home page provides a publication medium for anybody who presumes to a knowledge they do or do not possess. You can't avoid home pages because they pop up on search engines, but you *can* approach them with caution. For example, one student, investigating the topic "fad diets," searched the Web, only to find mostly commercial sites that were blatant in their commercial attempts to sell something and home pages that described personal battles with weight loss. Caution is vital. On this point see 4a, pages 40–42.

Usenet

Usenet newsgroups post information on a site. Like call-in radio shows, they invite opinions from a vast cross section of people, some reliable and some not. In most cases, participants employ a fake pseudonymous username, rendering their ideas useless for a documented paper.

Internet Chat Conversations

Chat rooms have almost no value for academic research. In most cases, you don't even know who you are chatting with, and the conversations are seldom about scholarly issues.

8b Selecting a Mix of Primary and Secondary Sources

Primary sources include novels, speeches, eyewitness accounts, interviews, letters, autobiographies, and the results of original research. Feel free to quote often from a primary source if it has direct relevance to your discussion. If you examine a poem by Dylan Thomas, you must quote the poem. If you examine President George W. Bush's domestic policies on health care, you must quote from White House documents.

For information about reading key parts of a book, article, or Internet site, see pages 116–120.

Secondary sources are writings *about* the primary sources, *about* an author, or *about* somebody's accomplishments. Examples of secondary sources are a report on a presidential speech, a review of new scientific findings, and an analysis of a poem. A biography provides a secondhand view of the life of a notable person. A history book interprets events. These evaluations, analyses, or interpretations provide ways of looking at primary works, events, and lives.

Do not quote liberally from secondary sources. Be selective. Use a well-worded sentence, not the entire paragraph. Incorporate a key phrase into your text, not eight or nine lines.

The subject area of a research paper determines in part the nature of the source materials. Use the following chart as a guide:

Citing from Primary and Secondary Sources

	Primary Sources	*Secondary Sources*
Literature	Novels, poems, plays, short stories, letters, diaries, manuscripts, auto-biographies, films, videos of live performances	Journal articles, reviews, biographies, critical books about writers and their works
Government, Political Science, History	Speeches, writings by presidents and others, the *Congressional Record*, reports of agencies and departments, documents written by historic figures	Newspaper reports, news magazines, political journals and newsletters, journal articles, history books
Social Sciences	Case studies, findings from surveys and question-naires, reports of social workers, psychiatrists, and lab technicians	Commentary and evalua-tions in reports, docu-ments, journal articles, and books
Sciences	Tools and methods, experiments, findings from tests and experiments, observations, discoveries, and test patterns	Interpretations and discussions of test data as found in journals and books (scientific books, which are quickly dated, are less valuable than up-to-date journals)
Fine Arts	Films, paintings, music, sculptures, as well as reproductions and synopses of these designed for research purposes	Evaluations in journal articles, critical reviews, biographies, and critical books about the authors and their works
Business	Market research and test-ing, technical studies and investigations, drawings, designs, models, memo-randums and letters, computer data	Discussion of the busi-ness world in news-papers, business magazines, journals, government documents, and books
Education	Pilot studies, term pro-jects, sampling results,	Analysis and evaluation of educational experi-

tests and test data, surveys, interviews, observations, statistics, and computer data	mentation in journals, pamplets, books, and reports

8c Evaluating Sources

Evaluating the Key Parts of an Article

Look closely at these parts of any article that looks promising.

1. The **title**. Look for the words that have relevance to your topic before you start reading the article. For example, "Children and Parents" may look ideal for child abuse research until you read the subtitle: "Children and Parents: Growing Up in New Guinea."
2. An **abstract**. Reading an abstract is the best way to ascertain if an essay or a book will serve your specific needs. Some are available at the beginning of printed articles; others are provided by abstracting services (e.g., *Psychological Abstracts*). Most articles found through the library's databases will feature an abstract that you should read before printing or downloading the entire article. Save a tree, read before printing.
3. The **opening paragraphs**. If the opening of an article shows no relevance to your study, abandon it.
4. The **topic sentence** of each paragraph of the body. These first sentences, even if you scan them hastily, will give you a digest of the author's main points.
5. The **closing paragraph(s)**. If the opening of an article seems promising, skim the closing for relevance.
6. **Author credits**. Learn something about the credentials of the writer. Magazine articles often provide brief biographical profiles of authors. Journal articles and Internet home pages generally include the author's academic affiliation and credentials.

Read an entire article only if a quick survey encourages you to further investigation. Student Victoria Aull, an elementary education major, scanned an article for her paper on the need for outdoor activities for children. Figure 8.1 shows how she highlighted key phrases with marginal comments that were germane to her study. Note that she recognizes the bias expressed throughout the environmental magazine, *Earth Island Journal*.

Evaluating the Key Parts of a Book

A **book** requires you to survey several items beyond those listed on page 116 for articles:

1. The **table of contents**. A book's table of contents may reveal chapters that pertain to your topic. Often, only one chapter is useful. For example, Richard Ellmann's book *Oscar Wilde* devotes one chapter, "The Age of Dorian," to

The Classroom Outside

Jason Mark

Growing up, I was lucky to have a large expanse of outdoor space in which to play. My parents owned a two-and-a-half acre lot on the north edge of Phoenix, AZ. Many of our neighbors had horses, and our home was a short dirt bike ride from the Mountain Preserve, one of the largest urban parks in the US. Much of my free time was spent scouting desert trails, exploring arroyos, and hunting for lizards and fools gold.

This writer and the magazine recognize the need for conservation and environmental preservation.

I never thought of the hours among the creosote and saguaros as "education"—it was just plain fun. But surely I learned some lessons during that time: the pattern of the seasons in the Sonoran Desert, the points of a compass, what a horny toad looks like. Simply being outside and having the freedom to satisfy a child's curiosity provided a crash course in ecology.

The ecology of natural areas can provide a valuable learning environment.

Unfortunately, a decreasing number of US children today are afforded similar opportunities for unstructured outdoor time. Suburban sprawl has paved over many meadows and creeks, and parental fears of crime and abduction keep many kids inside. Author Richard Louv has dubbed children's lack of engagement with the world "Nature Deficit Disorder." According to one statistic Louv cites, the radius that children travel away from their homes to play shrank by nearly 90 percent between 1970 and 1994. As one boy told Louv in the course of his research, he prefers playing inside…because that's where the electrical outlets are.

Urban sprawl is paving over many of the natural environments. It is sad that so many young people are more plugged in to indoor activities than experiencing the beauty of natural surroundings.

The implications of this trend are frightening. Watching TV, playing video games, or cruising the Internet may open windows of understandings into the workings of a complex post-industrial world. But at the same time those activities close other windows, and, I believe, limit children's understanding of the human experience. Too much time inside reduces young people's conception of what it means to be a physical creature on this fecund planet.

Although technology is important, we must open the windows to the natural world for all learners.

Several months after interviewing Oberlin College Professor David Orr for our Conversation (p. 50), I remain deeply unsettled by something he said to me: "The possibility of a divorce between humankind and nature is not a small issue.… I think that the danger of our becoming an indoor, primarily electronic species isn't small."

We must realize our connection to nature and pass that on to our children.

Thankfully, many organizations are working hard to prevent that from happening. Kids for the Bay is one of them—an Earth Island Institute-sponsored project that teaches young children about the importance of protecting the San Francisco Bay (p. 19). Another encouraging sign is the growing number of "Expeditionary earning" schools—elementary and high schools that use outdoor experiences to teach core subjects. The teaching methods, though unconventional, are proving successful; kids seem to respond to the kind of education in which real-life experiences reinforce what's learned in books.

Outdoor projects and classrooms are not novelties—they are essential to helping all learners experience real-life experiences.

(continued)

FIGURE 8.1 Article with highlighting and marginal comments on items that the student considered important to her thesis.
Source: *Earth Island Journal,* 22.4, 2008, p. 2.

As Adam Spangler reports in "Educational Trailblazers" (p. 46), students at many Expeditionary Learning schools are performing above average on standardized tests.

It's sad that in our urban, suburban, and exurban communities, such programs are exciting exceptions instead of everyday examples, because the stakes for our environmental future couldn't be higher. Unless children have the chance to fall in love with the natural world, they will have little desire to protect it.

An appreciation for the natural world is the only way that we can emphasize the importance of preservation and conservation of our natural resources to the rising generation.

■■■ **FIGURE 8.1** *(continued)*

Wilde's *The Picture of Dorian Gray*. If your research focuses on this novel, then the chapter, not the entire book, will demand your attention.

2. The **book jacket**, if one is available. For example, the jacket to Richard Ellmann's *Oscar Wilde* says:

> Ellmann's *Oscar Wilde* has been almost twenty years in the work, and it will stand, like his universally admired *James Joyce*, as the definitive life. The book's emotional resonance, its riches of authentic color and conversation, and the subtlety of its critical illuminations give dazzling life to this portrait of the complex man, the charmer, the great playwright, the daring champion of the primacy of art.

Such information can stimulate the reading and notetaking from this important book.

3. The **foreword, preface,** or **introduction**. An author's *preface* or *introduction* serves as a critical overview of the book, pinpointing the primary subject of the text and the particular approach taken. For example, Ellmann opens his book *Oscar Wilde* by saying:

> Oscar Wilde: we have only to hear the great name to anticipate that what will be quoted as his will surprise and delight us. Among the writers identified with the 1890s, Wilde is the only one whom everyone still reads. The various labels that have been applied to the age—Aestheticism, Decadence, the Beardsley period—ought not to conceal that fact that our first association with it is Wilde, refulgent, majestic, ready to fall.

This introduction describes the nature of the book: Ellmann will portray Wilde as the dominating literary figure of the 1890s. A *foreword* is often written by somebody other than the author. It is often insightful and worthy of quotation.

4. The **index**. A book's index lists names and terms with the page on which they are mentioned within the text. For example, the index to *Oscar Wilde* lists about eighty items under *The Picture of Dorian Gray*, among them:

homosexuality and, 312, 318
literature and painting in, 312–131
magazine publication of, 312, 319, 320

Home

Spring 2000

Issue Contents

Search

ISSUES online
IN SCIENCE AND TECHNOLOGY

Back Issues

The Delicate Balance: Environment, Economics, Development

JAMES G. WORKMAN

How to Fix Our Dam Problems

Thousands of aging dams should be repaired or destroyed, at a cost of billions. A cap-and-trade policy would speed the process and help pay the bills.

California is the world's eighth largest economy and generates 13% of U.S. wealth. Yet Governor Arnold Schwarzenegger says high temperatures, low rainfall, and a growing population have created a water crisis there. A third of the state is in extreme drought and, if there's another dry season, faces catastrophe. The governor fears that his economy could collapse without a $5.9 billion program to build more dams.

His concerns are widely shared in the United States—not to mention in dry Australia, Spain, China, and India. Yet as California desperately seeks new dam construction, it simultaneously leads the world in old dam destruction. It razes old dams for the same reasons it raises new dams: economic security, public safety, water storage efficiency, flood management, job creation, recreation, and adaptation to climate change. Dam-removal supporters include water districts, golf courses, energy suppliers, thirsty cities, engineers, farmers, and property owners.

With 1,253 dams risky enough to be regulated and 50 times that many unregistered small dams, California is a microcosm of the world. There are more than 2.5 million dams in the United States, 79,000 so large they require government monitoring. There are an estimated 800,000 substantial dams worldwide. But within the next two decades, 85% of U.S. dams will have outlived their average 50-year lifespan, putting lives, property, the environment, and the climate at risk unless they are repaired and upgraded.

Neither dam repair nor dam removal is a recent phenomenon. What is new is their scale and complexity as well as the number of zeros on the price tag. Between 1920 and 1956, in the Klamath River drainage 22 dams were dismantled at a total cost of $3,000. Today, the removal of four dams on that same river—for jobs, security, efficiency, safety, legal compliance, and growth—will cost upwards of $200 million.

Which old uneconomical dams should be improved or removed? Who pays the bill? The answers have usually come through politics. Pro-dam and anti-dam interests raise millions of dollars and press their representatives to set aside hundreds of millions more tax dollars to selectively subsidize pet dam projects. Other bills bail out private owners: A current House bill earmarks $40 million for repairs; another one sets aside $12 million for removals. The outcome is gridlock, lawsuits, debt spending, bloated infrastructure, rising risks, dying fisheries, and sick streams.

Dam decisions don't have to work that way. Rather than trust well-intentioned legislators, understaffed state agencies, harried bureaucrats, or nonscientific federal judges to decide the fate of millions of unique river structures, there's another approach. State and federal governments should firmly set in place safety and conservation standards, allow owners to make links between the costs and benefits of existing dams, and then let market transactions bring health, equity, and efficiency to U.S. watersheds. Social welfare, economic diversity, and ecological capital would all improve through a cap-and-trade system for water infrastructure. This system would allow mitigation and offsets from the vast stockpile of existing dams while improving the quality of, or doing away with the need for, new dam construction.

Aging dams and the cost involved with repairing or replacing the structures are economic and environmental concerns.

The economics regarding old dams is a local and national concern.

The construction as well as the razing of dams presents a difficult balance between those who need the water for their businesses and those who want to preserve our natural resources.

Failing dams can put a tremendous economic and environmental strain on local governments

Huge costs accompany the replacement and repair of old dams.

Old dams cause a gridlock over spending, infrastructure, and local climate.

All citizens have a stake in the repair, removal, and building of dams.

FIGURE 8.2 Internet article from *Issues in Science and Technology Online.*

An index, by its detailed listing, can determine the relevance of the book to your research.

Evaluating the Key Parts of an Internet Article

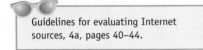

Guidelines for evaluating Internet sources, 4a, pages 40–44.

The techniques listed previously for evaluating periodical articles (page 116) apply also to Internet articles. In addition, examine:

1. The **home page**, if there is one. Prefer sites sponsored by universities and professional organizations. You may have to truncate the URL to find the home page where such information is featured. For example, this URL: **www.theatlantic.com/unbound/wordpolice/three/** can be truncated to **www.theatlantic.com/**, which is the magazine's home page.
2. The **hypertext links** to other sites whose quality can again be determined by the domain tags *.edu, .org, or .gov*. Be wary of sites that have the tag *.com*.

Figure 8.2 displays a sponsored Web site that student researcher Danny Ortiz discovered in his search of sources about the deterioration of dams in the water-deprived areas. It shows an online article by James G. Workman accompanied by his marginal notes to key ideas. Examine your Internet articles in like manner.

8d   Outlining a Source

You can frame an outline to capture an author's primary themes by listing statements that reveal the major issues and any supporting ideas. A quick outline of the Workman article, page 119, might look like this:

> Aging dams and the cost involved with repairing or replacing the structures.
>
> We must think globally, for the need for more dams is vital to the economy of the state of California as well as the economy of the nation.
>
> The construction as well as the razing of dams present a difficult balance between those who need the water for their businesses and those who want to preserve our natural resources.

Because they only have a life span of 50 years, failing dams can put a tremendous economic and environmental strain on local governments.

Astronomical costs accompany the replacement and repair of old dams.

Added to the tremendous cost of dam improvements and removal is the gridlock over spending, infrastructure, and local climate.

In truth, all citizens have a stake in the repair, removal, and building of dams.

This quickly drawn outline by Danny Ortiz provides an overview of the article with the issues clearly labeled. Ortiz can go in search of other sources that address these issues.

8e Summarizing a Source

A summary condenses into a brief note the general nature of a source. Writing a summary forces you to grasp the essence of the material. You might even use it in your paper with your evaluation and comments. The summary could serve as the heart of an annotated bibliography, which is a citation with a summary attached (see pages 122-124). Here is Danny Ortiz's summary of the Workman article (see page 119).

James Workman offers his views on environmental and economic cost involved with repairing or replacing the structures. Because they only have a life span of 50 years, failing dams can put a tremendous economic and environmental strain on local governments. Workman encourages us to think globally, for the need for more dams is vital to the economy of the state of California as well as the economy of the nation. The construction as well as the razing of dams presents a difficult balance between those who need the water for their businesses and those who want to preserve our natural resources. Added to the tremendous cost of dam improvements and removal is the gridlock over spending, infrastructure, and local climate. Workman wants to make all citizens aware of the tremendous costs involved with the repair, removal, and building of dams.

This summary can serve the researcher as he develops the paper, and it can become a part of the paper as part of the review of the literature (see pages 124-130).

Responding to a Source

- Read and make marginal notes on your sources. See pages 116–120 for details and an example.

- Search out scholarly materials—books and journals—by accessing your college library's resources. Don't depend entirely on the Internet.

- If appropiate, use a mix of quotations from primary sources, such as a novel, as well as paraphrases and quotations from secondary sources. See pages 114–116 for a list of both types.

- Assess the nature of the source for any bias it might contain. See page 107 and pages 166–168 for details.

- Read and highlight the key parts of the source, whether it is an article, book, or Internet site. See pages 116–120 for further details.

- Outline key ideas to identify the issues. See pages 120–121 for an example.

- Write a summary that captures the essence of the article. See page 121 for an example.

8f Preparing an Annotated Bibliography

An *annotation* is a summary of the contents of a book or article. A *bibliography* is a list of sources on a selected topic. Thus, an annotated bibliography does two important things: (1) it gives a bibliographic list of a selection of sources, and (2) it summarizes the contents of each book or article. Writing an annotated bibliography may at first appear to be busywork, but it will help you evaluate the strength of your sources.

The annotated bibliography that follows summarizes a selection of sources on the topic of gender communication.

Holz 1

Kaci Holz

Dr. Bekus

English 1010

Mar. 10, 2008

Annotated Bibliography

Armstrong, Colleen, "Deborah Tannen Comes to Class: Implications of

Gender and Conversation in the Classroom." *English Journal* 85.2

(1996): 15. Print. In a conversation with a male student, Armstrong thought she was "helpful" and "supportive" when she "nodded vigorously" and punctuated his words with "yes." The male thought she was "rude" and "intrusive." Concerned at the failure of conversation, Armstrong read Deborah Tannen's *You Just Don't Understand*, which helped Armstrong understand the ways men and women interrupt each other. Men see interruptions as "conversational bullying." Women see them as "cooperative overlapping." What Armstrong thought was support and involvement the male student saw as manipulation.

"Bill and coo." *The Economist* 321 (1991): 107. Print. The author of this article is not given. He/she describes a debate held at the Cooper Union in New York between Deborah Tannen and John Bly, two authors "whose work has discussed the female and male perspectives on understanding between the sexes." Many people expected this debate to be "a battle of the sexes," but instead it was "a high minded debate between two earnest intellectuals before a large and attentive audience." Both authors praised each other's ideas and research in the field. Bly claimed Tannen's book to be "a lively but serious examination of the different conversational styles of men and women." Tannen also complimented Bly's book *Iron John*, "which, unusually, puts the blame for the failure of boys to grow up on their fathers, not their mothers."

Deborah Tannen and Robert Bly: Men and Women Talking Together. New York Cooper Union. Mystic Fire Video, 1993. Film. This video presents two of the most popular and exciting people at the forefront of men's and women's issues, talking to each other about gender styles. Each brings an informed perspective on how men and women approach each other and conversation itself. Bly and Tannen agree that "it is crucial to describe both the differences and similarities, so that men and women can respect each other, and in the process, present a model of how that is done" (back cover of the videocassette).

Gergen, Mary. Rev. of *Talking Difference: On Gender and Language*, by Mary Crawford. *Archives of Sexual Behavior* 30.3 (2001): 338–.

InfoTrac. Web. 28 Sept. 2002. In her review of Crawford's book, Gergen suggests that the "differences between the ways men and women talk suggest that we might as well have come from different planets." Today, some view it as necessary to take a quick course in conversational translations. Gergen says Crawford made in-depth inquiries into issues of how conversation affects relations, power, and discrimination.

Glass, Lillian. *He Says, She Says: Closing the Communication Gap between the Sexes*. New York: Putnam, 1992. Print. Glass's book begins with the author's interest in gender communication. The first chapter is a Sex Talk Quiz that the reader can take to check his or her responses. The second chapter addresses "the evolution of sex differences in communication." Glass addresses the issue that different hormones found in men's and women's bodies make them act differently and therefore communicate differently. In later chapters Glass discusses brain development, environmental factors, and treatment of infants, and ends with recommendations for improving communication and thus the relationships with the other sex.

Tannen, Deborah. "Boys Will Be Boys." *The Argument Culture: Moving from Debate to Dialogue*. New York: Random House, 1998. Print. In Chapter 6 of *The Argument Culture* Tannen addresses the issue that boys or men "are more likely to take an oppositional stance toward other people and the world" and "are more likely to find opposition entertaining—to enjoy watching a good fight, or having one." She says girls try to avoid fights. She also claims that a girl tries to offer a view that would benefit the opponent. A boy, on the other hand, just argues for what is best for him. She concludes that patterns of opposition and conflict result from both biology and culture.

8g Preparing a Review of the Literature on a Topic

The *review of literature* presents a set of summaries in essay form for two purposes:

1. It helps you investigate the topic because it forces you to examine and then describe how each source addresses the problem.

2. It organizes and classifies the sources in some reasonable manner for the benefit of the reader.

Thus, you should relate each source to your central subject, and you should group the sources according to their support of your thesis. For example, the brief review that follows explores the literature on the subject of gender communication. It classifies the sources under a progression of headings: the issues, the causes (both environmental and biological), the consequences for both men and women, and possible solutions.

Like Kaci Holz in the paper below, you may wish to use headings that identify your various sections.

Holz 1

Kaci Holz

Dr. Bekus

April 23, 2008

English 1010

Gender Communication:

A Review of the Literature

Several theories exist about different male and female communication styles. These ideas have been categorized here to establish the issues, show causes for communication failures, the consequences for both men and women, and suggestions for possible solutions.

The Issues

Deborah Tannen, Ph.D., is a professor of sociolinguistics at Georgetown University. In her book *You Just Don't Understand: Men and Women in Conversation*, she claims there are basic gender patterns or stereotypes that can be found. Tannen says that men participate in conversations to establish "a hierarchical social order," while women most often participate in conversations to establish "a network of connections" (Tannen, *Don't Understand* 24–25). She distinguishes between the way women use "rapport-talk" and the way men use "report-talk" (74).

In similar fashion, Susan Basow and Kimberly Rubenfeld in "'Troubles Talk': Effects of Gender and Gender Typing," explore in detail the sex roles and how they determine and often control the speech of each gender. They notice that "women may engage in 'troubles talk' to enhance communication; men may avoid such talk to enhance autonomy and dominance" (186).

In addition, Kawa Patel asserts that men and women "use conversation for quite different purposes." He provides a "no" answer to the question in his title, "Do Men and Women Speak the Same Language?" He claims that women converse to develop and maintain connections, while men converse to claim their position in the hierarchy they see around them. Patel asserts that women are less likely to speak publicly than are men because women often perceive such speaking as putting oneself on display. A man, on the other hand, is usually comfortable with speaking publicly because that is how he establishes his status among others (Patel).

Similarly, masculine people are "less likely than androgynous individuals to feel grateful for advice" (Basow and Rubenfeld 186).

Julia T. Woods' book *Gendered Lives* claims that "male communication is characterized by assertion, independence, competitiveness, and confidence [while] female communication is characterized by deference, inclusivity, collaboration, and cooperation" (440). This list of differences describes why men and women have such opposing communication styles.

In another book, Tannen addresses the issue that boys, or men, "are more likely to take an oppositional stance toward other people and the world" and "are more likely to find opposition entertaining— to enjoy watching a good fight, or having one" (Tannen, *Argument* 166). Girls try to avoid fights.

Causes

Two different theories suggest causes for gender differences— the environment and biology.

Environmental Causes. Tammy James and Bethann Cinelli mention, "The way men and women are raised contributes to differences in conversation and communication..." (41).

Another author, Susan Witt, in "Parental Influence on Children's Socialization to Gender Roles," discusses the various findings that support the idea that parents have a great influence on their children during the development of their self-concept. She states, "Children learn at a very early age what it means to be a boy or a girl in our society" (253). She says that parents "[dress] infants in gender-specific colors, [give] gender-differentiated toys, and [expect] different behavior from boys and girls" (Witt 254).

Patel notices a cultural gap, defining culture as "shared meaning." He goes on to comment that problems come about because one spouse enters marriage with a different set of "shared meanings" than the other. The cultural gap affects the children. Patel also talks about the "Battle of the Sexes" as seen in conflict between men and women. Reverting back to his "childhood gender pattern" theory, Patel claims, "Men, who grew up in a hierarchical environment, are accustomed to conflict. Women, concerned more with relationship and connection, prefer the role of peacemaker."

Like Patel, Deborah Tannen also addresses the fact that men and women often come from different worlds and different influences. She says, "Even if they grow up in the same neighborhood, on the same block, or in the same house, girls and boys grow up in different worlds of words" (Tannen, *Don't Understand* 43).

Biological Causes. Though Tannen often addresses the environmental issue in much of her research, she also looks at the biological issue in her book *The Argument Culture*. Tannen states, "Surely a biological component plays a part in the greater use of antagonism among men, but cultural influence can override biological inheritance" (Tannen, *Argument* 205). She sums up the nature versus nurture issue by saying, "the patterns that typify women's and men's styles of opposition and conflict are the result of both biology and culture" (207).

Lillian Glass addresses the issue that different hormones found in men's and women's bodies make them act differently and therefore communicate differently. She also discusses how brain development has been found to relate to sex differences.

Judy Mann says, "Most experts now believe that what happens to boys and girls is a complex interaction between slight biological differences and tremendously powerful social forces that begin to manifest themselves the minute the parents find out whether they are going to have a boy or a girl" (qtd. in McCluskey 6).

Consequences of Gender Differences

Now that we have looked at different styles of gender communication and possible causes of gender communication, let us look at the possible results. Morgan and Coleman relate that divorce is one of the most stressful events a person can experience. They expound upon this point by stating, "The decision to divorce is typically made with ambivalence, uncertainty and confusion. It is a difficult step. The family identity changes, and the identities of the individuals involved change as well."

Through various studies, Tannen has concluded that men and women have different purposes for engaging in communication. In the open forum that Deborah Tannen led in 2004 (on compact disc), she explains the different ways men and women handle communication throughout the day. She explains that a man constantly talks during his workday in order to impress those around him and to establish his status in the office. At home he wants peace and quiet. On the other hand, a woman is constantly cautious and guarded about what she says during her workday. Women try hard to avoid confrontation and avoid offending anyone with their language. So when a woman comes home from work she expects to be able to talk freely without having to guard her words. The consequence? The woman expects conversation, but the man is tired of talking (Tannen, *He Said*).

Solutions

Answers for better gender communication seem elusive. What can be done about this apparent gap in communication between genders? In his article published in *Leadership*, Jeffrey Arthurs offers the obvious suggestion that women should make an attempt to understand the male model of communication and that men should make an attempt to understand the female model of communication.

However, in his article "Speaking Across the Gender Gap," David Cohen mentions that experts didn't think it would be helpful to teach men to communicate more like women and women to communicate more like men. This attempt would prove unproductive because it would go against what men and women have been taught since birth. Rather than change the genders to be more like one another, we could simply try to "understand" each other better.

In addition, Carolyn Crozier makes this observation, "The idea that women should translate their experiences into the male code in order to express themselves effectively ... is an outmoded, inconsistent, subservient notion that should no longer be given credibility in modern society." She suggests three things we can change: 1.) Change the norm by which leadership success is judged, 2.) Redefine what we mean by power, and 3.) Become more sensitive to the places and times when inequity and inequality occur (Crozier). Similarly, Patel offers advice to help combat "cross-cultural" fights. He suggests: 1.) Identify your fighting style, 2.) Agree on rules of engagement, and 3.) Identify the real issue behind the conflict (Patel).

McCluskey claims men and women need honest communication that shows respect, and they must "manage conflict in a way that maintains the relationship and gets the job done" (5). She says, "To improve relationships and interactions between men and women, we must acknowledge the differences that do exist, understand how they develop, and discard dogma about what are the 'right' roles of women and men" (5).

Obviously, differences exist in the way men and women communicate, whether caused by biological and/or environmental factors. We can consider the possible causes, the consequences, and possible solutions. Using this knowledge, we should be able to more accurately interpret communication between the genders.

Arthurs, Jeffrey. "He Said, She Heard: Any Time You Speak to Both Men
     and Women, You're Facing Cross-Cultural Communication."
     Leadership 23.1 (Winter 2002): 49. _Expanded Academic_. Web. 19
     Apr. 2008.

Basow, Susan A., and Kimberly Rubenfeld. "'Troubles Talk': Effects of
     Gender and Gender Typing." _Sex Roles: A Journal of Research_
     (2003): 183–. _Expanded Academic_. Web. 19 Apr. 2008.

Cohen, David. "Speaking Across the Gender Gap." _New Scientist_
     131.1783 (1991): 36. _Expanded Academic_. Web. 18 Apr. 2008.

Crozier, Carolyn Y. "Subservient Speech: Women Need to be Heard." 8
     Aug. 2005. Web. 15 Apr. 2008.

Glass, Lillian. _He Says, She Says: Closing the Communication Gap
     Between the Sexes_. New York: G. P. Putnam's Sons, 1992.
     Print.

James, Tammy, and Bethann Cinelli. "Exploring Gender-Based
     Communication Styles." _Journal of School Health_ 73 (2003):
     41–42. Print.

McCluskey, Karen Curnow. "Gender at Work." _Public Management_ 79.5
     (1997): 5–10. Print.

Morgan, Marni, and Marilyn Coleman. "Focus on Families: Divorce and
     Adults." Apr. 2007. Web. 17 Apr. 2008.

Patel, Kawa. "Do Men and Women Speak the Same Language?" 14 Nov.
     2007. Web. 18 Apr. 2008.

Tannen, Deborah. _The Argument Culture: Moving from Debate to
     Dialogue_. New York: Random House, 1998. Print.

———. _He Said, She Said: Exploring the Different Ways Men and
     Women Communicate_. Print. New York: Barnes & Noble, 2004.
     CD.

———. _You Just Don't Understand: Women and Men in Conversation_.
     New York: HarperCollins, 2001. Print.

Witt, Susan D. "Parental Influence on Children's Socialization to
     Gender Roles." _Adolescence_ 32 (1997): 253. Print.

Woods, Julia T. _Gendered Lives_. 6th ed. San Francisco: Wadsworth,
     2004. Print.

YOUR RESEARCH PROJECT

1. Examine your sources to test the validity of the list against the pyramid on page 108. Do you have enough sources from the upper tier of scholarly works? If not, go in search of journal articles and scholarly books to beef up the list. Do not depend on Internet articles entirely, even if every one is from a sponsored Web site.

2. Conduct a citation search (see pages 111–112 for details) on your topic, which will help you identify key people who have written on the subject several times and for several publications.

3. Examine the chart of primary and secondary sources on pages 115–116. Look for your discipline—literature, government, history—and then determine if you are using a mix of primary and secondary sources.

4. Respond to one of your sources by writing two items: (1) a rough outline of the contents of the source (see pages 120–121), and (2) a brief summary of the source (see page 121).

PEARSON
mycomplab

For more resources in research, writing, and documentation, go to MyCompLab.com

9 Writing Effective Notes and Creating Outlines

The primary reason for writing from research is to announce and publicize new findings. The accurate notes from your personal research will join with your carefully paraphrased notes from experts on the topic to form the support for your thesis. Your goal is to share verifiable information, but others can verify your work only if good records are kept and reported.

Gathering Printouts, Photocopies, Scanned Images, and Downloaded Data

Today's technology makes it fairly easy to collect material quickly and in volume. You can print online articles or save them to a file. You can use a scanner to make digital images of graphics as well as text. Plus, photocopy machines enable you to carry home a few sheets of paper instead of an entire book.

All this material will gradually make sense as you arrange it and use it. Warning: Keep *everything*. You will need to cite the source in the text and in a bibliography entry, so don't throw away a note, printout, or a photocopy.

Writing Notes of High Quality

Notetaking is the heart of research. If you write notes of high quality, they may need only minor editing to fit the appropriate places in your first draft. Prepare yourself to write different types of notes—quotations for well-phrased passages by authorities but also paraphrased or summarized notes to maintain your voice.

- *Personal notes* (9b), which express your own ideas or record data from field research.
- *Quotation notes* (9c), which preserve the wisdom and distinguished syntax of an authority.
- *Paraphrase notes* (9d), which interpret and restate what the authority has said.
- *Summary notes* (9e), which distill factual data that has marginal value; you can return to the source later if necessary.
- *Précis notes* (9f), which capture the essence of one writer's ideas in capsule form.
- *Field notes* (9g), which record interviews, questionnaire tabulations, laboratory experiments, and other types of field research.

9a Creating Effective Notes

Whether you write notes on a computer or by hand, you should keep in mind some basic rules, summarized in the checklist below.

Honoring the Conventions of Research Style

Your notetaking will be more effective from the start if you practice the conventions of style for citing a source, as advocated by the Modern Language Association (MLA), American Psychological Association (APA), Council of Science Editors (CSE), or Chicago Manual of Style (CMS), and as shown briefly below and explained later in this book.

MLA: Lawrence Smith states, "The suicidal teen causes severe damage to the psychological condition of peers" (34).

APA: Smith (2007) has commented, "The suicidal teen causes severe damage to the psychological condition of peers" (p. 34).

CSE number: Smith (4) has commented, "The suicidal teen causes severe damage to the psychological condition of peers."

CMS footnote: Lawrence Smith states, "The suicidal teen causes severe damage to the psychological condition of peers."[3]

Using a Computer for Notetaking

1. Record notes and save them using one of two methods:
   a. Write each note as a separate temporary file in a common directory so each can be moved later into the appropriate section of your draft via the Copy and Paste commands.

CHECKLIST

Writing Effective Notes

1. Write one item per note to facilitate the shuffling and rearranging of the data as you develop your paper during all stages of organization. Several notes can be kept in a computer file if each is labeled clearly.

2. List the source with name, year, and page to be ready for in-text citations and/or bibliographic entries.

3. Label each note (for example, "objectivity on television").

4. Write a full note in well-developed sentences to speed the writing of your first draft.

5. Keep everything (photocopy, scribbled note) in order to authenticate dates, page numbers, and full names.

6. Label your personal notes with "my idea" or "personal note" to distinguish them from the sources.

Identifying sources, 170–172

Darrel Abel in his third volume of *American*

Underscoring, 376

Literature narrates the hardships of the Samuel Clemens

family in Hannibal, yet Abel asserts that "despite such

Using lower-case after *that*, 188

hardships and domestic grief, which included the deaths

of a brother and sister, young Sam Clemens [Mark Twain]

Interpolations, 196–197

Single quotation marks, 188

had a happy and reasonably carefree boyhood" (11–12).

Page citations, 174–176

Abel acknowledges the value of Clemens's "rambling

Punctuation with quotations, 185–188

reminiscences dictated as an 'Autobiography' in his old

age" (12). Of those days Clemens says, "In the small

Ellipses points, 188–191

town . . . *everybody* [my emphasis] was poor, but didn't

know it; and everybody was comfortable, and did know it"

Signaling your emphasis of another's words, 192

(qtd. in Abel 12). Clemens felt at home in Hannibal with

One source quotes another, 177–178

everybody at the same level of poverty.

FIGURE 9.1 Conventions of style for writing notes.

b. Write all notes in a single file. Begin each new note with a code word or phrase. When you begin the actual writing of the paper, you can begin writing at the top of the file, which will push the notes down as you write.

2. You can record the bibliography information for each source you encounter by listing it in a BIBLIO file so that you build the necessary list of references in one alphabetical file. Chapters 14, 15, 16, and 17 give you the correct forms.

9b Writing Personal Notes

The content of a research paper is not a collection of ideas transmitted by experts in books and articles; it is an expression of your own ideas as supported by the scholarly evidence. Readers are primarily interested in *your* thesis statement, *your* topic sentences, and *your* personal view of the issues. Therefore, during your research, record your thoughts on the issues by writing plenty of personal notes in your research journal, or in your computer files. Personal notes are essential because they allow you to:

- Record your discoveries.
- Reflect on the findings.
- Make connections.
- Explore another point of view.
- Identify prevailing views and patterns of thought.

Personal notes should conform to these three standards:

1. The idea on the note is yours.
2. The note is labeled with "my idea," "mine," or "personal thought" so that later you can be certain it has not been borrowed.
3. The note is a rough summary, a sketch of ideas, or, preferably, a complete sentence or two.

A sample of a personal note follows:

Personal Thought

For me, organ donation might be a gift of life, so I have signed my donor card. At least a part of me will continue to live if an accident claims my life. My boyfriend says I'm gruesome, but I consider it practical. Besides, he might be the one who benefits, and then what will he say?

9c Writing Direct Quotation Notes

Quoting the words of another person is the easiest type of note to write. Quotation notes are essential because they allow you to:

- Capture the authoritative voice of the experts on the topic.
- Feature essential statements.
- Provide proof that you have researched the subject carefully.
- Offer conflicting points of view.
- Show the dialog that exists about the topic.

In the process, you will need to follow basic conventions:

1. Select quoted material that is important and well-phrased, not something trivial or something that is common knowledge. NOT "John F. Kennedy was a Democrat from Massachusetts" (Rupert 233) BUT "John F. Kennedy's Peace Corps left a legacy of lasting compassion for the downtrodden" (Rupert 233).

2. Use quotation marks. Do not copy the words of a source into your paper in such a way that readers will think *you* wrote the material.
3. Use the exact words of the source.
4. Provide an in-text citation to author and page number, like this (Henson 34–35), or give the author's name at the beginning of the quotation and put the page number after the quotation, like this example in MLA style:

> Barnill says, "More than 400 people each month receive the gift of sight through yet another type of tissue donation—corneal transplants. In many cases, donors unsuitable for organ donation are eligible for tissue donation" (2).

5. The in-text citation goes *outside* the final quotation mark but *inside* the period.
6. Try to quote key sentences and short passages, not entire paragraphs. Find the essential statement and feature it; do not force your reader to fumble through a long quoted passage in search of the relevant statement. Make the brief quotation a part of your sentence, in this way:

> Many Americans, trying to mend their past eating habits, adopt functional foods as an essential step toward a more health-conscious future. This group of believers spends "an estimated $29 billion a year" on functional foods (Nelson 755).

7. Quote from both primary sources (the original words by a writer or speaker) and secondary sources (the comments after the fact about original works). The two types are discussed immediately following.

Quoting Primary Sources

Quote from primary sources for four specific reasons:

1. To draw on the wisdom of the original author.
2. To let readers hear the precise words of the author.
3. To copy exact lines of poetry and drama.
4. To reproduce graphs, charts, and statistical data.

Selecting a Mix of Primary and Secondary Sources, page 115.

Cite poetry, fiction, drama, letters, and interviews. In other cases, you may want to quote liberally from a presidential speech, cite the words of a businessman, or reproduce original data. As shown in the next example, quote exactly, retain spacing and margins, and spell words as in the original.

Images of Frustration Have a Prominent Role in Eliot's "Prufrock":

> For I have known them all already,
>
> known them all:—
>
> Have known the evenings, mornings,
>
> afternoons,
>
> I have measured out my life with
>
> coffee spoons;
>
> I know the voices dying with a
>
> dying fall
>
> Beneath the music of a farther room.
>
> So how should I presume?

Quoting Secondary Sources

Quote from secondary sources for three specific reasons:

1. To display excellence in ideas and expression by experts on the topic.
2. To explain complex material.
3. To set up a statement of your own, especially if it spins off, adds to, or takes exception to the source as quoted.

The overuse of direct quotation from secondary sources indicates either (1) that you did not have a clear focus and copied verbatim just about everything related to the subject, or (2) that you had inadequate evidence and used numerous quotations as padding. Therefore, limit quotations from secondary sources by using only a phrase or a sentence, as shown here:

> The geographical changes in Russia require "intensive political
> analysis" (Herman 611).

If you quote an entire sentence, make the quotation a direct object. It tells *what* the authority says. Headings on your notes will help you arrange them.

> Geographic Changes in Russia
>
> In response to the changes in Russia, one critic notes, "The
> American government must exercise caution and conduct intensive
> political analysis" (Herman 611).

More examples of handling quoted materials, Chapter 11, pages 169–193.

Blend two or more quotations from different sources to build strong paragraphs, as shown here:

> Functional foods are helping fight an economic battle against
> rising health care costs. Clare Hasler notes, "The U.S. population is

getting older," which means more people are being diagnosed and treated for disease (68). These individuals are putting a huge financial strain on the health care system with their need for expensive antibiotics and hospital procedures. Dr. Herbert Pierson, director of the National Cancer Institute's $20 million functional food program, states, "The future is prevention, and looking for preventive agents in foods is more cost effective than looking for new drugs" (qtd. in Carper xxii).

9d Writing Paraphrased Notes

A paraphrase is the most difficult note to write. It requires you to restate, in your own words, the thought, meaning, and attitude of someone else. With *interpretation*, you act as a bridge between the source and the reader as you capture the wisdom of the source in approximately the same number of words. Use paraphrase for these reasons:

- To maintain your voice in the paper.
- To sustain your style.
- To avoid an endless string of direct quotations.
- To interpret the source as you rewrite it.

Keep in mind these five rules for paraphrasing a source:

1. Rewrite the original in about the same number of words.
2. Provide an in-text citation of the source (the author and page number in MLA style).
3. Retain exceptional words and phrases from the original by enclosing them within quotation marks.
4. Preserve the tone of the original by suggesting moods of satire, anger, humor, doubt, and so on. Show the author's attitude with appropriate verbs: "Edward Zigler condemns . . . defends . . . argues . . . explains . . . observes . . . defines."
5. To avoid unintended plagiarism, put the original aside while paraphrasing to avoid copying word for word. Compare the finished paraphrase with the original source to be certain the paraphrase truly restates the original and uses quotation marks with any phrasing or standout words retained from the original.

HINT: When instructors see an in-text citation but no quotations marks, they will assume that you are paraphrasing, not quoting. Be sure their assumption is true.

Here are examples that show the differences between a quotation note and a paraphrased one.

Quotation:

Heredity   Hein 294

Fred Hein explains, "Except for identical twins, each person's heredity is unique" (294).

Paraphrase:

Heredity   Hein 294

Fred Hein explains that heredity is special and distinct for each of us, unless a person is one of identical twins (294).

Quotation (more than four lines):

Heredity   Hein 294

Fred Hein clarifies the phenomenon:

> Since only half of each parent's chromosomes are transmitted to a child and since this half represents a chance selection of those the child could inherit, only twins that develop from a single fertilized egg that splits in two have identical chromosomes. (294)

As shown above, MLA style requires a 10-space indention.

Paraphrase:

Heredity   Hein 294

Hein specifies that twins have identical chromosomes because they grow from one egg that divides after it has been fertilized. He affirms that most brothers and sisters differ because of the "chance selection" of chromosomes transmitted by each parent (294).

As shown in the example above, place any key wording of the source within quotation marks.

9e   Writing Summary Notes

The *summary note* describes and rewrites the source material without great concern for style or expression. Your purpose at the moment will be quick, concise writing without careful wording. If the information is needed, you can rewrite it later in a clear, appropriate prose style and, if necessary, return to the source for revision. Use summary notes for these reasons:

- To record material that has marginal value.
- To preserve statistics that have questionable value for your study.
- To note an interesting position of a source speaking on a closely related subject but not on your specific topic.
- To reference several works that address the same issue, as shown in this example:

> The logistics and cost of implementing a recycling program have been examined in books by West and Loveless and in articles by Jones et al., Coffee and Street, and Abernathy.

Success with the summary requires the following:

1. Keep it short. It has marginal value, so don't waste time fine-tuning it.
2. Mark with quotation marks any key phrasing you cannot paraphrase.
3. Provide documentation to the author and page number. However, a page number is unnecessary when the note summarizes the entire article or book, not a specific passage.

> TV & reality   Epstein's book
>
> _____
>
> Now dated but cited by various sources, the 1973 book by Epstein seems to lay the groundwork for criticism in case after case of distorted news broadcasts.

This sort of summary might find its way into the final draft, as shown here:

> Television viewers, engulfed in the world of communication, participate in the construction of symbolic reality by their perception of and belief in the presentation. Edward Jay Epstein laid the groundwork for such investigation in 1973 by showing in case after case how the networks distorted the news and did not, perhaps could not, represent reality.

9f   Writing Précis Notes

A précis note differs from a quick summary note. It serves a specific purpose, so it deserves a polished style for transfer into the paper. It requires you to capture in just a few words the ideas of an entire paragraph, section, or chapter. Use the précis for these reasons:

- To review an article or book.
- To annotate a bibliography entry.

- To provide a plot summary.
- To create an abstract.

Success with the précis requires the following:

1. Condense the original with precision and directness. Reduce a long paragraph to a sentence, tighten an article to a brief paragraph, and summarize a book in one page.
2. Preserve the tone of the original. If the original is serious, suggest that tone in the précis. In the same way, retain moods of doubt, skepticism, optimism, and so forth.
3. Write the précis in your own language. However, retain exceptional phrases from the original, enclosing them in quotation marks. Guard against taking material out of context.
4. Provide documentation.

Use the Précis to Review Briefly an Article or Book

Note this example of the short review:

On the "Donor Initiative"   2008 Web site

The National Community of Organ and Tissue Sharing has a Web site devoted to its initiatives. Its goal is to communicate the problem—for example, more than 55,000 people are on the waiting lists. It seeks a greater participation from the public.

With three sentences, the writer has made a précis of the entire article.

Preparing a review of literature, pages 124–130.

Use the Précis to Write an Annotated Bibliography

An annotation is a sentence or paragraph that offers explanatory or critical commentary on an article or book. It seldom extends beyond two or three sentences. The difficulty of this task is to capture the main idea of the source.

"Top Ten Myths about Donation and Transplantation." Web. October 10, 2008. This site dispels the many myths surrounding organ donation, showing that selling organs is illegal, that matching donor and recipient is highly complicated, and secret back room operations are almost impossible.

"Preparing an Annotated Bibliography," pages 122–124.

Use the Précis in a Plot Summary Note

In just a few sentences, a précis summarizes a novel, short story, drama, or similar literary work, as shown by this next note:

> *Great Expectations* by Charles Dickens describes young Pip, who inherits money and can live the life of a gentleman. But he discovers that his "great expectations" have come from a criminal. With that knowledge, his attitude changes from one of vanity to one of compassion.

Furnish a plot summary in your paper as a courtesy to your readers to cue them about the contents of a work. The précis helps you avoid a full-blown retelling of the whole plot.

Use the Précis As the Form for an Abstract

An abstract is a brief description that appears at the beginning of an article to summarize the contents. It is, in truth, a précis. Usually, it is written by the article's author, and it helps readers make decisions about reading or skipping the article. You can find entire volumes devoted to abstracts, such as *Psychological Abstracts* and *Abstracts of English Studies*. An abstract is required for most papers in the social and natural sciences. Here's a sample:

Abstract using APA style, pages 301–303.

Abstract

The functional food revolution has begun! Functional foods, products that provide benefits beyond basic nutrition, are adding billions to the nation's economy each year. So what is their secret? Why are functional foods a hit? Functional foods are suspected to be a form of preventive medicine. This news has made the public swarm and food nutritionists salivate. Consumers hope that functional foods can calm some of their medical anxieties. Many researchers believe that functional foods may be the answer to the nation's prayers for lower health care costs. This paper goes behind the scenes, behind all the hype, in its attempt to determine if functional foods are an effective form of preventive medicine. The paper identifies several functional foods, locates the components that make them work, and explains the role that each plays in the body.

9g Writing Notes from Field Research

You sometimes will be expected to conduct field research. This work

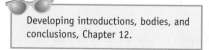
The report of empirical research, section 6e, pages 91–92.

requires different kinds of notes kept on charts, cards, notepads, laboratory notebooks, a research journal, or the computer.

If you **interview** knowledgeable people, make careful notes during the interview and transcribe those notes to your draft in a polished form. A tape recorder can serve as a backup to your notetaking.

If you conduct a **questionnaire,** the results will become valuable data for developing notes and graphs and charts for your research paper.

If you conduct **experiments, tests,** and **measurements,** the findings serve as your notes for the results section of the report and will give you the basis for the discussion section.

9h Creating Outlines Using Academic Models

A General All-Purpose Model

If you are uncertain about the design of your paper, start with this barebones model and expand it with your material. Readers, including your instructor, are accustomed to this sequence for research papers. It offers plenty of leeway.

Identify the subject.
> Explain the problem.
> Provide background information.
> Frame a thesis statement.

Analyze the subject.
> Examine the first major issue.
> Examine the second major issue.
> Examine the third major issue.

Discuss your findings.
> Restate your thesis and point beyond it.
> Interpret the findings.
> Provide answers, solutions, or a final opinion.

To the introduction you can add a quotation, an anecdote, a definition, or comments from your source materials. Within the body, you can compare, analyze, give evidence, trace historical events, and handle other matters. In the conclusion, you can challenge an assumption, take exception to a prevailing point of view, and reaffirm your thesis. Flesh out each section, adding subheadings as necessary, to create an outline.

Developing introductions, bodies, and conclusions, Chapter 12.

Writing theory in APA Style, Chapter 15.

Model for Advancing Your Ideas and Theories

If you want to advance a theory in your paper, use this next design, but adjust it to eliminate some items and add new elements as necessary.

Introduction:
> Establish the problem or question.
> Discuss its significance.
> Provide the necessary background information.
> Introduce experts who have addressed the problem.
> Provide a thesis statement that addresses the problem from a fresh perspective, if at all possible.

Body:
> Evaluate the issues involved in the problem.
> Develop a past-to-present examination.
> Compare and analyze the details and minor issues.
> Cite experts who have addressed the same problem.

Conclusion:
> Advance and defend your theory as it grows out of evidence in the body.
> Offer directives or a plan of action.
> Suggest additional work and research that is needed.

Model for the Analysis of Creative Works

If you plan to analyze musical, artistic, or literary works, such as an opera, a set of paintings, or a novel, adjust this next model to your subject and purpose.

Introduction:
> Identify the work.
> Give a brief summary in one sentence.
> Provide background information that relates to the thesis.
> Offer biographical facts about the artist that relate to the specific issues.
> Quote and paraphrase authorities to establish the scholarly traditions.
> Write a thesis statement that establishes your particular views of the literary work.

Body:
> Provide evaluative analysis divided according to such elements as imagery, theme, character development, structure, symbolism, narration, and language.

Conclusion:
> Keep a fundamental focus on the artist of the work, not just the elements of analysis as explained in the body.
> Offer a conclusion that explores the contributions of the artist in accord with your thesis statement.

Model for Argument and Persuasion Papers

If you write persuasively or argue from a set position, your paper should conform in general to this next model. Select the elements that fit your design.

Introduction:
> In one statement, establish the problem or controversial issue your paper will examine.
> Summarize the issues.
> Define the key terminology.
> Make concessions on some points of the argument.
> Use quotations and paraphrases to clarify the controversial nature of the subject.
> Provide background information to relate the past to the present.
> Write a thesis to establish your position.

Body:
> Develop arguments to defend one side of the subject.
> Analyze the issues, both pro and con.
> Give evidence from the sources, including quotations as appropriate.

Conclusion:
> Expand your thesis into a conclusion that makes clear your position, which should be one that grows logically from your analysis and discussion of the issues.

Model for Analysis of History

If you are writing a historical or political science paper that analyzes events and their causes and consequences, your paper should conform, in general, to the following plan.

Introduction:
> Identify the event.
> Provide the historical background leading up to the event.
> Offer quotations and paraphrases from experts.
> Give the thesis statement.

Body:
> Analyze the background leading up to the event.
> Trace events from one historic episode to another.
> Offer a chronological sequence that explains how one event relates directly to the next.
> Cite authorities who have also investigated this event in history.

Conclusion:
> Reaffirm your thesis.
> Discuss the consequences of this event, explaining how it altered the course of history.

Model for a Comparative Study

A comparative study requires that you examine two schools of thought, two issues, two works, or the positions taken by two persons. The paper examines the similarities and differences of the two subjects, generally using one of three arrangements for the body of the paper.

Introduction:
  Establish A.
  Establish B.
  Briefly compare the two.
  Introduce the central issues.
  Cite source materials on the subjects.
  Present your thesis.

Body (choose one):

Examine A.	Compare A and B.	Issue 1
Examine B.	Contrast A and B.	Discuss A and B.
Compare and	Discuss the central	Issue 2
contrast A and B.	issues.	Discuss A and B.
		Issue 3
		Discuss A and B.

Conclusion:
  Discuss the significant issues.
  Write a conclusion that ranks one side over the other, or
  Write a conclusion that rates the respective genius of each side.

Remember that the models provided above are general guidelines, not iron-clad rules. Adjust each as necessary to meet your special needs.

9i   Writing a Formal Outline

Not all papers require a formal outline, nor do all researchers need one. A short research paper can be created from key terms, a list of issues, a rough outline, and a first draft. As noted earlier in this chapter, rough or informal outlines will help you to make sure you cover the key points and guide your research. However, a formal outline can be important because it classifies the issues of your study into clear, logical categories with main headings and one or more levels of subheadings. An outline will change miscellaneous notes, computer drafts, and photocopied materials into an ordered progression of ideas.

> **HINT:** A formal outline is not rigid and inflexible; you may, and should, modify it while writing and revising. In every case, treat an outline or organizational chart as a tool. Like an architect's blueprint, it should contribute to, not inhibit, the construction of a finished product.

You may wish to experiment with the Outline feature of your computer software, which will allow you to view the paper at various levels of detail and to highlight and drop the essay into a different organization.

Using Standard Outline Symbols

List your major categories and subtopics in this form:

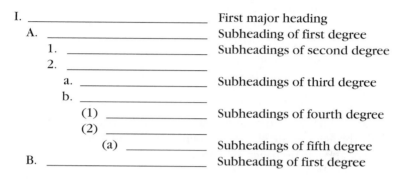

The degree to which you continue the subheads will depend, in part, on the complexity of the subject. Subheads in a research paper seldom carry beyond subheadings of the third degree, the first series of small letters.

An alternative form, especially for papers in business and the sciences, is the *decimal outline*, which divides material by numerical divisions:

1. _____
    1.1. _____
        1.1.1. _____
        1.1.2. _____
        1.1.3. _____
    1.2. _____
        1.2.1. _____
        1.2.2. _____
2. _____

Writing a Formal Topic Outline

If your purpose is to arrange quickly the topics of your paper without detailing your data, build a topic outline of balanced phrases. The topic outline may use noun phrases:

III. The senses

    A. Receptors to detect light

        1. Rods of the retina

        2. Cones of the retina

It may also use gerund phrases:

III. Sensing the environment

    A. Detecting light

        1. Sensing dim light with retina rods

        2. Sensing bright light with retina cones

And it may also use infinitive phrases:

III. To use the senses

    A. To detect light

        1. To sense dim light

        2. To sense bright light

No matter which grammatical format you choose, you should follow it consistently throughout the outline. Student Sarah Bemis's topic outline follows. Her paper appears on pages 347–357.

I. Diabetes defined

    A. A disease without control

        1. A disorder of the metabolism

        2. The search for a cure

    B. Types of diabetes

        1. Type 1, juvenile diabetes

        2. Type 2, adult-onset diabetes

II. Health complications

    A. The problem of hyperglycemia

        1. Signs and symptoms of the problem

        2. Lack of insulin

    B. The conflict of the kidneys and the liver

        1. Effects of ketoacidosis

        2. Effects of arteriosclerosis

III. Proper care and control

    A. Blood sugar monitoring

        1. Daily monitoring at home

        2. Hemoglobin test at a laboratory

    B. Medication for diabetes

        1. Insulin injections

        2. Hypoglycemia agents

C. Exercise programs

    1. Walking

    2. Swimming

    3. Aerobic workouts

D. Diet and meal planning

    1. Exchange plan

    2. Carbohydrate counting

IV. Conclusion: Balance of all the factors

Writing a Formal Sentence Outline

The sentence outline requires full sentences for each heading and subheading. It has two advantages over the topic outline:

1. Many entries in a sentence outline can serve as topic sentences for paragraphs, thereby accelerating the writing process.
2. The subject/verb pattern establishes the logical direction of your thinking (for example, the phrase "Vocabulary development" becomes "Television viewing can improve a child's vocabulary").

Consequently, the sentence outline brings into the open any possible organizational problems rather than hiding them as a topic outline might do. The time invested in writing a complete sentence outline, like writing complete, polished notes (see 9a, pages 133–142), will pay off when you write the rough draft and revise it.

Jamie Johnston's sentence outline is shown in the following example. Turn to pages 325–337 to see the complete paper. As shown here, the thesis statement should appear as a separate item in the outline. It is the main idea of the entire paper, so try not to label it as Item I in the outline. Otherwise, you may search fruitlessly for parallel ideas to put in II, III, and IV. (See also pages 194–195 on using the thesis in the opening.)

Outline

Thesis: Prehistoric humans were motived by biological instincts toward warfare rather than cultural demands for a share of limited resources.

  I. The conflict of "noble savage" versus prehistoric warriors has surfaced in recent literature.

    A. Some literature has advocated the existence of harmony and peace among early tribes.

      1. Rousseau argued for a noble savage in the 1700s.

      2. The Bible speaks of the Garden of Eden.

B. Recent research suggests that wars have existed since the dawn of life.

    1. LaBlanc cites evidence from the Southwest Indians.

    2. Yates reports on Chinese weapons from 28,000 BC.

    3. Ferrill has examined cave paintings.

II. The evidence points clearly to the existence of prehistoric wars.

    A. Anthropologists have uncovered skeletal remains of captives who were executed.

        1. Victims were skinned alive.

        2. Victims were decapitated.

        3. Massacres occurred in Europe, North and South America, Japan, and other parts of the world.

    B. Weapons of mass destruction (on their terms) have been unearthed along with fortifications.

        1. Clubs, slings, daggers, spears, and bows give testimony to early fighting.

        2. Fortress cities prove that villagers attempted to protect themselves from ravaging hordes.

III. Many reasons for prehistoric fighting have been advanced.

    A. Some fought to capture resources of various kinds.

        1. Humans were captured to serve as slaves, concubines, and sacrificial victims of religious ceremonies.

        2. Food, water, and cattle were targets of desperate tribes during famines.

        3. Gold, silver, bronze, and copper were prized commodities and worthy of a good battle.

        4. Trade routes and key locations were subject to dispute.

    B. Some fought for personal reasons and points of honor.

        1. Revenge was often a motivating factor for attacks on a village.

        2. Religion motived warriors to search out not only religious icons but sacrificial victims.

        3. Defending the tribe's honor was sometimes motivation for desperate battles.

IV. At issue is the primary motivating factor that prompted mass carnage at the dawn of civilization.

    A. Some argue that society as a whole wants to preserve its culture and will fight to maintain it.

    B. Others argue that human beings by nature are aggressive and love a good fight in the search for power over others.

YOUR RESEARCH PROJECT

1. Look carefully at each of the sources you have collected so far—books, photocopies of journal articles, and Internet printouts. Try writing a summary or précis of each one. At the same time, make decisions about material worthy of direct quotation and material that you wish to paraphrase or summarize.

2. Decide how you will keep your notes—in a research journal, on handwritten note cards, or in computer files. *Note:* The computer files will serve you well because you can transfer them into your text and save typing time.

3. Write various types of notes—that is, write a few that use direct quotations, some that paraphrase, and some that summarize.

4. Conscientiously and with dedication, write as many personal notes as possible. These will be your ideas, and they will establish your voice and position. Don't let the sources speak for you; let them support your position.

5. If you have access to Take Note! or some other notetaking program, take the time to consider its special features. You can create notes, store them in folders, and even search your own files by keyword, category, and reference.

6. Sketch out an outline for your project. List your general thesis and, below that, establish several divisions that will require careful and full development. Test more than one plan. Do you need several criteria of judgment? causal issues? arguments? evidence from field research? Which seems to work best for you?

7. Select one of the models, as found on pages 143–146, and develop it fully with the information in your sketch outline (see #6 immediately above).

8. If you are familiar about the design of Web pages, you probably realize that the hierarchical ideas have value because readers can click on links that will carry them deeper into the files. Test your outline by constructing a plan like the one below, filling the blanks downward from the large block (thesis statement) to major issues (medium blocks) to evidence

(small blocks). The chart, which you can redraw on a sheet of paper, looks something like this:

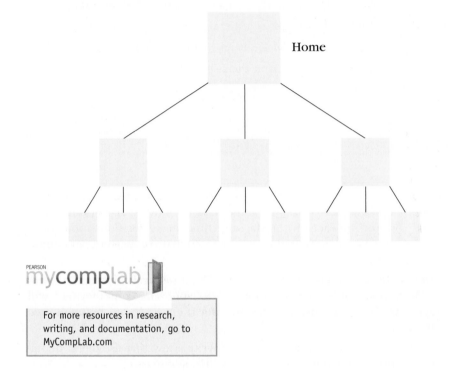

Home

10 Drafting the Paper in an Academic Style

As you draft your paper, your voice should flow smoothly and logically from one idea to the next. You should adopt an academic style, understanding that such a style requires precision but not necessarily long, polysyllabic words pulled from a thesaurus.

Try to present a fair, balanced treatment of the subject. Do not load the paper with favorable citations at the expense of contradictory evidence. In fact, mentioning opposing viewpoints early in a report gives you something to work against and may strengthen the conclusion.

A research paper may examine a subject in depth, but it also examines *your* knowledge and the strength of *your* evidence. You may need to retrace previous steps—reading, researching, and notetaking. Ask your instructor to examine the draft, not so much for line editing but for the big picture, to see if you have met the assignment and not oversimplified the issues.

Be practical

- Write what you know and feel, not what you think somebody wants to hear.
- Write portions of the paper when you are ready, not only when you arrive there by outline sequence.
- If necessary, leave blank spots on the page to remind you that more evidence is required.
- Skip entire sections if you are ready to develop later paragraphs.

Be uninhibited

- Initial drafts must be attempts to get words on the page rather than to create a polished document.
- Write without fear or delay.
- Be conscientious about references.
- Cite the names of the sources in your notes and text.
- Enclose quotations in your notes and text.
- Preserve the page numbers of the sources.

10a Focusing Your Argument

Your writing style in a research paper should be factual, but it should also reflect your take on the topic. Your draft will evolve more quickly if you focus

153

on the central issue(s). Each paragraph then amplifies your primary claim. Your aim or purpose is the key to discovering an argument. Do you wish to persuade, inquire, or negotiate?

Persuasion means convincing the reader that your position is valid and, perhaps, asking the reader to take action. For example:

> We need to establish green zones in every city of this country to control urban sprawl and to protect a segment of the natural habitat for the animals.

Inquiry is an exploratory approach to a problem in which you examine the issues without the insistence of persuasion. It is a truth-seeking adventure. For example:

> Many suburban home dwellers complain that deer, raccoons, and other wild animals ravage their gardens, flowerbeds, and garbage cans; however, the animals were there first. Thus, we may need a task force to examine the rights of each side of this conflict.

Negotiation is a search for a solution. It means you attempt to resolve a conflict by inventing options or a mediated solution. For example:

> Suburban neighbors need to find ways to embrace the wild animals that have been displaced rather than voice anger at the animals or the county government. Perhaps green zones and wilderness trails would solve some of the problems; however, such a solution would require serious negotiations with real estate developers who want to use every square foot of every development.

Often, the instructor's research assignment will tell you whether you want to persuade, inquire, or negotiate. But if it doesn't, try to determine early in the process where your research is heading.

Maintaining a Focus on Objective Facts and Subjective Ideas

As an objective writer, you should examine the problem, make your claim in a thesis statement, and provide supporting evidence. As a subjective writer, you should argue with a touch of passion; you must believe in your position on the issues. For this reason, complete objectivity is unlikely in any research paper that puts forth an intellectual argument in the thesis statement (see pages 22–24). Of course, you must avoid being overly subjective, as by demanding, insisting, and quibbling. Moderation of your voice, even during argument, suggests control of the situation, both emotionally and intellectually.

Your objective and subjective analysis alerts the audience to your point of view in two ways:

Ethical appeal. If you project the image of one who knows and cares about the topic, the reader will recognize and respect your deep interest in the subject and your carefully crafted argument. The reader will also appreciate your attention to research conventions.

Logical appeal. For readers to believe in your position, you must provide sufficient evidence in the form of statistics, paraphrases, and direct quotations from authorities on the subject.

10b Refining the Thesis Statement

A thesis statement expresses a theory you hope to support with your evidence and arguments. It is a proposition you want to maintain, analyze, and prove. It performs three tasks:

1. It sets the argument to control and focus the entire paper.
2. It provides unity and a sense of direction.
3. It specifies to the reader the point of the research.

For example, one student started with the topic "exorbitant tuition." He narrowed his work to "tuition fees put parents in debt." Ultimately, he crafted this thesis:

> The exorbitant tuition at America's colleges is forcing out the poor and promoting an elitist class.

This statement, a conclusion he must defend, focuses the argument on the fees and their effects on enrollment. Without such focus, the student might have drifted into other areas, confusing himself and his readers.

These same issues apply also to the use of the enthymeme or the hypothesis, as discussed earlier (see pages 23–24).

ENTHYMEME: America's colleges are promoting an elitist class because exorbitant tuition forces out the poor and limits their access to higher education.

HYPOTHESIS: This study will gather evidence on this proposition: Poor students are being locked out of higher education by the rapidly rising costs of tuition and registration fees.

Writing a thesis, enthymeme, or hypothesis, pages 22–24.

Using Questions to Focus the Thesis

If you have trouble focusing on a thesis statement, ask yourself a few questions. One of the answers might serve as the thesis.

- **What is the point of my research?**

  THESIS: A delicate balance of medicine, diet, and exercise can control diabetes mellitus to offer a comfortable lifestyle for millions.

  ENTHYMEME: Because diabetes attacks the body in several ways, a person needs a careful balance of medicine, diet, and exercise.

  HYPOTHESIS: The objective of this study is to examine the effects of a balanced program of medication, diet, and exercise for a victim of diabetes.

- **What do I want this paper to do?**

  THESIS: The public needs to understand that advertisers who use blatant sexual images have little regard for moral scruples and ordinary decency.

- **Can I tell the reader anything new or different?**

  THESIS: The evidence indicates clearly that most well water in the county is unsafe for drinking.

- **Do I have a solution to the problem?**

  THESIS: Public support for safe houses will provide a haven for children who are abused by their parents.

- **Do I have a new slant and new approach to the issue?**

  THESIS: Personal economics is a force to be reckoned with, so poverty, not greed, forces many youngsters into a life of crime.

- **Should I take the minority view of this matter?**

  THESIS: Give credit where it is due: Custer may have lost the battle at Little Bighorn, but Crazy Horse and his men, with inspiration from Sitting Bull, *won* the battle.

- **What exactly is my theory about this subject?**

  THESIS: Because they have certain medicinal powers, functional foods can become an economic weapon in the battle against rising health care costs.

- Will an enthymeme serve my purpose by making a claim in a *because* clause?

  ENTHYMEME: Sufficient organ and tissue donation, enough to satisfy the demand, remains almost impossible because negative myths and religious concerns dominate the minds of many people.

- Will a hypothesis serve my purposes?

  HYPOTHESIS: An education program to dispel negative myths and religious concerns will build a greater base of organ and tissue donors.

- What are the keywords surrounding this issue that I might use in framing the thesis statement?

  HYPOTHESIS: The objective is examination of issues with regard to supply and demand, the political power struggles that are emerging, and the ethical and perhaps even moral implication engulfing the world's scattered supply of fresh water.

Adjust or Change Your Thesis during Research If Necessary

Be willing to abandon your preliminary thesis if research leads you to new and different issues. For example, one writer began research on child abuse with this preliminary thesis: "A need for a cure to child abuse faces society each day." Investigation, however, narrowed her focus: "Parents who abuse their children should be treated as victims, not criminals." The writer moved, in effect, to a specific position from which to argue that social organizations should serve abusing parents in addition to helping abused children.

CHECKLIST

Writing the Final Thesis

You should be able to answer "yes" to each question that follows.

Does the thesis:

1. Express your position in a full, declarative statement that is not a question, not a statement of purpose, and not merely a topic?

2. Limit the subject to a narrow focus that grows out of research?

3. Establish an investigative, inventive edge to the discovery, interpretation, or theoretical presentation?

4. Point forward to the conclusion?

5. Conform to the title and the evidence you have gathered?

10c Writing an Academic Title

A clearly expressed title, like a good thesis statement, will control your writing and keep you on course. Although writing a final title may not be feasible until the paper is written, the preliminary title can provide specific words of identification to keep you on track. For example, one writer began with this title: "Diabetes." Then, to make it more specific, the writer added another word: "Diabetes Management." As research developed and she realized the role of medicine, diet, and exercise for victims, she refined the title even more: "Diabetes Management: A Delicate Balance of Medicine, Diet, and Exercise." Thereby, she and her readers had a clear idea of what the paper was to do—that is, explore methods for managing diabetes. Note that long titles are standard in scholarly writing. Consider the following strategies for writing your title.

1. Name a general subject, followed by a colon and a phrase that focuses or shows your slant on the subject.

   Organ and Tissue Donation and Transplantation: Myths, Ethical Issues, and Lives Saved

   The World's Water Supply: The Ethics of Distribution

2. Name a general subject and narrow it with a prepositional phrase.

   Gothic Madness in Three Southern Writers

3. Name a general subject and cite a specific work that illuminates the topic.

   Analysis of Verbal Irony in Swift's A Modest Proposal

4. Name a general subject and follow it by a colon and a phrase that describes the type of study.

   Black Dialect in Maya Angelou's Poetry: A Language Study

5. Name a general subject and follow it by a colon and a question.

   AIDS: Where Did It Come From?

6. Establish a specific comparison.

Religious Imagery in N. Scott Momaday's *The Names* and Heronimous Storm's *Seven Arrows*

As you develop a title, be sure to avoid fancy literary titles that fail to label issues under discussion.

Poor: "Foods, Fads, and Fat"
Better: "Nutritional Foods: A Survey"
Best: "Nutritional Foods: A Powerful Step on the Path of Preventive Medicine"

For placement of the title, see "Title Page or Opening Page," page 216.

10d Drafting the Paper from Your Research Journal, Notes, and Computer Files

To begin writing your research essay, you may work systematically through a preliminary plan or outline. You may also begin by writing what you know at the time. Either way, keep the pieces of your manuscript under control; your notes will usually keep you focused on the subject, and your thesis statement will control the flow and direction of your argument. Yet you must let the writing find its own way, guided but not controlled by your preliminary plans. Consult also the model (see pages 143–146) that best fits your design.

Writing from Your Notes

Use your notes and research journal to:

1. Transfer personal notes, with modification, into the draft.
2. Transcribe précis notes and paraphrased materials directly into the text.
3. Quote primary sources.
4. Quote secondary sources from notes.

Weave source material into the paper to support *your* ideas, not as filler. Your notes will let the essay grow, blossom, and reach up to new levels of knowledge. You can do this in several ways, and you may even have a method beyond the four mentioned here.

Method one requires separate note files within a specially named directory, as explained on pages 133–134. During the drafting stage, you can use the Insert, Copy, or Read command to transfer your notes into your text.

Method two assumes you have placed all your notes in one file. Begin writing your paper in a new file. As you need a note, minimize this text file and maximize your file of notes, or use two windows. Find the note you wish to transfer, highlight it, copy it, and then paste it into your file.

Method three assumes you have placed all your notes within one file and labeled each with a code word or title. Begin drafting your paper at the top

interaction with the "characters" in this made-for-television "drama" happens all the time. If we read a book or attend a play, we question the text, we question the presentation, and we determine for ourselves what it means to us.

Writing in the Proper Tense

Verb tense often distinguishes a paper in the humanities from one in the natural and social sciences. MLA style requires the present tense to cite an author's work (e.g., "Patel *explains*" or "the work of Scoggin and Roberts *shows*"). The CMS footnote style also asks for present tense.

> APA and CSE styles require both the past tense or present perfect tense to cite an author's work. Chapter 15, pages 283–284, and Chapter 17, pages 342–344.

MLA style requires that you use the present tense for your own comments and those of your sources because the ideas and the words of the writers remain in print and continue to be true in the universal present. Therefore, when writing a paper in the humanities, use the historical present tense, as shown here:

"Always forgive your enemies; nothing annoys them so much," writes Oscar Wilde about adversaries and forgiveness.

Yancy argues that sociologist Norman Guigou has a "fascination with the social causes rather than community solutions to homelessness" (64).

Use the past tense in a humanities paper only for reporting historical events. In the next example, past tense is appropriate for all sentences except the last:

Great works of art had been created for ages, but Leonardo da Vinci was the first to paint the atmosphere, the air in which the subject sat and which occupied the space between the eye and the thing seen. This technique continues to influence modern paintings, which place subjects in lights and shadows as well as natural settings.

Using the Language of the Discipline

Every discipline and every topic has its own vocabulary. Therefore, while reading and taking notes, jot down words and phrases relevant to your research study. Get comfortable with them so you can use them effectively.

For example, a child abuse topic requires the language of sociology and psychology, thereby demanding an acquaintance with these terms:

social worker	maltreatment	aggressive behavior
poverty levels	behavioral patterns	incestuous relations
stress	hostility	battered child
formative years	recurrence	guardians

Similarly, a poetry paper might require such terms as *symbolism, imagery, rhythm, persona*, and *rhyme*. Many writers create a terminology list to strengthen their command of appropriate nouns and verbs. However, nothing will betray a writer's ignorance of the subject matter more quickly than awkward and distorted technical terminology. For example, the following sentence uses big words, but it distorts and scrambles the language:

> The enhancement of learning opportunities is often impeded by a pathological disruption in a child's mental processes.

The words may be large, but what does the passage mean? Probably this:

> Education is often interrupted by a child's abnormal behavior.

Using Source Material to Enhance Your Writing

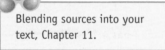

Blending sources into your text, Chapter 11.

Readers want to see your thoughts and ideas on a subject. For this reason, a paragraph should seldom contain source material only; it must contain a topic sentence to establish a point for the research evidence. Every paragraph should explain, analyze, and support a thesis, not merely string together a set of quotations.

The following passage cites effectively two sources.

> Organ and tissue donation is the gift of life. Each year many people confront health problems due to diseases or congenital birth defects. Tom Taddonia explains that tissues such as skin, veins, and valves can be used to correct congenital defects, blindness, visual impairment, trauma, burns, dental defects, arthritis, cancer, and vascular and heart disease (23). Steve Barnill says, "More than 400 people each month receive the gift of sight through yet another type of tissue donation—corneal transplants. In many cases, donors unsuitable for organ donation are eligible for tissue donation" (356). Barnill notes that tissues are now used in orthopedic surgery, cardiovascular surgery, plastic surgery, dentistry, and podiatry (358). Even so, not enough people are willing to donate organs and tissues.

This passage illustrates four points. A writer should:

1. Weave the sources effectively into a whole.
2. Use the sources as a natural extension of the discussion.
3. Cite each source separately, one at a time.
4. Provide separate in-text citations to pages or footnote numerals.

This means you must read carefully so you can select key ideas and phrasing. It also means you should be accurate and precise.

Writing in the Third Person

Write your paper with third-person narration that avoids "I believe" and "It is my opinion." Rather than saying, "I think objectivity on television is nothing more than an ideal," drop the opening two words and say, "Objectivity on television is nothing more than an ideal." Readers will understand that the statement is your thought. However, attribute human functions to yourself or other persons, not to nonhuman sources:

> **WRONG:** The study considered several findings.

> **Correct:** The study reported the findings of several sources.

The study can report its findings, but it can't consider them.

Writing with the Passive Voice in an Appropriate Manner

Instructors often caution young writers against using the passive voice, which is often less forceful than an active verb. However, research writers sometimes need to shift the focus from the actor to the receiver, as shown here:

> **PASSIVE:** Forty-three students of a third-grade class at Barksdale School were observed for two weeks.

> **ACTIVE:** I observed forty-three students of a third-grade class at Barksdale school.

In the previous examples, the passive voice is preferred because it keeps the focus on the subject of the research, not the writer. Also, as a general rule, avoid the first person in research papers. Here are additional examples of the effective use of the passive voice:

> The soil was examined for traces of mercury.

> President Jackson was attacked repeatedly for his Indian policy by his enemies in Congress.

> Children with attention disorders are often targeted for drug treatment.

As you see, the sentences place the focus on the soil, the President, and the children.

10e Using Visuals Effectively in a Research Essay

Graphics and visuals enable you to analyze trends and relationships in numerical data. Use them to support your text. Most computers allow you to create tables, line graphs, or pie charts as well as diagrams, maps, and other original designs. You may also import tables and illustrations from your sources. Place these graphics as close as possible to the parts of the text to which they relate. It is acceptable to use full-color art if your printer will print in colors; however, use black for the captions and date.

A table, as shown in the example in Figure 10.1, is a systematic presentation of materials, usually in columns. A figure is any non-text item that is not a table, such as a blueprint, a chart, a diagram, a drawing, a graph, a photo, a photostat, a map, and so on. Figure 10.2 is a sample figure that illustrates a room layout. Use graphs appropriately. A line graph, such as the example shown in Figure 10.3, serves a different purpose than does a circle

Table 2[a]

Mean Sources of Six Values Held by College Students According to Sex

All Students		Men		Women	
Pol.	40.61	Pol.	43.22	Aesth.	43.86
Rel.	40.51	Theor.	43.09	Rel.	43.13
Aesth.	40.29	Econ.	42.05	Soc.	41.13
Econ.	39.45	Soc.	37.05	Econ.	36.85
Soc.	39.34	Aesth.	36.72	Theor.	36.50

[a]Carmen J. Finley, et al. (165).

◼◼◼◼ FIGURE 10.1
Sample table with in-text citation source.

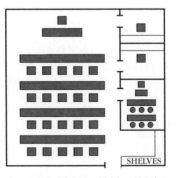

Figure 4: Audio Laboratory with Private Listening Rooms and a Small Group Room

◼◼◼◼ FIGURE 10.2
Sample figure with caption.

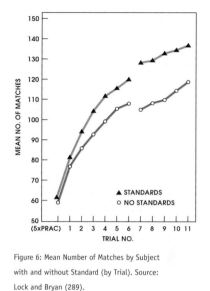

Figure 6: Mean Number of Matches by Subject with and without Standard (by Trial). Source: Lock and Bryan (289).

FIGURE 10.3
Sample graph with clear labels and caption.

(pie) chart, and a bar graph plots different information than does a scatter graph. Figures provide a visual amplification of the text. For example, a photograph of John Keats would reinforce and augment a research paper on the British poet.

Your figures, photographs, and tables should conform to the following guidelines:

- Present only one kind of information in each one, and make it as simple and as brief as possible. Frills and fancy artwork may distract rather than attract the reader.
- Place small figures and tables within your text; place large figures, sets of figures, or complex tables on separate pages in an appendix.
- Place the figure or table as near to your textual discussion as possible, but it should not precede your first mention of it.
- In the text, explain the significance of the figure or table. Describe the item so that your reader may understand your observations without reference to the item itself, but avoid giving too many numbers and figures in your text. Refer to figures and tables by number (for example, "Figure 5") or by number and page reference ("Table 4, 16"). Avoid using vague references (such as "the table above," "the following illustration," or "the chart below").
- Write a caption for the figure or table so that your reader can understand it without reference to your discussion.
- Number figures consecutively throughout the paper with Arabic numbers, preceded by "Fig." or "Figure" (for example, "Figure 4").
- Number tables consecutively throughout the paper with Arabic numerals, preceded by "Table" (for example, "Table 2").

- Insert a caption or number for each column of a table, centered above the column or, if necessary, inserted diagonally or vertically above it.
- When inserting an explanatory or a reference note, place it below both a table and an illustration; then use a lowercase letter as the identifying superscript (as shown in the table in Figure 10.1), not an Arabic numeral. Sources are abbreviated as in-text citations, and full documentation must appear on the Works Cited page.

File Formats

Illustration and information graphics are usually large files, so you will need to compress them with a compression format, either JPEG or GIF, so named for their file name extensions: ".jpg" and ".gif." In general, JPEGs work best for photographs and GIFs work best for line drawings.

Making your own graphics file is complex but rewarding. It adds a personal creativity to your research paper. Use one of the following techniques:

- *Use a graphics program*, such as Macromedia Freehand or Adobe Illustrator. With such software you can create a graphics file and save it as a JPEG or GIF. Also useful are Adobe Photoshop and JASC Paintshop Pro, which are designed primarily for working with photographs.
- *Use a scanner* to copy your drawings, graphs, photographs, and other matter.
- *Create original photographs with a digital camera.* Consult the owner's manual to learn how to create JPEGs or GIFs from your photography.
- *Create your own information graphics* in Microsoft PowerPoint or Excel.

As long as you create JPEG files or GIF files for your graphics, you can transport the entire research paper to a Web site.

10f Avoiding Sexist and Biased Language

Racial and gender fairness is one mark of the mature writer. The best writers exercise caution against words that may stereotype any person, regardless of gender, race, nationality, creed, age, or disability. If the writing is precise, readers will not make assumptions about race, age, and disabilities. Therefore, do not freely mention sexual orientation, marital status, ethnic or racial identity, or a person's disability. The following guidelines will help you avoid discriminatory language:

Age

Review the accuracy of your statement. It is appropriate to use *boy* and *girl* for children of high school age and under. *Young man* and *young woman* or *male adolescent* and *female adolescent* can be appropriate, but *teenager* carries a certain bias. Avoid *elderly* as a noun; use *older persons*, as in "Fifteen older patients suffered senile dementia of the Alzheimer's type."

Gender

Gender is a matter of our culture that identifies men and women within their social groups. *Sex* tends to be a biological factor (see the following discussion of sexual orientation).

1. Use plural subjects so that nonspecific, plural pronouns are grammatically correct. For example, do you intend to specify that Judy Jones maintains *her* lab equipment in sterile condition or to indicate that technicians, in general, maintain *their* own equipment?
2. Reword the sentence so a pronoun is unnecessary:

   Correct: The doctor prepared the necessary surgical [not *his*] equipment without interference.

   Correct: Each technician must maintain the laboratory [not *her*] equipment in sterile condition.

3. Use pronouns denoting gender only when necessary to specify gender or when gender has been previously established.

   Larissa, as a new laboratory technician, must learn to maintain her equipment in sterile condition.

4. The use of *woman* and *female* as adjectives varies, as in *female athlete* and *woman athlete*. Use *woman* or *women* in most instances (e.g., *a woman's intuition*) and *female* for species and statistics, (e.g., *four female subjects, 10 males and 23 females, a female chimpanzee*). The word *lady* has fallen from favor (i.e., avoid *lady pilot*).
5. The first mention of a person requires the full name (e.g., Ernest Hemingway, Joan Didion) and thereafter requires only the use of the surname (e.g., Hemingway, Didion). At first mention, use Emily Brontë, but thereafter use Brontë, *not* Miss Brontë. In general, avoid formal titles (e.g., Dr., Gen., Mrs., Ms., Lt., or Professor). Avoid their equivalents in other languages (e.g., Mme, Dame, Monsieur).
6. Avoid *man and wife* and *7 men and 16 females*. Keep the terms parallel by saying *husband and wife* or *man and woman* and *7 male rats and 16 female rats*.

Sexual Orientation

The term *sexual orientation* is preferred over the term *sexual preference*. It is preferable to use the terms *lesbians* and *gay men* rather than *homosexuals*. The terms *heterosexual, homosexual*, and *bisexual* can be used to describe both the identity and the behavior of subjects.

Ethnic and Racial Identity

Some people prefer the term *Black*, others prefer *African American*, and still others prefer *person of color*. The terms *Negro* and *Afro-American* are now dated and inappropriate. Use *Black* and *White*, not the lowercase *black* and *white*. In like manner, some individuals may prefer *Hispanic, Latino, Mexican*, or *Chicano*. Use the term *Asian* or *Asian American* rather than *Oriental*. *Native American* is a broad term that includes *Samoans, Hawaiians*, and *American Indians*. A good rule of thumb is to specify a person's nationality, tribe, or ethnic group when it is known (*Mexican, Korean, Comanche*, or *Nigerian*).

Disability

In general, place people first, not their disability. Rather than *disabled person* or *retarded child*, say *a person who has scoliosis* or *a child with Down's syndrome*. Avoid saying *a challenged person* or *a special child* in favor of *a person with* or *a child with*. Remember that a *disability* is a physical quality, while a *handicap* is a limitation that might be imposed by non-physical factors, such as stairs, poverty, or social attitudes.

YOUR RESEARCH PROJECT

1. Examine your own thesis using the Final Thesis Checklist on pages 157–158. Revise your thesis as necessary.

2. Consider your focus to determine if you will persuade, inquire, negotiate (see pages 153–154) or perhaps use a focus as explained in Chapter 1: evaluation, definition, proposal, causal argument, analogy, precedence (see pages 5–8).

3. Write an academic title for your paper—one that clearly describes the nature of your work (see pages 158–159).

4. After you draft a significant portion of the paper, review it carefully for each of these items: coherence, proper tense, third-person voice, and the language of the discipline.

For more resources in research, writing, and documentation, go to MyCompLab.com

11 Blending Reference Material into Your Writing by Using MLA Style

Your in-text citations should conform to standards announced by your instructor. This chapter explains the MLA style, as established by the Modern Language Association. It governs papers in freshman composition, literature, English usage, and foreign languages.

MLA style, pages 239–281
APA style, pages 282–309
CMS style, pages 310–337
CSE style, pages 338–357

The MLA style puts great emphasis on the writer of the source, asking for the full name of the scholar on first mention but last name only thereafter and last name only in parenthetical citations. Other styles emphasize the year of publication as well as the author. Still other styles use merely a number in order to emphasize the material, not the author or date.

11a Blending Reference Citations into Your Text

As you might expect, writing a research paper carries with it certain obligations. You should gather scholarly material on the topic and display it prominently in your writing. In addition, you should identify each source used with the authority's name or the title of the work with a page number, except for unprinted sources and most Internet sources, which will not require a page number. As a general policy, keep citations brief. Remember, your readers will have full documentation to each source on the Works Cited page (see Chapter 14).

Making a General Reference without a Page Number

Sometimes you will need no parenthetical citation.

The women of Thomas Hardy's novels are the special focus of three essays by Nancy Norris, Judith Mitchell, and James Scott.

Beginning with the Author and Ending with a Page Number

Introduce a quotation or a paraphrase with the author's name and close it with a page number, placed inside the parentheses. Try always to use this standard citation because it informs the reader of the beginning and the end of borrowed materials, as shown here:

> Herbert Norfleet states that the use of video games by children improves their hand and eye coordination (45).

In the following example, the reader can easily trace the origin of the ideas.

> Video games for children have opponents and advocates. Herbert Norfleet defends the use of video games by children. He says it improves their hand and eye coordination and that it exercises their minds as they work their way through various puzzles and barriers. Norfleet states, "The mental gymnastics of video games and the competition with fellow players are important to young children for their physical, social, and mental development" (45). Yet some authorities disagree with Norfleet for several reasons.

Putting the Page Number Immediately after the Name

Sometimes, notes at the end of a quotation make it expeditious to place the page number immediately after the name.

> Boughman (46) urges car makers to "direct the force of automotive airbags *upward* against the windshield" (emphasis added).

Putting the Name and Page Number at the End of Borrowed Material

You can, if you like, put cited names with the page number at the end of a quotation or paraphrase.

> "Each DNA strand provides the pattern of bases for a new strand to form, resulting in two complete molecules" (Justice, Moody, and Graves 462).

In the case of a paraphrase, you should give your reader a signal to show when the borrowing begins, as shown next:

> One source explains that the DNA in the chromosomes must be copied perfectly during cell reproduction (Justice, Moody, and Graves 462).

Use last names only within the parenthetical citation *unless your list contains more than one author with the same last name*, in which case you should add the author's first initial—for example, (H. Norfleet 45) and (W. Norfleet 432). If the first initial is also shared, use the full first name: (Herbert Norfleet 45).

> **HINT:** In MLA style, do not place a comma between the name and the page number.

11b Citing a Source When No Author Is Listed

When no author is shown on a title page, cite the title of the article, the name of the magazine, the name of a bulletin or book, or the name of the publishing organization. You should abbreviate or use an acronym (e.g., BBC, NASA).

> **HINT:** Search for the author's name at the bottom of the opening page, at the end of the article, at an Internet home page, or in an e-mail address.

Citing the Title of a Magazine Article

Use a shorted version of the title when no author is listed:

> The impending separation of Northern and Southern states which led to the American Civil War was most clearly realized as the nation prepared for the Presidential election of 1860. According to a recent article in America's Civil War magazine, nine states in the south "firmly refused to include Republican candidate Abraham Lincoln on the ballot" ("Open Fire").

The Works Cited entry would read:

> "Open Fire!" *America's Civil War.* May 2008: 12. Print.

Citing the Title of a Report

> One bank showed a significant decline in assets despite an increase in its number of depositors (Annual Report, 2008, 23).

Citing the Name of a Publisher or a Corporate Body

> The report by the Clarion County School Board endorsed the use of Channel One in the school system and said that "students will

benefit by the news reports more than they will be adversely affected by advertising" (CCSB 3–4).

11c Citing Nonprint Sources That Have No Page Number

On occasion you may need to identify nonprint sources, such as a speech, the song lyrics from a CD, an interview, or a television program. Since no page number exists, omit the parenthetical citation. Instead, introduce the type of source—for example, lecture, letter, interview—so readers do not expect a page number.

Thompson's lecture defined *impulse* as "an action triggered by the nerves without thought for the consequences."

Mrs. Peggy Meacham said in her phone interview that prejudice against young black women is not as severe as that against young black males.

11d Citing Internet Sources

Identify the Source with Name or Title

Whenever possible, identify the author of an Internet article. Usually, no page number is listed.

Hershel Winthrop interprets Hawthorne's stories as the search for holiness in a corrupt Puritan society.

If you can't identify an author, give the article title or Web site information.

One Web site claims that any diet that avoids carbohydrates will avoid some sugars that are essential for the body ("Fad Diets").

Identify the Nature of the Information and Its Credibility

As a service to your reader, indicate your best estimate of the scholarly value of an Internet source. For example, the next citation explains the role of the Center for Communications Policy:

The UCLA Center for Communication Policy, which conducted an intensive study of television violence, has advised against making the television industry the "scapegoat for violence" by advocating a focus on "deadlier and more significant causes: inadequate parenting, drugs, underclass rage, unemployment and availability of weaponry."

Here's another example of an introduction that establishes credibility:

John Armstrong, a spokesperson for Public Electronic Access to Knowledge (PEAK), states:

As we venture into this age of biotechnology, many people predict gene manipulation will be a powerful tool for improving the quality of life. They foresee plants engineered to resist pests, animals designed to produce large quantities of rare medicinals, and humans treated by gene therapy to relieve suffering.

Note: To learn more about the source of an Internet article, as in the case immediately above, learn to search out a home page. The address for Armstrong's article is **http://www.ifgene.org/overview.htm**. By truncating the address to **http://www.ifgene.org/** you can learn about the organization that Armstrong represents.

If you are not certain about the credibility of a source—that is, it seemingly has no scholarly or educational basis—do not cite it, or describe the source so readers can make their own judgments:

An Iowa non-profit organization, the Mothers for Natural Law, says—but offers no proof—that eight major crops are affected by genetically engineered organisms—canola, corn, cotton, dairy products, potatoes, soybeans, tomatoes, and yellow crook-neck squash ("What's on the Market").

Omitting Page and Paragraph Numbers to Internet Citations

In general, you should not list a page number, paragraph number, or screen number to an Internet site.

- You cannot list a screen number because monitors differ.
- You cannot list a page number of a downloaded document because computer printers differ.
- Unless they are numbered in the document, you cannot list paragraph numbers. Besides, you would have to go through and count every paragraph.

The marvelous feature of electronic text is that it is searchable, so your readers can find your quotation quickly with the Find or Search features. Suppose you have written the following:

> The Television Violence Report advices against making the
> television industry the "scapegoat for violence" by advocating a focus
> on "deadlier and more significant causes: inadequate parenting, drugs,
> underclass rage, unemployment and availability of weaponry."

A reader who wants to investigate further can consult your Works Cited page, find the Internet address (URL), use a browser to locate the article, and use Find for a phrase, such as "scapegoat for violence." That's much easier on you than numbering all the paragraphs and easier on the reader than counting them.

Some academic societies are urging scholars who publish on the Internet to number their paragraphs, and that practice may catch on quickly. Therefore, you should provide a paragraph number if the author of the Internet article has numbered each paragraph.

> The Insurance Institute for Highway Safety emphasizes restraint
> first, saying, "Riding unrestrained or improperly restrained in a motor
> vehicle always has been the greatest hazard for children" (par. 13).

Provide a page number only if you find original page numbers buried within the electronic article. For example, a database like JSTOR reproduces original images of works and thereby provides original page numbers, as with the article by Harold R. Walley shown in Figure 11.1. Cite these pages just as you would a printed source.

> One source says the "moralizing and philosophical speculation" in
> *Hamlet* is worthy of examination, but to Shakespeare these were
> "distinctly subsidiary to plot and stage business . . ." (Walley 778).

11e   Citing Indirect Sources

Sometimes the writer of a book or article quotes another person from an interview or personal correspondence, and you may want to use that same quotation. For example, in a newspaper article in *USA Today*, page 9A, Karen S. Peterson writes this passage in which she quotes two people:

> Sexuality, popularity, and athletic competition will create anxiety for junior high kids and high schoolers. Eileen Shiff says, "Bring up the topics. Don't wait for them to do it; they are nervous and they want to appear cool." Monitor the amount of time high schoolers spend working for money, she suggests. "Work is important, but school must be the priority." Parental intervention in a child's school career that worked in junior high may not work in high school, psychiatrist Martin Greenburg adds. "The interventions can be construed by the adolescent as negative, overburdening and interfering with the child's

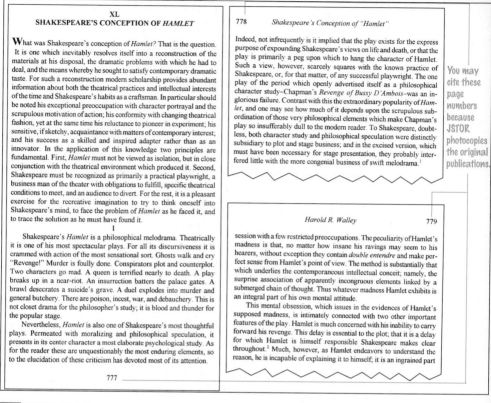

FIGURE 11.1 You may cite these page numbers.

ability to care for himself." He adds, "Be encouraging, not critical. Criticism can be devastating for the teen-ager."

Suppose you want to use the quotation above by Martin Greenburg. You must quote the words of Greenburg *and* put Peterson's name in the parenthetical citation as the person who wrote the article, as shown in the following:

> After students get beyond middle school, they begin to resent interference by their parents, especially in school activities. They need some space from Mom and Dad. Martin Greenburg says, "The interventions can be construed by the adolescent as negative, overburdening and interfering with the child's ability to care for himself" (qtd. in Peterson 9A).

On the Works Cited page, you will list Peterson's name with the bibliography entry for her article, but you will not list Greenburg's name there because he is not the author of the article.

CHECKLIST

Using Links to Document Internet Sources

If you are publishing your project on your own Web page, you have the opportunity to send your readers to other sites via hypertext links. If you do so, follow these guidelines:

1. You may activate a hot key (hypertext link) in your document that will automatically send your reader to one of your sources.
2. Identify the linked source clearly so readers know where the link will take them.
3. Be selective; don't sprinkle your document with excessive links. You want the reader to stay with you, not wander around on the Internet.
4. The links are part of your documentation, so cite these linked sources in your Works Cited list.

In other words, in the text you need a double reference that introduces the speaker and includes a clear reference to the book or article where you found the quotation or the paraphrased material. Without the reference to Peterson, nobody could find the article. Without the reference to Greenburg, readers would assume Peterson spoke the words.

HINT: If you can locate the original source of the quotation, cite it rather than use the double reference.

11f Citing Frequent Page References to the Same Work

If you quote more than once from the same page within a paragraph and no other citations intervene, you may provide one citation at the end for all the references.

> When the character Beneatha denies the existence of God in Hansberry's *A Raisin in the Sun,* Mama slaps her in the face and forces her to repeat after her, "In my mother's house there is still God." Then Mama adds, "There are some ideas we ain't going to have in this house. Not long as I am at the head of the family" (37).

Also, when you make frequent references to the same source, you need not repeat the author's name in every instance. Note the following example:

The consumption of "healing foods," such as those that reduce blood pressure, grows in popularity each year. Clare Hasler says that when the medicinal properties of functional food gain the support of clinical evidence, functional foods can become an economical weapon in the battle against rising health care costs. In addition, functional foods may be a promising addition to the diet of people who suffer from deadly disease. As executive director of the Functional Foods for Health Program at the University of Illinois, she claims, "Six of the ten leading causes of death in the United State are believed to be related to diet: cancer, coronary heart disease, stroke, diabetes, atherosclerosis, and liver disease" ("Western Perspective" 66).

HINT: If you are citing from two or more novels in your paper—let's say John Steinbeck's *East of Eden* and *Of Mice and Men*—provide both title (abbreviated) and page(s) unless the reference is clear: (*Eden* 56) and (*Mice* 12-13).

11g Citing Material from Textbooks and Large Anthologies

Reproduced below is a poem that you might find in many literary textbooks.

The Red Wheelbarrow
> so much depends
> upon
> a red wheel
> barrow
> glazed with rain
> water
> beside the white chickens
> > *William Carlos Williams*

If you quote lines of the poem, and if that is all you quote from the anthology, cite the author and page in the text and put a comprehensive entry in the Works Cited list.

Text:

For Williams, "so much depends" on the red wheel barrow as it sits "glazed with rain water beside the white chickens" (477).

Works Cited entry:

Williams, William Carlos. "The Red Wheelbarrow." *The Literary Experience*. Compact ed. Ed. Bruce Beiderwell and Jeffrey M. Wheeler. Boston: Thomson, Wadsworth, 2008. 477. Print.

Suppose, however, that you also take quotations from other poems in the textbook.

In "Stopping by Woods on a Snowy Evening," Robert Frost looks for an escape into the desolate solitude of the snowy woods, saying "The woods are lovely, dark, and deep" but realizes that his commitments outweigh his personal ambitions, "But I have promises to keep / And miles to go before I sleep" (61).

T. S. Eliot describes the fog as a "yellow smoke" that "Slipped by the terrace, made a sudden leap" (499).

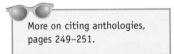

More on citing anthologies, pages 249–251.

Now, with three citations to the same anthology, you should list in your Works Cited the anthology used, as edited by Beiderwell and Wheeler, and also use shortened citations for Williams, Frost, and Eliot, with each referring to the lead editor's name, in this case *Bruce Beiderwell*.

Eliot, T. S. "The Love Song of J. Alfred Prufrock." Beiderwell. 499–503. Print.

Frost, Robert. "Stopping by Woods on a Snowy Evening." Beiderwell. 61. Print.

Beiderwell, Bruce, and Jeffrey M. Wheeler, eds. *The Literary Experience*. Compact Edition. Boston: Thomson, Wadsworth, 2008. Print.

Williams, William Carlos. "The Red Wheelbarrow." Beiderwell. 477. Print.

11h Adding Extra Information to In-Text Citations

As a courtesy to your reader, add extra information within the citation. Show parts of books, different titles by the same writer, or several works by different writers. For example, your reader may have a different anthology than yours, so a clear reference, such as (*Great Expectations* 81; chap. 4), will enable the reader to locate the passage. The same is true with a reference to

(*Romeo and Juliet* 2.3.65–68). The reader will find the passage in almost any edition of Shakespeare's play. Here's a reference to Herman Melville's *Moby-Dick* that shows both page and chapter:

> Melville uncovers the superstitious nature of Ishmael by stressing Ishmael's fascination with Yojo, the little totem god of Queequeg (71; chap. 16).

One of Several Volumes

These next two citations provide three vital facts: (1) an abbreviation for the title, (2) the volume used, and (3) the page number(s). The Works Cited entry will list the total number of volumes (see pages 257–258).

> In a letter to his Tennessee Volunteers in 1812 General Jackson chastised the "mutinous and disorderly conduct" of some of his troops (*Papers* 2: 348–49).

> Joseph Campbell suggests that man is a slave yet also the master of all the gods (*Masks* 2: 472).

However, if you use only one volume of a multivolume work, you need to give only page numbers in the parenthetical reference. Then include the volume number in the Works Cited entry (see page 258):

> Don Quixote's strange adventure with the Knight of the Mirrors is one of Cervantes's brilliant short tales (1,908–14).

If you refer to an entire volume, there is no need for page numbers:

> The Norton Anthology includes masterpieces of the ancient world, the Middle Ages, and the Renaissance (Mack et al., vol. 1).

Two or More Works by the Same Writer

In this example, the writer makes reference to two novels, both abbreviated. The full titles are *Tess of the D'Urbervilles* and *The Mayor of Casterbridge*.

> Thomas Hardy reminds readers in his prefaces that "a novel is an impression, not an argument" and that a novel should be read as "a study of man's deeds and character" (*Tess* xxii; *Mayor* 1).

If the author appears in the parenthetical citation, place a comma after the name: (Hardy, *Tess* xxii; Hardy, *Mayor* 1). If anything other than a page number appears after the title, follow the title with a comma: (Worth, "Computing," par. 6).

The complete titles of the two works by Campbell referenced in the following example are *The Hero with a Thousand Faces* and *The Masks of God*, a four-volume work.

> Because he stresses the nobility of man, Joseph Campbell suggests that the mythic hero is symbolic of the "divine creative and redemptive image which is hidden within us all . . ." (*Hero* 39). The hero elevates the human mind to an "ultimate mythogenetic zone—the creator and destroyer, the slave and yet the master, of all the gods" (*Masks* 1: 472).

Several Authors in One Citation

You may wish to cite several sources that treat the same topic. Put them in alphabetical order to match that of the Works Cited page, or place them in the order of importance to the issue at hand. Separate them with semicolons.

> Several sources have addressed this aspect of gang warfare as a fight for survival, not just for control of the local neighborhood or "turf" (Robertson 98–134; Rollins 34; Templass 561–65).

Additional Information with the Page Number

Your citations can refer to special parts of a page—for example, footnote, appendix, graph, table—and can also specify emphasis on particular pages.

> Horton (22, n. 3) suggests that Melville forced the symbolism, but Welston (199–248, esp. 234) reaches an opposite conclusion.

However, use a semicolon to separate the page number from the edition used, a chapter number, or other identifying information: (Wollstonecraft 185; ch. 13, sec. 2).

11i Punctuating Citations Properly and Consistently

Keep page citations outside quotation marks but inside the final period, as shown here:

> "The benefits of cloning far exceed any harm that might occur" (Smith 34).

In MLA style, use no comma between the name and the page within the citation (for example, Jones 16–17, *not* Jones, 16–17). Do not use *p.* or *pp.* with the page number(s) in MLA style. However, if an author's name begins a citation to paragraph numbers or screen numbers, *do* include a comma after the author's name (Richards, par. 4) or (Thompson, screens 6–7).

Commas and Periods

Place commas and periods inside quotation marks unless the page citation intervenes. The example below shows: (1) how to put the mark inside the quotation marks, (2) how to interrupt a quotation to insert the speaker, (3) how to use single quotation marks within the regular quotation marks, and (4) how to place the period after a page citation.

> "Modern advertising," says Rachel Murphy, "not only creates a
> marketplace, it determines values." She adds, "I resist the advertiser's
> argument that they 'awaken, not create desires'" (192).

Sometimes you may need to change the closing period to a comma. Suppose you decide to quote this sentence: "Scientific cloning poses no threat to the human species." If you start your sentence with the quotation, you will need to change the period to a comma, as shown:

> "Scientific cloning poses no threat to the human species,"
> declares Joseph Wineberg in a recent article (357).

However, retain question marks or exclamation marks; no comma is required:

> "Does scientific cloning pose a threat to the human species?"
> wonders Mark Durham (546).

Let's look at other examples. Suppose this is the original material:

> The Russians had obviously anticipated neither the quick discovery
> of the bases nor the quick imposition of the quarantine. Their diplo-
> mats across the world were displaying all the symptoms of improvi-
> sation, as if they had been told nothing of the placement of the
> missiles and had received no instructions what to say about them.—
> From: Arthur M. Schlesinger, Jr., *A Thousand Days* (New York:
> Houghton, 1965), 820.

Punctuate citations from this source in one of the following methods in accordance with MLA style:

> "The Russians," writes Schlesinger, "had obviously anticipated
> neither the quick discovery of the [missile] bases nor the quick
> imposition of the quarantine" (820).

> Schlesinger notes, "Their diplomats across the world were
> displaying all the symptoms of improvisation . . ." (820).

> Schlesinger observes that the Russian failure to anticipate an
> American discovery of Cuban missiles caused "their diplomats across
> the world" to improvise answers as "if they had been told nothing of
> the placement of the missiles . . ." (820).

Note that the last example correctly changes the capital *T* of "their" to lower case to match the grammar of the restructured sentence, and it does not use ellipsis points before "if" because the phrase flows smoothly into the text.

Semicolons and Colons

Both semicolons and colons go outside the quotation marks, as illustrated by these three examples:

> Zigler admits that "the extended family is now rare in contemporary
> society"; however, he stresses the greatest loss as the "wisdom and daily
> support of older, more experienced family members" (42).

> Zigler laments the demise of the "extended family": that is, the
> family suffers by loss of the "wisdom and daily support of older, more
> experienced family members" (42).

> Brian Sutton-Smith says, "Adults don't worry whether *their* toys
> are educational" (64); nevertheless, parents want to keep their
> children in a learning mode.

The third example, immediately above, shows how to place the page citation after a quotation and before a semicolon.

Use the semicolon to separate two or more works in a single parenthetical reference:

> (Roman, *Dallas* 16; Manfred 345)

> (Steinbeck, *Grapes* 24; Stuben xii)

Question Marks and Exclamation Marks

When a question mark or an exclamation mark serves as part of the quotation, keep it inside the quotation mark. Put the page citation immediately after the name of the source to avoid conflict with the punctuation mark.

> Thompson (16) passionately shouted to union members, "We can
> bring order into our lives even though we face hostility from every
> quarter!"

If you place the page number at the end of the quotation, retain the original exclamation mark or question mark, follow with the page reference, and then a sentence period outside the citation.

Thompson passionately shouted to union members, "We can bring order into our lives even though we face hostility from every quarter!" (16).

Retain questions marks and exclamation marks when the quotation begins a sentence; no comma is required.

"We face hostility from every quarter!" declared the union leader.

Question marks appear inside the closing quotation mark when they are part of the original quotation; otherwise, they go outside.

The philosopher Brackenridge (16) asks, "How should we order our lives?"

and

The philosopher Brackenridge asks, "How should we order our lives?" (16).

but

Did Brackenridge say that we might encounter "hostility from every quarter" (16)?

Single Quotation Marks

When a quotation appears within another quotation, use single quotation marks with the shorter one. The period goes inside both closing quotation marks.

George Loffler (32) confirms that "the unconscious carries the best of human thought and gives man great dignity, but it also has the dark side so that we cry, in the words of Shakespeare's Macbeth, 'Hence, horrible shadow! Unreal mockery, hence.'"

Remember that the period always goes inside quotation marks unless the page citation intervenes, as shown below:

George Loffler confirms that "the unconscious carries the best of human thought and gives man great dignity, but it also has the dark side so that we cry, in the words of Shakespeare's Macbeth, 'Hence, horrible shadow! Unreal mockery, hence'" (32).

11j Indenting Long Quotations

Set off long prose quotations of four lines or more by indenting 1 inch or 10 spaces, which is usually two clicks of the tab key. Do not enclose the indented material within quotation marks. If you quote only one paragraph or the beginning of one, do *not* indent the first line an extra five spaces. Maintain normal double spacing between your text and the quoted materials. Place the parenthetical citation *after* the final mark of punctuation. As shown below, the parenthetical citation might be a title to an Internet article rather than to page numbers:

> The number of people who need transplants continues to increase, but the number of donors fails to meet these needs. Tommy G. Thompson, secretary for the Department of Health and Human Services commented on the current state of organ donation:
>
> > Citing the growing need for organ donation to save and improve lives, Tommy G. Thompson, within his first 100 days as HHS Secretary, announced his commitment to develop a new national effort to encourage organ donation. That commitment, also known as the Gift of Life Donation Initiative, led to 2007's record transplant totals through which the number of transplant candidates who died waiting for an organ fell below 6,000 for the first time in six years. ("New Record")
>
> With the ever increasing number of organ donors needed, why don't people give of themselves? The most recognized reason for the shortage of donors is directly related to the myths that are associated with organ and tissue donation.

If you quote more than one paragraph, indent all paragraphs an extra three (3) spaces or a quarter-inch. However, if the first sentence quoted does not begin a paragraph in the original source, do not indent it an extra three spaces.

> Zigler makes this observation:
> With many others, I am nevertheless optimistic that our nation will eventually display its inherent greatness and successfully correct the many ills that I have touched upon here.
>
> > Of course, much remains that could and should be done, including increased efforts in the area of family planning, the widespread implementation of Education for Parenthood programs, an increase in the availability of homemaker and child care services, and a reexamination of our commitment to doing what is in the best interest of every child in America. (42)

11k Citing Poetry

Quoting Two Lines of Poetry or Less

Incorporate short quotations of poetry (one or two lines) into your text.

> In Part 3, Eliot's "The Waste Land" (1922) remains a springtime search for nourishing water: "Sweet Thames, run softly, for I speak not loud or long" (line 12) says the speaker in "The Fire Sermon," while in Part 5 the speaker of "What the Thunder Said" yearns for "a damp gust / Bringing rain" (73–74).

As the example demonstrates:

1. Set off the material with quotation marks.
2. Indicate separate lines by using a virgule (/) with a space before and after it.
3. Place line documentation within parentheses immediately following the quotation mark and inside the period. Do not use the abbreviations *l.* or *ll.*, which might be confused with page numbers; use *lines* initially to establish that the numbers represent lines of poetry, and thereafter use only the numbers.
4. Use Arabic numerals for books, parts, volumes, and chapters of works; acts, scenes, and lines of plays; and cantos, stanzas, and lines of poetry.

Quoting Three Lines of Poetry or More

Set off three or more lines of poetry by indenting 1 inch or 10 spaces, as shown below. Use double-spaced lines. A parenthetical citation to the lines of indented verse follows the last line of the quotation. If the parenthetical citation will not fit on the last line, place it on the next line, flush with the right margin of the poetry text.

> The king cautions Prince Henry:
>
> > Thy place in council thou has rudely lost,
> > Which by thy younger brother is supplied,
> > And art almost an alien to the hearts
> > Of all the court and princes of my blood.
> >
> > (3.2.32–35)

Refer to act, scene, and lines only after you have established Shakespeare's *Henry IV, Part 1* as the central topic of your study; otherwise, write (1H4 3.2.32–35). If you are citing from more than one play, always add an abbreviation for the play (1H4 1.1.15–18).

Indenting Turnovers for Long Lines of Poetry

When quoting a line of poetry that is too long for your right margin, indent the continuation line 3 spaces or a quarter-inch more than the greatest indentation.

> Plath opens her poem with these lines:
>
>> Love set you going like a fat gold watch.
>>
>> The midwife slapped your footsoles,
>>
>>> and your bald cry
>>
>> Took its place among the elements. (lines 1–3)

You may also indent less to make room for the words:

> Plath opens her poem with these lines:
>
>> Love set you going like a fat gold watch.
>>
>> The midwife slapped your footsoles, and your bald cry
>>
>> Took its place among the elements. (lines 1–3)

For using ellipsis points with poetry, see page 190.

Retaining Internal Quotations within a Block

While you should not use quotation marks around a block quotation, *do* retain any internal quotation marks:

> With his sonnet "Spring," Shakespeare playfully describes the cry
> of the cuckoo bird:
>
>> The cuckoo then, on every tree,
>>
>> Mocks married men; for thus sings he, "Cuckoo!
>>
>> Cuckoo, cuckoo!" O word of fear,
>>
>> Unpleasing to a married ear! (524)

Providing Translations

When a quotation is run into the text, use double quotation marks for translations placed within parentheses but single quotations around a translation without the parentheses:

> Chaucer's setting is Spring, when "zephyrs ("west winds") have
> breathed softly all about . . ." (line 5).
>
> Chaucer's setting is Spring, when "zephyrs 'west winds' have
> breathed softly all about . . ." (line 5).

Do not place quotation marks around quotations and translations set off from the text in a block. Place the block of translation below the block of poetry.

Ramon Magrans has translated this Lorca poem in a literal manner:

Alto pinar!

Cuatro palomas por el aire van.

Cuatro palomas

Vuelan y tornan

Llevan heridas

sus cuatro sombras

Bajo pinar!

Cuatro palomas en la tierra están.

Above the pine trees

four pigeons fly through the air.

Four pigeons

fly and turn around

Wounded, they carry

their four shadows.

Below the pine trees

four pigeons lie on the earth.

11l Handling Quotations from a Play

Set off from your text any dialog of two or more characters. Begin with the character's name, indented one inch and written in all capital letters. Follow the name with a period, and then start the character's lines of dialog. Indent subsequent lines of dialog an additional quarter-inch or three spaces.

At the end of *Oedipus Rex*, Kreon chastises Oedipus, reminding him that he no longer has control over his own life nor that of his children.

KREON.   Come now and leave your children.

OEDIPUS.   No! Do not take them from me!

KREON.   Think no longer

            That you are in command here, but rather think

            How, when you were, you served your own

                destruction.

11m Altering Initial Capitals in Quoted Matter

In general, you should reproduce quoted materials exactly, yet one exception is permitted for logical reasons. Restrictive connectors, such as *that* and *because*, create restrictive clauses and eliminate a need for the comma. Without a comma, the capital letter is unnecessary. In the following example, "The," which is capitalized as the first word in the original sentence, is changed to lowercase because it continues the grammatical flow of the student's sentence.

> Another writer argues that "the single greatest impediment to our improving the lives of America's children is the myth that we are a child-oriented society" (Zigler 39).

Otherwise, write:

> Another writer argues, "The single greatest. . . ."

11n Omitting Quoted Matter with Ellipsis Points

You may omit portions of quoted material with three spaced ellipsis points, as shown in the following examples.

Context

In omitting passages, be fair to the author. Do not change the meaning or take a quotation out of context.

Correctness

Maintain the grammatical correctness of your sentences—that is, avoid fragments and misplaced modifiers. You don't want your readers to misunderstand the structure of the original. When you quote only a phrase, readers will understand that you omitted most of the original sentence, so no ellipsis is necessary.

> Phil Withim recognizes the weakness in Captain Vere's "intelligence and insight" into the significance of his decisions regarding Billy Budd (118).

Omission within a Sentence

Use three ellipsis points (periods) with a space before each and a space after the last.

> Phil Withim objects to the idea that "such episodes are intended to demonstrate that Vere . . . has the intelligence and insight to perceive the deeper issue" (118).

Omission at the End of a Sentence

If an ellipsis occurs at the end of your sentence, use three periods with a space before each following a sentence period—that is, you will have four periods with no space before the first or after the last. A closing quotation mark finishes the punctuation.

> R. W. B. Lewis (62) declares that "if Hester has sinned, she has
> done so as an affirmation of life, and her sin is the source of life. . . ."

However, if a page citation also appears at the end in conjunction with the ellipsis, use three periods with a space before each and put the sentence period after the final parenthesis. Thus, you will have three ellipsis points with a space before each, the closing quotation mark followed by a space, the parenthetical citation, and the period.

> R. W. B. Lewis declares that "if Hester has sinned, she has done
> so as an affirmation of life, and her sin is the source of life . . ." (62).

Omission at the Beginning of a Sentence

Most style guides discourage the use of ellipsis points for material omitted from the beginning of a source, as shown here:

> He states: ". . . the new parent has lost the wisdom and daily
> support of older, more experienced family members" (Zigler 34).

The passage would read better without the ellipsis points:

> He states that "the new parent has lost the wisdom and daily
> support of older, more experienced family members" (Zigler 34).

Another option is this one, as stipulated by the *Chicago Manual of Style*: "If a quotation that is only part of a sentence in the original forms a complete sentence as quoted, an initial lower case letter may be changed to a capital where the structure of the text suggests it."

> He states: "The new parent has lost the wisdom and daily support
> of older, more experienced family members" (Zigler 34).

Here's another example:

> R. W. B. Lewis declares, "If Hester has sinned, she has done so as
> an affirmation of life, and her sin is the source of life . . ." (62).

Omission of Complete Sentences and Paragraphs

Use a closing punctuation mark and three spaced ellipsis points when omitting one or more sentences from within a long quotation. Here's an omission in which one sentence ends, another sentence or more is omitted, and a full sentence ends the passage.

> Zigler reminds us that "child abuse is found more frequently in a single (female) parent home in which the mother is working. . . . The unavailability of quality day care can only make this situation more stressful" (42).

Here's an omission from the middle of one sentence to the middle of another:

> Zigler reminds us that "child abuse is found more frequently in a single (female) parent home in which the mother is working, . . . so the unavailability of quality day care can only make this situation more stressful" (42).

Omissions in Poetry

If you omit a word or phrase in a quotation of poetry, indicate the omission with three or four ellipsis points, just as you would with omissions in a prose passage. However, if you omit a complete line or more from the poem, indicate the omission by a line of spaced periods that equals the average length of the lines. Note that the parenthetical citation shows two sets of lines.

> Elizabeth Barrett Browning asks:
>
>> Do ye hear the children weeping, O my brothers,
>>> Ere the sorrow comes with years?
>> They are leaning their young heads against their mothers,
>>> And *that* cannot stop their tears.
>
> . . . .
>
>> They are weeping in the playtime of the others,
>> In the country of the free. (1–4, 11–12)

Avoid Excessive Use of Ellipsis Points

Many times, you can be more effective if you incorporate short phrases rather than quote the whole sprinkled with many ellipsis points. Note how this next passage incorporates quotations without the use of ellipsis.

> The long-distance marriage, according to William Nichols, "works best when there are no minor-aged children to be considered," the two people are "equipped by temperament and personality to spend a considerable amount of time alone," and both are able to "function in a mature, highly independent fashion" (54).

Ellipsis in the Original

If the original passage has ellipsis by the author, and you wish to cut additional words, place brackets around your ellipsis points to distinguish them from the author's ellipsis points. If the original says:

Shakespeare's innovative techniques in working with revenge tragedy are important in *Hamlet* . . . while the use of a Senecan ghost is a convention of revenge tragedy, a ghost full of meaningful contradictions in calling for revenge is part of Shakespare's dramatic suspense.

If you cut the middle phrase, use this form:

> One writer says, "Shakespeare's innovative techniques in working with revenge tragedy are important in *Hamlet*,. . . [. . .] a ghost full of meaningful contradictions in calling for revenge is part of Shakespare's dramatic suspense."

11o Altering Quotations with Parentheses and Brackets

You will sometimes need to alter a quotation to emphasize a point or to make something clear. You might add material, italicize an important word, or use the word *sic* (Latin for "thus" or "so") to alert readers that you have properly reproduced the material even though the logic or the spelling of the original might appear to be in error. Use parentheses or brackets according to these basic rules.

Parentheses

Use parentheses to enclose your comments or explanations that fall outside a quotation, shown in these examples:

> The problem with airbags is that children (even those in protective seats) can be killed by the force as the airbag explodes. Boughman (46) urges car makers to "direct the force of automotive airbags *upward* against the windshield" (emphasis added).
>
> Roberts (22) comments that "politicians suffer a conflict with honoure" (sic).

Brackets

Use brackets for interpolation, which means inserting your own comment into a text or quotation. The use of brackets signals the insertion. Note the following rules.

Use Brackets to Clarify

> This same critic indicates that "we must avoid the temptation to read it [*The Scarlet Letter*] heretically" (118).

Use Brackets to Establish Correct Grammar within an Abridged Quotation

"John F. Kennedy [was] an immortal figure of courage and dignity in the hearts of most Americans," notes one historian (Jones 82).

He states: "[The] new parent has lost the wisdom and daily support of older, more experienced family members" (Zigler 34).

Use Brackets to Note the Addition of Underlining

He says, for instance, that the "extended family is now rare in contemporary society, and with its demise the new parent has *lost the wisdom* [my emphasis] and daily support of older, more experienced family members" (Zigler 42).

Use Brackets to Substitute a Proper Name for a Pronoun

"As we all know, he [Kennedy] implored us to serve the country, not take from it" (Jones 432).

Use Brackets with Sic to Indicate Errors in the Original

Lovell says, "John F. Kennedy, assassinated in November of 1964 [sic], became overnight an immortal figure of courage and dignity in the hearts of most Americans" (62).

HINT: The assassination occurred in 1963. However, do not burden your text with the use of "sic" for historical matter in which outmoded spellings are obvious, as with: "Faire seemly pleasauance each to other makes."

Use Brackets with Ellipsis Points

See the example on pages 191–192.

YOUR RESEARCH PROJECT

1. Examine your handling of the sources. Have you introduced them clearly so the reader will know when the borrowing began? Have you closed them with a page citation, as appropriate? Have you placed quotation marks at the beginning and the end of borrowed phrases as well as borrowed sentences?

2. If you have used online sources, look at them again to see if the paragraphs on the online site are numbered. If so, use the paragraph numbers in your citation(s); if not, use no numbers—not the numbers on any printout and not paragraph numbers if you must count them.

3. Look at your source material to find a table, graph, figure, or photograph you might insert into your paper as additional evidence. Be certain that you have labeled it correctly (see pages 164–166 for examples).

4. Make a critical journey through your text to be certain you have made an informed choice about the documentation style you need. Normally, instructors will inform you. In general, use MLA style for papers in freshman composition and literature classes; use APA style for papers in the social sciences; use the footnote style for papers in history and the fine arts; use CSE number style for papers in the applied sciences.

For more resources in research, writing, and documentation, go to MyCompLab.com

12 Writing the Introduction, Body, and Conclusion

The three parts of your paper—the introduction, the body, and the conclusion—demand special considerations. For most papers, follow the guidelines offered in this chapter. However, some scientific papers will demand different elements (see 15a, pages 282–283).

12a Writing the Introduction of the Paper

Use the first few paragraphs of your paper to establish the nature of your study. In brief, the introduction should establish the problem, the body should present the evidence, and the conclusion should arrive at answers, judgments, proposals, and closure. Most important, let the introduction and body work *toward* a demonstrative conclusion. The introduction should be long enough to establish the required elements described in the checklist on page 195.

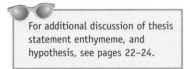

For additional discussion of thesis statement enthymeme, and hypothesis, see pages 22–24.

How you work these essential elements into the framework of your opening will depend on your style of writing. They need not appear in this order, nor should you cram all these items into a short opening paragraph. Feel free to write two or three paragraphs of introduction, letting it run over onto the next page, if necessary. When crafting your introduction, use more than one of the techniques described in the following approaches.

Provide the Thesis Statement

Generally, the controlling statement will appear early in the introduction to establish the agenda for the paper or appear late in the introduction to set the stage for the analysis to come in the body. For example, this opening features the thesis first:

Thesis —

Created by an act of Congress in 1933 and signed into law by President Franklin D. Roosevelt, the Tennessee Valley Authority Act created stability on the waterways and in the lives of citizens in the mid-south. With its establishment of

---

CHECKLIST

Writing the Introduction

Subject Identify your specific topic, and then define, limit, and narrow it to one issue.

Background Provide relevant historical data. Discuss a few key sources that touch on your specific issue. If writing about a major figure, give relevant biographical facts, but not an encyclopedia-type survey. (See "Provide Background Information," pages 196–197.)

Problem The point of a research paper is to explore or resolve a problem, so identify and explain the complications you see. The examples shown in the following sections demonstrate this technique.

Thesis Within the first few paragraphs, use your thesis sentence to establish the direction of the study and to point your readers toward your eventual conclusions.

a series of dams, the TVA controlled the drainage of 42,000 square miles of and waterways. That same control harnessed the power of the rivers to create electricity for residents of the area.

Provide the Enthymeme

The enthymeme, as explained on pages 23–24, uses a *because* clause to make a claim. It also determines the direction your paper will take. Notice the enthymeme that closes this opening paragraph:

Here we are, a civilized world with reasonably educated people, yet we constantly fight with each other. These are not sibling squabbles either; people die in terrible ways. We wonder, then, if there was ever a time when men and women lived in harmony with one another and with nature and the environment. The Bible speaks of the Garden of Eden, and the French philosopher Jean-Jacques Rousseau advanced the idea in the 1700s of the "noble savage," and that "nothing could be more gentle" than an ancient colony of people

(LaBlanc 15). Wrong! There has never been a "noble savage,"

Enthymeme — as such, because even prehistoric human beings fought

frequent wars for numerous reasons.

Provide a Hypothesis

The hypothesis, as explained on pages 22–24, is a theory that needs testing in the lab, in the literature, and/or by field research to prove its validity. Writers may list it as an objective, as in this example:

Diabetes is a disease that affects approximately 11

million people in the U.S. alone. Its complications lead to

approximately 350,000 deaths per year and cost the nation

$20,373 billion per year in medical care, in the direct cost

of complications, and in the indirect costs of loss of

productivity related to the disease (Guthrie and Guthrie 1).

The condition can produce devastating side effects and a

multitude of chronic health problems. Diabetes currently

has no known cure, but it can be controlled. The objective

of this study is to examine how well diabetes can be

Hypothesis — controlled by a combination of medication, monitoring,

diet, and exercise.

Relate to the Well Known

The next passage will appeal to the popular interest and knowledge of the reader:

Television flashes images into our living rooms, radios

invade the confines of our automobiles, and local

newspapers flash their headlines to us daily. However, one

Popular appeal — medium that has gained great popularity and influence

within the past decade is the specialized magazine.

Provide Background Information

Writers may trace the historical nature of a topic, give biographical data about a person, or provide a geographic description. A summary of a novel, long poem, or other work can refresh a reader's memory about details of plot, character, and so forth.

> First published in 1915, *Spoon River Anthology* by
> Edgar Lee Masters gives readers candid glimpses into the life
> of a small town at the turn of the twentieth century.

Background —
> Speaking from beyond the grave, the narrator of each poem
> gives a portrait of happy, fulfilled people or draws pictures
> of lives filled with sadness and melancholy.

This passage offers *essential* background matter, not information irrelevant to the thesis. For example, explaining that Eudora Welty was born in Jackson, Mississippi, in 1909 would contribute little to the following opening:

Background —
> In 1941 Eudora Welty published her first book of short
> stories, *A Curtain of Green.* That group of stories was
> followed by *The Wide Net* (1943) and *The Bride of the*
> *Innisfallen* (1955). Each collection brought her critical
> acclaim, but taken together the three volumes established
> her as one of America's premier short story writers.

Review the Literature

Cite a few books and articles relevant to the specific issue to introduce literature connected with the topic. This paragraph gives distinction to your introduction because it establishes the scholarship on the subject. It also distinguishes your point of view by explaining the logical connections and differences between previous research and your work:

> Throughout his novella *Billy Budd,* Herman
> Melville intentionally uses biblical references as a
> means of presenting different moral principles by which
> people may govern their lives. The story depicts the

Review of
literature —
> "loss of Paradise" (Arvin 294); it serves as a gospel story
> (Weaver 37–38); and it hints at a moral and solemn
> purpose (Watson 319). The story explores the biblical
> passions of one man's confrontation with good and evil
> (Howard 327–28; Mumford 248). This paper will examine
> the biblical references.

Review the History and Background of the Subject

The opening passage normally reviews the history of the topic, often with quotations from the sources, as shown below in APA style:

> Autism, a neurological dysfunction of the brain which commences before the age of thirty months, was identified by Leo Kanner (1943). Kanner studied eleven cases, all of which showed a specific type of childhood psychosis that was different from other childhood disorders, although each was similar to childhood schizophrenia. Kanner described the characteristics of the infantile syndrome as:
>
> 1. Extreme autistic aloneness
> 2. Language abnormalities
> 3. Obsessive desire for the maintenance of sameness
> 4. Good cognitive potential
> 5. Normal physical development
> 6. Highly intelligent, obsessive, and cold parents

Background information

> Medical studies have reduced these symptoms to four criteria: onset within thirty months of birth, poor social development, late language development, and a preference for regular, stereotyped activity (Rutter, 2008; Watson, 2007; Waller, Smith, and Lambert, 2006). In the United States, autism affects one out of 2,500 children, and is not usually diagnosed until the child is between two and five years of age (Lambert and Smith, 2006).

Take Exception to Critical Views

This opening procedure identifies the subject, establishes a basic view taken by the literature, and then differs with or takes exception to the critical position of other writers, as shown in the following example:

> Lorraine Hansberry's popular and successful *A Raisin in the Sun*, which first appeared on Broadway in 1959, is a problem play of a black family's determination to escape a Chicago ghetto to a better life in the suburbs. There is agreement that this escape theme explains the drama's conflict and its role in the black movement (e.g., Oliver,

Archer, and especially Knight, who describes the Youngers as "an entire family that has become aware of, and is determined to combat, racial discrimination in a supposedly democratic land" [34]). Yet another issue lies at the heart of the drama. Hansberry develops a modern view of black matriarchy in order to examine both the cohesive and the conflict-producing effects it has on the individual members of the Younger family.

Exception to prevailing views

Challenge an Assumption

This type of introduction presents a well-known idea or general theory in order to question it, analyze it, challenge it, or refute it.

Christianity dominates the religious life of most Americans to the point that many assume that it dominates the world population as well. However, despite the denominational missionaries who have reached out to every corner of the globe, only one out of every four people on the globe is a Christian, and far fewer than that practice their faith. In truth, Christianity does not dominate religious beliefs around the globe.

Challenge to an assumption

Provide a Brief Summary

When the subject is a literary work, historic event, educational theory, or similar item, a brief summary will refresh the reader's memory.

The chief legacy of the two Bush administrations might well be one of waging war. George Bush liberated Kuwait with the 1991 war against Iraq, but he withdrew after accomplishing that mission rather than overthrow Saddam Hussein and his government in Baghdad. Later, George W. Bush retaliated against the Taliban of Afghanistan in late 2001 after the 9/11 tragedy. Then, in 2003, George W. Bush attacked Iraq again to remove Saddam Hussein from power. This study will examine the literature to confirm the hypothesis that Bush and Bush will be remembered as war presidents.

Summary

Summary

Alice Walker's *The Color Purple* narrates the ordeal of a young black girl living in Georgia in the early years of the twentieth century. Celie writes letters to God because she has no one else to help her. The letters are unusually strong and give evidence of Celie's painful struggle to survive the multiple horrors of her life.

Define Key Terms

Sometimes an opening passage must explain difficult terminology, as in the following example:

Definition

Occurring in one of every 3,900 babies born, cystic fibrosis remains one of the most common fatal genetic disorders in the United States. Approximately 30,000 American children and young adults have cystic fibrosis (Tariev 224). Cystic fibrosis causes the body to secrete an abnormally thick, sticky mucus that clogs the pancreas and the lungs, leading to problems with breathing and digestion, infection, and ultimately, death. Thirty years ago most infants with cystic fibrosis died in early childhood, but today more than 60 percent of babies born with cystic fibrosis reach adulthood, thanks in part to gene therapy. With continued advances in diagnosing and treating the disease, the prognosis for future generations will be significantly improved.

Supply Data, Statistics, and Special Evidence

Concrete evidence can attract the reader and establish the subject. For example, a student working with demographic data might compare the birth and death rates of certain sections of the world. In Europe, the rates are almost constant, while the African nations have birth rates that are 30 percent higher than the death rates. Such statistical evidence can be

Sample introduction in a student paper using these techniques, pages 303–304.

a useful tool in many papers. Just remember to support the data with clear, textual discussion.

12b Writing the Body of the Research Paper

> Sample research papers with well-developed paragraphs, pages 222–238

When writing the body of the paper, you should classify, compare, and analyze the issues. Keep in mind three key elements, as shown in the checklist on page 202.

The length of your paragraphs ought to be from four sentences up to twelve or even fifteen. You can accomplish this task only by writing good topic sentences and by developing them fully. The techniques described in the following paragraphs demonstrate how to build substantive paragraphs for your paper.

Organize by Chronology

Use *chronology* and *plot summary* to trace historical events and to survey a story or novel. You should, almost always, discuss the significance of the events. This first example traces historical events.

Time sequence established

> Following the death of President Roosevelt in April 1945, Harry S. Truman succeeded to the Presidency. Although he was an experienced politician, Truman "was ill prepared

---

CHECKLIST

Avoiding Certain Mistakes in the Introduction

Avoid a purpose statement, such as "The purpose of this study is . . . " unless you are writing reports of empirical research, in which case you *should* explain the purpose of your study (see Chapter 15, "Writing in APA Style").

Avoid repetition of the title, which should appear on the first page of the text anyway.

Avoid complex language or difficult questions that may puzzle the reader. However, general rhetorical questions are acceptable.

Avoid simple dictionary definitions, such as "Webster defines *monogamy* as marriage with only one person at a time." See page 204 for an acceptable opening that features definition.

Avoid humor, unless the subject deals with humor or satire.

Avoid hand-drawn artwork, clip art, and cute lettering unless the paper's subject matter requires it (for example, "The Circle as Advertising Symbol"). *Do* use computer graphics, tables, illustrations, and other designs that are appropriate to your subject.

CHECKLIST

Writing the Body of the Paper

Analysis	Classify the major issues of the study and provide a careful analysis of each in defense of your thesis.
Presentation	Provide well-reasoned statements at the beginning of your paragraphs, and supply evidence of support with proper documentation.
Paragraphs	Offer a variety of development to compare, show process, narrate the history of the subject, show causes, and so forth.

to direct a foreign policy," especially one that "called for the use of the atomic bomb to bring World War II to an end" (Jeffers 56). Consideration must be directed at the circumstances of the time, which led up to Truman's decision that took the lives of over 100,000 individuals and destroyed four square miles of the city of Hiroshima. Consideration must be given to the impact that this decision had on the war, on Japan, and on the rest of the world. Consideration must be directed at the man who brought the twentieth century into the atomic age.

The next passage shows the use of plot summary.

Quick plot summary

> John Updike's "A & P" is a short story about a young grocery clerk named Sammy who feels trapped by the artificial values of the small town where he lives and, in an emotional moment, quits his job. The store manager, Lengel, is the voice of the conservative values in the community. For him, the girls in swimsuits pose a disturbance to his store, so he expresses his displeasure by reminding the girls that the A & P is not the beach (1088). Sammy, a liberal, believes the girls may be out of place in the A & P only because of its "fluorescent lights," "stacked packages," and "checkerboard green-and-cream rubber-tile floor," all artificial things (1086).

HINT: Keep the plot summary short and relate it to your thesis, as shown by the first sentence in the previous passage. Do not allow the plot summary to extend beyond one paragraph; otherwise, you may retell the entire story. Your task is to make a point, not retell the story.

Compare or Contrast Issues, Critical Views, and Literary Characters

Employ *comparison* and *contrast* to show the two sides of a subject, to compare two characters, to compare the past with the present, or to compare positive and negative issues. The next passage compares and contrasts differences in forest conservation techniques.

When a "controlled burn" gets out of hand and burns an entire town, defenders of controlled burns have a serious public relations problem. Thus, to burn or not to burn the natural forests in the national parks is the question. The pyrophobic public voices its protests while environmentalists praise the rejuvenating effects of a good forest fire. It is difficult to convince people that not all fire is bad. The public has visions of Smokey the Bear campaigns and mental images of Bambi and Thumper fleeing the roaring flames. Perhaps the public could learn to see beauty in fresh green shoots, like Bambi and Faline do as they returned to raise their young. Chris Bolgiano explains that federal policy evolved slowly "from the basic impulse to douse all fires immediately to a sophisticated decision matrix based on the functions of any given unit of land" (22). Bolgiano declares that "timber production, grazing, recreation, and wilderness preservation elicit different fire-management approaches" (23).

Comparison and contrast

Develop Cause and Effect

Write *cause-and-effect* paragraphs to develop the reasons for a circumstance or to examine its consequences. An example is shown here that not only explains with cause and effect, but also uses the device of *analogy*, or metaphoric comparison—in this case, of bread dough and the uniform expansion of the universe.

> To see how the Hubble Law implies uniform, centerless expansion of a universe, imagine that you want to make a loaf of raisin bread. As the dough rises, the expansion pushes the raisins away from each other. Two raisins that were originally about one centimeter apart separate more slowly than raisins that were about four centimeters apart. The uniform expansion of the dough causes the raisins to move apart at speeds proportional to their distances. Helen Write, in explaining the theory of Edwin Powell Hubble, says the farther the space between them, the faster two galaxies will move away from each other. This is the basis for Hubble's theory of the expanding universe (369).

Analogy — [bracket marking lines from "to make a loaf" through "their distances."]

Cause and effect — [bracket marking lines from "Edwin Powell Hubble, says" through "other."]

Define Your Key Terminology

Use *definition* to explain and expand upon a complex subject. This next example, by Katie Hebert, defines *functional foods*:

> Functional foods, as defined by the Australian National Food Authority, are:

> > A class of foods that have strong putative metabolic and reulatory (physiological) roles over and above those seen in a wide range of common foods; a class of foods that achieve a defined endpoint that can be monitored (e.g., reduction in blood pressure, reduction in plasma-borne risk markers); and products referred to as special dietary foods. (Head, Record, and King S17)

Definition —

Explain a Process

Draft a *process* paragraph that explains, one by one, the steps necessary to achieve a desired end:

Process

Blood doping is a process for increasing an athlete's performance on the day of competition. To perform this procedure, technicians drain about one liter of blood from the competitor about 10 months prior to the event. This time allows the "hemoglobin levels to return to normal" (Ray 79). Immediately prior to the athletic event, the blood is reintroduced by injection to give a rush of blood into the athlete's system. Ray reports that the technique produces an "average decrease of 45 seconds in the time it takes to run five miles on a treadmill" (80).

Ask Questions and Provide Answers

Framing a question as a topic sentence gives you the opportunity to develop a thorough answer with specific details and evidence. Look at how this approach is used in this example:

Question

Does America have enough park lands? The lands now designated as national and state parks, forests, and wild land total in excess of 33 million acres. Yet environmentalists call for additional protected land. They warn of imbalances in the environment. Dean Fraser, in his book, *The People Problem*, addresses the question of whether we have enough park land:

> Yosemite, in the summer, is not unlike Macy's the week before Christmas. In 1965 it had over 1.6 million visitors; Yellowstone over 2 million. The total area of federal plus state-owned parks is now something like 33 million acres, which sounds impressive until it is divided by the total number of annual visitors of something over 400 million. . . . (33)

Answer

We are running short of green space, which is being devoured by highways, housing projects, and industrial development.

Cite Evidence from the Source Materials

Citing evidence from authorities in the form of quotations, paraphrases, and summaries to support your topic sentence is another excellent way to build a paragraph. This next passage combines commentary by a critic and a poet to explore Thomas Hardy's pessimism in fiction and poetry.

Several critics reject the impression of Thomas Hardy as a pessimist. He is instead a realist who tends toward optimism. Thomas Parrott and Willard Thorp make this comment about Hardy in *Poetry of the Transition*:

Evidence from a source

> There has been a tendency in the criticism of Hardy's work to consider him as a philosopher rather than as a poet and to stigmatize him as a gloomy pessimist. This is quite wrong. (413)

The author himself felt incorrectly labeled, for he has written his own description:

> As to pessimism. My motto is, first correctly diagnose the complaint—in this case human ills— and ascertain the cause: then set about finding a remedy if one exists. The motto of optimists is: Blind the eyes to the real malady, and use empirical panaceas to suppress the symptoms.
> (*Life* 383)

Hardy is dismayed by these "optimists," so he has no desire to be lumped within such a narrow perspective.

Use a Variety of Other Methods

Many methods exist for developing paragraphs; among them are the *description* of a scene in a novel, *statistics* in support of an argument, *historical evidence* in support of a hypothesis, *psychological theory*, and others. You must make the choices, basing your decision on your subject and your notes. Employ the following methods as appropriate to your project.

- Use *classification* to identify several key issues of the topic, and then use *analysis* to examine each issue in detail. For example, you might classify several types of fungus infections, such as athlete's foot, dermatophytosis, and ringworm, and then analyze each.

- Use specific *criteria of judgment* to examine performances and works of art. For example, analyze the films of George Lucas with a critical response to story, theme, editing, photography, sound track, special effects, and so forth.
- Use *structure* to control papers on architecture, poetry, fiction, and biological forms. For example, a short story might have six distinct parts you can examine in sequence.
- Use *location* and *setting* for arranging papers in which geography and locale are key ingredients. For example, examine the settings of several novels by William Faulkner, or build an environmental study around land features (e.g., lakes, springs, sinkholes).
- Use *critical responses to an issue* to evaluate a course of action. For example, an examination of President Truman's decision to use the atomic bomb in World War II would invite you to consider several minor reasons and then to study Truman's major reason(s) for his decision.
- Dividing the body by important *issues* is standard fare in many research papers.

12c Writing the Conclusion of the Research Paper

The conclusion of a research paper should offer the reader more than a mere summary. Use the following checklist to review your conclusion.

How you work these elements into your conclusion will depend on your style of writing. They need not appear in this order, nor should you crowd all

---

CHECKLIST

Writing the Conclusion

Thesis Reaffirm your thesis statement.

Judgment Reach a decision or judgment about the merits of the subject, be it a work of art, an author's writing, a historical moment, or a social position.

Discussion Discuss the implications of your findings.

Directive Offer a plan of action or a proposal that will put into effect your ideas. (Not required of every paper.)

Ending Use the final paragraph, especially the final sentence, to bring the paper to closure.

the items into one paragraph. The conclusion can extend over several paragraphs and require more than one page. When drafting the conclusion, consider using several of the techniques described here.

Restate the Thesis and Reach beyond It

As a general rule, restate your thesis statement; however, do not stop and assume that your reader will generate final conclusions about the issues. Instead, establish the essential mission of your study. In the example below, one student opens her conclusion by reestablishing her thesis statement and then moves quickly to her persuasive, concluding judgments.

Thesis restated in the conclusion

Functional foods appear to exert a strong preventive effect on the two diseases that take most American lives than any other—coronary heart disease and cancer. High cholesterol levels cause coronary heart disease, the factor responsible for 24 percent of the fatalities that occur in the United States (Blumberg 3). Foods high in antioxidants (i.e., Vitamin C, E, and beta-carotene), omega-3 fatty acids, and soluble fiber, along with green and black tea, have been proven to be an effective form of preventive medicine for individuals at risk of developing coronary heart disease. Second only to coronary heart disease, "cancer is the cause of death in 22 percent of Americans" (4). Functional foods have exhibited similar strength in the fight for cancer prevention. By incorporating functional foods, such as insoluble fiber, garlic, and green and black tea into the diet, an individual can lower his or her risk of being diagnosed with cancer. Although this finding does not mean one should cancel all future doctor appointments, it has shown that individuals who eat functional foods are a step ahead in the battle for disease prevention.

Close with an Effective Quotation

Sometimes a source may provide a striking commentary that deserves special placement, as shown by this example:

W. C. Fields had a successful career that extended from vaudeville to musical comedy and finally to the movies. In his private life, he loathed children and animals, and he fought with bankers, landladies, and the police. Off screen, he maintained his private image as a vulgar, hard-drinking cynic until his death in 1946. On the screen, he won the hearts of two generations of fans. He was beloved by audiences primarily for acting out their own contempt for authority. The movies prolonged his popularity "as a dexterous comedian with expert timing and a look of bibulous rascality," but Fields had two personalities, "one jolly and one diabolical" (Kennedy 990).

Effective quotation

Return the Focus of a Literary Study to the Author

While the body of a literary paper should analyze characters, images, and plot, the conclusion should explain the author's accomplishments. The following closing shows how one writer focused on the author:

As to the issues of the country versus the city and the impact of a market economy, Jonathan Swift advances the conservative position of the early eighteenth century, which lamented the loss of the rural, agrarian society, with its adherence to tradition and a stable social hierarchy. His position focused on the social outcomes: unemployment, displacement, and the disenfranchisement of a significant portion of the populace. Unlike his London contemporaries, Swift resided in the economic hinterland of Ireland, so he had a more direct view of the destructive population shifts from rural to urban.

Focus on the author

Ultimately, Swift's commentary in *A Modest Proposal* is important because it records a consciousness of a continuing problem, one that worsens with the intensification of the urban rather than rural growth. It continues to plague the twenty-first–century world, from America to Africa and from Russia to Latin America.

Focus on the author

Compare the Past to the Present

You can use the conclusion rather than the opening to compare past research to the present study or to compare the historic past with the contemporary scene. For example, after explaining the history of two schools of treatment for autism, one writer switches to the present, as shown in this excerpt:

Future in
contrast to
the present

> There is hope in the future that both the cause and the cure for autism will be found. For the present, new drug therapies and behavior modification offer some hope for the abnormal, SIB actions of a person with autistism. Since autism is sometimes outgrown, childhood treatment offers the best hope for the autistic person who must try to survive in an alien environment.

Offer a Directive or Solution

After analyzing a problem and synthesizing issues, offer your theory or solution, as demonstrated in the previous example in which the writer suggests that "childhood treatment offers the best hope for the autistic person who must try to survive in an alien environment." Note also this closing:

A directive
or solution

> All of the aspects of diabetes management can be summed up in one word: balance. Diabetes itself is caused by a lack of balance of insulin and glucose in the body. In order to restore that balance, a diabetic must juggle medication, monitoring, diet, and exercise. Managing diabetes is not an easy task, but a long and healthy life is very possible when the delicate balance is carefully maintained.

Discuss Test Results

In scientific writing (see Chapters 15 and 17), your conclusion, labeled "discussion," must explain the ramifications of your findings and identify any limitations of your scientific study, as shown:

Test results

> The results of this experiment were similar to expectations, but perhaps the statistical significance, because of the small subject size, was biased toward the delayed conditions of the curve. The subjects were, perhaps, not representative of the total population because of their prior exposure to test procedures. Another factor that may have affected the curves was the presentation of the data. The images on the screen were available for five seconds, and that amount of time may have enabled the subjects to

CHECKLIST

Avoiding Certain Mistakes in the Conclusion

- **Avoid** afterthoughts or additional ideas. Now is the time to end the paper, not begin a new thought. If new ideas occur to you as you write your conclusion, don't ignore them. Explore them fully in the context of your thesis and consider adding them to the body of your paper or modifying your thesis. Scientific studies often discuss options and possible alterations that might affect test results (see the previous section, "Discuss Test Results").

- **Avoid** the use of "thus," "in conclusion," and "finally" at the beginning of the last paragraph. Readers can see plainly the end of the paper.

- **Avoid** ending the paper without a sense of closure.

- **Avoid** questions that raise new issues; however, rhetorical questions that restate the issues are acceptable.

- **Avoid** fancy artwork.

store each image effectively. If the time period for each image were reduced to one or two seconds, there could be lower recall scores, thereby reducing the differences between the control group and the experimental group.

YOUR RESEARCH PROJECT

1. Review your opening to determine whether it builds the argument and sets the stage for analysis to come in the body. Consider adding paragraphs like those described on pages 194–200: Relate the well known, provide background information, review the literature, review the history of the subject, take exception to prevailing views, challenge an assumption, provide a summary of the issues, define key terms, supply statistical evidence.

2. After finishing the first draft, review the body of your paper. Has your analysis touched on all the issues? Have you built paragraphs of substance, as demonstrated on pages 201–207? Judge the draft against the checklist for the body on page 202.

3. Evaluate your conclusion according to the checklist on page 207. If you feel it's necessary, build the conclusion by these techniques: Elaborate on the thesis, use an effective quotation, focus on a key person, compare the past and the present, offer a directive or solution, or discuss test results (see pages 207–211 for a discussion of these techniques).

For more resources in research,
writing, and documentation, go to
MyCompLab.com

13 Revising, Proofreading, and Formatting the Rough Draft

Once you have the complete paper in a rough draft, the serious business of editing begins. First, revise the paper on a global scale, moving blocks of material to the best advantage and into the proper format. Second, edit the draft with a line-by-line examination of wording and technical excellence. Third, proofread the final version to ensure that your words are spelled correctly and the text is grammatically sound.

13a Conducting a Global Revision

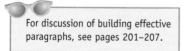
For discussion of developing the introduction, see pages 194–200.

Revision can turn a passable paper into an excellent one and change an excellent one into a radiant one. First, revise the whole manuscript by performing the tasks in the checklist as shown on page 214.

Revising the Introduction

Examine your opening for the presence of several items:

- Your thesis
- A clear sense of direction or plan of development
- A sense of involvement that invites the reader into your investigation of a problem

Revising the Body

For discussion of building effective paragraphs, see pages 201–207.

Use the following bulleted list as a guide for revising each individual paragraph of the body of your paper.

- Cut out wordiness and irrelevant thoughts, even to the point of deleting entire sentences that contribute nothing to the dynamics of the paper.
- Combine short paragraphs with others or build one of greater substance.

CHECKLIST

Global Revision

1. Skim through the paper to check its unity. Does the paper maintain a central proposition from paragraph to paragraph?
2. Transplant paragraphs, moving them to more relevant and effective positions.
3. Delete sentences that do not further your cause.
4. As you cut, copy, and paste, remember to rewrite and blend the words into your text.
5. If your outline must be submitted with your draft, revise it to reflect these global revisions.

- Revise long, difficult paragraphs by dividing them or by using transitions effectively (see "Writing with Unity and Coherence," pages 160–161).
- For paragraphs that seem short, shallow, or weak, add more commentary and more evidence, especially quotations from the primary source or critical citations from secondary sources.
- Add your own input to paragraphs that rely too heavily on the source materials.
- Examine your paragraphs for transitions that move the reader effectively from one paragraph to the next.

Revising the Conclusion

For discussion of writing the conclusion, see pages 207–211.

Examine the conclusion to see that it meets these criteria:

- It is drawn from the evidence.
- It is developed logically from the introduction and the body.
- It expresses your position on the issues.

Participating in Peer Review

Part of the revision process for many writers, both students and professionals, is peer review. This has two sides. First, it means handing your paper to a friend or classmate, asking for opinions and suggestions. Second, it means reviewing a classmate's research paper. You can learn by reviewing as well as by writing.

Since this task asks you to make judgments, you need a set of criteria. Your instructor may supply a peer review sheet, or you can use the "Peer

Peer Review

1. Are the subject and the accompanying issues introduced early?

2. Is the writer's critical approach to the problem presented clearly in a thesis statement? Is it placed effectively in the introduction?

3. Do the paragraphs of the body have individual unity? That is, does each one develop an important idea and only one idea? Does each paragraph relate to the thesis?

4. Are sources introduced, usually with the name of the expert, and then cited by a page number within parentheses? Keep in mind that Internet sources, in most cases, do not have page numbers.

5. Is it clear where a paraphrase begins and where it ends?

6. Are the sources relevant to the argument?

7. Does the writer weave quotations into the text effectively while avoiding long quotations that look like filler instead of substance?

8. Does the conclusion arrive at a resolution about the central issue?

9. Does the title describe clearly what you have found in the contents of the research paper?

Review" checklist provided here. Criticize the paper constructively on each point. If you can answer each question with a *yes*, your classmate has performed well. For those questions you answer *no*, you owe it to your classmate to explain what seems wrong. Make suggestions. Offer tips. Try to help!

13b Formatting the Paper to MLA Style

The format of a research paper consists of the following parts:

1. Title page
2. Outline
3. Abstract
4. The text of the paper
5. Content notes
6. Appendix
7. Works Cited

Items 4 and 7 are required for a paper in the MLA style; use the other items to meet the needs of your research. *Note:* A paper in APA style (see Chapter 15) requires items 1, 3, 4, and 7, and the order differs for items 5–7.

Title Page or Opening Page

A research paper in MLA style does not need a separate title page unless you include an outline, abstract, or other prefatory matter. Place your identification in the upper left corner of your opening page, as shown here:

1 inch from
top of page

1/2 inch in the header position   Howell 1

Pamela Howell

Professor Magrans

English 102c

17 May 2008

Identifying
information

Creative Marriages

Judging by recent divorce rates, it would seem that the
traditional marriage fails to meet the needs . . .

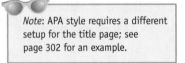

Note: APA style requires a different setup for the title page; see page 302 for an example.

If you do include prefatory matter, such as an outline, you need the title page with centered divisions for the title, the author, and the course identification.

An Interpretation of Melville's

Use of Biblical Characters

in *Billy Budd*

by

Melinda Singleton

English II, Section 108b

Dr. Crampton

April 23, 2008

Follow these guidelines for writing a title page in MLA style:

1. Use an inverted pyramid to balance two or more lines.
2. Use capitals and lowercase letters without underlining and without quotation marks. Published works that appear as part of your title require italicizing (books) or quotation marks (short stories). Do not use a period after a centered heading.
3. Place your full name below the title, usually in the center of the page.
4. Employ separate lines, centered, to provide the course information, institution, instructor, date, or program (e.g., Honors Program).
5. Provide balanced margins for all sides of the title page.

Outline

Print your outline with the finished manuscript only if your instructor requires it. Place it after the title page on separate pages and number these pages with small Roman numerals, beginning with ii (for example, ii, iii, iv, v), at the upper right corner of the page, just after your last name (e.g., Spence iii). For information on writing an outline, see section 9h, pages 143–146, and the sample outlines on pages 147–151.

Abstract

Include an abstract for a paper in MLA style only if your instructor requires it. (APA style requires the abstract; see section 15f, pages 301–308.) An abstract provides a brief digest of the paper's essential ideas in about 100 words. To that end, borrow from your introduction, use some of the topic sentences from your paragraphs, and use one or two sentences from your conclusion.

In MLA style, place the abstract on the first page of text (page 1) one double-space below the title and before the first lines of the text. Indent the abstract five spaces as a block, and indent the first line an additonal five spaces. Use quadruple spacing at the end of the abstract to set it off from the text, which follows

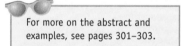

For more on the abstract and examples, see pages 301–303.

immediately after. You may also place the abstract on a separate page between the title page and first page of text.

Remember that the abstract is usually read first and may be the *only* part read; therefore, make it accurate, specific, objective, and self-contained (i.e., it makes sense alone without references to the main text). Note this example:

Wu 1

Child Abuse: A View of the Victims

Abstract

This study examines the problems of child abuse, especially the fact that families receive attention after abuse occurs, not before. With abuse statistics on the rise, efforts devoted to prevention rather than coping should focus on parents in order to discover those adults most likely to commit abuse because of heredity, their own childhood, the economy, and other causes of depression. Viewing the parent as a victim, not just a criminal, will enable social agencies to institute preventive programs that may control abuse and hold together family units.

Quadruple
space

Text ———

Family troubles will most likely affect the delicate members of our society, the children. The recognition of causal elements . . .

The Text of the Paper

Double-space throughout the entire paper except for the title page (page 216) and the separation of the abstract from the first line of text (page 217). In general, you should *not* use subtitles or numbered divisions for your paper, even if it becomes twenty pages long. Instead, use continuous paragraphing without subdivisions or headings. However, some scientific and business reports require subheads (see Chapters 15 and 17).

If the closing page of your text runs short, leave the remainder of the page blank. Do not write "The End" or provide artwork as a closing signal. Do not start Notes or Works Cited on this final page of text.

Content Endnotes Page

Label this page with the word *Notes* centered at the top edge of the sheet, at least one double-space below your page-numbering sequence in the upper right corner. Double-space between the *Notes* heading and the first note.

For discussion of content notes, see pages 318–319.

Number the notes in sequence with raised superscript numerals to match those within your text. Double-space all entries and double-space between them.

Appendix

Place additional material, if necessary, in an appendix preceding the Works Cited page. This is the logical location for numerous tables and illustrations, computer data, questionnaire results, complicated statistics, mathematical proofs, and detailed descriptions of special equipment. Double-space appendixes and begin each appendix on a new sheet. Continue your page numbering sequence in the upper right corner of the sheet. Label the page *Appendix*, centered at the top of the sheet. If you have more than one appendix, use *Appendix A, Appendix B*, and so forth.

Works Cited

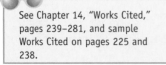

See Chapter 14, "Works Cited," pages 239–281, and sample Works Cited on pages 225 and 238.

Center the heading *Works Cited* 1 inch from the top edge of the sheet. Continue the page-numbering sequence in the upper right corner. Double-space throughout. Set the first line of each entry flush left and indent subsequent lines five spaces. If your software supports it, use the hanging indent.

13c Editing before Typing or Printing the Final Manuscript

For discussion of unity, coherence, and effective writing, see pages 160–163.

The cut-and-paste revision period is complemented by careful editing of paragraphs, sentences, and individual words. Travel through the paper to study your sentences and word choice. Look for ways to tighten and condense. Use the checklist provided here to guide your editing.

Note the editing by one student in Figure 13.1. As shown, this writer conscientiously deleted unnecessary material, added supporting statements, related facts to one another, rearranged data, added new ideas, and rewrote for clarity.

Using the Computer to Edit Your Text

Remember to click on Tools and use the spelling and grammar checkers to spot spelling errors and to perform several tasks related to grammar and

CHECKLIST

Editing

1. Cut phrases and sentences that do not advance your main ideas or that merely repeat what your sources have already stated.

2. Determine that coordinated, balanced ideas are appropriately expressed and that minor ideas are properly subordinated.

3. Change most of your *to be* verbs (is, are, was) to stronger, active verbs.

4. Maintain the present tense in most verbs.

5. Convert passive structures to active if possible.

6. Confirm that you have introduced paraphrases and quotations so that they flow smoothly into your text. Use a variety of verbs for the instructions (*Winston argues, Thomas reminds, Morganfield offers*).

7. Use formal, academic style, and guard against clusters of monosyllabic words that fail to advance ideas. Examine your wording for its effectiveness within the context of your subject.

In some cases   is   see
~~One critic calls~~ television "junk food" (Fransecky

717), and ~~I think~~ excessive viewing ~~does~~ distracts
      (see esp. Paul Witty as qtd. in Postman 41)
from other activities, yet television can and does
      and shows   of our best
bring cultural programs some ~~good~~ novels. It does,
according to the evidence,
improve children's vocabularies, encourages their

      and school
reading, and inspires their writing. Television should
      s the traditional classroom curriculum
not be ~~an~~ antagonist; ~~it should complement school~~
should seek and find harmony with the preschool television
~~work.~~
curriculum.

FIGURE 13.1 Example of editing on a manuscript page.

mechanics—for example, looking for parentheses you have opened but not closed, unpaired quotation marks, passive verbs, and other items. Pay attention to these caution flags. *Caution:* The spellchecker will not discern incorrest usage of "its" and "it's." However, you must edit and adjust your paper by *your* standards with due respect to the computer analysis. Remember, it is your paper, not the computer's. You may need to use some long words and write some long sentences, or you may prefer the passive voice to emphasize the receiver of the action, not the actor.

13d Proofreading on the Screen and on the Printed Manuscript

First, proofread your paper on the screen with a program that will check your spelling, grammar, and style, as mentioned previously. Check your formatting for double-spacing, 1-inch margins, running heads, page numbers, and so forth.

Check the entries in your Works Cited section for precision and completeness in the citations. Also, be sure that each is formatted with a hanging indention.

Consult Appendix A, "Glossary: Rules and Techniques for Preparing the Manuscript in MLA Style," for instructions on handling abbreviations, margins, numbering, punctuation, and other matters.

After editing the text on screen to your satisfaction, print out a hard copy of the manuscript. You should proofread this final paper version with great care because the software will not have caught every error. Be sure your in-text citations are correct and confirm that you have a corresponding bibliography entry for each.

Proofreading

1. Check for errors in sentence structure, spelling, and punctuation.

2. Check for correct hyphenation and word division. Remember that *no* words should be hyphenated at the ends of lines. If you are using a computer, turn off the automatic hyphenation option.

3. Read each quotation for the accuracy of your own wording and of the words within your quoted materials. Look, too, for your correct use of quotations marks.

4. Be certain that in-text citations are correct and that each corresponding source is listed on your Works Cited page.

5. Double-check the format—the title page, margins, spacing, content notes, and many other elements, as explained on pages 215-218 and in the glossary on pages 369-376.

YOUR RESEARCH PROJECT

1. Examine once again the intellectual argument of your first draft. Is it clearly established in the opening and then reaffirmed in the closing?

2. Do the paragraphs of the body develop systematically the evidence to support your claim or thesis? Examine each paragraph for relevance.

3. Examine again your title. Does it meet the criteria set forth on page 215?

4. If you participated in a peer review, consider carefully the recommendations and judgments of your reviewer. There's always a tendency to dismiss words of criticism, but you need to learn that constructive criticism exists at all levels of collegiate and professional life.

5. Read aloud to yourself a portion of the paper. Does it have an academic style? If not, read pages 160-163 and begin editing.

6. Read through the two papers that follow next in this chapter, pages 222-238, to get a feel for the academic style of writing. Try to duplicate that style.

13e Sample Papers in MLA Style

Short Literary Research Paper

Anthony Murphy's assignment was to analyze the work of poet Wilfred Owen and to assess its literary significance in its historical context—World War I, in this case. His literary research paper conforms to the style and format specified for MLA-style research papers.

Murphy 1

Anthony Murphy

English 1102

Dr. Pasch

November 1, 2008

Murphy opens with background information.

Wilfred Owen—Battlefront Poet

In the summer of 1917, World War I was at its peak. Countries were being torn apart, men were being slaughtered by the thousands, and the civilians were starving. But out of the mists of this carnage came one of the greatest war poets of the twentieth century. With his horrific imagery, and antiwar themes, Owen shows readers the darker side of war. Although his life was cut short, the poems of Wilfred Owen describe for readers around the world the consequences of war.

Murphy establishes the concept he will explore.

Born in March 1893 in a house near Oswestry, England, Wilfred Owen spent most of his childhood reading the scriptures and learning the ways of the church. As a committed Christian and with a "pious mother. . . [urging] him to become an Anglican priest," according to Rich Geib, Owen seriously considered entering the ministry. Instead he decided to attend the University of London, where unfortunately he was denied a scholarship and therefore had to work as a reverend's liaison to pay his tuition. By the age of nineteen, Owen had already immersed himself in poetry, being especially impressed with Keats and Shelley (Roberts). After a few years of college, he made his way to Bordeaux, France, to work as a private tutor at the Berlitz School. It was here that Owen first received word that war had broken out between the European nations.

During the first year of the War, Owen frequently visited soldiers who had been wounded during battle. After being influenced by what he saw in the hospitals and national propaganda encouraging young men to enlist, Owen decided to join the military (Roberts; Geib) In the fall of 1915, Owen left France and headed to England to enlist in the Army. In June he became a second lieutenant and made a brief statement at his commissioning: "I came out in order to help these boys—directly by leading them as well as an officer can" (qtd.

Murphy cites the authorities on Owen in brief but effective ways.

in Geib). After Owen's commission, he was given a platoon under the Manchester division, which was sent to the trenches of France in January 1917. It was these first days of battle "where his outlook on life changed permanently" (Geib). For months he dodged bullets and bombs only to see his men be killed daily. In April, Owen's luck ran out, and his trench was hit with a stream of explosions. Suffering from shell shock, he was evacuated to Craiglockhart War Hospital. It was here that Owen would meet the inspiration to his destiny.

Siegfried Sassoon was already an acclaimed poet when Owen met him. Sassoon became a mentor to Owen and introduced him to renowned poets Robert Graves and H. G. Wells ("Wilfred Owen"). Sassoon also helped Owen in his writing of the poems "Anthem for Doomed Youth" and "Dulce et Decorum Est." With Sassoon's assistance, Owen spent the next several months developing and writing his poetry. In June 1918, Owen was sent back to the lines to join his regiment, but not before completing numerous poems. As noted by Dr. Stuart Lee, it was here at Craiglockhart where "[Owen] wrote many of the poems for which he is remembered today."

Owen rejoined the 2nd Manchester Regiment in Scarborough, and was immediately sent back to France. In October, as the Great War was coming to an end, Owen's unit was still on the offensive. As Owen's men entered the town of Amiens, they were attacked by a German machine gun. Owen advanced the German position and defeated the enemy single handedly. Due to his heroic acts he was awarded the Military Cross for Bravery (Multimedia). On November 11, 1918, the Armistice was signed and World War I had officially ended. People all over the world were cheering and celebrating, including the parents of Wilfred Owen. But on the afternoon of that day Owen's parents received a telegram informing them that their son had been killed just seven days prior.

"It was only when the war and his life came to an end that his poetry was truly recognized" ("Examine"). After two years, Owen's poems were finally published, thanks to the work of his mentor Siegfried Sassoon. In December 1920, Sassoon published a book called *Poems of Wilfred Owen* that consisted of ten of Owen's best poems with each poem introduced by Sassoon. One poem that was not put into the book was "Disabled." "'Disabled' presents a poignant picture of a young soldier 'legless, sewn short at elbow' . . . and shows what he had been before against what he is left with," writes Kenneth Simcox of the Wilfred Owen Association.

> He sat in a wheeled chair, waiting for dark,
>
> And shivered in his ghastly suit of grey,
>
> Legless, sewn short at elbow. Through the park
>
> Voices of boys rang saddening like a hymn,
>
> Voices of play and pleasure after day,
>
> Till gathering sleep had mothered them from him. (l.1–5)

Lines of the poem are identified, line breaks are maintained, and the line numbers are listed.

"Disabled" is a perfect example of Owen's antiwar feelings. There is a sense of negativity just from the title alone (Groves). The character in the story is never given a name, which adds a feeling of worthlessness to his life ("Examine"). The poem further relates how the soldier only went to war to impress the girls, and now all people do is pity him rather than thank him. The soldier never really wanted to go to war, but pressure led him to do so. Paul Groves describes the pressure by stating, "the soldier was already a football hero . . . and now the soldier must become a war hero as well." The poem was written not only to have pity for these soldiers, but to reflect the personal conflict Owen had with his enlistment. "Disabled" shows that people have different reasons for going to war and illustrates the effects that war has on men, both mentally and physically (Groves). The overall message of "Disabled" however, is do not let others dictate your life.

This section demonstrates the manner in which Murphy interprets one of the poems, citing from it and explaining the implications in light of the poetic theme.

With the signing of the Armistice, peace was finally realized for a brief period of time. Wilfred Owen opened the minds of many readers after the war by showing that soldiers just do not always sign-up willingly and that battle during or after war is never glorious. Although he is gone, Wilfred Owen's life lives on through the poems he left the world—"My subject is War, and the pity of War. The Poetry is in the pity" (qtd. in Geib).

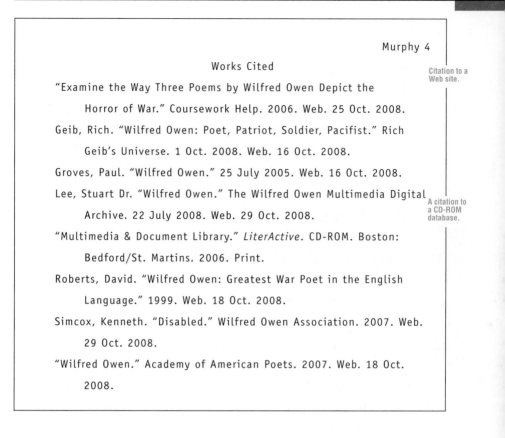

Murphy 4

Works Cited

Citation to a Web site.

"Examine the Way Three Poems by Wilfred Owen Depict the
   Horror of War." Coursework Help. 2006. Web. 25 Oct. 2008.

Geib, Rich. "Wilfred Owen: Poet, Patriot, Soldier, Pacifist." Rich
   Geib's Universe. 1 Oct. 2008. Web. 16 Oct. 2008.

Groves, Paul. "Wilfred Owen." 25 July 2005. Web. 16 Oct. 2008.

Lee, Stuart Dr. "Wilfred Owen." The Wilfred Owen Multimedia Digital
   Archive. 22 July 2008. Web. 29 Oct. 2008.

A citation to a CD-ROM database.

"Multimedia & Document Library." *LiterActive*. CD-ROM. Boston:
   Bedford/St. Martins. 2006. Print.

Roberts, David. "Wilfred Owen: Greatest War Poet in the English
   Language." 1999. Web. 18 Oct. 2008.

Simcox, Kenneth. "Disabled." Wilfred Owen Association. 2007. Web.
   29 Oct. 2008.

"Wilfred Owen." Academy of American Poets. 2007. Web. 18 Oct.
   2008.

Sample Research Paper

Kaci Holz, using MLA style for format and documentation, develops a comprehensive analysis of a communication issue: the ways men and women communicate with one another. She pinpoints several key issues, and along the way she reviews and summarizes the research literature on the subject and shares it with her readers.

Holz 1

Kaci Holz

Dr. Bekus

April 29, 2008

English 2010

A title page
is not
required, but
provide your
name, the
instructor's
name, date,
and course.

Gender Communication

Men and women are different. Obvious enough, right? Not so

obviously, men and women have different communication styles.

During the first four weeks of existence, the human embryo is

neither male nor female (Starr and Taggart 190). During this time,

if human embryos could talk, gender communication is not an issue.

However, after the first four weeks, the human embryo starts to

develop either male or female reproductive organs (Starr and

Taggart 190). With these male or female developments come other

differences. Men and women develop different communication styles

because of biological and environmental differences.

The opening
statement is
followed by
a source to
give support
to the topic.

Holz establishes
the thesis
statement as a
transition to the
supporting
evidence.

There are numerous theories about the differences between

male and female communication styles. In her book *You Just Don't

Understand,* Professor Deborah Tannen addresses several issues

surrounding the patterns of conversation styles between men and

women. While she stresses that not all men and not all women

communicate in the same ways, she claims there are basic gender

patterns or stereotypes that can be found. In her studies of

sociolinguistics at Georgetown University, Tannen says that men

participate in conversations to establish "a hierarchical social

order" (*Don't Understand* 24), while women most often participate

in conversations to establish "a network of connections" (25). She

distinguishes the way women most often converse as "rapport-talk,"

and the way men most often converse as "report-talk" (74).

The writer pro-
vides a brief
review of the lit-
erature on the
topic in the next
three para-
graphs.

Tannen continues to differentiate between the male

communication style and the female communication style by

describing each one's purpose for communicating. She explains that

women often communicate to gain sympathy or understanding for a

Holz 2

particular problem. However, men often respond to such communication with their typical "report-talk" by trying to offer solutions to a woman's problems. These opposing communication styles often conflict and cause problems. The miscommunication is caused by different purposes for communicating. The woman wants sympathy, while the man thinks she wants him to solve her problems (Tannen, *Don't Understand* 49–53).

Other theorists concur with Tannen. Susan Basow and Kimberly Rubenfeld notice that "women may engage in 'troubles talk' to enhance communication; men may avoid such talk to enhance

A line drawing, photograph, map, or graph should be labeled *Figure*, usually abbreviated, assigned a number, and given a caption or title.

Fig. 1 Miscommunication between men and women is often caused by the different purposes men and women have for communicating.

Holz 3

autonomy and dominance" (186). In addition, Phillip Yancey's article in *Marriage Partnership* also asserts that men and women "use conversation for quite different purposes" (71). He claims that women converse to develop and maintain connections, while men converse to claim their position in the hierarchy they see around them. Yancey asserts that women are less likely to speak publicly than are men because women often perceive such speaking as putting oneself on display. A man, on the other hand, is usually comfortable with speaking publicly because that is how he establishes his status among others (Yancey 71). Similarly, masculine people are "less likely than androgynous individuals to feel grateful for advice" (Basow and Rubenfeld 186).

Gender communication can be enhanced when couples focus on interaction categories such as being trustworthy, concise, decisive, and so on. Table 1 displays the key components to enhancing gender communication. As this chart from Carl Brecheen and Paul Faulkner's book *What Every Family Needs* illustrates, every couple must remain positive to nurture and strengthen the relationship through rapport talk. It is also telling to consider that barriers such as commands or directions in a blunt manner inhibit true communication that is built up through tact and sensitivity.

For Table, type the table and the caption flush left on separate lines above the table, using capital letters to begin key words.

Table 1

Rules for Fantastic Communication

Be Knowledgeable	It takes time to truly know someone; there is no shortcut. Too often, couples refuse to spend time studying needs, thoughts, or aspirations.
Be Loving	Anyone can carry on a beautiful relationship when his or her spouse is doing all the right things. Forgiveness of faults establishes love.

(Continued)

Holz 4

Be Transparent	Just as a window lets light shine through, we must also reveal our innermost thoughts and hidden feelings to develop true communication.
Be Trustworthy	Trust develops confidence, faith, and hope. At the same time, trust removes suspicion and doubt from discussions.
Be Positive	Effective communication will maximize the positive and minimize the negative. Couples must define and stress what is important.
Be Sensitive	Effective communication will balance ideas, judgments, or facts with emotions, such as joy, fear, and expectation in a relationship.
Be a Communicator	Slight clues are often enough reason to stop and check to determine whether the listener is truly understanding your message.
Be a Listener	Our culture is built on talk, not conversation. A good listener learns to listen to what is *not* said and the hidden meanings of ideas.
Be Concise	We must think and then rethink before we give a response. Words fly fast, and when not given careful consideration, our words can be hurtful.
Be Decisive	Couples will never *find* time to talk; they must instead *make* time. Effective communication is established through a resolute commitment.

Source: Brecheen, Carl, and Paul Faulkner. *What Every Family Needs*. Nashville: Gospel Advocate, 1994. 88–98. Print.

Give the source
of a table below
the table.

Holz 5

Many more differences in communication patterns of men and women can be found. Richard L. Weaver pointed out another author who identifies different communication styles for men and women. In "Leadership for the Future: A New Set of Priorities," Weaver refers to Dr. Julia T. Wood's book *Gendered Lives*. According to Weaver, Wood claims that "male communication is characterized by assertion, independence, competitiveness, and confidence, while female communication is characterized by deference, inclusivity, collaboration, and cooperation" (qtd. in Weaver 440). This list of differences describes why men and women have such opposing communication styles.

In another book, Deborah Tannen also discusses opposition in communication among men and women. In chapter six of *The Argument Culture*, entitled "Boys Will Be Boys: Gender and Opposition," Tannen addresses the issue that boys, or men, "are more likely to take an oppositional stance toward other people and the world" and "are more likely to find opposition entertaining—to enjoy watching a good fight, or having one" (*Argument* 166). Tannen goes into detail by giving examples from real life and research studies of how boys and girls play and fight differently. She claims that boys tend to cause fights, while girls try to avoid fights. A girl often tries to convince her opponent that her view would benefit the opponent. A boy, on the other hand, just argues for what is best for him (*Argument* 170–174). Tannen addresses other gender opposition factors, such as how men and women insult differently, men's negotiating status and women's forging bonds, the paradox of male and female fighting, conflict on the job, watching fights for fun, and talking in public (*Argument* 184–205).

There are numerous differences in the communication styles of men and women; moreover, there are distinct causes for these differences. Two different theories involve biological factors and/or environmental factors. Lillian Glass, another linguistics researcher,

Two works by the same author require an abbreviated title to the work within the parenthetical citation.

Holz reaffirms her thesis to keep the reader focused on the topic.

Holz 6

examines "the evolution of sex differences in communication" (61) in *He Says, She Says: Closing the Communication Gap between the Sexes*. Glass addresses the issue that different hormones found in men and women's bodies make them act differently and therefore communicate differently. She also discusses how brain development has been found to relate to sex differences. Glass writes extensively about how environmental factors, specifically the way we treat boy and girl infants, directly affect the ways we learn to communicate (64–73). Added to this research, one additional source states: "The way men and women are raised contributes to differences in conversation and communication" (James and Cinelli 41).

In "Parental Influence on Children's Socialization to Gender Roles," Susan Witt discusses the various findings that support the idea that parents have a great influence on their children during the development of their self-concept. She states, "Children learn at a very early age what it means to be a boy or a girl in our society" (253). Things that affect a child's idea of self-concept are the things they encounter early and throughout life such as: "parent-child interactions, role modeling, reinforcement for desired behaviors, parental approval or disapproval, friends, school, those around them, media, television" (Witt 253). Witt sums her theory up by saying, "Through all these socialization agents, children learn gender stereotyped behavior. As children develop, these stereotypes become firmly entrenched beliefs, and thus, they are a part of the child's self-concept" (253).

To further demonstrate the environmental factor that influences learned gender characteristics, Witt discusses how parents treat sons and daughters differently from the time they are babies. She says that parents "dress infants in gender-specific colors, give gender-differentiated toys, and expect different behavior from boys and girls" (Witt 254). At play and in chores, parents tend to "encourage their sons and daughters to participate

The writer clarifies the influence of environment on gender characteristics.

in sex-typed activities" (Witt 254). Witt claims that women have even admitted a preference to having male children over female children in order to "please their husbands, to carry on the family name, and to be a companion to the husband" (254). Conversely, Witt found that women want daughters "to have a companion for themselves and to have fun dressing a girl and doing her hair" (254). These choices affect a child's learned patterns of communication. The environmental factors around a child help determine how a child will act and how he or she will communicate with others.

Discussing the environmental factor, Phillip Yancey explores the fact that many times a communication difference between genders exists simply because of their different roots (69). Two people who come from two different families often have different ideas of how men and women should communicate. Different families have different conversation styles, different fighting styles, and different communication styles overall. Yancey addresses the communication problems between genders as a cultural gap, defining culture as "shared meaning" (68). "Some problems come about because one spouse enters marriage with a different set of 'shared meanings' than the other" (Yancey 69).

Yancey goes into detail about the issue "that boys and girls grow up learning different styles of communicating" (70). So not only does the cultural gap between families sometimes pose a problem, the gender gap between the way boys and girls are raised can also impair efficient communication. Yancey points out:

> Boys tend to play in large groups that are hierarchically
> structured, with a leader who tells the others what to do
> and how to do it. Boys reinforce status by giving orders
> and enforcing them; their games have winners and losers
> and are run by elaborate rules. In contrast, girls play in small

Holz 8

> groups or in pairs, with 'best friends.' They strive for
> intimacy, not status. These gender patterns continue into
> adulthood. (70)

The page reference for an indented quotation goes outside the final period.

The different ways that boys and girls play help to explain different ways that boys and girls, or men and women, communicate.

Most of us have heard of the "Battle of the Sexes" as seen in conflict between men and women. Reverting back to his "childhood gender pattern" theory, Yancey claims that "men, who grew up in a hierarchical environment, are accustomed to conflict. Concerned more with relationship and connection, women prefer the role of peacemaker" (71). Men often use and value criticism, but women avoid and dislike outright criticism for fear of offending (Yancey 71–72).

Like Yancey, Deborah Tannen also addresses the fact that men and women often come from different worlds, or from different influences. Men are taught to be masculine and women are taught to be feminine. She says, "Even if they grow up in the same neighborhood, on the same block, or in the same house, girls and boys grow up in different worlds of words" (*Don't Understand* 43). Tannen distinguishes between the way boys are talked to and the way girls are talked to, and she addresses the differences between the way boys play and the way girls play (*Don't Understand* 43–47).

Though Tannen often addresses the nurture, or environmental issue in much of her research, she also looked at the nature, or biological issue in her book *The Argument Culture*. Tannen states, "Surely a biological component plays a part in the greater use of antagonism among men, but cultural influence can override biological inheritance" (205). She sums up the nature versus nurture issue by saying, "the patterns that typify women's and men's styles of opposition and conflict are the result of both biology and culture" (207).

Holz 9

Numerous authorities believe that the causes of different styles of gender communication are biological, while others attribute causes to environmental factors. Still more people contend that men and women have different communication styles because of a combination of biological and environmental factors. With these differences in the styles of gender communication and possible causes of gender communication, one must consider the possible results.

Let us look briefly at a hypothetical situation that will demonstrate different gender communication styles. We will examine the results of this situation to grasp an understanding of possible results in life. Consider the following scenario. A husband and wife have just arrived home after a long day of work in the business world. The wife asks her husband, "How was your day?" And the husband replies, "Fine." The wife is offended by this simplistic response and expresses her hurt by saying, "That's it? 'Fine'? Why don't you ever talk to me?" In confusion as to where this statement has come from, the husband defends himself declaring, "What are you talking about? I do talk to you. I'm talking to you right now!" They both blow each other off and refuse to talk to each other for the rest of the night. What went wrong in this conversation? The resulting failure of communication happened because men and women have different communication styles that directly affect intentional and perceived meaning from one to the other. Perhaps the communication failure above can be explained when backed by an understanding of the differences between the purposes and the ways that men and women communicate. Let us take this specific example and examine the results as compared to theories about gender communication.

In this scenario, the husband and wife are exhibiting different communication styles that directly relate to their own gender. Through various studies, Tannen has concluded that men and women have different purposes for engaging in communication. In *You Just*

Holz provides a scenario to illustrate the validity of her research.

Don't Understand, Tannen states, "For girls, talk is the glue that holds relationships together" (85). Boys, on the other hand, use language when "they feel the need to impress, or when they are in situations where their status is in question" (85). Tannen goes on to explain the different ways men and women handle communication throughout the day. She explains that a man constantly talks during his workday in order to impress those around him and to establish his status in the office. When a man comes home from work, he is tired of talking. He expects to be able to be silent in his home where he does not have to impress anyone or establish his status (86).

On the other hand, a woman is constantly cautious and guarded about what she says during her workday. Women try hard to avoid confrontation and avoid offending anyone with their language. So when a woman comes home from work, she expects to be able to talk freely without having to guard her words. Can we see the controversy that the man's expectation to be silent and the woman's expectation to talk can cause?

With Tannen's input, hopefully we can begin to see the differences in the communication styles of the wife and the husband. When the wife asked, "How was your day?" she expected a detailed response because her purpose of communication was to strengthen her relationship with her husband. She honestly wanted to know what specific things happened during her husband's workday so that she would be able to sympathize with what he was feeling and become closer to him. She wanted to talk freely because she had been busy guarding her words all day.

The husband's response of "fine" was direct and to the point because he felt no need to communicate further. At home with his wife, he was not in a situation in which he needed to impress anyone or establish status. He simply answered the question that was asked of him and was willing to leave it at that. He wanted to be silent because he had been working hard at communication all day.

The scenario is analyzed and conclusions are presented to the reader.

Though the intentions of both husband and wife seem innocent enough when looking at them with the thought of different communication styles in mind, the husband and wife obviously didn't see the other's response as innocent. Because the wife didn't receive the in-depth description she was expecting, she was disappointed. Tannen says that "when a woman who expects her partner to talk to her is disappointed that he doesn't, she perceives his behavior as a failure of intimacy: He's keeping things from her; he's lost interest in her; he's pulling away" (*Don't Understand* 83). Can we imagine the wife's pain now?

The husband did not sense her pain. When his wife came back with "That's it? 'Fine?' Why don't you ever talk to me?" this just triggered anger and defense. Because the wife and the husband had different purposes for and different ways of communicating, they misinterpreted each other. This misinterpretation led to anger, and the anger led to frustration and the abandonment of communication.

The results of gender communication can look bleak. What can we do about this apparent gap in communication between genders? Some researchers have offered several solutions. In his article published in *Leadership*, Jeffrey Arthurs has the suggestion that women should make an attempt to understand the male model of communication and that men should make an attempt to understand the female model of communication (49). Having men that can better understand women and having women that can better understand men cannot be a bad thing. Even a general study of the different communication styles could benefit men and women by helping them understand possible misinterpretations before cross-gender communication is abandoned.

In his article "Speaking Across the Gender Gap," David Cohen mentions that experts did not think it would be helpful to teach men to communicate more like women and women to communicate more like men. This attempt would prove unproductive because it would go against what men and women have been taught since birth. Rather than change the genders to be more like one another, we could simply try to understand each other better. By doing a little research and a little thoughtful consideration about the differences in gender communication styles, men and women would be able to communicate more successfully.

Richard Weaver has observed, "The idea that women should translate their experiences into the male code in order to express themselves effectively is an outmoded, inconsistent, subservient notion that should no longer be given credibility in modern society" (439). He suggests three things we can change: 1.) Change the norm by which leadership success is judged, 2.) Redefine what we mean by power, and 3.) Become more sensitive to the places and times when inequity and inequality occur (Weaver 439). Phillip Yancey also offers advice to help combat "cross-cultural" fights. He suggests: 1.) Identify your fighting style, 2.) Agree on rules of engagement, and 3.) Identify the real issue behind the conflict (Yancey 71). In truth, men and women must understand one another, communicate honestly and respectfully, and manage conflict in a way that maintains the relationship to get the job done. Moreover, we must acknowledge the differences that do exist, understand how they develop, and discard dogma about what are the "right" roles of women and men.

By acknowledging that there are differences between the way men and women communicate, whether caused by biological and/or environmental factors, we can be on the watch for circumstances that might lead to miscommunications, as well as consider the possible causes, results, and solutions discussed previously. Using this knowledge, we should be able to more accurately interpret communication between genders. The next cross-gendered misinterpretation we face, we should stop for a moment to consider the differing gender before we make things worse or abandon communication all together.

Holz reaffirms her thesis in the final paragraph.

Begin the Works Cited on a new page.

A source from an electronic database.

An article from an academic journal found on the Internet.

Internet sources require the word "Web" preceding the date of access.

Works Cited

Arthurs, Jeffrey. "He Said, She Heard: Any Time You Speak to Both Men and Women, You're Facing Cross-Cultural Communication." *Leadership* 23.1 (Winter 2002): 49. Print.

Basow, Susan A., and Kimberly Rubenfeld. "'Troubles Talk': Effects of Gender and Gender Typing." *Sex Roles: A Journal of Research*. 48 (2003): 183–187. *EBSCOhost*. Web. 24 Apr. 2008.

Brechen, Carl, and Paul Faulkner. *What Every Family Needs*. Nashville: Gospel Advocate, 1994. 88–98. Print.

Cohen, David. "Speaking Across the Gender Gap." *New Scientist* 131 (1991): 36. *EBSCOhost*. Web. 23 Apr. 2008.

Glass, Lillian. *He Says, She Says: Closing the Communication Gap between the Sexes*. New York: Penguin, 1993. Print.

James, Tammy, and Bethann Cinelli. "Exploring Gender-Based Communication Styles." *Journal of School Health* 73 (2003): 41–42. Abstract. Web. 25 Apr. 2008.

Starr, Cecie, and Ralph Taggart. *Biology: The Unity and Diversity of Life*. 11th ed. Florence, KY: Cengage, 2007. Print.

Tannen, Deborah. *The Argument Culture: Moving from Debate to Dialogue*. New York: Random House, 1998. Print.

---. *You Just Don't Understand: Women and Men in Conversation*. New York: HarperCollins. 2007. Print.

Weaver, Richard L. "Leadership for the Future: A New Set of Priorities." *Vital Speeches of the Day* 61 (1995): 438–441. *EBSCOhost*. Web. 22 Apr. 2008.

Witt, Susan D. "Parental Influence on Children's Socialization to Gender Roles." *Adolescence* 32 (1997): 253. Print.

Yancey, Phillip. "Do Men and Women Speak the Same Language?" *Marriage Partnership* 10 (1993): 68–73. *EBSCOhost*. Web. 24 Apr. 2008.

14 Works Cited: MLA Style

The final step in your research project is to complete your Works Cited page. List only those materials actually used in your manuscript, including works mentioned within content endnotes and in captions to tables and illustrations. Preparing the Works Cited list will be relatively simple if you have carefully developed your working bibliography as a computer file with detailed publication data on each source cited in the paper (see pages 62–63).

Keep in mind that on occasion somebody might use your Works Cited listing for research of his or her own. The MLA documentation style gives all scholars in the field a consistent way to consult the sources. Inaccurate records might prevent an easy retracing of your steps.

Select a heading that indicates the nature of your list.

Works Cited for a list of works including books, articles, films, recordings, Internet sources, and so on that are quoted or paraphrased in the research paper.

Works Consulted if your list includes non-print items such as an interview, letter, or speech as well as printed works.

Annotated Bibliography for a list of references that includes a description of the contents of each source (see pages 122–124).

Selected Bibliography for a list of readings on the subject.

> For examples of Works Cited pages, see pages 225 and 238. For an example of an annotated bibliography, see pages 122–124.

The title "Works Cited" is usually most appropriate, because it lists scholarly works of printed books and articles, Web sources, and non-print items.

Works pertinent to the paper but not quoted or paraphrased, such as an article on related matters, can be mentioned in a content endnote (see pages 319–322) and then listed in the Works Cited.

14a Formatting the Works Cited Page

Arrange items in alphabetic order by the surname of the author using the letter-by-letter system. Ignore spaces in the author's surname. Consider the first names only when two or more surnames are identical. Note how the following examples are alphabetized letter by letter. When no author is listed, alphabetize by the first important word of the title. Imagine lettered spelling for unusual items. For example, "#2 Red Dye" should be alphabetized as though it were "Number 2 Red Dye."

> Dempsey, Morgan
> "Facing Your Failures"
> Lawrence, Jacob
> Lawrence, Melissa
> McPherson, James Alan
> "Miracles and Tragedies in West Virginia Coal Mines"
> Saint-Exupéry, Antoine de
> St. James, Christopher

When two or more entries cite coauthors that begin with the same name, alphabetize by the last names of the second authors:

> Huggins, Marjorie, and Devin Blythe
> Huggins, Marjorie, and Stephen Fisher

The list of sources may also be divided into separate alphabetized sections for primary and secondary sources, for different media (articles, books, Internet sources), for different subject matter (biography, autobiography, letters), for different periods (Neoclassic period, Romantic period), and for different areas (German viewpoints, French viewpoints, American viewpoints).

Place the first line of each entry flush with the left margin and indent succeeding lines one-half inch. Double-space each entry as well as between all entries. Use one space after periods and other marks of punctuation.

Set the title "Works Cited" one inch down from the top of the sheet and double-space between it and the first entry. The following example illustrates a sample Works Cited page.

HINT: MLA style uses italics in place of underlining for titles.

Mims 13

Works Cited

Calvert, John H. "The Key Deception." *Intelligent Design Network.* 19

Oct. 2006. Web. 18 Sept. 2008.

Evans, Hestia, Lady Evans, and Dugald Steer, Eds. *Mythology.*

Cambridge, MA: Candlewick, 2007. Print.

Haug, Matthew C. "Of Mice and Metaphysics: Natural Selection and

Realized Population-Level Properties." *Philosophy of Science* 74.4

(2007): 431–51. Print.

Hill, Christopher T. "The Post-Scientific Society." *Issues in Science and

Technology Online* 24.1 (2007). Web. 20 Sept. 2008.

Hudson, Robert G. "The Empirical Basis to Skepticism." *Minerva: An*
Internet Journal of Philosophy 11 (2007). Web. 22 Sept. 2008.

Martin, Thomas R. "Religion, Myth, and Community." *An Overview of*
Classical Greek History from Homer to Alexander. 3 Apr. 1999. Web.
18 Sept. 2008.

Stratton, Jerry. "Secular Humanist Pantheon." *The Biblyon Broadsheet*.
1 Apr. 2007. Web. 17 Sept. 2008.

Weisman, Alan. *The World without Us*. New York: St. Martin's, 2007. Print.

Wilson, David S. *Darwin's Cathedral: Evolution, Religion, and the Nature*
of Society. Chicago: U of Chicago P, 2003. Print.

---. *Evolution for Everyone: How Darwin's Theory Can Change the Way We*
Think about Our Lives. New York: Dell, 2007. Print.

Index to Works Cited Models: MLA Style

(continued on page 242)

(continued from page 241)

Index to Works Cited Models: MLA Style

Index to Works Cited Models: MLA Style

(continued on page 244)

(continued from page 243)

Index to Works Cited Models: MLA Style

Index to Works Cited Models: MLA Style

14b Works Cited Form—Books

Enter information for books in the following order. Items 1, 3, and 7 are required; add other items according to the circumstances explained in the text that follows.

1. Author(s)
2. Chapter or part of book
3. Title of the book
4. Editor, translator, or compiler
5. Edition
6. Volume number of book
7. Place, publisher, and date
8. Page numbers
9. Number of volumes
10. Medium of publication—"Print."

The following example shows three primary divisions of a Works Cited entry for a book—Author's Name. *Title of the Book.* Publication Information.

Kennedy, Randall. *Sellout: The Politics of Racial Betrayal.* New York: Pantheon, 2008. Print.

Items 1, 3, 7, and 10 are always required book entries on the Works Cited page. Add other items according to the circumstances.

Carroll, Lewis. "The Walrus and the Carpenter." *The Best Poems of the English Language.* Ed. Harold Bloom. New York: HarperCollins, 2004. 757–60. Print.

Following is a detailed breakdown of the components found in the previous entry:

Author Name. "Title for Section of the Book." *Book Title in Italics.*

Name of the editor. City, State of Publication: Name of Publisher,

Year of Publication. Page Numbers. Medium of Publication.

Author's Name

List the author's name, surname first, followed by given name or initials, and then a period:

Gingrich, Newt.

Always give authors' names in the fullest possible form, for example, "Jimmerson, Aundra V." rather than "Jimmerson, A. V." unless, as indicated on the title page of the book, the author prefers initials. If you spell out an abbreviated name, put square brackets around the material added:

Tolkien, J[ohn] R [onald] R[euel].

With pseudonyms you may add the real name, enclosing the addition in brackets.

Carroll, Lewis [Charles Lutwidge Dodgson].

Omit a title, affiliation, or degree that appears with the author's name on the title page.

If the title page says:	*In the Works Cited use:*
Sir John Gielgud	Gielgud, John
Sister Margaret Grayson	Grayson, Margaret
Barton O'Connor, Ph.D.	O'Connor, Barton

However, do provide an essential suffix that is part of a person's name:

Justin, Walter, Jr.
Peterson, Robert J., III.

Title of the Book

State the title of the book, including any subtitle. Use italics for the entire title, including any colon, subtitle, or punctuation. Place a period after the entire title, unless it ends in another punctuation mark.

Gingrich, Newt. *Real Change: From the World That Fails to the World That Works.*

Publication Information

Provide the city of publication, the publisher's name, the year of publication, and the medium of publication. The word *Print* is given as the medium of publication for books and periodicals.

> Gingrich, Newt. *Real Change: From the World That Fails to the World*
>
> *That Works.* Washington, DC: Regnery, 2008. Print.

Include the abbreviation for the state or country only if necessary for clarity:

> Brunstetter, Wanda E. *A Sister's Test.* Uhrichsville, OH: Barbour, 2007. Print.

If more than one place of publication appears on the title page, the first city mentioned is sufficient. If successive copyright dates are given, use the most recent (unless your study is specifically concerned with an earlier, perhaps definitive, edition). A new printing does not constitute a new edition.

If the place, publisher, date of publication, or pages are not provided, use one of these abbreviations:

n.p.	No place of publication listed
n.p.	No publisher listed
n.d.	No date of publication listed
n. pag.	No pagination listed

> Lewes, George Henry. *The Life and Works of Goethe.* 1855. 2 vols. Rpt.
>
> as vols. 13 and 14 of *The Works J. W. von Goethe.* Ed. Nathan
>
> Haskell Dole. London: Nicolls, n.d. 14 vols. Print.

Provide the publisher's name in a shortened form, such as "Bobbs" rather than "Bobbs-Merrill Co., Inc." A publisher's special imprint name should be joined with the official name, for example, Anchor-Doubleday.

Abbreviations to publisher's names are listed on page 370.

> Miller, Sue. *The Senator's Wife.* New York: Knopf, 2008. Print.

Cite page numbers to help a reader find a particular section of a book.

> Lawrence, Cooper. "The Influence of Self-Esteem." *The Cult*
>
> *of Perfection.* Guilford, CT: Globe Pequot, 2008. 175–97.
>
> Print.

The following list provides examples and explains the correct form for books listed on a Works Cited page.

Author, Anonymous

Begin with the title. Do not use *anonymous* or *anon.* Alphabetize by the title, ignoring initial articles, *A*, *An*, or *The*.

The Song of Roland. Trans. W. S. Merwin. New York: Random, 2006. Print.

Author, Pseudonymous but Name Supplied

Slender, Robert [Freneau, Philip]. *Letters on Various and Important
        Subjects*. Philadelphia: Hogan, 1799. Print.

Author, Listed by Initials with Name Supplied

Rowling, J[oanne] K[athleen]. *Harry Potter and the Deathly Hallows*.
        New York: Scholastic, 2007. Print.

Authors, Two

Preston, Douglas, and Lincoln Child. *The Wheel of Darkness*. New York:
        Warner, 2008. Print.

Authors, Three

Evans, Hestia, Lady Evans, and Dugald Steer, Eds. *Mythology*.
        Cambridge, MA: Candlewick, 2007. Print.

Authors, More Than Three

Use "et al.," which means "and others," or list all the authors. See the two examples that follow:

Garrod, Andrew C., et al. *Adolescent Portraits: Identity, Relationships,
        and Challenges*. 6th ed. Boston: Allyn & Bacon, 2007. Print.

Orlich, Donald C., Robert J. Harder, Richard C. Callahan, and Ola
        M. Brown. *Teaching Strategies: A Guide to Effective Instruction*.
        Boston: Houghton Mifflin, 2006. Print.

Author, Corporation or Institution

A corporate author can be an association, a committee, or any group or institution when the title page does not identify the names of the members.

American Medical Association. *Health Professions Career and Education
        Directory 2008–2009*. New York: Random, 2008. Print.

List a committee or council as the author even when the organization is also the publisher, as in this example:

Consumer Reports. *Consumer Reports Electronics Buying Guide 2008*.
        New York: Consumer Reports, 2008. Print.

Author, Two or More Books by the Same Author

When an author has two or more works, do not repeat his or her name with each entry. Rather, insert a continuous three-dash line flush with the left margin, followed by a period. Also, list the works alphabetically by the title (ignoring *a*, *an*, and *the*), not by the year of publication. In the following example, the *Wh* of *Whiteout* precedes the *Wo* of *World*.

> Follett, Ken. *Hornet Flight*. New York: New American Library, 2002.
>
>> Print.
>
> ---. *Whiteout*. New York: Penguin, 2004. Print.
>
> ---. *World without End*. New York: Dutton, 2007. Print.

The three dashes stand for exactly the same name(s) as in the preceding entry. However, do not substitute three hyphens for an author who has two or more works in the Works Cited when one is written in collaboration with someone else:

> Gaiman, Neil. *Anansi Boys*. New York: HarperTorch, 2006. Print.
>
> ---. *Stardust*. New York: HarperCollins, 2007. Print.
>
> Gaiman, Neil, and Terry Pratchett. *Good Omens: The Nice and Accurate*
>
>> *Prophecies of Agnes Nutter, Witch*. New York: HarperTorch, 2006. Print.

If the person edited, compiled, or translated the work that follows on the list, place a comma after the three hyphens and write *ed.*, *comp.*, or *trans.* before you give the title. This label does not affect the alphabetic order by title.

> Finneran, Richard J., ed. *The Tower: A Facsimile Edition*. New York:
>
>> Simon & Schuster, 2004. Print.
>
> ---, ed. *Yeats Reader*. New York: Scribner, 2002. Print.

Author, Two or More Books by the Same Multiple Authors

When you cite two or more books by the same authors, provide the names in the first entry only. Thereafter, use three hyphens, followed by a period.

> Axelrod, Rise B., and Charles R. Cooper. *Concise Guide to Writing*. 4th
>
>> ed. Boston: St. Martin's, 2005. Print.
>
> ---. *St. Martin's Guide to Writing*. 8th ed. Boston: St. Martin's, 2007. Print.

Anthology, or a Compilation

In general, works in an anthology have been published previously and collected by an editor. Supply the names of authors as well as editors. Many times the prior publication data on a specific work may not be readily available; therefore, use this form:

> Glaspell, Susan. "Trifles." *The Literary Experience*. Compact Edition.
>
>   Eds. Bruce Beiderwell and Jeffrey M. Wheeler. Boston: Thomson,
>
>   Wadsworth, 2008. 550–61. Print.

> If you use several works from the same anthology, you can shorten the citation by citing the short work and by making cross references to the larger one; see "Cross-References to Works in a Collection," page 251.

Provide the inclusive page numbers for the piece, not just the page or pages that you have cited in the text.

The Bible

Do not italicize the word Bible or the books of the Bible. Common editions need no publication information, but do italicize special editions of the Bible.

> The Bible. Print. [Denotes King James version]

> *The Geneva Bible*. 1560. Facsim. rpt. Madison: U of Wisconsin P, 1961.
>
>   Print.

> *NRSV [New Revised Standard Version] Study Bible*. New York:
>
>   HarperCollins, 2007. Print.

A Book Published before 1900

For older books that are now out of print, you may omit the name of the publisher and use a comma, instead of a colon, to separate the place of publication from the year. If it has no date listed, use "n.d." If it has no publisher or place of publication mentioned, use "n.p."

> Dewey, John. *The School and Society*. Chicago, 1899. Print.

Chapter or Part of the Book

> If you cite from an anthology or collection, list the title of the specific story, poem, essay, and so on. See "Anthology, or a Compilation," page 249, or "Collection, Component Part," page 251.

List the chapter or part of the book on the Works Cited page only when it is separately edited, translated, or written, or when it demands special attention. For example, if you quote from a specific chapter of a book, let's say Chapter 6 of Michael Pollan's book,

the entry should read:

> Pollan, Michael. *In Defense of Food*. New York: Penguin, 2008. Print.

Your in-text citation will have listed specific page numbers, so there is no reason to mention a specific chapter, even though it is the only portion of Pollan's book that you read.

Classical Works

> Homer. *The Odyssey*. Trans. W.H.D. Rouse. New York: Penguin, 2007. Print.

You are more likely to find a classic work in an anthology, which would require this citation:

> Sophocles. *Oedipus the King*. *The Literary Experience*. Compact Edition.
>
> Ed. Bruce Beiderwell, and Jeffrey M. Boston: Thomson Wadsworth,
>
> 2008. 64–111. Print.

Collection, Component Part

If you cite from one work in a collection of works by the same author, provide the specific name of the work and the corresponding page numbers. This next entry cites one story from a collection of stories by the same author:

> Berry, Jedediah. "Inheritance." *Best New American Voices 2008*. Ed.
>
> Richard Bausch. Orlando, FL: Harcourt, 2007. 42–57. Print.

Cross-References to Works in a Collection

If you are citing several selections from one anthology or collection, provide a full reference to the anthology (as explained on page 249) and then provide references to the individual selections by providing the author and title of the work, the last name of the editor of the collection, and the inclusive page numbers used from the anthology.

> Lithgow, John, ed. *The Poet's Corner*. New York: Grand Central, 2007. Print.
>
> Parker, Dorothy. "Afternoon." Lithgow 226–29.
>
> Shelley, Percy Bysshe. "To a Skylark." Lithgow 193.
>
> Wordsworth, William. "I Wandered Lonely as a Cloud." Lithgow 270.

Edition

Indicate the edition used, whenever it is not the first, in Arabic numerals ("3rd ed."), by name ("Rev. ed.," "Abr. ed."), or by year ("1999 ed."), without further punctuation:

> Fenoglio-Preiser, Cecilia, et al. *Gastrointestinal Pathology: An Atlas and*
>
> *Text*. 3rd ed. Philadelphia: Lippincott, Williams, & Wilkins 2008.
>
> Print.

Indicate that a work has been prepared by an editor, not the original author:

> Crane, Stephen. *Maggie: A Girl of the Streets and Other Selected Stories*.
>
> Ed. with Intro. by Alfred Kazin. New York: Signet, 2006. Print.

If you wish to show the original date of the publication, place the year immediately after the title, followed by a period. *Note:* The title of an edition in a series is capitalized.

> Hardy Thomas. *Far from the Madding Crowd.* 1874. Ed. Joslyn T. Pine.
>
> Mineola, NY: Dover, 2007. Print.

Editor, Translator, Illustrator, or Compiler

If the name of the editor or compiler appears on the title page of an anthology or compilation, place it first:

> Pollack, Harriet, and Christopher Metress, eds. *Emmett Till in Literary*
>
> *Memory and Imagination.* Baton Rouge: Louisiana State U P, 2008.
>
> Print.

If your in-text citation refers to the work of the editor, illustrator, or translator (e.g., "The Ciardi edition caused debate among Dante scholars") use this form with the original author listed after the work, preceded by the word *By*:

> Kirkpartick, Robin, trans. *The Purgatorio.* By Dante. New York: Penguin,
>
> 2008. Print.
>
> Dore Gustave, illus. *The Raven.* By Edgar Allan Poe. Gloucester, UK:
>
> Book Depository, 2008. Print.
>
> Kerrigan, William, Stephen M. Fallon, and John Rumrich, eds. *Complete*
>
> *Poetry and Essential Prose of John Milton.* New York: Random,
>
> 2007. Print.

Otherwise, mention an editor, translator, or compiler of a collection *after* the title with the abbreviations Ed., Trans., or Comp., as shown here:

> Yeats, W. B. *Sophocles' Oedipus at Colonus.* Ed. Jared Curtis. Ithica, NY:
>
> Cornell U P, 2008. Print.

Encyclopedia, Dictionary, or Reference Book

Treat works arranged alphabetically as you would an anthology or collection, but omit the name of the editor(s), the volume number, place of publication, publisher, and page number(s). If the author is listed, begin the entry with the author's name; otherwise, begin with the title of the article. If the article is signed with initials, look elsewhere in the work for a complete name. Well-known works, such as the first two examples that follow, need only the edition and the year of publication.

> "Tumult." *The American Heritage College Dictionary.* 4th ed. 2007. Print.
>
> Ward, Norman. "Saskatchewan." *Encyclopedia Americana.* 2008 ed.
>
> Print.

If you cite a specific definition from among several, add *Def.* (Definition), followed by the appropriate number/letter of the definition.

"Level." Def. 4a. *The American Heritage College Dictionary*. 4th ed.

2007. Print.

Less-familiar reference works need a full citation, as shown in the next examples:

"Probiotics." *Mayo Clinic Book of Alternative Medicine*. Ed. Brent Bauer,

M.D. New York: Time, 2007. Print.

"Clindamycin." *Complete Guide to Prescription and Nonprescription Drugs*

2008. Eds. H. Winter Griffith and Stephen Moore. New York:

Perigee, 2008. Print.

If you cite material from a chapter of one volume in a multivolume set, you must include the volume number. Although not required, you may also provide the total number of volumes. Conform to the following entry format:

Saintsbury, George. "Dickens." *The Cambridge History of English*

Literature. Ed. A. W. Ward and A. R. Waller. Vol. 13. New York:

Putnam's, 1917. 14 vols. Print.

Introduction, Preface, Foreword, or Afterword

If you are citing the person who has written the introduction to a work by another author, start with the name of the person who wrote the preface or foreword. Give the name of the part being cited, neither underscored nor enclosed within quotation marks. Place the name of the author in normal order after the title preceded by the word *By*. Follow with publication information and end with the inclusive page numbers.

Wilson, E. O. Foreword. *A Contract with the Earth*. By Newt Gingrich and

Terry L. Maple. Baltimore: Johns Hopkins U P, 2007. ix–x. Print.

Frantz, Sarah S. G. Introduction. *Love and Friendship*. By Jane Austin.

New York: Barnes and Noble, 2007. vii–xvii. Print.

If the author has written the prefatory matter, not another person, use only the author's last name after the word *By*.

Miller, Dan. Introduction. *No More Mondays*. By Miller. New York:

Currency, 2008. 1–10. Print.

Use this form only if you cite from the introduction and not the main text.

> For more details about this type of citation, see "Chapter or Part of the Book," page 250, and "Anthology, or a Compilation," page 249.

Manuscript or Typescript

Chaucer, Geoffrey. *The Canterbury Tales.* MS Harley 7334. British
     Museum, London.

Tabares, Miguel. "Voices from the Ruins of Ancient Greece."
     Unpublished essay, 2008.

Play, Classical

Shakespeare, William. *Othello.* Ed. Daniel Vitkus. Rpt. of the 1623 ed.
     Comedies, Histories, and Tragedies. New York: Barnes and Noble
     Shakespeare, 2007. Print.

Today, classical plays are usually found in anthologies, which will require this form:

Shakespeare, William. *Hamlet.* The Literary Experience. Compact Edition.
     Eds. Bruce Beiderwell and Jeffrey M. Wheeler. Boston: Thomson,
     Wadsworth, 2008. 709–817. Print.

Play, Modern

Contemporary plays may be published independently or as part of a collection.

Shepard, Sam. *Kicking a Dead Horse.* New York: Knopf, 2008. Print.

Poem, Classical

Classical poems are usually translated, so you will often need to list a translator and/or editor. If the work is one part of a collection, show which anthology you used.

> If you cite the translator's or editor's preface or notes to the text, put the name of the translator or editor first. See page 252.

Dante. *The Divine Comedy.* Trans. Sean O'Brien. New York: Macmillan,
     2008. Print.

Dante. *Inferno. The Divine Comedy.* Trans. John Ciardi.
The Norton Anthology of World Masterpieces. Ed. Sarah Lawall et al. New
     York: Norton, 1999. 1303–1429. Print.

Poem, Modern Collection

Use this form that includes the inclusive page numbers if you cite one short poem from a collection.

> Lee, Li-Young, "Descended from Dreamers." *Behind My Eyes*. New York:
>
> Norton, 2008. 60-61. Print.

Use this next form if you cite from one book-length poem.

> Eliot, T. S. *Four Quartets*. *The Complete Poems and Plays 1909–1950*.
>
> New York: Harcourt, 1952. 115-45. Print.

Do not cite specific poems and pages if you cite several different poems of the collection. Your in-text citations should cite the specific poems and page numbers (see page 185). Your Works Cited entry would then list only the name of the collection.

> Eliot, T. S. *The Complete Poems and Plays 1909–1950*. New York:
>
> Harcourt, 1952. Print.

Reprinted Works

Use the following form if you can quickly identify original publication information.

> Tan, Amy. "Mother Tongue." *Threepenny Review* 1989: n. pag. Rpt. in *Rotten*
>
> *English*. Ed. Dohra Ahmad. New York: Norton, 2007. 503-10. Print.

Republished Book

If you are citing from a republished book, such as a paperback version of a book published originally in hardback, provide the original publication date after the title and then provide the publication information for the book from which you are citing.

> Stevenson, Robert Louis. *Treasure Island*. 1883. Gloucester, UK: Book
>
> Depository, 2008. Print.

Although it is not required, you may wish to provide supplementary information. Give the type of reproduction to explain that the republished work is, for example, a facsimile reprinting of the text.

> Laughlin, Ruth. *Caballeros: The Romance of Santa Fe and the Southwest*.
>
> 1945. Facsim. rpt. Santa Fe, NM: Sunstone, 2008. Print.

Give facts about the original publication if the information will serve the reader. In this next example the republished book was originally published under a different title.

> Arnold, Matthew. "The Study of Poetry." *Essays: English and American*. Ed.
>
> Charles W. Eliot. 1886. New York: Collier, 1910. Rpt. of the General
>
> Introduction to *The English Poets*. Ed. T. H. Ward. 1880. Print.

Screenplay

Baumbach, Noah. *Margot at the Wedding: The Shooting Script.* Screenplay. New York: Newmarket, 2008. Print.

Series, Numbered and Unnumbered

If the work is one in a published series, show the name of the series, abbreviated, without quotation marks or italics, the number of this work in Arabic numerals, and a period:

Wallerstein, Ruth C. *Richard Crashaw: A Study in Style and Poetic Development.* U of Wisconsin Studies in Lang. and Lit. 37. Madison: U of Wisconsin P, 1935. Print.

Sourcebooks and Casebooks

Gitomer, Jeffrey. "The Secret of Self-Belief." *Little Green Book of Getting Your Way.* New York: Pearson, 2007. 20–21. Print.

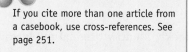

If you cite more than one article from a casebook, use cross-references. See page 251.

If you can identify the original facts of publication, include that information also:

Ellmann, Richard. "Reality." *Yeats: The Man and the Masks.* New York: Macmillan, 1948. Rpt. in *Yeats: A Collection of Critical Essays.* Ed. John Unterecker. Twentieth Century Views. Englewood Cliffs: Prentice, 1963. 163–74. Print.

Title of the Book

Show the title of the work italicized, followed by a period. Separate any subtitle from the primary title by a colon and one space even though the title page has no mark of punctuation or the card catalog entry has a semicolon.

Budiansky, Stephen. *The Bloody Shirt.* New York: Viking, 2008. Print.

If an italicized title to a book incorporates another title that normally receives italics, do not underscore or italicize the shorter title nor place it within quotation marks. In the title below, *Absalom and Acidophil* is the shorter title; it does not receive italics.

Schilling, Bernard N. *Dryden and the Conservative Myth: A Reading of* Absalom and Acidophil. New Haven: Yale UP, 1961. Print.

Title of a Book in Another Language

In general, use lowercase letters for foreign titles except for the first major word and proper names. Provide a translation in brackets if you think it necessary (e.g., *Étranger* [*The Stranger*] or Praha [Prague]).

Eco, Umberto. *Historia de la belleza.* New York: Random House, 2007. Print.

Pauly, Daniele. *Barragan: L'espace et l'ombre, le mur et la couleur.* New
    York: Birkhauser Verlag, 2008. Print.

Translator

List the translator's name first only if the translator's work (preface, foreword, afterword, notes) is the focus of your study.

Marquez, Gabriel Garcia. *Memories of My Melancholy Whores.* Trans.
    Edith Grossman. New York: Knopf, 2005. Print.

Volumes

If you are citing from only one volume of a multivolume work, provide
the number of that volume in the works cited entry with information for that
volume only. In your text, you will need to specify only page numbers, for
example, (Borgese 45–51).

Chircop, Aldo, Moira L. McConnell, and Scott Coffen-Smout, eds. *Ocean
    Yearbook.* Vol. 22. Chicago: U of Chicago P, 2008. Print.

Although additional information is not required, you may provide the
inclusive page numbers, the total number of volumes, and the inclusive dates
of publication.

Lauter, Paul, ed. "New Generations: Postmodernity and Difference." *The
    Heath Anthology of American Literature.* 5th ed. Vol. E. Boston:
    Houghton Mifflin, 2006. 2345–54. 5 vols. Print.

If you are citing from two or more volumes of a multivolume work, your
in-text citation will need to specify volume and page (2: 120–21); then the
Works Cited entry will need to show the total number of volumes in Arabic
numerals, as shown here.

Hersen, Michel. *Handbook of Psychological Assessment, Case
    Conceptualization, and Treatment.* 2 vols. Indianapolis: Wiley,
    2007. Print.

If you are citing from volumes that were published over a period of years,
provide the inclusive dates at the end of the citation. Should the volumes still
be in production, write *to date* after the number of volumes and leave a space
after the dash that follows the initial date.

Walsch, Neale Donald. *Conversations with God: An Uncommon Dialogue.*
    3 vols. New York: Penguin, 1996–98. Print.

Cassidy, Frederic, ed. *Dictionary of American Regional English.*
    3 vols. to date. Cambridge: Belknap-Harvard UP, 1985– . Print.

If you are using only one volume of a multivolume work and the volume has an individual title, you can cite the one work without mentioning the other volumes in the set.

> Crane, Stephen. *Wounds in the Rain. Stephen Crane: Tales of War.*
>
>   Charlottesville: UP of Virginia, 1970. 95–284. Print.

As a courtesy to the reader, you may include supplementary information about an entire edition.

> Crane, Stephen. *Wounds in the Rain. Stephen Crane: Tales of War.*
>
>   Charlottesville: UP of Virginia, 1970. Vol. 6 of *The University of*
>
>   *Virginia Edition of the Works of Stephen Crane.* Ed. Fredson
>
>   Bowers. 95–284. 10 vols. 1969–76. Print.

14c   Works Cited Form—Periodicals

For journal or magazine articles, use the following order:

1. Author(s)
2. Title of the article
3. Name of the periodical—*italicized*
4. Series number (if it is relevant)
5. Volume and issue number (for journals)—(e.g., 70.4)
6. Date of publication
7. Page numbers
8. Medium of publication—"Print."

> Lindberg, Erik. "Expert Energy-saving Tips." *The Family Handyman* June
>
>   2008: 44–46. Print.

Following is a detailed breakdown of the components found in the previous entry:

> Author's Name. "Title of Article." *Title of Periodical* Publication Date:
>
>   Page Numbers. Medium of Publication.

Give the name of the journal or magazine in full, italicized, and with no following punctuation. Omit any introductory article, such as *The*.

> Panning, Anne. "All-U-Can-Eat." *Kenyon Review* 29.4 (Fall 2007):
>
>   21–40. Print.

Be sure to include the volume as well as issue number for journals immediately after the title of the journal. In this example, the volume and issue number is

29.4. If no issue number is provided, then simply give the volume number, 29, for example. Magazine entries on the Works Cited page do not need to mention the volume or issue number because they are usually printed on a weekly basis; hence, the date is more useful for locating a magazine article.

The formatting of Works Cited entries for periodicals are explained and illustrated in the following examples.

Abstract in an Abstracts Journal

If you have cited from an abstract found in a journal devoted to abstracts, not full articles, begin the citation with information on the original work and then give information on the abstracts journal. Use either item number or page number according to how the journal provides the abstracts.

> Gabriel, Adrian T., Timm Meyer, and Guido Germano. "Molecular
>
> Graphics of Convex Body Fluids." *Journal of Chemistry Theory and*
>
> *Computation* 70.3 (2008): 192–93. Chemical Abstracts 101 (2008):
>
> item 5523. Print.

Add the word *Abstract* if the title does not make clear that you have used an abstract, not a full article.

> Crowell, Sheila E., et al. "Parent-Child Interactions, Peripheral
>
> Serotonin, and Self-inflicted Injury in Adolescents." *Journal of*
>
> *Consulting and Clinical Psychology* 76.1 (2008): 15–21. Abstract.
>
> PsycLIT 2008–18544. Print.

Use the next form when you cite from *Dissertation Abstracts International (DAI)*. The page number features A, B, or C to designate the series used: A—Humanities, B—Sciences, C—European dissertations. Before volume 30 (1969) the title was *Dissertation Abstracts*, so use *DA* for those early volumes.

> Nicholson, Andre Wesley. "Criticisms and Critiques: An Analysis of
>
> Proofreading Marks of College English Professors." Diss. Southern
>
> Tech. U, 2008. DAI 66 (2008): 2957D. Print.

Author(s)

Show the author's name flush with the left margin, without a numeral and with succeeding lines indented five spaces. Enter the surname first, followed by a comma, followed by a given name or initials, followed by a period:

> Kleine-Ahlbrandt, Stephanie, and Andrew Small. "China's New
>
> Dictatorship Diplomacy." *Foreign Affairs* 87.1 (Jan./Feb. 2008):
>
> 38–56. Print.

Author, Anonymous

"Italy." *Biblical Archeology Review* Jan./Feb. 2008: 88. Print.

Interview, Published

Rosenfeld, Jordan E. Interview with Tess Gerritsen. "Mistress of

Suspense." *Writer's Digest* Feb 2008: 50–55. Print.

Journal, with All Issues for a Year Paged Continuously

Pavalko, Eliza K., Fang Gong, and J. Scott Long. "Women's Work, Cohort

Change, and Health." *Journal of Health & Social Behavior* 48.4

(2007): 352–68. Print.

Journal, with Each Issue Paged Anew

Add the issue number after the volume number, because page numbers alone are not sufficient to locate the article within a volume of six or 12 issues when each issue has separate pagination. Adding the month or season with the year will also serve the researcher.

McCorkle, Jill. "Cuss Time." *The American Scholar* 77.1 (Win. 2008):

59–62. Print.

If a journal uses only an issue number, treat it as a volume number:

Michta, Andrew A. "Double or Nothing." *The National Interest* 93

(Jan./Feb. 2008): 54–57. Print.

Loose-Leaf Collection

Clemmitt, Marcia. "Climate Change." *CQ Researcher* 16.4 (27 Jan. 2006):

75+. Print.

Magazine

With magazines, the volume number offers little help for finding an article. For example, one volume of *Time* (52 issues) will have page 16 repeated 52 times. For this reason, you need to insert an exact date (month and day) for weekly and fortnightly (every two weeks) publications. Do not list the volume and issue numbers.

Lobel, Hannah. "Shame on Us." *Utne* Jan./Feb. 2008: 36–37. Print.

The month suffices for monthly and bimonthly publications:

Le Guin, Ursula K. "Staying Awake." *Harper's* Feb. 2008: 76–84. Print.

Microform

Some reference sources, such as *NewsBank*, republish articles on microfiche. If you use such a microform, enter the original publication information first and then add the pertinent information about the microform, as shown.

> Chapman, Dan. "Panel Could Help Protect Children." *Winston-Salem*
>
> *Journal* 14 Jan 1990: 14. Microform. *Newsbank: Welfare and Social*
>
> *Problems* 12 (1990): fiche 1, grids A8–11.

Notes, Editorials, Queries, Reports, Comments, and Letters

Magazine and journals publish many pieces that are not full-fledged articles. Identify this type of material if the title of the article or the name of the journal does not make clear the nature of the material (e.g., "Letter" or "Comment").

> Maltby, Richard E., Jr. "Be My Valentine: Heart Transplants." Puzzle.
>
> *Harper's* Feb. 2008: 95. Print.
>
> Perina, Kaja. "Waiting for Attraction to Strike." Editor's note.
>
> *Psychology Today* 41.1 (Jan./Feb. 2008): 7. Print.
>
> Waring-Flood, Clive. "Market Changes." Editorial. *Silvershotz* 4.4
>
> (2007): 2. Print.

Reprint of a Journal Article

> Vail, Kathleen. "Climate Control." *American School Board Journal* 192.6
>
> (June 2005): 12–19. Print. *Education Digest* Dec. 2005: 4–11.

Review, in a Magazine, Newspaper, or Journal

Name the reviewer and the title of the review. Then write *Rev. of* and the title of the work being reviewed, followed by a comma, and the name of the author or producer. If necessary, identify the nature of the work within brackets immediately after the title.

> Macowlay, Scott. "Wrong Turn." Rev. of *Taxi to the Dark Side,* by Alex
>
> Gibney. *Filmmaker.* 16.2 (Win. 2008): 56+. Print.

If the name of reviewer is not provided, begin the entry with the title of the review.

> "Nikon D300: A New Standard?" Rev. of Nikon D300. *Photography*
>
> *Monthly* Feb. 2008: 96+. Print.

If the review has no title, omit it from the entry.

> Benedict-Nelson, Andrew. Rev. of *The Summer Isles,* by Ian R. MacLeod.
>
> *Bookmarks* 32 (Jan./Feb.2008): 19. Print.

Skipped Pages in an Article

Supply inclusive page numbers (202–09, 85–115, or 1112–24), but if an article is paged here and there throughout the issue (for example, pages 74, 78, and 81–88), write only the first page number and a plus sign with no intervening space.

> Larson, Christine. "Keeping Your Brain Fit." *U.S. News & World Report*
>
> 11 Feb. 2008: 41+. Print.

Special Issue

If you cite one article from a special issue of a journal, you may indicate the nature of this special issue, as shown next.

> Bedusa, Jennie. "Photographer Focus: Connie Imboden." *Focus.* Spec.
>
> Issue of *Focus* 15 (Feb. 2008): 72–79. Print

If you cite several articles from the special issue, begin the primary citation with the name of the editor.

> Perloff, Stephen, ed. Spec. Issue of *Focus* 15 (Feb. 2008): 1–209. Print.

See also "Cross-References to Works in a Collection," page 251.

When that entry is established, cross-reference each article used in the following manner.

> Lambert, Patricia. "Bet's Bench." Photograph. *Perloff,* 119.

Speech or Address, Published

> United States. President. "State of the Union." *Weekly Compilation of*
>
> *Presidential Documents* pd04fe08 txt-11 (1 Feb. 2008): 117–25. Print.

Title of the Article

Show the title within quotation marks followed by a period inside the closing quotation marks.

> Theil, Stefan. "Europe's Philosophy of Failure." *Foreign Policy*
>
> (Jan./Feb. 2008): 54–60. Print.

Title, Omitted

> Granderson, Milton. *Oakleaf Journal of Conservation* 23.3 (2008):
>
> 93–94. Print.

Title, within the Article's Title

Rammelkamp, Charles. "Origins of Shakespeare's *Romeo and Juliet*."

   Renaissance 13.1 (Issue #59): 42–44. Print.

> See also "Title of a Book in Another
> Language," page 256.

Title, Foreign

Correa, Armando, and Maria Morales. "La Importancia de Ser." *People en*

   Espanol Diciembre/Enero 2006: 136–41. Print.

Volume, Issue, and Page Numbers for Journals

Some journals are paged continuously through all issues of an entire year, so listing the month of publication is unnecessary. For clarity, provide the volume and issue number, as well as the page numbers. Give the issue number following the volume number, separated by a period.

Greenspoon, Leonard J. "Casting Pearls before Swine." *Biblical*

   Archeology Review 34.1 (Jan./Feb. 2008): 13. Print.

14d Works Cited Form—Newspapers

Provide the name of the author, the title of the article, and the name of the newspaper as it appears on the masthead, omitting any introductory article (e.g., *Wall Street Journal*, not *The Wall Street Journal*). If the city of publication is not included in the name of a newspaper published locally, add the city in square brackets, not italicized, after the name: "*Times-Picayune* [New Orleans]." Provide the complete date—day, month (abbreviated), and year. Omit any volume and issue numbers.

Provide a page number as listed (e.g., 21, B-7, 13C, D4). For example, *USA Today* uses "6A" but the *New York Times* uses "A6." There is no uniformity among newspapers on this matter, so list the page accurately as an aid to your reader. If the article is not printed on consecutive pages, for example, if it begins on page 1 and skips to page 8, write the first page number and a plus (+) sign (see the entry below). Finally, provide the medium of publication—"Print."

Newspaper in One Section

Samuels, Christina A. "Embracing 'Response to Intervention.'" *Education*

   Week 23 Jan. 2008: 23–24. Print.

Newspaper with Lettered Sections

Kaufman, Marc, and Josh White. "Bull's-eye: Navy Missle Scores Hit on

   Falling Satellite." *Denver Post* 21 Feb. 2008: 1A+. Print.

Newspaper with Numbered Sections

Berger, Susan. "Animal Rescuers, Officials Clash." *Chicago Tribune* 26

Nov. 2005, sec. 1: 1. Print.

Newspaper Editorial with No Author Listed

"Stifling Online Speech." Editorial. *New York Times* 21 Feb. 2008: A22.

Print.

Newspaper Column, Cartoon, Comic Strip, or Advertisement

Add a description to the entry to explain that the citation refers to something other than a regular news story.

Williams, Dick. "Honesty for Taxpayers." Column. *Atlanta Business*

Chronicle 15 Feb. 2008: 26A. Print.

Newspaper Article with City Added

In the case of locally published newspapers, add the city in square brackets (see also the sample entry immediately above).

Kuyper, Tom. "Giving Awards Does Have a Special Value in Youth

Sports." *Leaf Chronicle* [Clarksville, TN] 2 July 2008: C1. Print.

Newspaper Edition or Section

When the masthead lists an edition, add a comma after the date and name the edition (*late ed., city ed.*), followed by a colon and then the page number.

Feagans, Brian. "True Feel for the Circus." *The Atlanta Journal-*

Constitution 21 Feb. 2008, home ed.: A1+. Print.

Newspaper in a Foreign Language

"Les Grands de ce monde reunis a Saint-Petersbourg." *Le Monde* 30 mai

2003: 1. Print.

14e Works Cited Form—Government Documents

Since the nature of public documents is so varied, the form of the entry cannot be standardized. Therefore, you should provide sufficient information so that the reader can easily locate the reference. As a general rule, place information in the Works Cited entry in this order (but see below if you know the author, editor, or compiler of the document):

1. Government
2. Body or agency

3. Subsidiary body
4. Title of document
5. Identifying numbers
6. Publication facts
7. Medium of publication

When you cite two or more works by the same government, substitute three hyphens for the name of each government or body that you repeat:

United States. Cong. House.

---. ---. Senate.

---. Dept. of Justice.

Congressional Papers

Senate and House sections are identified by an S or an H with document numbers (e.g., S. Res. 16) and page numbers (e.g., H2345–47).

United States. Cong. Senate. *Natural Resource Protection Cooperative*
   Agreement Act. 110th Cong., 1st sess. S. Bill 110–10. Washington,
   DC: GPO, 2007. Print.

---. ---. ---. *911 Modernization Act*. 110th Cong., 1st sess. S. Bill
   110–38. Washington, DC: GPO, 2007. Print.

If you provide a citation to the *Congressional Record*, you should abbreviate it and provide only the date and page numbers.

Cong. Rec. 13 Feb. 2008: S937–57. Print.

Executive Branch Documents

United States. Dept. of State. *Foreign Relations of the United States:*
   Diplomatic Papers, 1943. 5 vols. Washington, DC: GPO, 1943–44.
   Print.

---. President. *2008 Economic Report of the President*. Washington, DC:
   GPO, 2008. Print.

Documents of State Governments

Publication information on state papers will vary widely, so provide sufficient data for your reader to find the document.

2007–2008 Statistical Report. Nashville: Tennessee Board of Regents,
   2008. TBR A-001-03. Print.

Tennessee Election Returns, 1796–1825. Microfilm. Nashville:
   Tennessee State Library and Archives, n.d. M-Film JK 5292 T46.
   Print.

"Giles County." *2006–07 Directory of Public Schools*. Nashville: State

Dept. of Educ., n.d. 61. Print.

Legal Citations and Public Statutes

Use the following examples as guidelines for developing your citations, which can usually appear as parenthetical citations in your text, but not on the Works Cited page.

Illinois. Revised Statutes Annotated. Sec. 16-7-81. 2008. Print.

Noise Control Act of 2007. Pub. L. 92–574. 2007. Stat. 86. Print.

People v. McIntosh. California 321 P.3d 876, 2001–6. 1970. Print.

State v. Lane. Minnesota 263 N. W. 608. 1935. Print.

U.S. Const. Art. 2, sec. 1. Print.

14f   Works Cited Form—Internet Sources

Modern technology makes it possible for you to have access to information at your computer. In particular, the Internet opens a cornucopia of information from millions of sources. Other electronic sources include e-mail and databases.

Because of their length and the fluid changes of the network, the *MLA Style Manual*, 3rd edition, no longer recommends the inclusion of URLs in the Works Cited entries for Web publications. Instead, researchers may document the medium of documentation by providing the word "Web," followed by a period, just before the date of access. Rather than typing the URL, readers are now more likely to find resources on the Web by searching for the name of the author or the title of the article. This streamlining of entries will benefit the researcher while still allowing the reader the necessary documentation information for the source.

Citing Sources Found on the Internet

Include these items as appropriate to the source:

1. Author/editor name
2. Title of the article within quotation marks, or the title of a posting to a discussion list or forum followed by the words *online posting*, followed by a period.
3. If the document has a printed version, provide the publication information and the date.
4. Information on the electronic publication, such as the title of the site, the date of the posting, and the sponsoring organization, followed by a period.
5. The medium of publication—"Web."
6. Date of your access, followed by a period.

For discussion of the Internet's special format, see pages 39–46. For making judgments about the validity of Internet sources, see pages 42–43.

NOTE: Do not include page numbers unless the Internet article shows original page numbers from the printed version of the journal or magazine. Do not include the total number of paragraphs nor specific paragraph numbers unless the original Internet article has provided them.

World Wide Web Sites

Titles of books and journals from online sources should be shown in italics.

Abstract

Brown, Gregory G., et al. "Performance of Schizophrenia and Bipolar
    Patients on Verbal and Figural Working Memory Tasks." Abstract.
    Journal of Abnormal Psychology 116.4 (2007): 741. Web. 10 May 2008.

Advertisement

"R.M.S. Titanic, Inc." Advertisement. Arizona Science Center, 2008.
    Web. 14 Feb. 2008.

Anonymous Article

"What's Your PSI? Test Your Tire Safety Knowledge." *National Highway
    Traffic Safety Administration*. NHTSA, n.d. Web. 23 Sept. 2008.

Archive or Scholarly Project

British Poetry Archive. Ed. Jerome McGann and David Seaman. U of
    Virginia Lib, 2006. Web. 19 Apr. 2008.

Article from an Online Magazine

"Controlling Anger—Before It Controls You." *APA Online*. American
    Psychological Association, 10 May 2008. Web. 30 Sept. 2008.

Article from a Scholarly Journal

Osilla, Karen Chan, et al. "A Brief Intervention for At-Risk Drinking in
    an Employee Assistance Program." *Journal of Studies on Alcohol
    and Drugs* 69 (2008): 14–20. Web. 2 Dec. 2008.

Article Written for the Internet

"History of Elba." *Elba on line*, 2008. Web. 12 Apr. 2008.

Audio Program Online

See the entry for "Television or Radio Program," page 280.

Blogs and Chat Rooms

Carella, Lucinda, narr. "Speaking to an Elderly Parent." *Medhealth Metapage.*

Medical Health and Resources, 13 Sept. 2008. Web. 28 Oct. 2008.

Chat rooms seldom have great value, but on occasion you might find something that you wish to cite; if so, use this form.

"Weight Loss Support." *Yahoo! Chat.* Yahoo!, 30 May 2008. Web. 4 Oct.

2008.

Cartoon

Parker, Brant. "How Come You Don't Celebrate Valentine's Day?"

Cartoon. *Wizard of Id.* 14 Feb. 2008. Web. 29 Feb. 2008.

Chapter or Portion of a Book

Add the name of the chapter after the author's name.

Dewey, John. "Waste in Education." *School and Society.* Chicago: U of

Chicago P, 1907. Web. 14 Sept. 2008.

Database

Most libraries have converted their computer searches to online databases, such as Lexis-Nexis, ProQuest Direct, EBSCOhost, Electric Library, InfoTrac, and others. Omit the identifying numbers for the database or the key term used in the search. Following are examples.

"America's Children: Key National Indicators of Well-Being, 2007."

Federal Interagency Forum on Child and Family Statistics. 2007.

ERIC. Web. 8 Dec. 2008.

Brezina, Timothy. "Teenage Violence toward Parents as an Adaptation

to Family Strain: Evidence from a National Survey of Male

Adolescents." *Youth and Society* 30 (1999): 416–44. *MasterFILE*

Elite. Clarksville Montgomery County Library, Clarksville, TN. Web.

23 Feb. 2008.

Esslin, Martin. "Theater of the Absurd." *Grolier Multimedia*

Encyclopedia. 2007 ed. Web. 22 Oct. 2007.

Lee, Catherine C. "The South in Toni Morrison's *Song of Solomon*:

Initiation, Healing, and Home." *Studies in the Literary*

Imagination 31 (1998): 109–23. *InfoTrac.* Web. 19 Sept. 2008.

Sloan, T. A. "Pilates: Your Ticket to a Longer, Leaner You." *Discovery*
Health 30 Oct. 2007. *EBSCOhost*. Web. 23 Jan. 2008.

Editorial

Elliott, Jim. "Fear Mongering Undermines U.S. Constitution."
Editorial. *The Billings Outpost Online,* 21 Feb. 2008. Web.
21 Feb. 2008.

E-mail

Wright, Ellen. "Online Composition Courses." Message to the author. 24
May 2008. E-mail.

Encyclopedia Article Online

"Kurt Vonnegut, Jr." *Encyclopedia Britannica Online*. Encyclopedia
Britannica, 2007. Web. 9 Nov. 2007.

Film or Video Online

"Epiphany: Festival of Lights." *The History of the Orthodox Christian*
Church. GoTelecom Online, 2008. Web. 24 Oct. 2008.

Home Page for an Academic Course

Wilkins, John, Trisch Longbrake, and Tom Barrett. "Uses of Science in
Society." Dept. of Physics, Ohio State U, 15 Dec. 2007. Web. 12
Jan. 2008.

Home Page for an Academic Department

"Department of Lauguage and Literature." Home page. Dept. of Language
and Literature, Clayton State U, 2008. Web. 12 Sept. 2008.

Home Page for an Academic Site

Since you are not citing a specific article, you can refer to home pages in
your text, but not in the Works Cited.

"Robert Penn Warren: 1905–1989." Home page. *Modern American*
Poetry, Dept. of English, U of Illinois, Urbana-Champaign, 2008.
Web. 2 Apr. 2008.

Home Page for a Personal Web Site

Giovanni, Nikki. Home Page. Dept. of English, Virginia Tech U, 2008.
Web. 2 Apr. 2008.

Interview

Kowars, Kacey. Interview with Pete Hamill, author of *North River. Kacey Kowars Show,* 18 Jul. 2007. Web. 24 Mar. 2008.

Journal Article

Stillar, Scott. "Shocking the Cultureless: The Crucial Role of Culture Shock in Racial Identity Transformation." *Electronic Journal of Sociology* (2007): 1–16. Web. 22 Jan. 2008.

Manuscript

Girondo, Oliverio. *Scarecrow & Other Anomalies.* Trans. Gilbert Alter-Gilbert. MS. 2002. Web. 24 Aug. 2008.

Map

"Virginia—1735." Map. *U.S. County Formation Maps, 1643–Present.* Genealogy, Inc., 1999. Web. 24 Sept. 2008.

Newsletter

Oswald, Tom. "Tobacco Smoke Linked to Workplace Death." *MSU News Bulletin* 39.12 (21 Feb. 2008). Web. 28 Feb. 2008.

Newspaper Article, Column, Editorial

Tettamanti, Maria. "Boulevard of Dreams." *Miamiherald.com.* Miami Herald, 22 Feb. 2008. Web. 28 Feb. 2008.

Novel

Conrad, Joseph. "Chapter 1." *Heart of Darkness. 1902.* Web. 26 Sept. 2008.

Online Posting for E-mail Discussion Groups

Supply the name of the list's moderator and the Internet site, if known; otherwise show the e-mail address of the list's moderator.

Chapman, David. "An Electoral System for Iraq." Online Posting. Democracy Design Forum, 21 June 2005. Web. 27 Nov. 2008.

Photo, Painting, Sculpture

MLA style does not require you to label the type of work, as shown in the example of a photograph. Usually, the text will have established the nature of the work. However, if you feel that clarification is necessary, as in the case of "The Blessed Damozel," which is both a painting and a poem, you may wish to designate the form.

"Boy and Bear." Bronze sculpture. Marshall M. Fredericks Sculpture
Museum, 2007. Web. 29 Aug. 2008.

Joscelyn, Steven. "Leadenhall Market." Photograph. Pbase, 2008. Web.
12 Aug. 2008.

Rossetti, Dante. "The Blessed Damozel." 1875–78. Painting. *Rossetti
Archive*, 2008. Web. 30 Sept. 2008.

Poem, Song, or Story

Dylan, Bob. "Tangled Up in Blue." 1975. Song lyrics. *BobDylan.com*,
2008. Web. 13 Mar. 2008.

Hardy, Thomas. "To a Lady." *Wessex Poems and Other Verses*. 1898.
Project Bartleby. Great Books Online, 2008. Web. 10 Oct. 2008.

Report

"Spam Summit: The Next Generation of Threats and Solutions." Federal
Trade Commission, Nov. 2007. Web. 4 Dec. 2007.

Serialized Article

Brenner, Sydney. "The Next 100 Years of Biology." The Discovery Lecture
Series. Vanderbilt Medical Center, 14 Sept. 2006. Web.
20 Oct. 2008.

Song

See "Poem, Song, or Story" on page 271.

Sound Clip, Speech, or Recording

See "Television or Radio Program" on page 271.

Story

See "Poem, Song, or Story" on page 271.

Television or Radio Program

Simon, Scott. "Bhangra's DJ Rekha Takes the Dance Floor."
Weekend Edition. National Public Radio, 16 Feb. 2008. Web.
9 Mar. 2008.

University Posting, Online Article

Wetterich, Chris. "Smoke Free." Online posting. U of Illinois at
Springfield, Feb. 2008. Web. 28 Feb. 2008.

Video

See "Film or Video Online," page 269.

14g Works Cited Form—Citing CD-ROM and Database Sources

CD-ROM technology provides information in four different ways, and each method of transmission requires an adjustment in the form of the entry for your works cited page.

Full-Text Articles with Publication Information for the Printed Source

See also page 277 for citing SIRS in its loose-leaf form.

Full-text articles are available from national distributors, such as Information Access Company (InfoTrac), UMI-Pro-Quest (ProQuest), Silverplatter, or SIRS CD-ROM Information Systems. (*Note*: Most of these sources are also available online.) Conform to the examples that follow.

Brand, Madeleine. "Walking the Immigration Line." *National Public Radio*. NPR, 24 Jan. 2008. CD-ROM. *EBSCOhost.* EBSCOhost Research Database, May 2008.

Weise, Elizabeth. "Agreement Could Bring End to Animal Testing." *USA Today* 14 Feb. 2008: n.p. CD-ROM. *SIRS Researcher.* Boca Raton, FL: SIRS, 2008.

HINT: Complete information may not be readily available; for example, the original publication data may be missing. In such cases, provide what is available.

"Nor Any Drop to Drink." *Economist* 385 (8 Dec. 2007): 41. CD-ROM. *EBSCOhost.* EBSCOhost Research Database, May 2008.

Full-Text Articles with No Publication Information for a Printed Source

Sometimes the original printed source of an article or report will not be provided by the distributor of the CD-ROM database. In such a case, conform to the examples that follow, which provide limited data.

"Faulkner Biography." *Discovering Authors*. CD-ROM. Detroit: Gale, 2008.

"U.S. Population by Age: Urban and Urbanized Areas." *2007 U.S. Census Bureau*. CD-ROM. US Bureau of the Census. 2007.

Complete Books and Other Publications on CD-ROM

Cite this type of source as you would a book, and then provide information to the electronic source that you accessed.

The Bible. Life Application Study Bible. CD-ROM. Carol Stream, IL:
     Tyndale House, 2007.

English Poetry Full-Text Database. Re. 2. CD-ROM. Cambridge, Eng.:
     Chadwyck, 2008.

"John F. Kennedy." *InfoPedia*. CD-ROM. N.p.: Future Vision, n.d.

Poe, Edgar Allan. "Fall of the House of Usher." *Electronic Classical*
     Library. CD-ROM. Garden Grove, CA: World Library, 2007.

Abstracts to Books and Articles Provided by the National Distributors

As a service to readers, the national distributors have members of their staff write abstracts of articles and books if the original authors have not provided such abstracts. As a result, an abstract that you find on InfoTrac and ProQuest may not be written by the original author, so you should not quote such abstracts. You may quote from abstracts that say, "Abstract written by the author." Some databases *do* have abstracts written by the original authors. In either case, you need to show in the Works Cited entry that you have cited from the abstract, so conform to the example that follows, which provides name, title, publication information, the word *abstract*, the name of the database italicized, the medium (CD-ROM), the name of the vender, and—if available to you—the electronic publication date (month and year).

Peekhaus, Wilhelm. "Privacy for Sale—Business as Usual in the 21st
     Century: An Economic and Normative Critique." *Journal of*
     Information Ethics 16.1 (Spring 2007): 83–98. Abstract.
     CD-ROM. *EBSCOhost.* 29 Jan. 2008.

Nonperiodical Publication on CD-ROM or Diskette

Cite a CD-ROM, diskette, or cassette tape as you would for a book with the addition of a descriptive word. If relevant, show the edition (3rd ed.), release (Rel. 2), or version (Ver. 3). Conform to the examples that follow:

Lester, James D., Jr. *Introduction to Greek Mythology: Computer Slide*
     Show. 12 lessons on CD-ROM. Morrow, GA: Clayton State U, 2008.

2007 Statistics on Child Abuse—Montgomery County, Tennessee. Rel. 2.
     Diskette. Clarksville, TN: Harriett Cohn Mental Health Center, 2008.

Encyclopedia Article

For an encyclopedia article on a compact disc, use the following form.

"Abolitionist Movement." *Compton's Interactive Encyclopedia*. CD-ROM.
     The Learning Company, 2007.

Multidisc Publication

When citing a multidisc publication, follow the term *CD-ROM* with the total number of discs or with the disc that you cited from.

Springer, Alice G. *Barron's AP Spanish—2008*. 6th ed. CD-ROM. Disc 3.

Hauppauge, NY: Barron's, 2008.

14h Works Cited Form—Other Electronic Sources

Citing a Source That You Access in More Than One Medium

Some distributors issue packages that include different media, such as CD-ROM and accompanying microfiche or a diskette and an accompanying videotape. Cite such publications as you would a nonperiodical CD-ROM (see "Multidisc Publication," page 274) with the addition of the media available with this product.

Franking, Holly. *The Martensville Nightmare*. Ver. 1.0. Diskette. CD-ROM.

Prairie Village: Diskotech, 2005.

Silver, Daniel J. "The Battle of the Books." Rev. of *The Western Canon:*

The Books and School of the Ages, by Harold Bloom. CD-ROM.

Resource/One. UMI-ProQuest. Feb. 1995.

Chaucer, Geoffrey. "Prologue." *Canterbury Tales*. Videocassette. CD-ROM.

Princeton: Films for the Humanities and Sciences, 2006.

14i Works Cited Form—Other Sources

Advertisement

Provide the title of the advertisement, within quotation marks, or the name of the product or company, not within quotation marks, the label *Advertisement*, and publication information.

"Teaching for Intelligence: Believe to Achieve Conference."

Advertisement. *Education Week*, 23 Jan. 2008: 2. Print.

OnStar. Advertisement. CNN. 4 Aug. 2008. Television.

Art Work

If you actually experience the work itself, use the following form.

Remington, Frederic. *Mountain Man*. Bronze sculpture. Metropolitan

Museum of Art, New York. Visual art.

If the art work is a special showing at a museum, use the form of this next example.

> Sloan, John. "Seeing the City: Sloan's New York." Art Exhibition.
>
> Westmoreland Museum of American Art, Greensburg, PA. 27 Feb.
>
> 2008. Visual art.
>
> "Beth Campbell: Following Room." Whitney Museum of American Art,
>
> New York. 10 Feb. 2008. Visual art.

Use this next form to cite reproductions in books and journals.

> Raphael. *School of Athens*. The Vatican, Rome. *The World Book-*
>
> *Encyclopedia*, 2007 ed. Print.

If you show the date of the original, place the date immediately after the title.

> Raphael. *School of Athens*. 1510–1511. The Vatican, Rome. *The World*
>
> *Book-Encyclopedia*. 2007 ed. Print.

Broadcast Interview

> Reed, Philip. "Car Loans." Interview. CNN. Cable News Network, 23 Feb.
>
> 2008. Television.

Bulletin

> *The South Carolina Market Bulletin*. Columbia, SC: South Carolina
>
> Department of Agriculture, 21 Feb. 2008. Print.
>
> Maryland State Bar Association's Public Awareness Committee.
>
> *Appointing a Guardian*. Baltimore: Maryland State Bar Association.
>
> 2008. Print.

Cartoon

If you cannot decipher the name of the cartoonist and cannot find a title, use this form.

> Cartoon. *Education Week* 23 Jan. 2008: 36. Print.

Sometimes you will have the artist's name but not the name of the cartoon.

> Rickert, David. Cartoon. *English Journal* Jan. 2008: 94. Print.

Some cartoons are reprinted in magazines.

Ramirez. "Peace." Cartoon. Rpt. in *Weekly Standard* 2 June 2005: 13.

Print.

Computer Software

Publisher Deluxe 2007. Redmond, WA: Microsoft, 2007. CD-ROM.

Conference Proceedings

Caunt-Nulton, Heather, Samantha Kulatilake, and I-hao Woo, eds.

BUCLD-31: Proceedings of the Thirty-first Boston University

Conference on Language Development. Apr. 2007. Somerville, MA:

Cascadilla, 2007. Print.

> If you cite only the abstract of a dissertation, see "Abstract in an Abstracts Journal," page 259, for the correct form.

Dissertation, Published

Wu, Zhaohong. *Automated Optimal Design of Dynamic Systems*. Diss. U

Texas at Austin, 2007. Austin: U Texas, 2007. Print.

Dissertation, Unpublished

Patel-McCune, Santha. "An Analysis of Homophone Errors in the Writing

of 7th Grade Language Arts Students: Implications for Middle

School Teachers." Diss. Southern Tech. U, 2008. Print.

Film, Videocassette, or DVD

Cite the title of a film, the director, the distributor, and the year.

Harry Potter and the Half-Blood Prince. Dir. David Yates. Warner Bros.

Video, 2008. DVD.

If relevant to your study, add the names of performers, writers, or producers after the name of the director.

Juno. Dir. Jason Reitman. Screenplay by Diablo Cody. Newmarket, 2008. DVD.

If the film is a DVD, videocassette, filmstrip, slide program, or videodisc, add the type of publication medium after the date. You can also add the date of the original film, if relevant.

Crimmins, Morton. "Robert Lowell—American Poet." Lecture. Western

State U, 2007. Videocassette.

Citizen Kane. Dir. Orson Welles. 1941. Warner, 2002. DVD.

If you are citing the accomplishments of the director or a performer, begin the citation with that person's name.

Caird, John, and Gavin Taylor, dir. *Les Miserables.* 1995. Perf. Colm

Wilkinson, Philip Quast, Ruthie Henshall, and Jenny Galloway.

BBC, 2008. DVD.

If you cannot find certain information, such as the original date of the film, cite what is available.

Altman, Robert, dir. *The Room.* Perf. Julian Sands, Linda Hunt, and

Annie Lennox. Prism. Videocassette.

Interview, Unpublished

See also "Interview, Published," page 260, and "Broadcast Interview," page 275.

For an interview that you conduct, name the person interviewed, the type of interview (e.g., telephone interview, personal interview, e-mail interview), and the date.

Carter, Luella. "Growing Georgia Greens." Personal interview. 5 Mar. 2008.

Letter, Personal

Knight, Charles. Letter to the author. 21 Oct. 2008. MS.

Letter, Published

Eisenhower, Dwight. "Letter to Richard Nixon." 20 April 1968. *Memoirs*

of Richard Nixon. By Richard Nixon. New York: Grosset, 1978.

Print.

Loose-Leaf Collections

If you cite an article from *SIRS, Opposing Viewpoints*, or other loose-leaf collections, provide both the original publication data and then add information for the loose-leaf volume, as shown in this next example:

Teicher Khadaroo, Stacy. "Suicide Prevention Program Focuses on

Teens." *Christian Science Monitor* 3 Jan. 2008: n.p. Print. Boca

Raton: SIRS, 2008. Art. 24.

Krasney, Ben. *City Crime Rankings: Crime in Metropolitan America.* 14th

ed. *CQ Researcher* 18 Nov. 2007: 416. Washington, DC: CQ Press,

2007. Print.

Manuscript (MS) and Typescript (TS)

Glass, Malcolm. Journal 3, MS. Malcolm Glass Private Papers,

Clarksville, TN.

Williams, Ralph. "Walking on the Water." 2009. TS.

Map

Treat a map as you would an anonymous work, but add a descriptive label, such as *map*, *chart*, or *survey*, unless the title describes the medium.

County Boundaries and Names. United States Base Map GE-50, No. 86.

Washington, DC: GPO, 2007. Print.

Pennsylvania. Map. Chicago: Rand, 2008. Print.

Miscellaneous Materials (Program, Leaflet, Poster, Announcement)

"Earth Day." Poster. Louisville. 20 Mar. 2008. Print.

"Spring Family Weekend." Program. Nashville: Fisk U. 1 Apr. 2008.

Print.

Musical Composition

For a musical composition, begin with the composer's name, followed by a period. Italicize the title of an opera, ballet, or work of music identified by name, but do not italicize or enclose within quotation marks the form, number, and key when these are used to identify an instrumental composition.

Mozart, Wolfgang A. *Jupiter.* Symphony No. 41. London: n.p., 1999. CD.

Treat a published score as you would a book.

Legrenzi, Giovanni. *La Buscha.* Sonata for Instruments. *Historical*

Anthology of Music. Ed. Archibald T. Davison and Willi Apel.

Cambridge, MA: Harvard UP, 1950. 70–76. Print.

Pamphlet

Treat a pamphlet as you would a book.

Federal Reserve Board. *Consumer Handbook to Credit Protection Laws.*

Washington, DC: GPO, 2007. Print.

Westinghouse Advanced Power Systems. *Nuclear Waste Management: A*

Manageable Task. Madison, PA: Author, n.d. Print.

Performance

Treat a performance (e.g., play, opera, ballet, or concert) as you would a film, but include the site (normally the theater and city) and the date of the performance.

Oklahoma Statehood: A Cherokee Perspective. Cherokee Heritage Center,
Tahlequah, OK. 12 Apr. 2008. Performance.

Macbeth. By William Shakespeare. Folger Elizabethan Theatre,
Washington, D.C.: 29 Mar. 2008. Performance.

If your text emphasizes the work of a particular individual, begin with the
appropriate name.

Szymanski, Natalie, Connie Sirois, Rachel Breneman, and Tom
Thompson. "Developing Relevant and Responsible Writing
Instruction." Conf. on Coll. Composition and Communication
Convention. Hilton Riverside, New Orleans, 3 Apr. 2008.
Address.

Ebersole, Christine, and Billy Stritch. "American Songbook." The Allen
Room, New York. 29 Feb. 2008. Address.

Essman, Susie, comedian. Zanies, Chicago. 20 Mar. 2008. Address.

Public Address or Lecture

Identify the nature of the address (e.g., Lecture, Reading), include the site
(normally the lecture hall and city), and the date of the performance.

Holl, Scott. "Taking Your Ancestors to Church: Finding Clues in
Ecclesiastical Records." St. Louis Genealogical Soc., St. Louis. 1
Mar. 2008. Address.

Recording on Record, Tape, or Disk

If you are not citing a compact disc, indicate the medium (e.g., audiocassette, audiotape [reel-to-reel tape], or LP [long-playing record]).

"Chaucer: The Nun's Priest's Tale." *Canterbury Tales.* Narr. in Middle
English by Alex Edmonds. London, 2005. Audiocassette.

Dylan, Bob. "The Times They Are A-Changin'." *Bob Dylan's Greatest Hits.*
CBS, 1967. CD.

Reich, Robert B. *Locked in the Cabinet: A Political Memoir.* 4
audiocassettes abridged. New York: Random Audio, 1997.
Audiocassette.

Hancock, Herbie "Both Sides Now." *River: The Joni Letters.* n.p.: Verve,
2007. CD.

Do not underscore, italicize, or enclose within quotation marks a private
recording or tape. However, you should include the date, if available, as well
as the location and the identifying number.

Drake, Marc. Early Settlers of the Smokey Mountains. Rec. Feb. 2007. U

of Knoxville. Knoxville, TN. UTF.34.82. Audiotape.

Cite a libretto, liner notes, or booklet that accompanies a recording in the form shown in the following example.

Crow, Sheryl. Booklet. *Detours*. By Sheryl Crow. A&M, 2008. Print.

Report

Unbound reports are placed within quotation marks; bound reports are treated as books.

McGruder Dynamics. *2008 Annual Report.* Atlanta: McGruder, 2008. Print.

Franco, Lynn. "Confidence Slips Amid Fragile Economy." The Conference

Board. New York: CBS/Broadcast Group, 23 Jan. 2006. Print.

Reproductions, Photographs, and Photocopies

Blake, William. *Comus*. Plate 4. "Blake's *Comus* Designs." *Blake Studies*

4 (Spring 1972): 61. Print.

Michener, James A. "Structure of Earth at Centennial, Colorado." Line

drawing in *Centennial*. By Michener. New York: Random, 1974. 26.

Print.

Table, Illustration, Chart, or Graph

Tables or illustrations of any kind published within works need a detailed label (chart, table, figure, photograph, and so on).

"Communication Strategies Used by New Language Learners." Figure.

English Journal 97.3 (Jan. 2008): 23. Print.

Alphabet. Chart. Columbus: Scholastic, 2008. Print.

Television or Radio Program

If available or relevant, provide information in this order: the episode (in quotation marks), the title of the program (italicized), title of the series (not italicized nor in quotation marks), name of the network, call letters and city of the local station, and the broadcast date. Add other information (such as narrator) after the episode or program narrated or directed or performed. Place the number of episodes, if relevant, before the title of the series.

"Border Security and Immigration Security." Host: Brian Lamb.

Washington Journal. C-SPAN. 22 Feb 2006. Television.

"Elton John." *Larry King Live*. Host Larry King. CNN. 25 Feb. 2008.

Television.

Pride and Prejudice. By Jane Austin. 3 episodes. Masterpiece

Theatre. Introd. Russell Baker. NPT, Nashville. 3 Feb. 2008.

Television.

Thesis

See "Dissertation, Unpublished," page 276.

Transparency

Sharp, La Vaughn, and William E. Loeche. *The Patient and Circulatory*

Disorders: A Guide for Instructors. 54 transparencies, 99 overlays.

Philadelphia: Lorrenzo, 2005. Print.

Unpublished Paper

Schuler, Wren. "Prufrock and His Cat." Unpublished essay, 2008. Print."

For more resources in research,
writing, and documentation, go to
MyCompLab.com

15 Writing in APA Style

Your instructor may require you to write the research paper in APA style, which is governed by *The Publication Manual of the American Psychological Association*, 5th edition, 2001. This style has gained wide acceptance in the social sciences, and versions similar to it are used in the biological sciences, business, and earth sciences. Research is paramount in the sciences; in fact, the APA style guide says, "No amount of skill in writing can disguise research that is poorly designed or managed." Thus, you will need to execute your project with precision.

15a Writing Theory, Reporting Test Results, or Reviewing Literature

In the sciences, you may choose between three types of articles, or your instructor will specify one of these:

- Theoretical articles
- Reports of empirical studies
- Review articles

Theoretical Article

For a sample theoretical article, see the student paper on pages 302–309, which examines the trend of eliminating recess in elementary schools to gain more instructional time.

The theoretical article draws on existing research to examine a topic. This is the type of paper you will most likely write as a first-year or second-year student. You will need to trace the development of a theory or compare theories by examining the literature to arrive at the current thinking about topics such as autism, criminal behavior, dysfunctional families, and learning disorders. The theoretical article generally accomplishes four aims:

1. Identifies a problem or hypothesis that has historical implications in the scientific community.
2. Traces the development and history of the evolution of the theory.
3. Provides a systematic analysis of the articles that have explored the problem.
4. Arrives at a judgment and discussion of the prevailing theory.

282

Report of an Empirical Study

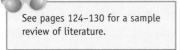

For additional details about field research, consult Chapter 6, pages 84–93.

When you conduct field research and perform laboratory testing, you must report the details of your original research. The empirical report accomplishes these four purposes:

1. Introduces the problem or hypothesis investigated and explains the purpose of the work.
2. Describes the method used to conduct the research.
3. Reports the results and the basic findings.
4. Discusses, interprets, and explores the implications of the findings.

You will need to work closely with your instructor to accomplish each of these stages.

Review Article

See pages 124–130 for a sample review of literature.

You may be required to write a critical evaluation of a published article, a book, or a set of articles on a common topic. The purpose is to examine the state of current research—and, in some cases, to determine if additional work might be in order. A review article sets out to accomplish several goals:

1. Define a problem or issue that is the subject of discussion.
2. Summarize the article(s) or book(s) under review.
3. Analyze the literature to discover strengths, weaknesses, or inconsistencies in the research.
4. Recommend additional research that might grow logically from the work under review.

15b Writing in the Proper Tense for an APA Paper

Verb tense is an indicator that distinguishes papers in the humanities from those in the natural and social sciences. MLA style, as shown in previous chapters, requires you to use present tense when you refer to a cited work ("Jeffries *stipulates*" or "the work of Mills and Maguire *shows*"). In contrast, APA style requires you to use past tense or present perfect tense ("Jeffries *stipulated*" or "the work of Mills and Maguire *has demonstrated*"). The APA style does require present tense when you discuss the results (e.g., "*the results confirm*" or "*the study indicates*") and when you mention established knowledge (e.g., "*the therapy offers some hope*" or "*salt contributes to hypertension*"). The following paragraphs, side by side, show the differences in verb tenses for MLA and APA styles.

MLA style:	APA style:
The scholarly issue at work here is the construction of reality. Cohen, Adoni, and Bantz label the construction a social process "in which human beings act both as the creators and products of the social world" (34). These writers identify three categories (34–35).	The scholarly issue at work here is the construction of reality. Cohen, Adoni, and Bantz (2008) labeled the construction a social process "in which human beings act both as the creators and products of the social world" (p. 34). These writers have identified three categories.

APA style, shown on the right, requires that you use the present tense for generalizations and references to stable conditions, but it requires the present perfect tense or the past tense for sources cited (e.g., the sources *have tested* a hypothesis or the sources *reported* the results of a test). This next sentence uses tense correctly for APA style:

> The danger of steroid use exists for every age group, even youngsters. Lloyd and Mercer (2009) reported on six incidents of liver damage to 14-year-old swimmers who used steroids.

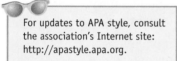

For updates to APA style, consult the association's Internet site: http://apastyle.apa.org.

As shown in this example, use the present tense (*exists*) for established knowledge and the present perfect (*has reported*) or the past tense (*reported*) for a citation.

15c Using In-Text Citations in APA Style

APA style uses the following conventions for in-text citations:

- Cites last names only.
- Cites the year, within parentheses, immediately after the name of the author. Include only the year in the text citation even if the reference includes a month.
- Cites page numbers with a direct quotation but not with a paraphrase.
- Uses "p." or "pp." before page numbers.

Citing Last Name Only and the Year of Publication

An in-text citation in APA style requires the last name of the author and the year of publication.

> Nguyen (2008) has advanced the idea of combining the social sciences and mathematics to chart human behavior.

If you do not use the author's name in your text, place the name(s) within the parenthetical citation.

One study has advanced the idea of combining the social sciences and mathematics to chart human behavior (Nguyen, 2008).

Providing a Page Number

If you quote the exact words of a source, provide a page number and use "p." or "pp." Place the page number in one of two places: after the year (2008, p. B4) or at the end of the quotation.

Nguyen (2008) has advanced the idea of "soft mathematics," which is the practice of "applying mathematics to study people's behavior" (p. B4).

Citing a Block of Material

Present a quotation of forty words or more as a separate block, indented five spaces or ½ inch from the left margin. (*Note*: MLA style uses ten spaces or one inch). Because it is set off from the text in a distinctive block, do not enclose it with quotation marks. Do not indent the first line an extra five spaces; however, *do* indent the first line of any additional paragraphs that appear in the block an extra five spaces—that is, ten spaces from the left margin. Set parenthetical citations outside the last period.

Albert (2009) reported the following:

Whenever these pathogenic organisms attack the human body and begin to multiply, the infection is set in motion. The host responds to this parasitic invasion with efforts to cleanse itself of the invading agents. When rejection efforts of the host become visible (fever, sneezing, congestion), the disease status exists. (pp. 314–315)

Citing a Work with More Than One Author

When one work has two or more authors, use *and* in the text but use *&* in the citation.

Werner and Throckmorton (2008) offered statistics on the toxic levels of water samples from six rivers.

but

It has been reported (Werner & Throckmorton, 2008) that toxic levels exceeded the maximum allowed each year since 1983.

For three to five authors, name them all in the first entry (e.g., Torgerson, Andrews, Smith, Lawrence, & Dunlap, 2007), but thereafter use "et al." (e.g.,

Torgerson et al., 2007). For six or more authors, employ "et al." in the first and in all subsequent instances (e.g., Fredericks et al., 2008).

Citing More Than One Work by an Author

Use lowercase letters (a, b, c) to identify two or more works published in the same year by the same author—for example, (Thompson, 2008a) and (Thompson, 2008b). Then use "2008a" and "2008b" in your List of References (see page 292 for examples). If necessary, specify additional information:

> Horton (2006; cf. Thomas, 2008a, p. 89, and 2008b, p. 426)
> suggested an intercorrelation of these testing devices, but after
> multiple-group analysis, Welston (2008, esp. p. 211) reached an
> opposite conclusion.

Citing Indirect Sources

Use a double reference to cite a person who has been quoted in a book or article—that is, use the original author(s) in the text and cite your source for the information in the parenthetical citation.

> In other research, Massie and Rosenthal (2007) studied home
> movies of children diagnosed with autism, but determining criteria was
> difficult due to the differences in quality and dating of the available
> videotapes (cited in Osterling & Dawson, 2008, p. 248).

Citing from a Textbook or Anthology

If you make an in-text citation to an article or chapter of a textbook, casebook, or anthology, use the in-text citation to refer only to the person(s) you cite:

> One writer stressed that two out of every three new jobs in this
> decade will go to women (Ogburn 2008).

The list of references will clarify the nature of this reference to Ogburn (see page 293).

Citing Classical Works

If an ancient work has no date of publication, cite the author's name followed by n.d. within parentheses.

> Seeing psychic emotions as . . . (Sophocles, n.d.).

Cite the year of any translation you have used, preceded by *trans.*, and give the date of the version used, followed by *version*.

Plato (trans. 1963) offered a morality that . . .

Plato's *Phaedrus* (1982 version) explored . . .

If you know the original date of publication, include it before the date of the translation or version you have used.

In his "Poetics," Aristotle (350 B.C.E.) viewed the structure of the plot as a requisite to a good poem.

Note: Entries on your References page need not cite major classical works and the Bible. Therefore, identify in your text the version used and the book, chapter, line, verse, or canto.

In Exodus 24:3-4 Moses erects an altar and "twelve pillars according to the twelve tribes of Israel" (King James version).

The Epic of Gilgamesh shows, in part, the search for everlasting life (Part 4).

In the Iliad, Homer takes great efforts in describing the shield of Achilles (18:558-709).

Abbreviating Corporate Authors in the Text

The names of groups that serve as authors, such as corporations, associations, and government agencies, are usually spelled out each time they appear. The names of some corporate authors may be abbreviated after a first, full reference:

One source questioned the results of the use of aspirin for arthritis treatment in children (American Medical Association [AMA], 2009).

Thereafter, refer to the corporate author by initials: (AMA, 2009). It is important to give enough information in the text citation for the reader to locate the entry in the reference list without difficulty.

Citing a Work with No Author

When a work has no author listed, cite the title as part of the in-text citation (or use the first few words of the material).

The cost per individual student has continued to rise rapidly ("Tuition Crises," 2008, p. B-3).

Citing Personal Communications

E-mail, telephone conversations, memos, and conversations do not provide recoverable data, so APA style excludes them from the list of references. Consequently, you should cite personal communications in the text only. In so doing, give the initials as well as the last name of the source, provide the date, and briefly describe the nature of the communication.

> M. Gaither (personal communication, August 24, 2008) described the symptoms of Wilson's disease.

Citing Internet Sources in Your Text

In 2007, APA published the *APA Style Guide to Electronic References*, updating the clarifying citation guidelines for electronic sources. The 2007 update includes a number of significant changes from the 2001 APA style guide. The examples and guidance offered here reflect these 2007 updates. In general, citations for electronic sources include the same basic information as for print sources, with the following qualifications.

Omit a page or paragraph number.   The marvelous feature of electronic text is that it is searchable, so your readers can find your quotation quickly with the Find feature. Suppose you have written the following:

> The Internet Report presented by the University of South Carolina (2009) advised policy makers with "a better understanding of the impact the Internet is having in our society."

A reader who wants to investigate further will find your complete citation, including the Internet address of the article, in your References list. After finding the article via a browser (e.g., Safari or Internet Explorer), the investigator can press Edit, then Find, and type in a key phrase, such as *better understanding of the impact.* The software will immediately move the cursor to the passage shown above. That is much easier than counting through forty-six paragraphs.

Provide a paragraph number.   Some scholars who write on the Internet number their paragraphs. Therefore, if you find an online article that has numbered paragraphs, by all means supply that information in your citation.

> The Insurance Institute for Highway Safety (2008) has emphasized restraint first, and said, "A federal rule requiring special attachments to anchor infant and child restraints in vehicles is making installation easier, but not all child restraints fit easily in all vehicles" (par. 1).

> Recommendations for treating non-insulin-dependent diabetes mellitus (NIDDM), the most common type of diabetes, include a diet that is rich in carbohydrates, "predominantly from whole grains, fruit, vegetables, and low-fat milk" (Yang, 2007, par. 3).

Provide a page number.   In a few instances, you will find page numbers buried within brackets here and there throughout an article. These refer to the page numbers of the printed version of the document. In these cases, you should cite the page just as you would a printed source. Here is the Internet source with the page numbers buried within the text to signal the break between page 17 and page 18:

> What is required is a careful reading of Chekhov's subtext, that elusive [pp17–18] literature that lingers in psychological nuances of the words, not the exact words themselves.—Ward

The page number may be included in the citation:

> One source argued the merits of Chekhov's subtext and its "psychological nuances of the words" (Ward, 2007, p. 18).

World Wide Web Sites

Internet article

> Commenting on the distinction between a Congressional calendar day and a legislative day, Dove (2008) stated that "a legislative day is the period of time following an adjournment of the Senate until another adjournment."

> "Reports of abuses in the interrogation of suspected terrorists raise the question of how—or whether—we should limit the interrogation of a suspected terrorist when our national security may be at stake" (Parry & White, 2008, abstract).

Online newspaper article

> Ochberg (2008) commented on the use of algae in paper that "initially has a green tint to it, but unlike bleached paper which turns yellow with age, this algae paper becomes whiter with age."

Online magazine

> *BusinessWeek Online* (2008) reported that the idea of peer-to-peer computing is a precursor to new Web applications.

Government document

> The Web site *Thomas* (2008) has outlined the amendments to the *American Energy Independence and Security Act of 2008,* which calls for

all the federal revenues from oil production to fund many forms of
alternative energy and the programs that help Americans deal with
high energy and food prices.

Other Electronic Sources

E-mail

The Publication Manual of the American Psychological Association
stipulates that personal communications, which others cannot retrieve,
should be cited in the text only and not mentioned at all in the bibliography.

One technical writing instructor (March 8, 2008) has bemoaned
the inability of hardware developers to maintain pace with the
ingenuity of software developers. In his e-mail message, he indicated
that educational institutions cannot keep pace with the hardware
developers. Thus, "students nationwide suffer with antiquated
equipment, even though it's only a few years old"
(dplattner@cscc.edu).

Electronic mailing list posting

Listserv groups have gained legitimacy in recent years, so in your text you
might wish to give an exact date and provide the e-mail address *only* if the
citation has scholarly relevance and *only* if the list has an academic sponsor,
such as an instructor of an online class.

R. D. Brackett (online discussion, May 7, 2008) has identified the
book *Echoes of Glory* for those interested in detailed battlefield maps
of the American Civil War.

A. G. Funder (January 5, 2009) argued against the "judgmental
process."

FTP sites

Patel (2007) has shown in the following graph that "enrollment in
radiology programs of study has increased by 67% in the past ten years."

CD-ROM

Grolier's Multimedia Encyclopedia (2008) explained that in recent
decades huge swaths of the rain forest have been toppled; as the trees
disappeared, so, too, did the flora and fauna that thrived under their canopy.

15d Preparing the List of References

Use the title *References* for your bibliography page. Like the body of the paper, your reference list should be double-spaced throughout. Alphabetize the entries letter by letter—remembering, for example, that Adkins, Y. R., precedes Adkinson, A. G., even though *o* precedes the *y* for the first entry. Every reference used in your text, except personal communications and major classical

---

Index to Bibliographic Models: APA Style

(continued on page 292)

(continued from page 291)

Bulletin 298	Symposium, Report 299
Government Document 298	Usenet, Telnet, FTP, Message 299
Message Posted to an Online Discussion Group or Forum 298	Article from a Library Database 299
Message Posted to an Electronic Mailing List 298	**CD-ROM**
Newsgroup, Message 298	Abstract 299
Virtual Conference, Report 298	Encyclopedia Article 300
	Full-Text Article 300

works, should appear in your alphabetical list of references at the end of the paper. Type the first line of each entry flush left and indent succeeding lines five spaces. Italicize names of books, periodicals, and volume numbers. Underline the punctuation mark at the end of names and volume numbers.

Book

> Walsh, J. (2008). *Libertarian nation: The call for a new agenda.*
>
> Aberdeen, WA: Silver Lake.

List the author (surname first and then initials for given names), year of publication within parentheses, title of the book italicized and with only first word of the title and any subtitle capitalized (but do capitalize proper nouns), place of publication, and publisher. In the publisher's name omit the words *Publishing, Company*, and *Inc.*, but otherwise give a full name: Florida State University Press; Addison, Wesley, Longman; HarperCollins.

List chronologically, not alphabetically, two or more works by the same author—for example, Fitzgerald's 2007 publication would precede the 2008 publication.

> Fitzgerald, R. A. (2007). Crimson glow . . .
>
> Fitzgerald, R. A. (2008). Walking . . .

References with the same author in the same year are alphabetized and marked with lowercase letters—*a, b, c*—immediately after the date:

> Craighead, T. B. (2009a). Marketing trends . . .
>
> Craighead, T. B. (2009b). Maximizing sales . . .

Entries of a single author precede multiple-author entries beginning with the same surname without regard for the dates:

Watson, S. M. (2007). Principles . . .

Watson, S. M., & Wheaton, A. F. (2008). Crimes . . .

References with the same first author and different second or third authors should be alphabetized by the surname of the second author:

Bacon, D. E., & Smithson, C. A. (2007). Arctic explorers . . .

Bacon, D. E., & Williamson, T. (2008). Seasons in . . .

If, *and only if*, the work is signed *Anonymous*, the entry begins with the word *Anonymous* spelled out, and the entry is alphabetized as if *Anonymous* were a true name. If no author is given, the title moves to the author position, and the entry is alphabetized by the first significant word of the title.

Part of a Book

List author(s), date, chapter or section title, editor (with name in normal order) preceded by "In" and followed by "(Ed.)" or "(Eds.)," the name of the book, (italicized), page numbers to the specific section of the book cited (placed within parentheses), place of publication, and publisher.

Litt, T. (2007). The monster. In Z. Smith (Ed.) *The book of other people* (pp. 133–138). New York: Penguin.

If no author is listed, begin with the title of the article.

Mount of Olives. (2008). *Essential visual history of the Bible.*
Washington, DC: National Geographic.

Encyclopedia or Dictionary

Fitch, P. T. Escrow. (2006). *Dictionary of banking terms* (5th ed.). New
York: Barrons.

Moran, J. M. (2008). Weather. *World book encyclopedia* (2008 ed., Vol.
21, pp. 156–171). Chicago, World Book.

Book with Corporate Author

American Medical Association. (2008). *American Medical Association complete medical encyclopedia.* New York: Random House.

Periodical
Journal

List author(s), year, title of the article without quotation marks and with only the first word (and any proper nouns) capitalized, name of the journal italicized and with all major words capitalized, volume number italicized, inclusive page numbers *not* preceded by "p." or "pp."

> Barot, R. (2008). The body project: Notes on Carl Phillips. *Pleindes, 28(1)*, 90–103.

Article Retrieved from Database

You do not need to include the database name or retrieval date for most common databases.

> Peekhaus, W. (2007). Privacy for sale—business as usual in the 21st century: An economic and normative critique. *Journal of Information Ethics, 16*, 83–98.

Magazine

List author, the date of publication—year, month without abbreviation, and the specific day for magazines published weekly and fortnightly (every two weeks)—title of the article without quotation marks and with only the first word capitalized, name of the magazine in italics with all major words capitalized, the volume number if it is readily available, and inclusive page numbers if you do not provide the volume number. If a magazine prints the article on discontinuous pages, include all page numbers.

> Kokmen, L. (2008, March/April). Environmental justice for all. *Utne*, 42–46.
>
> Townsend, S., & Evans, K. (2008, March/April). Minga: The communal work tradition of Bolivia. *Native People's Arts and Lifeways*, 48–51.

Newspaper

List author, date (year, month, and day), title of article with only first word and proper nouns capitalized, complete name of newspaper in initial capitals and italicized, and the section with all discontinuous page numbers.

> Manasso, T. G. (2008, April 7). Lands of waste and debt. *Barron's*, 46.

Abstract
Abstract as the Cited Source

> Hendriks, A. J., & Mulder, C. (2008, April). Scaling of offspring number and mass to plant and animal size: Model and meta-analysis [Abstract]. *Oecologia, 155*, 705–716.

Abstract of an Unpublished Work

> Darma, J. (2008). *Political institutions under dictatorship* [Abstract]. Unpublished manuscript, Knoxville: University of Tennessee.

Review

Archambeau, R. (2008) A portrait of Reginald Shepherd as Philoctetes. [rev. article]. *Pleiades, 28, The New England Journal of Medicine, 354,* 731–739.

Report

Gorman, L. (2008). Reporting insurance fraud (No. 2008–2). Hartford, CT: Insurance Institute.

Nonprint Material
Computer Program

Microsoft Office 2007 Excel. (2007). [Computer program]. Redmond, WA: Microsoft.

DVD, Videotape, Film

Edwards, B. (Director). (1961). *Breakfast at Tiffany's* [DVD]. Hollywood, CA: Paramount.

Interviews, Letters, and Memos

Barstow, I. (2008, May 22). "Palm reading as prediction" [Interview]. Chattanooga, TN.

Unpublished Raw Data from a Study, Untitled Work

Barstow, I. (2008, May 22). "Homophone errors in essays of 100 9th grade writers" [Unpublished raw data]. Emporia, KS.

Internet Sources

The following information conforms to the 2007 APA Style Guide to Electronic References. When citing electronic sources in your APA references, include the following information if available:

1. Author/editor last name, followed by a comma, the initials, and a period.
2. Year of publication, followed by a comma, then month and day for magazines and newspapers, within parentheses, followed by a period.
3. Title of the article, not within quotations and not underscored, with the first word and proper nouns capitalized, followed by the total number of paragraphs within brackets only if that information is provided. *Note*: You need not count the paragraphs yourself; in fact, it's better that you don't. This is also the place to describe the work within brackets, as with [Abstract] or [Letter to the editor].
4. Name of the book, journal, or complete work, italicized, if one is listed.
5. Volume number, if listed, italicized.

6. Page numbers only if you have that data from a printed version of the journal or magazine. If the periodical has no volume number, use "p." or "pp." before the numbers; if the journal has a volume number, omit "p." or "pp.").

7. For undated or in-press sources only, include the word *Retrieved*, followed by the date you accessed the source.

8. The DOI (digital object identifier), or URL if a DOI is not available. Line breaks in URLs should come *before slashes* or other punctuation marks.

Web Sites

Article from an Online Journal

Hudson, R. G. (2007). The empirical basis to skepticism. *Minerva: An Internet Journal of Philosophy*. Retrieved September 22, 2008, from http://www.mic.ul.ie/stephen/vol11/Skepticism.html

Article with DOI Assigned

Cole, N. D. (2004). Gender differences in perceived disciplinary fairness. *Gender, Work and Organization, 11(3)*, 254–279. doi: 10.1111/j.1468-0432.2004.00231.x

Article from a Printed Journal, Reproduced Online

Haug, M. C. (2007). Of mice and metaphysics: Natural selection and realized population-level properties *Philosophy of Science, 74*, 431–51.

Add the URL if page numbers are not indicated, as shown in the following entry:

Fluchel, R. W. (2006). For feet that never leave asphalt. *Missouri Conservationist, 67(2)*. Retrieved from http://mdc.mo.gov /conmag/2006/02/10.htm

Article from an Internet-Only Newsletter

Pyke, B. (2008). The e-health revolution: Interview with professor Peter Yellowlees. *Telehealth News.* Retrieved from http://www .telehealth.net/interviews/yellowlees.html

Document Created by a Private Organization, No Date

Internet Engineering Task Force. (n.d.). *Active IETF Working Groups*. Retrieved from http://www.ietf.org/html.charters/wg-dir.html

Chapter or Section in an Internet Document

Benton Foundation. (2008). *Getting to February 2009: Implementing the digital TV transition* (sec. 1). Retrieved from http://www.benton.org/index.php?q_node/1257

Standalone Document, No Author Identified, No Date

Remember to begin the reference with the title of the document if the author of the document is not identified.

Web Surveyor. (n.d.). *Learn more about surveys*. Retrieved December 2,
2008, from http://www.websurveyor.com/resources/online-survey-
resources.asp

Document from a University Program or Department

Henry, S. (2007). *Department of language and literature writing*
guidelines. Retrieved from Clayton State University, Department of
Arts & Sciences site: http://a-s.clayton.edu/langlit/guidelines
/default.html.

Report from a University, Available on a Private Organization's Web Site

University of Illinois at Chicago, Health Research and Policy Centers.
(2008). *Partners with tobacco use research centers: Advancing*
transdisciplinary science and policy studies. Retrieved from
the Robert Wood Johnson Foundation Web site: http:
//www.rwjf.org/portfolios/resources/grant.jsp?id=
039787&iaid_143

Abstract

Brown, G. G., et al. (2007). Performance of schizophrenia and bipolar
patients on verbal and figural working memory tasks [Abstract],
Journal of Abnormal Psychology, 116. Retrieved from http:
//content.apa.org/journals/abn/116/4/741.

Article from a Printed Magazine, Reproduced Online

Rowe, M. (2008, March/April). How sportswriting lost its game. *Utne.*
Retrieved from http://www.utne.com/2008-04-03/Media
/How-Sportswriting-Lost-Its-Game.aspx

Article from an Online Magazine, No Author Listed

Controlling anger—Before it controls you. (2008, May 10).
APA Online. Retrieved from http://www.apa.org/topics
/controlanger.html

Note: Avoid listing page numbers for online articles.

Article from an Online Newspaper

Tettamanti, M. (2008, February 22). Boulevard of dreams. *Miami Herald*.

Retrieved from http://www.miami.com/boulevard-of-dreams-article

Bulletin

Bulletins are brief reports and brochures, usually printed in paperback form, which you should treat as a book.

Murphy, F. L., M.D. (2008). *What you don't know can hurt you.*

Preventive Health Center. Retrieved from http://www.md-phc

.com/education/fiber.html

Government Document

U.S. Cong. House. (2008, March 4). *Internet gambling regulation and tax enforcement act of 2008.* House Resolution 5523.

Retrieved from http://thomas.loc.gov/cgi-bin

/query//D?c110:1:./temp/~c110XFedvx::

Message Posted to an Online Discussion Group or Forum

Weiser, R. (2008, April 2). Big Green Discussion Group [Archives].

Environmental Discussion Group. Retrieved from

http://www.biggreen.org/pipermail/biggrean/2008-April/008315.html

Message Posted to an Electronic Mailing List

Oskoboiny, G. (2008, February 9). Fun with wiimotes: finger/head tracking, multi-point interaction. Message posted to Fogo mailing

list, archived at http://impressive.net/archives/fogo

/20080209224511.GA20759@impressive.net

Newsgroup, Message

Clease, G. V. (2008, November 5). Narrative bibliography [Msg. 39].

Message posted to jymacmillan@mail.csu.edu

Virtual Conference, Report

A virtual conference occurs entirely online, so there is no geographic location. Treat a report as a book.

Ali, H., & Shou, J. (2006, May 18). *Microarray data analysis.* Paper

presented at the Sixth Virtual Conference on Genomics and

Bioinformatics. Retrieved from http://midas.cs.ndsu.nodak.edu
/VGAB06/overview.htm

Symposium, Report

Morrison, S. (2008, May 12). The remote worker: An instruction
manual. Paper presented at the Gartner Symposium ITxpo,
Barcelona, Spain. Abstract retrieved from http:
//www.gartner.com/spr9/WebPages/SessionDetail.aspx?
EventSessionld=785

Usenet, Telnet, FTP, Message

Haas, H. (2008, August 5) Link checker that works with cold fusion
[Msg. 34]. Message posted to impressive.net/archives/fogo
/200000805113615.AI4381@w3.org

Article from a Library Database

University libraries, as well as public libraries, feature servers that supply articles in large databases, such as PsycInfo, ERIC, Academic Search Premiere, and others. For most common databases, APA no longer requires the database name as part of the citation.

America's children: Key national indicators of well-being. (2007).
Federal Interagency Forum on Child and Family Statistics.
Retrieved from ERIC database (ED427897).

Tavares, R., & Hogan, J. (2008, Winter). Fundamental foundations:
One-room school houses on the American plains. *Journal of
Social Foundations, 85,* 41.

CD-ROM

Material cited from a CD-ROM requires different forms.

Abstract

Nagorra, N., et al. (2005). Light levels and the presence of vision
phenotypes of primate species [CD-ROM]. *Journal of Sociobiology,
14,* 353–79. Abstract from Silverplatter File: PsychLIT item:
94-5458.

Encyclopedia Article

African American history: Abolitionist movement [CD-ROM]. (2008).

> *Encarta encyclopedia.* Redmond, WA: Microsoft.

Full-Text Article

Spence, D. (2008, August 10). Bible belt resistance and acceptance of

> alternative lifestyles in religion [CD-ROM]. *Red River Messenger.*

> p. A-11. Article from UMI ProQuest file (Item 5602–109).

15e Formatting an APA Paper

APA style applies to three types of papers: theoretical articles, reports of empirical studies, and review articles (as explained in section 15a). Each requires a different arrangement of the various parts of the paper.

Theoretical Paper

The theoretical paper should be arranged much like a typical research paper, with the additional use of centered side heads and italicized side heads to divide the sections.

The introduction should:

- Establish the problem under examination.
- Discuss its significance to the scientific community.
- Provide a review of the literature (see pages 124–130 for more information).
- Quote the experts who have commented on the issue.
- Provide a thesis sentence that gives your initial perspective on the issue.

The body of the theoretical paper should:

- Trace the various issues.
- Establish a past-to-present perspective.
- Compare and analyze the various aspects of the theories.
- Cite extensively from the literature on the subject.

The conclusion of the theoretical paper should:

- Defend one theory as it grows from the evidence in the body.
- Discuss the implications of the theory.
- Suggest additional work that might be launched in this area.

Report of Empirical Research

The general design of a report of original research, an empirical study, should conform to the following general plan.

The introduction should:

- Establish the problem or topic to be examined.
- Provide background information, including a review of literature on the subject.
- Give the purpose and rationale for the study, including the hypothesis that serves as the motivation for the experiment.

The body of the report of empirical research should:

- Provide a methods section for explaining the design of the study with respect to subjects, apparatus, and procedure.
- Offer a results section for listing in detail the statistical findings of the study.

The conclusion of a report of empirical research should:

- Interpret the results and discuss the implications of the findings in relation to the hypothesis and to other research on the subject.

Review Article

The review article is usually a shorter paper because it examines a published work or two without extensive research on the part of the review writer.

The introduction of the review should:

- Identify the problem or subject under study and its significance.
- Summarize the article(s) under review.

The body of the review should:

- Provide a systematic analysis of the article(s), the findings, and the apparent significance of the results.

The conclusion of the review should:

- Discuss the implications of the findings and make judgments as appropriate.

15f Writing the Abstract

You should provide an abstract with every paper written in APA style. An abstract is a quick but thorough summary of the contents of your paper. It is read first and may be the only part read, so it must be:

1. *Accurate*, in order to reflect both the purpose and content of the paper.
2. *Self-contained*, so that it (1) explains the precise problem and defines terminology, (2) describes briefly both the methods used and the findings, and (3) gives an overview of your conclusions—but see item 4 following.

3. *Concise and specific*, in order to remain within a range of 80 to 150 words.
4. *Nonevaluative*, in order to report information, not to appraise or assess the value of the work.
5. *Coherent and readable*, in a style that uses an active, vigorous syntax and that uses the present tense to describe results (e.g., the findings confirm) but the past tense to describe testing procedures (e.g., I attempted to identify).

For theoretical papers, the abstract should include:

- The topic in one sentence, if possible
- The purpose, thesis, and scope of the paper
- A brief reference to the sources used (e.g., published articles, books, personal observation)
- Your conclusions and the implications of the study

For a report of an empirical study (see also 6e, pages 91–92), the abstract should include the four items listed above for theoretrical papers, plus three more:

- The problem and hypothesis in one sentence if possible
- A description of the subjects (e.g., species, number, age, type)
- The method of study, including procedures and apparatus

15g Sample Paper in APA Style

The following paper demonstrates the format and style of a paper written to the standards of APA style. The paper requires a title page that establishes the running head, an abstract, in-text citations to name and year of each source used, and a list of references. Marginal notations explain specific requirements.

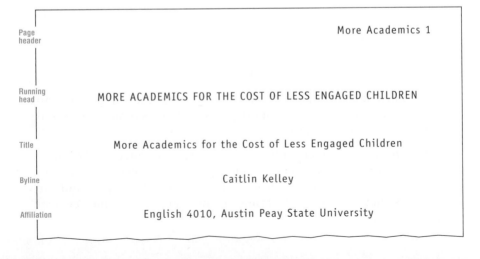

Page header   More Academics 1

Running head   MORE ACADEMICS FOR THE COST OF LESS ENGAGED CHILDREN

Title   More Academics for the Cost of Less Engaged Children

Byline   Caitlin Kelley

Affiliation   English 4010, Austin Peay State University

Abstract

The elimination of elementary school recess periods was investigated to examine the theoretical implications of depriving learners of these important mental and physical stimuli. The goal was to determine the effect of the modern trend to use recess time for longer academic periods. The social and psychological implications were determined by an examination of the literature, including comments from educational leaders. Results are mixed, as the end result of an increased emphasis on standardized testing will not be realized for several years. The social implications affect the mental and physical lives of school-aged children who are learning less about cooperation with their peers and more about remaining stagnant with little activity for lengthy periods of time.

The abstract provides a quick but thorough summary of the contents of your paper.

Caitlin Kelley
Professor Girdner
English 401
March 8, 2008

More Academics for the Cost of Less Engaged Children

Everyone remembers the days out on the playground when "you got skinned knees and bruises and sand in your eyes" (DeGregory, 2005). Growing up in the 1990s I remember the days when classes walked to the cafeteria for lunch, and students could sit next to whomever they wanted. When they were finished, they were free to play outside for 30 to 40 minutes on the playground. However, times are changing, and so are the rules. Not all school children have the luxury of free play on the hard top.

Establish the topic along with social and/or psychological issues that will be examined.

More Academics 4

In Pinellas County, Florida, in an elementary school of 800
students, one boy did not know what recess was. For a class

A theoretical study depends heavily on the literature, which must be cited correctly in APA form.

newspaper, this first grade student wrote that his favorite day to
have gym class was Friday because the children were allowed "Open
Court" because they were allowed to play whatever they wanted
without the instruction of the teacher. Lane DeGregory (2005), the
journalist who wrote the article, mentioned, "It sounds just like
recess. He's 7 years old and he doesn't know what recess is."
Because this elementary school does not have recess, the children
in Pinellas County only have 25 minutes every Friday to play with
one another, explore and make their own rules to games. However,
this school is not alone; according to Education World, "40 percent
of schools in the United States have cut recess or are considering
dropping it" (Poynter, 2008).

The question is why are nearly half of the elementary schools
around the country dropping free play and expression from the daily
lives of young children? The two prevailing reasons are that
eliminating free play reduces the risk of accidents and by eliminating
recess, students have more time in their day for academics, mostly
reading and math (Svensen, 2008). Contradicting these arguments are
mostly parents and doctors who feel that "recess provides children
with the opportunity to develop friendships, negotiate relationships
and build positive connections" (DeGregory, 2005). The elimination
and reduction of recess in elementary schools to allow more time
for academics is detrimental to the student's mental and physical
well-being.

Posing a question in the paper helps to re-emphasize the thesis.

So who is to say what is best for the children? The process of
eliminating or limiting recess is the decision of the principal of the
elementary school. According to Greg Toppo (2007, p. 1-A), "the
principal of each school respectively decides whether his or her
children need that extra time for play, or whether it would be better
spent on academics."

According to Patti Caplan, spokeswoman for the Howard County schools in Washington, DC, principals stated, "shortening recess by five minutes daily provides 25 minutes of additional instruction time each week" (Matthews, 2004, p. B1). Most schools take their students straight from lunch back to the classroom and start a lecture right away. This lack of a break often proves to be a problem because the students are restless and fidgety (Adelman & Taylor, 2008). In some schools, however, "with the principal's permission, a teacher can take his or her class outside for 15 minutes. For the kids, it's like a jailbreak" (DeGregory 2005). In the typical classroom, children sit in their seats for up to six hours each day. With academics and curriculum becoming harder, schools need those extra 25 minutes each day to teach students everything they will need to know in preparation for the ever-increasing glut of standardized tests. Schools are completely focused on academics, not only so that the students pass the standardized tests, but because "the federal government expects schools to have all children testing at the proficient level in science, language arts and math by the year 2014" (Nussbaum, 2006, p. C1). Unfortunately, these expectations are unable to be reached because of the bell curve; an average will be formulated by the low and high scores, illuminating the possibility of a perfect score. Specifically, not every student can learn and comprehend information in the same way. With the pressure of standardized tests and a more challenging curriculum, "Parents worry about the strain on their children" (Matthews, 2004, p. B1). For this reason, recess for children is even more important than ever. Ginny Mahlke, the principal of Wolftrap Elementary School in Fairfax, Virginia summed up the shift in a more stringent, performance-based curriculum:

> The increased demands on schools mean it is even
> more important now for students to get outside, relax,
> and get some exercise, for every minute spent at school

Use present tense verbs (take, proves) for what happens or can happen now.

Use the present perfect tense (will be formulated) for actions completed and for actions continued into the present time.

Indent block quotations 1 full tab.

is instructional time, right down to learning the skills of negotiating by deciding whose turn it is on the swing (Matthews, 2004, p. B1).

Sharing the opinion of Mahlke are 60 percent of principals who believe that their students do not learn well without a break because they are fidgety and cannot pay attention sitting in a chair for 6 hours at a time (Adelman & Taylor, 2008). Before the limitations of recess started in the 1980s, students enjoyed breaks for 10 to 20 minutes at a time in the morning, after lunch, and in the afternoon (Nussbaum, 2006, p. C1). In order to give students the recess and the healthy break they need in the middle of the day, some parents argue that if the school days were longer, there would be enough time for a recess break and enough time for the teaching required for the year. Then parents would not be "forced to choose between recess and instruction. Children need both" (Dulman & Sigall, 2006, p. A22).

The problems with eliminating recess do not just stop on an academic level. Cutting out play time for young children affects their social skills and their physical skills. Students need to learn to make up their own rules and play their own games. With recess, students can experience uninstructed play in contrast to being constantly directed all day (Widhalm, 2004, p. B1). On the playground, with adults serving only as supervisors, children learn to work through altercations, to make decisions, and also how to make friends. It is essential to have physical contact with other children in a world of technology where students often play with themselves. Scientists say that "children who are glued to their computers interact less with other children, become passive learners, and read less" (Devi 2006).

Recess is a physical activity for most children, which is constructive toward their health and well-being. "Research shows that between more schools eliminating recess and after-school programs . . . the amount of time kids spend being physically active is dwindling significantly" (Tracey, 2005). When children are taken outside for recess after lunch, they are exposed to and become used to playing outdoors, an activity that can be repeated in the home environment. Because of the stagnant environment of school, too many children would rather play inside with electronics than go outside. Even worse than children not getting the exercise they need is that schools are contributing to childhood obesity. Results from recent research revealed that "36% of schools sell treats such as chips, candy and ice cream in the school cafeteria" (Toppo, 2007, p. 1-A). If children had recess as an outlet to run around and play, the rates of childhood obesity would be cut because the children would be burning calories.

The other speculation as to why recess is being eliminated in schools is that children are being injured and schools are being sued by parents because of the injuries ("Tag—you're illegal!" 2006). This reason brings up the debate of whether or not children are being nurtured too much and whether they are being made into weaker human beings because of it. "An elementary school in Massachusetts that banned tag, dodge ball and all other 'contact' or 'chase' games" ("Tag—you're illegal!" 2006) has joined the bandwagon with many other schools that worry about the scratches and scrapes of its young children. Another town even "outlawed touching altogether" ("Tag—you're illegal!" 2006). It is no wonder why childhood obesity is such a prevalent issue in American society today. Children are not given the opportunity to exercise and have fun, even when they are allowed onto the playground.

Amazingly, only 60 percent of the nation's elementary schools still have a full 20 to 40 minute recess period after lunch (Poynter, 2008). Students in the 40 percent of elementary schools who are neglecting the benefits and needs of recess are suffering from it.

Use the past tense (outlawed, banned) to express actions that occurred at a specific time in the past.

More Academics 8

Children need recess to exercise their bodies and their minds, especially at such a young age when they are still growing and developing. Principals have reasons to back up their decisions for doing away with recess; however, there is more evidence that proves students need the time and exercise that a recess period provides. How will the elimination of recess affect that 40 percent of children in the United States who do not have play time during the day? Will it stunt their mental growth and become detrimental in the long run? At the present time it is too early to tell because these eliminations are so new; however, the more important question is whether elementary school children today can reach their full potential after being deprived of the mental and physical stimuli that can be experienced on the playground.

The conclusion can include a statement on the state of research in the area of study as well as questions for further research.

More Academics 9

References begin on a new page.

References

Citation for an online article from a research center at an institution.

Adelman, H., & Taylor, L. (2008). Attention problems:

Intervention and resources. UCLA Center for Mental Health

in Schools. Retrieved from http://smhp.psych.ucla.edu

/pdfdocs/Attention/attention.pdf

DeGregory, L. (2005, March 29). Boulevard of dreams. *St.*

Petersburg Times. Retrieved from http://www.sptimes.com

/2005/03/29/Floridian/Out_of_play.shtml

Devi, C. (2006, September 14). When starting them young is not

all. Retrieved from http://www.redorbit.com/news

/technology/655999/when_starting_them_

young_is_not_all/index.html?source=r_technology

Citation for a newspaper article.

Dulman, P. P., & Sigall, B. T. (2006, June 8). Find time for

learning and play. *Washington Post*, A22.

Matthews, J. (2004, April 9). Federal education law squeezes out

recess. *Washington Post*, B1.

More Academics 10

Nussbaum, D. (2006, December 10). Before children ask, what's recess? *New York Times*, C1.

Poynter, A. (2008). The end of recess. Retrieved from http://www.poynter.org/column.asp?id=2&aid=80426

Svensen, A. (2008). Banning school recess. Retrieved from http://school.familyeducation.com/educational-innovation /growth-and-development/38674.html

Tag—you're illegal! (2006, October 28). *Los Angeles Times*. Retrieved from http://www.latimes.com/news/opinion/la-ed-tag28oct28,0,59791.story?coll=la-opinion-leftrail

Toppo, G. (2007, May 16). School recess isn't exactly on the run. *USA Today*, 1-A. Retrieved from EBSCOhost database.

Tracy, K. (2005, October 6). The fruit fixation. *Variety*. Retrieved from http://www.variety.com/article /VR1117930289.html?categoryid=2075&cs=1

Widhalm, S. (2004, March 15). Sometimes you want a break: Benefits of recess outweigh lost class time, advocates say. *Washington Post*, B1.

Internet sources require the word "Retrieved" preceding the date of access

Citation for an article from a library's database.

PEARSON
mycomplab

For more resources in research,
writing, and documentation, go to
MyCompLab.com

16 The Footnote System: CMS Style

The fine arts and some fields in the humanities (but not literature) use traditional footnotes, which should conform to standards set by *The Chicago Manual of Style* (CMS), 15th ed., 2003. In the CMS system, you must place superscript numerals within the text (like this[15]), and place documentary footnotes on corresponding pages.

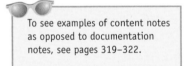

If you wish to group all your notes into one list, see the instructions on pages 318–319.

The discussion below assumes that notes will appear as footnotes; however, some instructors accept endnotes—that is, all notes appear together at the end of the paper, not at the bottom of individual pages (see pages 318–319).

There are two types of footnotes: One documents your sources with bibliographic information, but the other can discuss related matters, explain your methods of research, suggest related literature, provide biographical information, or offer information not immediately pertinent to your discussion.

To see examples of content notes as opposed to documentation notes, see pages 319–322.

If available, use the footnote or endnote feature of your software. It will not only insert the raised superscript number but also keep your footnotes arranged properly at the bottom of each page or keep your endnotes in a correct list. In most instances, the software will insert the superscript numeral, but it will not write the note automatically; you must type in the essential data in the correct style.

16a Inserting a Superscript Numeral in Your Text

Use Arabic numerals typed slightly above the line (like this[12]). In both Microsoft Word and WordPerfect, go to Font and select Superscript or go to Insert and select Footnote. Place a superscript numeral at the end of each quotation or paraphrase, with the number following immediately without a space after the final word or mark of punctuation, as in this sample:

Steven A. LeBlanc, an archeologist at Harvard University, along

with several other scholars, argues instead that "humans have been at each others' throats since the dawn of the species."[1] Robin Yates, for example, says the ancient ancestors of the Chinese used "long-range projectile weapons" as long ago as 28,000 BC for both hunting and "intrahuman conflict."[2] Arthur Ferrill observes, "When man first learned how to write, he already had war to write about."[3] Ferrill adds, "In prehistoric times man was a hunter and a killer of other men. The killer instinct in the prehistoric male is clearly attested by archeology in fortifications, weapons, cave paintings, and skeletal remains."[4]

The footnotes that relate to these in-text superscript numerals will appear at the bottom of the page, as shown here:

1. See Steven A. LeBlanc, *Constant Battles: The Myth of the Peaceful, Noble Savage* (New York: St. Martin's Press, 2004), 15, and also L. D. Cooper, *Rousseau, Nature, and the Problem of the Good Life* (University Park: Pennsylvania State Univ. Press, 2000).

2. Steven A. LeBlanc, "Prehistory of Warfare," *Archaeology* (May/June, 2003): 18.

3. Robin Yates, "Early China," in *War and Society in the Ancient and Medieval Worlds*, ed. Kurt Raaflaub and Nathan Rosenstein (Cambridge, Massachusetts: Center for Hellenic Studies, 2001), 9.

4. Arthur Ferrill, "Neolithic Warfare," http://eserver.org/history /neolithic-war.txt (accessed 6 April 2008).

However, you may place the notes at the back of your paper, so you should usually include a source's name in your text. The first example below implies a source that will be found in the footnote; the second expresses the name in the text. Some writers prefer the first approach, others the second.

Implied reference:

The organic basis of autism is generally agreed upon. Three possible causes for autism have been identified: behavioral syndrome, organic brain disorder, or a range of biological and psychosocial factors.[9]

Expressed reference:

Martin Rutter has acknowledged that the organic basis of autism is generally agreed upon. Rutter named three possible causes for autism: behavioral syndrome, organic brain disorder, or a range of biological and psychosocial factors.[10]

Writing Full or Abbreviated Notes

CMS style permits you to omit a bibliography page as long as you give full data to the source in each of your initial footnotes.

> 1. Douglas Preston and Lincoln Child, *The Wheel of Darkness* (New York: Warner, 2008), 49.

However, you may provide a comprehensive bibliography to each source and abbreviate all footnotes, even the initial ones, since full data will be found in the bibliography.

> 1. Preston & Child, *The Wheel of Darkness*, 49.

The bibliography entry would read this way:

> Preston, Douglas, and Lincoln Child. *The Wheel of Darkness*. New York: Warner, 2008.

Consult with your instructor on this matter if you are uncertain about the proper format for a specific course.

Index to Footnote Models

16b Formatting and Writing the Footnotes

Place footnotes at the bottom of pages to correspond with superscript numerals (as shown in section 16a). Some papers will require footnotes on almost every page. Follow these conventions:

1. **Spacing.** In academic papers not intended for publication, footnotes are commonly typed single-spaced and placed at the foot of the page, usually with a line space between each note. Drafts and manuscript intended for publication in print or on the Web should have all notes double-spaced and placed together on one page at the end of the paper. The student example on page 328 shows single-spaced footnotes. A Notes page with double spacing can be found on pages 318–319.
2. **Indention.** Indent the first line of the note five spaces or one inch (usually one click of the tab key).
3. **Numbering.** Number the footnotes consecutively throughout the entire paper with an indented number, a period, and space, as shown in the examples throughout this chapter.
4. **Placement.** Collect at the bottom of each page all footnotes to citations made on that page.
5. **Distinguish footnotes from text.** Separate footnotes from the text by triple spacing or, if you prefer, by a twelve-space bar line from the left margin.
6. **Footnote form.** Basic forms of notes should conform to the following styles.

Book

List the author, followed by a comma, the title underlined or italicized, the publication data within parenthesis (city: publisher, year), followed by a comma and the page number(s). Unless ambiguity would result, the abbreviations *p.* and *pp.* may be omitted.

1. Newt Gingrich, *Real Change: From the World that Fails to the World that Works* (Washington, DC: Regnery, 2008), 20–23.

List two authors without a comma:

2. Steven D. Levitt and Stephen J. Dubner, *Freakonomics: A Rogue Economist Explores the Hidden Side of Everything* (New York: HarperCollins Publishers, 2006), 18.

See pages 317–318 for further details about subsequent references and the use of Latinate phrases.

List three authors separated by commas. *Note:* Publisher's names are spelled out in full but the words *Company* or *Inc.* are omitted. Reference to an edition follows the title or the editors, if listed (see footnote 4).

3. Hestia Evans, Lady Evans, and Dugald Steer, *Mythology* (Cambridge, MA: Candlewick, 2007), 140–41.

For more than three authors, use *et al.* after mention of the lead author:

4. Andrew C. Garrod et al., eds., "Introduction," *Adolescent Portraits: Identity, Relationships, and Challenges,* 6th ed. (Boston: Allyn & Bacon, 2007), 3.

For a subsequent reference to an immediately preceding source, use "Ibid." in the roman typeface, not in italics and not underscored:

> 5. Ibid.

Collection or Anthology

> 6. Sandra Leiblum and Nicola Döring, "Internet Sexuality: Known Risks and Fresh Chances for Women," in *Sex and the Internet: A Guidebook for Clinicians*, ed. Al Cooper (New York: Brunner-Routledge, 2002), 20–21.

Journal Article

> 7. B. Corenblum and Christian A. Meissner, "Recognition of Faces of Ingroup and Outgroup Children and Adults," *Journal of Experimental Child Psychology* 93 (2006): 187.

Note: Use a colon before the page number of a journal but a comma before page numbers for magazines and books.

Magazine Article

> 8. R. L. Murray, "Killers in Green Coats," *Civil War Times*, April 2008, 26–33.

Newspaper Article

> 9. Karen Auge, "Lost in the System," *Denver Post*, 13 April 2008, 1A.
>
> 10. John Kirkenfeld, "Digging for More Dirt," *Mill City Daily News*, 23 July 2008, sec. 4, p. 1.

Note: the abbreviations *sec.* and *p.* are necessary to distinguish the 4 and the 1.

Review Article

> 11. Chris Dodge, review of *Arborsculpture: Solutions for a Small Planet*, by Richard Reames, *Utne* March–April 2006, 24.

Nonprint Source: Lecture, Sermon, Speech, Oral Report

> 12. Dick Weber, "The Facts about Preparing Teens to Drive" (lecture, Morrow High School, Morrow, GA, October 16, 2008).

Encyclopedia

13. *The World Book Encyclopedia*, 2007 ed., s.v. "Raphael."

Note: "s.v." means *sub verbo*, "under the word(s)."

Government Documents

14. United States. Dept. of the Treasury, "Financial Operations of Government Agencies and Funds," *Treasury Bulletin*, Washington, DC (June 2008): 134–141.

15. U.S., *Constitution*, art. 1, sec. 4.

16. United Kingdom, *Coroner's Act, 1954*, 2 & 3 Eliz. 2, ch.31.

Television

17. Bob Schieffer, *CBS News*, September 13, 2008.

Film on DVD

18. *Breakfast at Tiffany's*, DVD, directed by Blake Edwards (Hollywood, CA: Paramount, 1961).

Musical Work on VHS

19. Handel, George Frederic, *Messiah*, selections, VHS, Atlanta Symphony Orchestra and Chamber Chorus, Robert Shaw, conductor (Atlanta, GA: Video Imaging, 2008).

Biblical Reference

20. Matt. 10:5.

21. 1 Pet. 5:1–3 (New Revised Standard Version)

16c   Writing Footnotes for Electronic Sources

To cite electronic sources, *The Chicago Manual of Style* includes a publication date and the URL but not the date of access. The models below show these requirements. Adjust your sources accordingly.

Scholarly Project

22. *British Poetry Archive*, ed. Jerome McGann and David Seaman (University Of Virginia Library, 2008), http://etext.lib.virgina.edu /britpo.html.

Article Online, Limited Information

23. Arthur Ferrill, "Neolithic Warfare Frontline Educational Foundation," http://eserver.org/history/neolithic-war.txt.

Magazine Article Reproduced Online

24. James Owens, "Baby Mammoth CT Scan Reveals Internal Organs," *National Geographic News*, 11 April 2008 [magazine online], http://news.nationalgeographic.com/news/2008/04/080411-baby-mammoth.html.

Journal Article Reproduced Online

25. Kimberly A. Tyler and Katherine A. Johnson, "Exemplifying the Integrations of the Relational Developmental System: Synthesizing Theory, Research, and Application to Promote Positive Development and Social Justice," *Journal of Adolescent Research* 23 (2008): 245–55, http://jar.sagepub.com/cgi/reprint/23/3/245.

Journal Article Online with No Author Listed

26. Catherine D. DeAngelis and Joseph P. Thornton, "Preserving Confidentiality in the Peer Review Process," *Journal of the American Medical Association* 24 March 2008, http://jama.ama-assn.org/cgi/content/full/299.16.jed80000.

Article from a Scientific Database

At a minimum, show in this order the name of the database, the URL, a descriptive phrase or record locator (such as a number) to indicate the part of the database being cited, and an access date.

27. NASA/IPAC Extragalactic Database, http://nedwww.ipac.caltech.edu/ (object name IRAS F004000+4059; accessed July 13, 2008).

Article Accessed from a Database through the Library System

28. Victor Davis Hanson, "War Will Be War: No Matter the Era, No Matter the Weapons, and the Same Old Hell." *National Review*, 54 (2002); InfoTrac database, Art. A84943306.

Book Online

29. D. H. Lawrence, *Lady Chatterly's Lover*, 1928, http://bibliomania.com/fiction/dhl/chat.html.

CD-ROM Source

Place of publication and date may be omitted unless relevant.

30. The Old Testament, The Bible, CD-ROM, Bureau Development.

31. *Oxford English Dictionary*, 2nd ed. CD-ROM, version 2.0, Oxford University Press.

Electronic Mailing List, Archived

32. Warren Watts, e-mail to Victorian Association for Library Automation mailing list, September 23, 2008, http://www.vala.org.au/conf2008.htm.

Article from an Online Service

33. Randolph E. Schmid, "Dyslexia Differs by Language," *Discovery Health*, April 8, 2008, http://dsc.discovery.com/news/2008/04/08/dyslexia-language.html.

E-mail

Since e-mail is not retrievable, do not document with a footnote or bibliography entry. Instead, mention the nature of the source within your text by saying something like this:

Walter Wallace argues that teen violence stems mainly from the breakup of the traditional family (e-mail to the author).

16d Writing Subsequent Footnote References

After a first full footnote, references to the same source should be shortened to the author's last name and page number. When an author has two works mentioned, employ a shortened version of the title, e.g., "3. Jones, *Paine*, 25." In general, avoid Latinate abbreviations such as *loc. cit.* and *op. cit.*; however, whenever a note refers to the source in the immediately preceding note, you may use "Ibid." alone or "Ibid." with a page number, as shown on the next page. If the subsequent note does not refer to the one immediately above it, do not use "Ibid." Instead, repeat the author's last name (note especially the difference between notes 2 and 4):

1. Robert E. Slavin, *Educational Psychology: Theory and Practice,* 9th ed. (New York: ASCD, 2008), 23.

2. Ibid., 27.

3. Grant P. Wiggins and Jay McTighe, *Understanding by Design,* 2nd ed. (Alexandria, VA: ASCD, 2005), 91.

4. Slavin, 24.

5. Ibid., 27.

Note: Single-space footnotes but double-space between each note.

16e Writing Endnotes Rather Than Footnotes

With the permission of your instructor, you may put all your notes together as a single group of endnotes to lessen the burden of typing the paper. Most computer software programs will help you with this task by inserting the superscript numerals and by allowing you to type the endnotes consecutively at the end of the text, not at the bottom of each page. Follow these conventions:

1. Begin notes on a new page at the end of the text.
2. Entitle the page "Notes," centered, and placed two inches from the top of the page.
3. Indent the first line of each note one-half inch or five spaces. Type the number of the note followed by a period.
4. Double-space the endnotes.
5. Triple-space between the heading and the first note.

Conform to the following example:

Notes

1. Michael Hayutin, *Character Immunization: How to Raise Children Strong Enough to Resist Popular Culture* (Camp Cherman, OR: VMI, 2006), 24.

2. Ibid., 27.

3. Jean Illsley Clark, Connie Dawson, and David Bredehoft, *How Much Is Enough? Everything You Need to Know to Steer Clear of Overindulgence and Raise Likeable, Responsible, and Respectful Children* (New York: Avalon, 2004), 221.

4. Michele Borba, "10 Tips for Raising Moral Kids," http://www.moralintelligence.com/Pages/ArtBMI13.htm.

5. Hayutin, 28.

6. Abraham J. Heschel, *Man Is Not Alone: A Philosophy of Religion* (New York: Farrar, Straus, and Young, 1951), 221.

7. Ibid., 222.

8. Borba.

9. Hayutin, 28.

10. Borba.

16f Writing Content Footnotes or Content Endnotes

See the sample paper on pages 325–337 for its use of two content footnotes: number 1, page 328, and number 26, page 335.

As a general rule, put important matters in your text. Use a content note to explain research problems, conflicts in the testimony of the experts, matters of importance that are not germane to your discussion, interesting tidbits, credit to people and sources not mentioned in the text, and other matters that might interest readers.

HINT: After you have embedded most of your computer files in your draft, check the remaining files to find appropriate material for a few content endnotes.

Content notes should conform to these rules:

1. Content notes are *not* documentation notes; a full citation to any source mentioned in the note will appear elsewhere—in a documentation note or on the Bibliography page (see item 4.)
2. Content notes may be placed on a separate page(s) following the last page of text, but generally they appear as footnotes mixed among the documentation footnotes.
3. Content footnotes should be single-spaced, like your documentation footnotes. Content endnotes should be double-spaced, as shown in the next few examples.
4. Full information on sources mentioned in content notes must appear elsewhere in a footnote or in a separate Bibliography page at the end of the paper.
5. Unless ambiguity might result without them, do not use *p.* or *pp.* with page numbers.

The following samples demonstrate various types of content endnotes.

Related Matters Not Germane to the Text

1. The problems of politically correct language are explored in Adams, Tucker (4–5), Zalers, and also Young and Smith (583). These authorities cite the need for caution by administrators who would impose new measures on speech and behavior. Verbal abuse cannot be

erased by a new set of unjust laws. Patrick German offers several guidelines for implementing an effective but reasonable program (170–72).

Blanket Citation

2. On this point see Giarrett (3–4), de Young (579), Kinard (405–07), and Young (119).

3. Cf. Campbell (*Masks* 1: 170–225; *Hero* 342–45), Frazer (312), and Baird (300–44).

Note: Cf. means *compare.*

Literature on a Related Topic

4. For additional study of the effects of alcoholics on children, see especially the *Journal of Studies on Alcohol* for the article by Wolin et al. and the bibliography on the topic by Orme and Rimmer (285–87). In addition, group therapy for children of alcoholics is examined in Hawley and Brown.

Major Source Requiring Frequent In-Text Citations

5. All citations to Shakespeare are to the Fogler Library edition.

6. Dryden's poems are cited from the California edition of his *Works* and documented in the text with first references to each poem listing volume, page, and lines and with subsequent references citing lines only.

Reference to Source Materials

7. See also James Baird, who argues that the whiteness of Melville's whale is "the sign of the all-encompassing God" (257). Baird states: "It stands for what Melville calls at the conclusion of the thirty-fifth chapter of *Moby-Dick* 'the inscrutable tides of God'; and it is of these tides as well that the great White Whale himself is the quintessential emblem, the iconographic representation" (257).

NOTE: Either list Baird in the bibliography or include full bibliographic information with this footnote.

8. On this point see also the essay by Patricia Chaffee in which she examines the "house" as a primary image in the fiction of Eudora Welty.

Explanation of Tools, Methods, or Testing Procedures

9. Water samples were drawn from the identical spot each day at 8 a.m., noon, 4 p.m., and 8 p.m., with testing done immediately on site.

10. The control group continued normal dietary routines, but the experimental group was asked to consume nuts, sharp cheeses, and chocolates to test acne development of its members against that of the control group.

11. The initial sample was complete data on all twins born in Nebraska between 1920 and 1940. These dates were selected to provide test subjects 60 years of age or older.

> **NOTE:** A report of an empirical study in APA style would require an explanation of tools and testing procedures in the text under "Methods." See section 15e, pages 300–301.

Statistics

See also "Using Visuals Effectively in a Research Essay," pages 164–166.

12. Database results show 27,000 pupil-athletes in 174 high schools with grades 0.075 above another group of 27,000 non-athletes at the same high schools. Details on the nature of various *reward structures* are unavailable.

Acknowledgments of Assistance or Support

13. Funds to finance this research were graciously provided by the Thompson-Monroe Foundation.

14. This writer wishes to acknowledge the research assistance of Pat Luther, graduate assistant, Physics Department.

Variables or Conflicts in the Evidence

15. Potlatch et al. included the following variables: the positive acquaintance, the equal status norm, the various social norms, the negative stereotypes, and sexual discrimination (415–20). However, racial barriers cannot be overlooked as one important variable.

16. The pilot study at Dunlap School, where sexual imbalance was noticed (62 percent males), differed sharply with test results of other schools. The male bias at Dunlap thereby caused the writer to eliminate those scores from the totals.

16g Using the Footnote System for Papers in the Humanities

Several disciplines in the humanities—history, philosophy, religion, and theology—use footnotes. The following list demonstrates the format for the types of notes you might need to write for papers on religion or history. They are shown as endnotes, which should be double-spaced.

Sample Page of Notes to a Paper on a Religious Topic

Notes

1. Elaine Pagels and Karen L. King, *Reading Judas: The Gospel of Judas and the Shaping of Christianity* (New York: Penguin, 2008), 23–27.

2. Rob Brezsny, Promoia Is the Antidote for Paranoia: How the Whole World Is Conspiring to Shower You with Blessings (Berkeley, CA: Frog, 2005), 214–17.

3. Claude Levi-Strauss, *The Savage Mind* (Chicago: University of Chicago Press, 1966), chap. 9, esp. p. 312.

4. Ibid., 314.

5. E. E. Evans-Pritchard, *Theories of Primitive Religion* (Oxford: Clarendon Press, 1965), chap. 2.

6. Evans-Pritchard, *Nuer Religion* (Oxford: Clarendon Press, 1956), 85.

7. Evans-Pritchard, *Primitive Religion*, 46.

8. Humphries, P. T., "Marriage as Inspiration," Sermon (Bowling Green, KY: Primitive Baptist Church, 2008).

9. Romans 6:2.

10. *The Church and the Law of Nullity of Marriage*, Report of a Commission Appointed by the Archbishops of Canterbury and York in 1949 (London: Society for Promoting Christian Knowledge, 1955), 12–16.

Sample Page of Notes to a History Paper

Notes

1. Bill Bryson, *Shakespeare: The World as Stage* (New York: HarperCollins, 2007), 34.

2. Thomas Jefferson, "Notes on the State of Virginia" (1784), http://www.yale.edu/lawweb/avalon/jevifram.htm.

3. Darren Staloff, *Hamilton, Adams, Jefferson: The Politics of Enlightenment and the American Founding* (New York: Farrar, Straus, and Giroux, 2005), 56–60.

4. *Encyclopedia Britannica*, 2001 ed., s.v. "Declaration of Independence."

5. Henry Steele Commager, *The Nature and Study of History*, Social Science Seminar Series (Columbus, Ohio: Merrill, 2006), 10.

6. Dept. of the Treasury, "Financial Operations of Government Agencies and Funds," Treasury Bulletin (Washington, DC: GPO, June 1974), 134–41.

7. Constitution, Art. 1, sec. 4.

8. Great Britain, Coroner's Act, 1954, 2 & 3 Eliz. 2, ch. 31.

9. *State v. Lane*, Minnesota 263 N. W. 608 (1935).

10. Papers of Gen. A. J. Warner (P-973, Service Record and Short Autobiography), Western Reserve Historical Society.

16h Using the Footnote System for Papers in the Fine Arts

Several disciplines in the fine arts—art, dance, music, theater—use footnotes. The following list demonstrates the format for the types of footnotes you might need to write for topics that treat the fine arts.

Notes

1. Nancie Hudson, "Simply Irresistible: 5 Techniques for Writing Inviting Leads," *Writer* (2008): 38–39.

2. "Beethoven's Ninth in the News," http://www.fmcs.us/node/58.

3. Hudson, 39.

4. Sarah Dunant, *In the Company of the Courtesan* (New York: Random House, 2005), 286.

5. Aristophanes, *The Birds*, in *Five Comedies of Aristophanes*, trans. Benjamin B. Rogers (Garden City, N.Y.: Doubleday, 1955), 1.2.12–14.

6. Jean Bouret, *The Life and Work of Toulouse Lautrec*, trans. Daphne Woodward (New York: Abrams, n.d.), 5.

7. Cyrus Hoy, "Fathers and Daughters in Shakespeare's Romances," in *Shakespeare's Romances Reconsidered*, ed. Carol McGinnis Kay and Henry E. Jacobs (Lincoln: Univ. of Nebraska Press, 1978), 77–78.

8. Lionello Venturi, *Botticelli* (Greenwich, Conn.: Fawcett, n.d.), plate 32, p. 214.

NOTE: Add "p." for page only if needed for clarity.

9. Cotton Vitellius MSS, A., 15. British Museum.

10. *Ham.* 2.3.2.

16i Writing a Bibliography Page for a Paper That Uses Footnotes

In addition to footnotes or endnotes, you may be requested to supply a separate bibliography page that lists sources used in developing the paper. Use a heading that represents its contents, such as Selected Bibliography, Sources Consulted, or Works Cited.

See pages 336–337 for a sample of a complete bibliography for a research paper.

If your initial footnotes are completely documented, the bibliography is redundant. Check with your instructor before preparing one because it may not be required. Separate the title from the first entry with a triple space. Type the first line of each entry flush left; indent the second line and other succeeding lines five spaces or one inch. Alphabetize the list by last names of authors. Double-space the entries as shown. List alphabetically by title two or more works by one author. The basic forms are:

Book

Feith, Douglas J. *War and Decision: Inside the Pentagon at the Dawn of the War on Terrorism*. New York: HarperCollins, 2008.

Journal Article

Hardwick-Ivey, Amy R. "Vocabulary in Action: Strategies for Turning Students into Wordsmiths." *English Journal* 97 (March 2008): 56–61.

Newspaper

Aguilera, Elizabeth. "Higher Shreducation." *Denver Post* 14 April 2008, 1A+.

Internet Article

"Biography." Paul Laurence Dunbar Web site. http://www.dunbarsite .org/biopld.asp.

16j Sample Research Paper in the CMS Style

The essay that follows demonstrates the format and documentation style you should use for a research paper when the instructor asks that you use "footnotes," the Chicago style, or the CMS style, all of which refer to *The Chicago Manual of Style*. If permitted, notes may be placed at the end of the paper as double-spaced endnotes rather than at the bottom of the pages.

In the paper that follows, Jamie Johnston has researched the history of war back into prehistoric times. The student offers substantial evidence to prove that early tribes had a history of warfare and even brutality toward captives. The tools of war are reviewed, and then Johnston poses the crucial question: Why did early civilizations fight? He lists many reasons, such as fights for resources, slaves, precious metals, revenge, and honor. Ultimately, he poses the key issue: Was human behavior motivated by biology or culture? Johnston reaches an interesting conclusion, so read on.

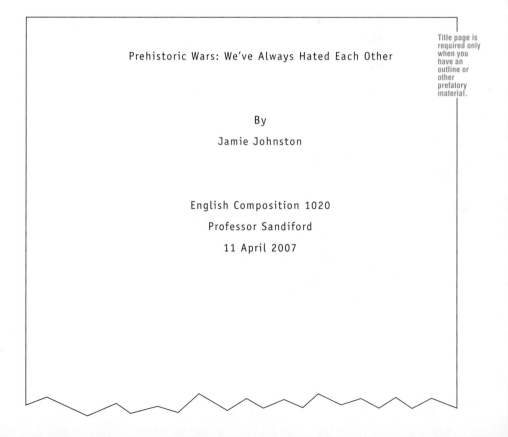

Prehistoric Wars: We've Always Hated Each Other

Title page is required only when you have an outline or other prefatory material.

By

Jamie Johnston

English Composition 1020

Professor Sandiford

11 April 2007

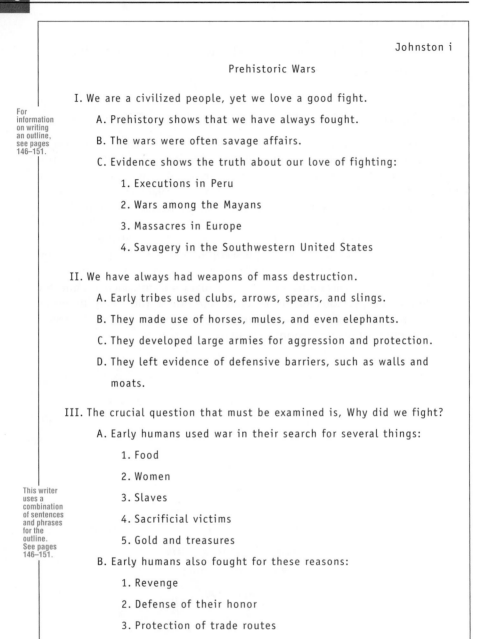

Johnston i

Prehistoric Wars

I. We are a civilized people, yet we love a good fight.

For information on writing an outline, see pages 146–151.

    A. Prehistory shows that we have always fought.

    B. The wars were often savage affairs.

    C. Evidence shows the truth about our love of fighting:

        1. Executions in Peru

        2. Wars among the Mayans

        3. Massacres in Europe

        4. Savagery in the Southwestern United States

II. We have always had weapons of mass destruction.

    A. Early tribes used clubs, arrows, spears, and slings.

    B. They made use of horses, mules, and even elephants.

    C. They developed large armies for aggression and protection.

    D. They left evidence of defensive barriers, such as walls and moats.

III. The crucial question that must be examined is, Why did we fight?

    A. Early humans used war in their search for several things:

        1. Food

        2. Women

This writer uses a combination of sentences and phrases for the outline. See pages 146–151.

        3. Slaves

        4. Sacrificial victims

        5. Gold and treasures

    B. Early humans also fought for these reasons:

        1. Revenge

        2. Defense of their honor

        3. Protection of trade routes

        4. Honor God and their religion

Johnston ii

IV. Ultimately, the cause for our warlike nature boils down to two

   primary causes.

   A. One group advances the theory that culture dictates our

     aggression.

     1. A desire for freedom demands war at times.

     2. Capitalism and world markets affect aggressive

       actions.

     3. Government and official control promote

       aggression.

   B. A second group advances the theory that biology is the

     motivating factor.

     1. Humans love a good fight.

     2. Tempers are explosive and sometimes uncontrollable.

     3. People want power over others.

     4. Civil law and moral behavior cannot be dictated to others.

> One advantage of sentence outline is that the material can launch the drafting of the paper itself. See pages 149–151.

Johnston 1

Prehistoric Wars: We've Always Hated Each Other

Here we are, a civilized world with reasonably educated people,

yet we constantly fight with others. These are not sibling squabbles

either; people die in terrible ways. We wonder, then, if there was ever

a time when men and women lived in harmony with one another and

with nature and the environment. The Bible speaks of the Garden of

Eden, and the French philosopher Jean-Jacques Rousseau advanced the

> Repeat the title on the opening page of text.

idea in the 1700s of the "noble savage," and that "nothing could be more gentle" than an ancient colony of people.[1] Wrong!

Steven A. LeBlanc, an archeologist at Harvard University, along with several other scholars, argues instead that "humans have been at each others' throats since the dawn of the species."[2] Robin Yates, for example, says the ancient ancestors of the Chinese used "long-range projectile weapons" as long ago as 28,000 B.C. for both hunting and "intrahuman conflict."[3] Arthur Ferrill observes, "When man first learned how to write, he already had war to write about."[4] Ferrill adds, "In prehistoric times man was a hunter and a killer of other men. The killer instinct in the prehistoric male is clearly attested by archaeology in fortifications, weapons, cave paintings, and skeletal remains."[5]

Evidence proves that savage fighting occurred in the ancient history of human beings. We have evidence of the types of weapons employed. We can also list reasons for the prehistoric fighting. This paper will examine those items, but the crux of the debate centers on the inducement or instinct. Were early humans motivated by biological

The writer uses the introduction to discuss historical evidence.

This section opens with the writer's thesis, and discusses reasons for prehistoric wars.

---

1. See Steven A. LeBlanc, *Constant Battles: The Myth of the Peaceful, Noble Savage* (New York: St. Martin's Press, 2004, 15, and also L. D. Cooper, *Rousseau, Nature, and the Problem of the Good Life* (University Park: Pennsylvania State Univ. Press, 1999.

2. Steven A. LeBlanc, "Prehistory of Warfare," *Archaeology* (May/June, 2003), 18.

3. Robin Yates, "Early China," in *War and Society in the Ancient and Medieval Worlds,* ed. Kurt Raaflaub and Nathan Rosenstein (Cambridge, Massachusetts: Center for Hellenic Studies, 2001), 9.

4. Arthur Ferrill, "Neolithic Warfare," Frontline Educational Foundation, http://eserver.org/history/neolithic-war.txt.

5. Ibid.

Citation for a magazine.

Citation for a book.

Citation for an Internet source.

instincts or by cultural demands for a share of limited resources?
That's the issue this paper will address.

First, we need to look briefly at the evidence. Kelly Hearn has
reported on the work of one forensic archeologist, Christina Conlee,
who has investigated a rare headless skeleton with a "ceramic head jar"
in the Nasca region of southern Peru.[6] The victim "was killed in a rite
of ancestral worship. This information provides new information on
human sacrifice in the ancient Andes and in particular on decapitation
and trophy heads."[7] Conlee has the proof of the executions, but not the
reason, although speculations center on religious ceremonies.
Anthropologists continue to study the "head jar" which is "painted with
two inverted human faces."[8] Other researchers suggest that the victims
were prisoners of war and not the losers of ritual combat. In either
case, the ancients were less than noble savages.

LeBlanc's book *Constant Battles* is a catalog of prehistoric
fighting, David Webster describes the savage fighting of the ancient
Mayans,[9] and Nick Thorpe in *British Archaeology* describes massacres
that occurred in Europe over 8,500 years ago—decapitation, scalping,

---

6. Kelly Hearn, "Decapitated Man Found in Peru Tomb with Ceramic
'Replacement' Head" *National Geographic News*, 6 June 2007, http:
//news.nationalgeographic.com/news/2007/06/070606-head-jar.html.

The word *Ibid.* refers to the immediately preceding note.

7. Ibid.

8. Ibid.

9. David Webster, "Ancient Maya Warfare," in *War and Society in
the Ancient and Medieval Worlds*, ed. Kurt Raaflaub and Nathan
Rosenstein (Cambridge, Massachusetts: Center for Hellenic Studies,
2001), 333–60.

Johnston 4

axe blows, and other nasty methods.[10] Indeed, articles are now available on wars in ancient Japan, Egypt, Greece,[11] and the Southwestern areas of the United States.[12]

    The weapons, too, have been uncovered: clubs, arrowheads, bows, slings, daggers, maces, and spears. Each weapon graduated upon the previous and served new purposes as armies gathered for combat. One source points out that "the bow and the sling were important for hunting, but the dagger and mace were most useful for fighting other humans."[13] The spear required close combat. The bow and arrow had a range of about 100 yards. The sling was a significant weapon because in the right hands it was accurate from long distances and very powerful with stones that could crush skulls. The mace gave way to the battle axe to cut through armor. Then with copper, bronze, and finally iron, the sword gained great popularity and remains a weapon of choice even today.[14]

    Horses, mules, and even elephants gave primitive armies mobility. Ultimately, however, the primary weapon was the soldier, and over time the ragged fighting groups were organized into armies that could march in columns and lay siege to other villages and cities. Accordingly, archeologists have examined walls, pits, ditches, moats, and barriers of all sorts, even villages with all the rooms built against each other, with access only from the roof.[15] Fortress cities were built on mountaintops, as with the Acropolis at Athens. And researchers

---

    10. Nick Thorpe, "Origins of War: Mesolithic Conflict in Europe," *British Archaeology* 52 (2000), http://www.birtarch.ac.uk/ba/ba52/ba52feat.html.

    11. See Donald Kagan and David Webster.

    12. See LeBlanc, "Prehistory of Warfare," and also *Constant Battles*.

    13. "Prehistoric Warfare," http://digilander.libero.it/tepec /prehistoric_warfare.htm.

    14. Ibid.

    15. LeBlanc, "Prehistory of Warfare," 20.

Johnston 5

have found an ancient Peruvian city high atop a mountain peak in the Andes.[16] Thus, archeologists have uncovered many offensive weapons but also gigantic earthen defenses, and the Great Wall of China springs forward as one great example.

Why fight? Many reasons have been advanced by different researchers, and we can take our pick from quite a list as armies went out in search of:

- Food, resources, water, and cattle
- Women for concubines and wives
- Slaves
- Sacrificial victims
- Gold, bronze, copper, and other valuable metals

And they fought to:

- Seek revenge.
- Protect and secure the best trade routes.
- Honor their God and their religion.
- Defend their honor.

John Shy argues that early people, like today, fought to protect their culture and way of life.[17] Michael Adams says the four principles used by the Allies in World War II would serve all armies

This section of the paper examines the causes for prehistoric wars.

---

16. D. L. Parsell, "City Occupied by Inca Discovered on Andean Peak in Peru," *National Geographic News*, 21 March 2002, http://news .nationalgeographic.com/news/2002/03/0314_0318_vilcabamba.html.

17. John Shy, "The Cultural Approach to the History of War," Abstract, *The Journal of Military History* 57 (1993), http://web4 .infotrac.galegroup.com.

of all times—"freedom from want, freedom from fear, freedom of speech, freedom of religion."[18] Thorpe offers this theory:

> My own belief is that warfare, in earliest prehistory, arose over matters of personal honour—such as slights, insults, marriages going wrong, or theft. In a small hunter-gatherer community, everyone is related. An attack on one group member is an attack on the whole family. A personal feud may quickly involve the whole community. From there it is a small step to war.[19]

Donald Kagan echoes that concept with his focus on the word *honor*: "If a state finds that its honor is at risk, that it is treated with contempt, the other two elements of the triad immediately become part of the story. Men get fearful that in light of this contempt others will take advantage and damage their real interests."[20] Yet I recall reading *Beowulf* for one of my classes, and Beowulf fought for *wergild* (money and riches), and he made no bones about it. Victory brings economic bonanzas. LeBlanc shows that ancient battles shifted from total annihilation of the enemy to economic control of villages, cities, and even large states. Conflict waged by complex societies results in a new twist. Warfare was controlled by the elite, and wealth and prestige began to play a role. The commoners became valuable as a

Use the computer's standard indention for block quotations.

---

18. Michael Adams, "The 'Good War' Myth and the Cult of Nostagia," *The Midwest Quarterly* 40 (1998), http://web4.infotrac.galegroup.com.

19. Thorpe.

20. Donald Kagan, "History's Largest Lessons" [interview by Fredric Smoler], *American Heritage* 48 (1997), http://web4.infotrac.galegroup.com.

means to supply wealth to the elite, so warfare began to include conquest instead of annihilation as a goal.[21] Thus, we must add "the search for wealth" as a prime reason for war in primitive times and also the present because it was whispered about George W. Bush's conquest of Iraq—he did it for the oil.

Ultimately, the key question about the cause of war, whether ancient or current, centers on one's choice between biology and culture. On the one side we have the historian, like Victor Hanson, who argues, "Culture largely determines how people fight. The degree to which a society embraces freedom, secular rationalism, consensual government, and capitalism often determines—far more than its geography, climate, or population—whether its armies will be successful over the long term."[22] Hanson adds, "No nation has ever survived once its citizenry ceased to believe that its culture was worth saving."[23]

The society as a whole wants to preserve its culture, in peace if possible. In 500 B.C.E. Herodotus said, "No one is so foolish that he prefers war to peace. In peace sons bury their fathers, in war fathers their sons."[24]

Yet, in my opinion (I have to reach my own conclusion here), the biological history of men and women suggests that we love a good fight. I recall reading an article that said twins inside the womb actually fight, and one fetus might actually devour or absorb the other

---

21. LeBlanc, *Constant Battles*, 194.

22. Victor Davis Hanson, "War Will Be War: No Matter the Era, No Matter the Weapons, and the Same Old Hell," *National Review* 54 (2002), http://web4.infotrac.galegroup.com.

23. Ibid.

24. Qtd. in Peter Jones, "Ancient and Modern," *Spectator* 291 (2003), http://web4.infotrac.galegroup.com.

Johnston 8

one. Siblings just naturally fight, as I did with my older sister and younger brother. His anger exploded one time, and he broke my arm by hitting me with a shovel. We all have witnessed the terrible fights at sporting events, and recently at Glenbrook North High School in Northbrook, Illinois, hazing turned into a terrible beating for some girls. Oh sure, we can give reasons for our eagerness to fight—to preserve our honor ("Don't diss me!"), to preserve our freedom ("Don't encroach!"), or because of fear ("Don't hit me 'cause I'll be hitting back even harder!"). Yet in a final analysis, people want power over others—men beat their wives, mothers overly spank their children, the better team overpowers an opponent, and, yes, a larger, stronger nation will demolish another if self-interest prevails.

This is human nature. The men of Al Qaeda who flew their suicide missions into the World Trade Center and the Pentagon knew exactly what they were doing—exercising their power. In effect, they said, "We'll show the United States that we can inflict great damage." Professor Donald Kagan observes:

> In the end what people really go to war about is power, by which I simply mean the ability to have their will prevail. . . . Every being and every nation requires power for two purposes. The first is to be able to do what it wishes to and must do, some of which will be good and perfectly natural things. Second, one needs power to keep others from imposing their will, to prevent evil things from being done.[25]

The sport of boxing continues to thrive, despite attempts to end it because of its brutality. The fans have a vicarious thrill as one boxer gets pounded to the canvas. At NASCAR races the greatest shouts occur as the fenders crash and cars go tumbling topsy-turvy down the

The writer's conclusion connects his thesis to the modern emphasis on war and terrorism.

---

25. Kagan.

Johnston 9

asphalt. The aggressive behavior of humans is not always a pretty sight, such as the eager willingness of some to loot and pilfer a neighborhood that has been hit by a tornado or other natural disaster.

At the same time, a country like ours governs itself, imposing order by law and moral behavior by religion.[26] Our government, our culture, and our sense of honor have prevailed in a world of nations gone berserk and lawless. Whether we should use our power to impose our sense of democracy on other countries is an international question without a clear answer. My brother, with the shovel in his hand, would say "yes."

---

26. When chaos develops, as in Baghdad during the 2003 war, lawless looting and violence emerge because neither the religious leaders nor an absent police force can maintain order. The breakdown of the culture opens a vacuum filled quickly by primitive behavior.

Bibliography

A separate bibliography is not required if you write initial footnotes with full data.

Adams, Michael. "The 'Good War' Myth and the Cult of Nostagia." *The Midwest Quarterly*, 40 (1998). http://web4.infotrac.galegroup.com.

Cooper, L. D. *Rousseau, Nature, and the Problem of the Good Life*. University Park: Pennsylvania State Univ. Press, 1999.

Ferrill, Arthur. "Neolithic Warfare," Frontline Educational Foundation. http://eserver.org/history/neolithic-war.txt.

Hanson, Victor Davis. "War Will Be War: No Matter the Era, No Matter the Weapons, and the Same Old Hell." *National Review* 54 (2002). http://web4.infotrac.galegroup.com.

Hearn, Kelly. "Decapitated Man Found in Peru Tomb with Ceramic 'Replacement' Head" *National Geographic News*, 6 June 2007, http://news.nationalgeographic.com/news/2007/06/070606-head-jar.html.

Jones, Peter. "Ancient and Modern." *Spectator* 291 (2003). http://web4.infotrac.galegroup.com.

Kagan, Donald. "History's Largest Lessons." Interview by Fredric Smoler. *American Heritage* 48 (1997). http://web4.infotrac.galegroup.com.

LeBlanc, Steven A. *Constant Battles: The Myth of the Peaceful, Noble Savage*. New York: St. Martin's Press, 2004.

---. "Prehistory of Warfare," *Archaeology* May/June, 2003.

Parsell, D. L. "City Occupied by Inca Discovered on Andean Peak in Peru." *National Geographic News*, 21 March 2002. http://news.nationalgeographic.com/news/2002/03/0314_0318_vilcabamba.html.

"Prehistoric Warfare." http://digilander.libero.it/tepec/prehistoric_warfare.htm.

Johnston 11

Shy, John. "The Cultural Approach to the History of War." *The Journal of Military History* 57 (1993). http://web4.nfotrac.galegroup .com.

Thorpe, Nick. "Origins of War: Mesolithic Conflict in Europe." *British Archaeology* 52 (2000). http://www.birtarch.ac.uk/ba/ba52 /ba52feat.html.

Webster, David. "Ancient Maya Warfare." In *War and Society in the Ancient and Medieval Worlds*. Ed. Kurt Raaflaub and Nathan Rosenstein. Cambridge, Massachusetts: Center for Hellenic Studies, 1999.

Yates, Robin. "Early China." In *War and Society in the Ancient and Medieval Worlds*. Ed. Kurt Raaflaub and Nathan Rosenstein. Cambridge, Massachusetts: Center for Hellenic Studies, 2001.

17 CSE Style for the Natural and Applied Sciences

The Council of Science Editors who produced the *CBE Style Manual* has established two forms for citing sources in scientific writing. One is the **citation-sequence** system for writing in the applied sciences, such as chemistry, computer science, mathematics, physics, and medicine. The second is the **name-year** system for use in the biological and earth sciences.

Citation-Sequence

The original description (3) contained precise taxonomic detail that differed with recent studies (4–6).

Name-Year

The original description (Roberts 1999) contained precise taxonomic detail that differed with recent studies (McCormick 2005a, 2005b, and Tyson and others 2004).

There are advantages and disadvantages to each system. The citation-sequence system saves space, and the numbers make minimal disruption to the reading of the text. But this system seldom mentions names, so readers must refer to the bibliography for the names of authors. Also, any disruption in the numbering sequence late in the composition may necessitate a renumbering of all references in the text and the bibliography.

The name-year system mentions authors' names in the text with the year to show timely application and historical perspective. Citations can be deleted or added without difficulty. But a long string of citations in the text can be more disruptive than numbers. In truth, the decision is usually not yours to make. The individual disciplines in the sciences have adopted one form or the other, as shown in the chart on pages 338–339.

Guide by Discipline

Agriculture, Name-Year, 17c–17d
Anthropology, Name-Year, 17c–17d

Archaeology, Name-Year, 17c–17d
Astronomy, Name-Year, 17c–17d

17a Writing In-Text Citations Using the CSE Citation-Sequence System

This system employs numbers to identify sources. Use this style with these disciplines: chemistry, computer science, mathematics, physics, and the medical sciences (medicine, nursing, and general health). In simple terms, the system requires an in-text *number*, rather than the year, and a list of References that are numbered to correspond to the in-text citations.

After completing a list of references, assign a number to each entry. Use one of two methods for numbering the list: (1) arrange references in alphabetical order and number them consecutively (in which case the numbers will appear in random order in the text), or (2) number the references consecutively as you put them into your text, interrupting that order when entering references cited earlier.

The number serves as the key to the source, as numbered in the References. Conform to the following regulations:

1. Place the number within parentheses (1) or brackets [2] or as a raised index numeral, like this.[5] A name is not required and is even discouraged, so try to arrange your wording accordingly. Full information on the author and the work will be placed in the references list.

   It is known (1) that the DNA concentration of a nucleus doubles during interphase.

   A recent study [1] has raised interesting questions related to photosynthesis, some of which have been answered [2].

   In particular, a recent study[1] has raised many interesting questions related to photosynthesis, some of which have been answered.[2]

2. If you include the authority's name, add the number after the name.

   Additional testing by Cooper (3) included alterations in carbohydrate metabolism and changes in ascorbic acid incorporation into the cell and adjoining membranes.

3. If necessary, add specific data to the entry:

   "The use of photosynthesis in this application is crucial to the environment" (Skelton,[8] p 732).

   The results of the respiration experiment published by Jones (3, Table 6, p 412) had been predicted earlier by Smith (5, Proposition 8).

17b Writing a References Page

Supply a list of references at the end of your paper. Number the entries to correspond to sources as you cite them in the text. An alternate method is to alphabetize the list and then number it. Label the list *References*. The form of the entries should follow the examples provided here.

Book

Provide a number and then list the author, title of the book, place of publication, publisher, year, and total number of pages (optional).

1. Goldschneider G. The precision approach to charting your life, career, and relationships. Philadelphia: Running; 2008. 928 p.

Article in a Journal

Provide a number and then list the author, the title of the article, the name of the journal, the year and month if necessary, volume number and issue number if necessary, and inclusive pages. The month or an issue number is necessary for any journal that is paged anew with each issue.

2. King R. Conservatism, institutionalism, and the social control of intergroup conflict. American Journal of Sociology 2008 Mar; 113.5:1351–93.

3. Monhanty S, Jayawardhana, R. The mystery of brown dwarf origins. Scientific American 2006 Jan;294(1):38–45.

Internet Articles and Other Electronic Publications

Add at the end of the citation an availability statement as well as the date you accessed the material. Use the form in number 4 for an article published on the Web. Use the form in number 5 for an periodical article that has been reproduced on the Web. Number 4 is online and number 5 is a printed journal [serial online].

4. Hirsch L. Complementary and alternative medicine. 2005. Available from http://kidshealth.org/teen/your_body/medical_care /alternative_medicine.html. Accessed 2008 Nov 8.

5. Woo JS, Kim DH, Allen, P. TRPC3-interacting triadic proteins in skeletal muscle. Biochem J. [serial online] 2008;411:399–405. Available from http://www.biochemj.org/bj/411/bj4110399.htm .Accessed 2008 May 18.

Magazine or Newspaper Article

Add a specific date and, for newspapers, cite a section letter or number.

6. Rosenwald M. The flu hunter. Smithsonian 2006 Jan:36–46.

7. [Anonymous]. Gas fumes—circulation trouble. The [Nashville] Tennessean 2008 Jun8;Sect D:3.

Proceedings and Conference Presentations

After supplying a number, give the name of the author or editor, the title of the presentation, name of the conference, type of work (report, proceedings, proceedings online, etc.), name of the organization or society, the date of the conference, and the place. If found on the Internet, add the URL and the date you accessed the information.

> For a sample of a "References" page using the number system, see pages 356–357.

8. Sneden GG, Gottlieb-Nudd A, Gottlieb NH. Linking real data to a program assessment and feedback model in state tobacco prevention and control programs [abstract online]. In: Abstracts: 19th National Conference on Chronic Disease Prevention and Control; 2005 Mar 1–3; Atlanta(GA). Available from http://www.cdc.gov/nccdphp /conference/pdf/AbstractBook.pdf. Accessed 2007 Nov 8.

Article from a Loose-Leaf Collection

9. [Anonymous]. Mariculture: Farming on the coastal plains. HRRS Research Collection 2008;2:287.

17c Writing In-Text Citations with Name and Year

The CSE Name-Year style applies to these disciplines:

Agriculture	Anthropology	Archeology
Astronomy	Biology	Botany
Geography	Geology	Zoology

When writing research papers in accordance with the Name-Year system, conform to the following rules:

1. Place the year within parentheses immediately after the authority's name:

   Stroyka (2007) ascribes no species-specific behavior to man.

   However, Adamson (2008) presents data that tend to be contradictory.

2. If you do not mention the authority's name in your text, insert the name, year, and page numbers within the parentheses:

   One source found some supporting evidence for a portion of the questionable data (Marson & Brown 2008, pp 23–32) through point bi-serial correlation techniques.

3. For two authors, employ both names in your text and in the parenthetical citation:

> Torgerson and Andrews (2008)

or

> (Torgerson and Andrews 2008)

Note: Unlike APA style, the CSE style does not use the ampersand (&). For three or more authors, use the lead author's name with "and others." *Note*: CSE style prefers English terms and English abbreviations rather than Latin words and abbreviations, such as *et al.*

In the text:	Torgerson and others (2008)
In the parenthetical citation:	(Torgerson and others 2008)

4. Use lowercase letters (a, b, c) to identify two or more works published in the same year by the same author—for example, "Thompson (2008a)" and "Thompson (2008b)." Then use "2008a" and "2008b" in your List of References.

5. If necessary, supply additional information:

> Alretta (2007a, 2007b; cf. Thomas, 2008, p 89) suggests an
> intercorrelation of these testing devices. But after multiple-group
> analysis, Welston (2008, esp. p 211) reached an opposite conclusion.

6. In the case of a reference to a specific page, separate the page number from the year with a comma and a space. Do not use a period after the "p."

   a. A quotation or paraphrase in the middle of the sentence:

   > Jones stated, "These data of psychological development suggest that
   > retarded adolescents are atypical in maturational growth" (2009, p 215),
   > and Jones attached the data that were accumulated during the study.

   b. A quotation or paraphrase that falls at the end of a sentence:

   > Jones (2009) found that "these data of psychological
   > development suggest that retarded adolescents are atypical in
   > maturational growth" (p 215).

   c. A long quotation, indented with the tab key and set off from the text in a block (and therefore without quotation marks):

   > Tavares (2007) found the following:
   >
   > Whenever these pathogenic organisms attack the human body and
   > begin to multiply, the infection is set in motion. The host
   > responds to this parasitic invasion with efforts to cleanse

itself of the invading agents. When rejection efforts of the host become visible (fever, sneezing, congestion), the disease status exists. (pp 314–315)

7. Punctuate the citations according to the following stipulations:
   a. Use a comma followed by a space to separate citations of different references by the same author or authors in same-year or different-year references:

   Supplemental studies (Johnson 2008a, 2008b, 2007) have shown . . .

   Supplemental studies (Randolph and Roberts 2007, 2008) have shown . . .

   b. Use a comma to separate two authors of the same work who have the same surname.

   (Ramirez SL, Montoya CB, and others 2008)

   Use commas with three or more authors:

   (Smith, Jones, Thompson, and others 2009)

   c. Use a semicolon followed by a space to separate citations to different authors:

   Supplemental studies (Smith, 2007; Barfield 2006, 2008; Barfield and Smith 2008; Wallace 2009) have shown . . .

17d Using Name-Year with Bibliography Entries

Alphabetize the list and label it *References*. Double-space the entries and use the hanging indention. When there are two to ten authors, all should be named in the reference listing. When there are eleven or more authors, the first ten are listed, followed by "and others." If the author is anonymous, insert "[Anonymous]." Place the year immediately after the author's name.

Article in a Journal

List the author, year, article title, journal title, volume number, and inclusive pages. Add an issue number for any journal that is paged anew with each issue.

McCabe ME, Hunt EA, Serwint JR. 2008. Pediatric residents' clinical and educational experiences with end-of-life care. Pediatrics 121:731–37.

Book

List the author, year, title, place of publication, publisher, and total number of pages (optional).

Weisman A. 2007. The world without us. New York: St. Martin's. 336 p.

Internet Articles and Other Electronic Publications

Add at the end of the citation an availability statement as well as the date you accessed the material.

Frank S. 2008. Find the perfect steam trap. Chemical Processing.
[online]. Available from http://www.chemicalprocessing.com
/articles/2007/013.html. Accessed 2008 May 17.

Journal Article Reprinted on the Internet

Provide original publication data as well as the Internet address and the date you accessed the material. Label it as *serial online*.

Linker D. 2006. Heidegger's revelation: The end of enlightenment
[abstract]. American Behavioral Scientist. [serial online];
49:733–749. Available from http://abs.sagepub.com/cgi/content
/abstract/49/5/733. Accessed 2007 Dec 3.

Magazine or Newspaper Article

Add a specific date and, if listed, a section letter or number.

McDaniel A. 2006 Jan–Feb. The three R's of ecofashion. Utne 133:81.

Human K. 2008 Apr 3. Climate change a moving target, experts say.
Denver Post A1.

Proceedings and Conference Publications

Give author, date, title of the presentation, name of conference, type of work (report, proceeding, proceedings online, etc.), name of the organization or society, and place of the conference. If found on the Internet, add the URL.

Sneden GG, Gottlieb-Nudd A, Gottlieb NH. 2005 Mar 1–3. Linking real
data to a program assessment and feedback model in state tobacco
prevention and control programs [abstract online]. In: Abstracts:
19th National Conference on Chronic Disease Prevention and
Control; Atlanta(GA). Available from http://www.cdc.gov/nccdphp
/conference/pdf/AbstractBook.pdf. Accessed 2007 Nov 8.

Article from a Loose-Leaf Collection

[Anonymous]. 2008. Mariculture: Farming on the coastal plains. HRRS
Research Collection 2:287.

Arranging the References List

The list of references should be placed in alphabetical order, as shown next.

References

[Anonymous]. 2006. Myths and facts about Perchlorate. Council on Water Quality. Available from http://www.councilonwaterquality .org/know/myths.html. Accessed 2008 Feb 22.

[Anonymous]. 2007. Perchlorate in California drinking water: Overview and links. California Department of Health Services. Available from http://www.dhs.ca.gov/ps/ddwem/chemicals/perchl /perchlindex.htm. Accessed 2008 Feb 22.

Hogue C. 2005. Federal policy on perchlorate evolves. Chemical and Engineering News. Available from http://pubs.acs.org/cen/news /83/i39/8339perchlorate.html. Accessed 2008 Feb 21.

Logan BE. 2005. Simultaneous wastewater treatment and biological electricity generation. Water Science and Technology 52(1–2):31–37.

Sanchez CA, Crump KS, Kreiger RI, Khandaker NR, Gibbs JP. 2005. Perchlorate and nitrate in leafy vegetables of north America. Environmental Science and Technology 39(24):9391–9397.

17e Sample Paper Using the CSE Citation-Sequence System

Student Sarah Bemis has researched problems with managing diabetes and presented the paper using the CSE citation-sequence system. As she cites a source in the text, she uses a number that also reappears on her References page. Accordingly, the references are not in alphabetical order. As is standard with writing in the sciences, an abstract is provided.

Diabetes Management:

A Delicate Balance

Balance the title, name, and affiliation.

By

Sarah E. Bemis

English 103: College Writing

Sister Winifred Morgan, O.P.

5 March 2008

Bemis ii

Abstract

Diabetes affects approximately 11 million people in the U. S. alone, leading to $350 billion in medical costs. Two types, I and II, have debilitating effects. The body may tolerate hyperglycemia for a short time, but severe complications can occur, such as arterioscleroses, heart disease, nerve damage, and cerebral diseases. New drugs continue to improve the lifestyle of a person with diabetes, but controlling blood sugar requires three elements working together—medication, diet, and exercise. This study examines the importance of each of the three. Patients need a controlled balance of the medication, diet, and exercise program.

An abstract of 100–200 words states the purpose, scope, and major findings of the report.

Bemis 1

Diabetes Management: A Delicate Balance

Use a number to register the use of a source.

Diabetes is a disease that affects approximately 11 million people in the U.S. alone (1), and its complications lead to hundreds of thousands of deaths per year and cost the nation billions in medical care for the direct cost of complications and for indirect costs of lost productivity related to the disease. The condition can produce devastating side effects and a multitude of chronic health problems. For this reason, it can be very frightening to those who do not understand the nature and treatment of the disease. Diabetes currently has no known cure, but it can be controlled. Diabetes research has made great advancements in recent years, but the most important insights into the management of this disease are those which seem the most simplistic. By instituting a healthy, balanced lifestyle, most persons with diabetes can live free of negative side effects.

The thesis or hypothesis is expressed at the end of the introduction.

Scientific writing requires careful definition, as shown here.

More than one source can be listed for one idea or concept.

Diabetes mellitus, according to several descriptions, is a disorder in which the body cannot properly metabolize glucose or sugar. The body's inability to produce or properly use insulin permits glucose to build up in the bloodstream. The excess sugar in the blood, or hyperglycemia, is what leads to the side effects of diabetes (2,3,4).

There are actually two types of diabetes. Type 1, or juvenile diabetes, is the name given to the condition in which the pancreas produces very little or no insulin. It is normally discovered during childhood, but can occur at any age (3). Adult onset, or Type II diabetes, occurs when the pancreas produces usable insulin, but not enough to counteract the amount of glucose in the blood. This often results from obesity or poor diet.

In both Type I and Type II diabetes, the problem has been identified as hyperglycemia (5). This buildup of glucose in the

Bemis 2

bloodstream leads to a number of dangerous side effects. The initial effects and indicators of hyperglycemia are frequent urination, intense thirst, increased hunger and fatigue. When glucose begins to build up in the blood, the kidneys begin to filter out the excess sugar into the urine. The amount of glucose the kidneys can filter varies with each person. In this process, all the water in the body's tissues is being used to produce urine to flush glucose from the kidneys. This is what leads to the intense thirst and frequent urination associated with hyperglycemia (5).

Causal analysis, as shown here, is a staple of scientific writing.

Because the body lacks the insulin needed to allow glucose into the cells, the glucose cannot be processed to produce energy. The cells signal the brain that they are not getting sugar and this causes hunger. However, no matter how much a victim of hyperglycemic diabetes eats, the cells will not be producing energy (6).

It has been shown (4) that with hyperglycemia the kidneys try to compensate for the excess of sugar and lack of energy. While the kidneys attempt to filter the sugar from the blood, the liver tries to produce energy by burning fat and muscle to produce ketones, a protein that the body attempts to burn in place of glucose. Ketones do not provide the energy the body requires but do produce chemicals toxic to the body. When too many ketones are present in the blood, ketoacidosis occurs (4).

Refer to the sources with the past tense verb or the present participle.

Guthrie and Guthrie (1) have demonstrated that ketoacidosis is a condition caused by high levels of hydrogen in the blood. This leads initially to a high blood pH, depleted saline fluids and dehydration. If untreated it can lead to a shut down of the central nervous system, coma or even death. In fact, many diabetes-related deaths are caused by ketoacidosis that has reached a comatose state. Ketoacidosis is characterized by

In addition to the number, you may mention the name(s) of your sources.

Bemis 3

frequent urination, dry mouth, extreme thirst, headache, rapid and deep respiration, increased heart rate, nausea, vomiting, disorientation and lethargy (1).

The American Academy of Family Physicians (4) has reported that hyperglycemia can cause other, more subtle, side effects. Because the body is not receiving the nourishment it requires, a victim of hyperglycemic diabetes often experiences poor tissue growth and repair. This can cause problems with growth and development in children and wound healing in adults as well as children. It has also been reported (7) that the immune system is also affected and that victims experience infection more often and more severely than a person without diabetes. Other conditions that frequently occur in conjunction with hyperglycemia in its early stages are depression and chronic fatigue (8). Many patients who experience hypoglycemia have difficulties controlling gain and loss of weight as well.

It has been shown (Guthrie and Guthrie 1) that the body may tolerate hyperglycemia over a short time period. However, if untreated, it leads to other chronic and often fatal health conditions. Arteri005cleroses occurs in hyperglycemic diabetics over time, resulting in decreased circulation and eyesight. This also may lead to heart disease, angina and heart attack, the most prevalent causes of death among diabetics (1). Also common is diabetic neuropathy, a degeneration of the nerves. This condition causes pain and loss of function in the extremities (1).

A person with diabetes is also at risk for many cerebral diseases. Both the large and small cerebral arteries of victims are prone to rupture, which can cause cerebral hemorrhage, thrombosis or stroke. Blockages in the carotid arteries can decrease blood flow to the brain, causing episodes of lightheadedness and fainting (1, p 201–202).

You may add page numbers to the reference as a courtesy to the reader.

Bemis 4

Diabetic nephropathy occurs when the kidneys are overloaded with glucose. Eventually, they begin to shut down. The kidneys of a person with uncontrolled diabetes are also susceptible to infection, resulting in decreased kidney function (1).

With all the complications victims experience, the outlook for a long and healthy life does not seem good for those diagnosed with the disease. However, all of these effects can be reduced, delayed, and even prevented with proper care and control. By monitoring blood sugar and reacting accordingly with medication, by special diets, and by exercise and a controlled lifestyle, persons with diabetes can avoid these serious health conditions (Hu and others 9).

The first aspect of diabetes care is blood sugar monitoring and medication. The two go hand in hand in that the patient must have the appropriate type and dosage of medication and must know blood sugar values and patterns in order to determine the correct regimen. Two main types of monitoring are necessary for diabetes control. Patients must perform home glucose monitoring on a daily basis. Advancements in this area in recent years have made this relatively effortless. Several glucose monitoring kits are available to the general public. These consist of a small, electronic machine that measures the amount of glucose in the blood, as well as the equipment necessary to obtain a small sample. With such equipment, patients can test and record blood sugars several times per day. This gives both short-term and long-term information by which they and their physicians can determine insulin dosages and meal plans.

Process analysis, as shown here, is often a staple of scientific writing.

In addition to daily monitoring, victims should visit their physician regularly. Doctors usually perform a test called a hemoglobin AIC, which gives a better indication of blood sugar control over a longer period of time than a home test. This

Bemis 5

should be done approximately every ninety days, as that is the time period over which blood cells are renewed. This test along with consideration of daily glucose values can help the physician determine overall control and effectiveness of the patient's routine. Regular visits also give the physician an opportunity to monitor the general health of the patient, including circulation, eyesight, infections, and organ infections.

The writer explores control element number one: methods of administering medication.

The treatment of diabetes usually involves medication. Since Type I diabetics produce very little or no insulin, insulin injections will always be necessary. For Type II, the treatment may be strictly dietary, dietary with oral hypoglycemic agents, or insulin therapy.

When insulin therapy is required, it is very important that the appropriate type and dosage is implemented. Many types of insulin are available. The main distinction among these types is in their action time, onset, peak-time, and duration. Different types of insulin begin to act at different rates. They also continue to act for different periods of time and hit peak effectiveness at different intervals (1). This is why it is important to have records of blood sugars at regular intervals over several weeks. From this it can be determined when and what type of insulin is needed most. Once it is determined what insulin regimen is appropriate, the patient must follow it closely. Routine is very important in controlling diabetes.

Patients with diabetes now have a few options when it comes to injection method. One may chose traditional manual injection, an injection aid, or an insulin pump. Injection aids can make using a needle easier and more comfortable or actually use air pressure to inject. The insulin pump is a device that offers convenience as well as improved control. The pump is a small battery-operated device that delivers insulin 24 hours a day through a small needle worn under the skin. The pump

Bemis 6

contains a computer chip which controls the amount of insulin delivered according to the wearer's personalized plan (10). The pump is meant for patients who do not wish to perform multiple injections, but are willing to test blood sugars frequently. The pump can help patients who have some trouble controlling their blood sugars by providing insulin around the clock. It also provides an element of freedom for persons with busy schedules.

Some Type II patients can control the disease with a combination of diet, exercise and an oral hypoglycemic agent. These drugs themselves contain no insulin. They traditionally lower blood glucose levels by stimulating the pancreas to produce insulin (1). Therefore, they are only appropriate for patients whose pancreas is still producing some insulin. Diabetes research has advanced in recent years, however. Some new drugs may be coming available in the new millennium. Creators of the pharmaceuticals are able to increase sensitivity to insulin and suppress the secretion of hormones that raise blood sugar. A number of new drugs that are aimed at taking the place of insulin therapy are currently in the final stages of research and development. Glucovance has been advanced as a valuable new medication (11). For now, the oral medications that are available can aid in keeping better control when properly paired with an effective diet and exercise plan.

While it is important to have the proper medication, the backbone of diabetes management is the meal plan. By making wise choices in eating, persons with diabetes can reduce stress on the body and increase the effectiveness of their medication. The basis of a good meal plan is balanced nutrition and moderation. Eating a low fat, low sodium, low sugar diet is the best way for a diabetic to ensure longevity and health. It is important for everyone to eat balanced meals on a routine

The writer now explores control element number two: methods of diet management.

Bemis 7

schedule. For victims of diabetes, it can help in blood sugar control and in preventing heart disease and digestive problems.

Two established meal plans are recommended for patients: the Exchange Plan and carbohydrate counting (12, 13). Both are based on The Diabetes Food Pyramid (Nutrition). The Food Pyramid divides food into six groups. These resemble the traditional four food groups, except that they are arranged in a pyramid in which the bottom, or largest, section contains the foods that should be eaten most each day. The top, or smallest, section contains the foods that should be eaten least, if at all. With any diabetic meal plan, the patient should eat a variety of foods from all the food groups, except the sweets, fats, and alcohol group. New directives by the American Diabetes Association offer helpful and authoritative guidance to help victims cope with their meal planning (14, 15).

The Exchange Plan provides a very structured meal plan. Foods are divided into eight categories, which are more specific than those of the Food Pyramid are. A dietician or physician determines a daily calorie range for the patient and, based on that range, decides how many servings she or he should eat from each category per meal. Portion sizes are determined and must be followed exactly. The patient then has the option to either choose foods that fit into the groups recommended for each meal or exchange foods from one group for foods from another.

Another meal plan patients can utilize is carbohydrate counting. This plan is less structured and gives the patient more flexibility in making meal choices. It also involves less planning. Once again, food is categorized, but into only three groups. The largest food group, carbohydrates, encompasses not only starches, but dairy products, fruits, and vegetables as well. The dietician or physician again assigns a calorie range. With this plan, however,

Bemis 8

only the number of carbohydrates per meal are assigned, and even this is flexible. This plan is recommended for those who know how to make balanced meal choices, but need to keep track of their food intake. Once again, portion sizes are important, and the patient must remember to eat the recommended amount of foods from each pyramid category (5, 11, 12).

The final element in successfully managing diabetes is exercise. It has been shown (16) that exercise can help stimulate the body to use glucose for energy, thus taking it out of the blood. Diabetic patients need regular exercise programs that suit their personal needs. Something as simple as a walking routine can significantly reduce blood glucose levels (16). Some patients may require as little as a fifteen-minute per day walk, where some may need a more involved workout. In each case, an exercise schedule works with meal plans, medication, and lifestyle. Also crucial to the success of an exercise routine is close monitoring of blood sugar. If glucose levels are too high or too low, exercise will have negative effects.

All of the aspects of diabetes management can be summed up in one word: balance. Diabetes itself is caused by a lack of balance of insulin and glucose in the body. In order to restore that balance, a person with diabetes must juggle medication, monitoring, diet, and exercise. Managing diabetes is not an easy task, but a long and healthy life is very possible when the delicate balance is carefully maintained.

The writer now explores control element number three: methods of exercise.

Bemis 9

References

1. Guthrie DW, Guthrie RA. Nursing management of diabetes mellitus. New York: Springer, 2002. 500 p.

2. [Anonymous]. Diabetes insipidus. American Academy of Family Physicians. Available from http://www.aafp.org/patientinfo/insipidu.html. Accessed 2008 Feb 20.

3. Clark CM, Fradkin JE, Hiss RG, Lorenz RA, Vinicor F, Warren-Boulton E. Promoting early diagnosis and treatment of type 2 diabetes. JAMA 2000;284:363–365.

4. [Anonymous]. Diabetes: Monitoring your blood sugar level. American Academy of Family Physicians. Available from http://familydoctor.org/355.xml. Accessed 2008 Feb 19.

5. Peters AL. Conquering diabetes. New York: Penguin, 2005. 368 p.

6. Schlosberg S. The symptoms you should never ignore. Shape 2000 Aug;19:136–142.

7. Inzucchi S. Diabetes mellitus manual. New York: McGraw-Hill, 2004. 360 p.

8. Roberts SS. The diabetes advisor. Diabetes Forecast 2005;58(11):41–42. Available from http://www.diabetes.org/diabetes-forecast/nov2005/toc.jsp. Accessed 2008 Feb 18.

9. Hu FB, Li TY, Colditz GA, Willett WC, Manson JE. Television watching and other sedentary behaviors in relation to risk of obesity and type 2 diabetes mellitus in women. JAMA 2003;289:1785–91.

10. [Anonymous]. Insulin pump therapy. Children with Diabetes 2007. Available from http://www.childrenwithdiabetes.com/pumps/. Accessed 2008 Feb 21.

11. [Anonymous]. Glucophage. Diabetes Healthsource. 2008. Available from http://www.glucophage.com. Accessed 2008 Feb 23.

12. McDermott MT. Endocrine Secrets. New York: Elsevier, 2004. 448 p.

13. Eades MR, Eades MD. Protein Power. New York: Warner, 2005. 464 p.

Citations on this page demonstrate the citation-sequence method, as explained on pages 339–342. For details on the name-year system, see pages 342–344.

Bemis 10

14. American Diabetes Association. The American diabetes association complete guide to diabetes. New York: McGraw-Hill; 2006. 518 p.

15. American Diabetes Association. Magic Menus for people with diabetes. Alexandria, VA: ADA; 2003. 244 p.

16. [Anonymous]. Exercise. American Diabetes Association [article online] 2008. Available from http://www.diabetes.org/weightloss-and-exercise/exercise/overview.jsp. Accessed 2008 Feb 22.

18 Creating Electronic Research Projects

This chapter suggests ways to create and publish your research project electronically. It begins with the easiest—putting a word-processed research paper on a disk for your instructor—and moves to the most difficult—designing a Web site and releasing the paper onto the Internet. This chapter will give you a sense of the possibilities of electronic research papers.

Creating your research paper electronically has a number of advantages:

- **It is easy.** Creating electronic research projects can be as simple as saving your paper in a computer file and publishing your paper electronically.
- **It offers multimedia potential.** Unlike paper documents, electronic documents enable you to include anything available in a digital form—including text, illustrations, sound, and video.
- **It can link your reader to more information.** Your readers can click a hyperlink to access additional sources of information. (A **hyperlink** or link is a highlighted word or image that, when clicked, lets readers jump from one place to another—for example, from your research paper to a Web site on your subject.)

18a Beginning the Electronic Project

Before you decide to create your research paper electronically, consider three questions to assist the development of the presentation:

1. **What support is provided by your school?** Most institutions have made investments in technology and the personnel to support it. Investigate how your college will help you publish in an electronic medium.
2. **Is electronic publishing suitable for your research topic?** Ask yourself what your readers will gain from reading an electronic text rather than the traditional paper version. Will an electronic format really help you get your ideas to readers?
3. **What form will it take?** Electronic research papers appear generally in one of the following forms:
   - A word-processed document (see section 18b)
   - An electronic slide show (see section 18c)
   - A Web site (see section 18d)

Each of these forms can be researched and produced using traditional methods, but the writing and presentation will differ.

18b Using Word Processing

The easiest way to create an electronic document is by using word processing programs such as Microsoft Word or Corel WordPerfect and then distributing your report in its electronic form rather than printing it out.

Most popular word processing programs include tools for handling features that will enhance your presentation:

- **Graphics.** Word processors can accommodate graphics in a variety of formats, including .gif and .jpg (see section 18f for more information on graphic formats).
- **Sound and video.** Word processors can include several common audio and video clip formats. Usually, the reader has to click on an icon to activate the clip.
- **Hyperlinks.** Readers can click to go to a Web site on the Internet for further reading.

There are unique advantages when using a word processor to create an electronic research paper. Using a word processor is familiar; you probably already use one to create your traditional research papers. It is also flexible; word processors give you more control over format and design.

However, using a word processor to create your electronic research paper has two disadvantages: The computer file created by your word processor can become quite large if you include graphics, sound, and video. Also, to view your paper, readers must own the same word-processing software and sometimes even the same version of the software. Nevertheless, a word processor works well in a classroom or computer laboratory that shares the same software.

18c Building Electronic Presentations

If you plan an oral presentation, an electronic slide show can help illustrate your ideas. Electronic presentations differ from word-processed documents in that each page, or slide, comprises one computer screen. By clicking, you can move to the next slide.

The most common programs for creating electronic presentations are Microsoft PowerPoint and Corel Presentations. Both help you create a series of slides for presentation on your computer screen or through a projector to a large screen. These programs allow you to include graphics, sound, and other elements. More complex, standalone presentations with multimedia animation—designed for distribution on CD-ROM or through the Internet—can be created with programs such as Macromedia Director and Hyperstudio.

For small audiences you can usually present the show on a computer screen. For larger audiences, you may need a wide-screen television or a data projector. Check with your instructor or school technology specialist to find out what presentation equipment is available.

As you create your electronic presentation, consider the following suggestions:

- Because each slide can hold only limited information, condense the content of each slide to key points and fill in the details orally.
- Use the slide show to support your oral presentation.
- If appropriate, include graphics from your research project in your slide show.
- End the slide show with a carefully designed closing slide or an empty slide so that people will know the presentation is finished.

If you distribute the slide show by disk, CD, or the Web, you will probably need to adjust the presentation by adding more information to the slides because your oral commentary will be unavailable to the viewer—or you can record your audio commentary for inclusion with the presentation.

18d Research Paper Web Pages and Sites

A Web site can be an exciting and flexible way to convey your research. It is also the easiest way to get your work out to a large audience. Like an electronic presentation, a research paper Web site can include graphics, sound, and video.

> For more information on building Web pages and sites, see the Beginner's Guide to HTML at http://www.cs .trinity.edu/About/The_Courses/cs301 /html/HTMLPrimerAll.html or http: //www.kean.edu/HomePages /beginnersGuide.htm.

Creating a Web page or a Web site involves collecting or making a series of computer files—some that contain the basic text and layout for your pages, and others that contain the graphics, sounds, or video that goes in your pages. These files are assembled together automatically when you view them in a Web browser.

Creating a Single Web Page

If you want to create a single Web page from your research paper, the easiest but most limited method is to save your word-processed research paper in HTML (Hyper Text Markup Language, the computer language that controls what Web sites look like). Different word-processing programs perform this process differently; so consult your software's help menu for specific instructions.

When the word processing software converts your document to HTML, it also converts any graphics you have included to separate graphics files. Together, your text and the graphics can be viewed in a Web browser like any other Web page.

Your research paper will look somewhat different in HTML format than in its word-processed format. In some ways, HTML is less flexible than word processing, but you can still use word-processing software to make changes to your new HTML-formatted paper.

NOTE: The reader will need to scroll down the screen to continue to read the document.

Creating a Web Site with Multiple Pages

A multiple-page Web site allows you to assemble a large number of shorter pages, which are easy for readers to access and read. It requires careful planning and organization.

Creating a multipage Web site means creating one Web page after another—you repeat the basic process to create each page, and you add links between pages so readers can navigate easily from one to the next. Start with a home page that includes a title, a basic description of your project, and an index with hyperlinks to the contents of your site. Navigational elements, like links to the home page and other major pages of your site, provide a way for readers to "turn the pages" of your report.

Using an Editor to Create Web Pages

The easiest way to create your pages is with a Web page editor such as Microsoft FrontPage, Adobe Page Mill, or Netscape Composer. These programs work differently, but they all do the same thing—create Web pages. Using them is like using a word processor: You enter or paste in text, insert graphics or other multimedia objects, and save the file.

Importing, Entering, and Modifying Text

You can create your text within the Web page editor or outside it. To import text, simply copy it from your word processor and paste it into your Web page editor. You can also specify fonts, font sizes, font styles (such as bold), alignment, lists with bullets, and numbered lists. Here are a few tips for entering text into a Web page:

- **Use bold rather than underlining for emphasis and titles.** On a Web site, links are often underlined, so any other underlining can cause confusion.
- **Do not use tabs.** HTML does not support tabs for indenting the first line of a paragraph. You also will not be able to use hanging indents for your bibliography.
- **Do not double-space.** The Web page editor automatically single spaces lines of text and double spaces between paragraphs.
- **Make all lines flush left** on the Works Cited Page; HTML does not support the hanging indentions.

Citing Your Sources in a Web Research Paper

If you are using MLA, APA, or CSE styles, include parenthetical citations in the text itself and create a separate Web page for references. Remember to include such a page in your plans. Do not put footnotes at the bottom of each of your Web pages. Instead, use endnotes and create a separate page that holds all of the notes, just as you would have a separate page for the Works Cited or References pages. Create each note number in the text as a link to the notes page so readers can click on the number to go to the note. Remember to have a link on the notes page or Works Cited page to take the reader back again to the text.

18e Planning Electronic Research Papers

Because creating an electronic research paper can be more complicated than creating a traditional paper, it's important to plan your project carefully.

Creating a Plan for Your Research Paper

The following questions will help you think through the planning of your project.

- **Assignment.** Does your instructor have specific requirements for this assignment you should keep in mind?
- **Project description.** What topic will you be writing on?
- **Purpose.** What are your reasons for creating an electronic project? Are you going to blend photographs of the 1960s with an essay on the Civil Rights Movement? Or provide audio examples in an essay on John F. Kennedy's speeches?
- **Audience.** Are you writing for the instructor, or will there be a broader audience, such as classmates or readers on the Web?
- **Format.** Will your research paper be a word-processed document, an electronic presentation, or a Web site?
- **Multimedia content.** What information, other than text, will you present? Do you have the tools available to scan or import multimedia?
- **Structure.** How will you organize your document?

Designing Your Electronic Research Paper

Reading any kind of electronic document can be difficult for the reader unless you take special care in designing it. Aim for the following:

- **A consistent look and feel.** Make your research paper look very consistent throughout. Presentation software usually includes ready-made templates that help you to create a consistent look and feel.
- **A subtle design.** It is easy to create a Web site or presentation that includes all the bells and whistles—but such documents are hard to navigate and even harder to read. Avoid distractions like blinking text, garish colors, or unnecessary animations.

For more information on Web site design, see the Yale C/AIM WWW Style Guide at http://www.webstyleguide.com/index .html?/.

- **Ease of navigation.** Include consistent navigation tools so readers can see where they are and where they can go next.
- **Legibility.** Because readers often access electronic documents through a computer screen, legibility is important.

Make the contrast between your text and background colors strong enough that readers can see the text easily. Avoid using the italic fonts, which are difficult to see on a computer screen.

18f Using Graphics in Your Electronic Research Paper

Graphics will give your electronic text some exciting features that are usually foreign to the traditional research paper. They go beyond words on a printed page to pictures, sound, video clips, animation, and a vivid use of full-color art.

Decorative graphics make the document look more attractive but seldom add to the paper's content. Most clip art, for example, is decorative.

Illustration graphics provide a visual amplification of the text. For example, a picture of Thomas Hardy would reinforce and augment a research paper on the British poet and novelist.

Information graphics, such as charts, graphs, or tables, provide data about your topic.

Graphic File Formats

Graphics usually take up a lot of space, but you can save them as either JPEG or GIF files to make them smaller. In fact, Web sites can use only graphics saved in these formats. Both formats compress redundant information in a file, making it smaller while retaining most of the image quality. You can recognize the file format by looking at the extension to the file name—GIFs have the extension .gif, and JPEGs have the extension .jpg or .jpeg. GIF stands for Graphical Interchange Format, which develops and transfers digital images. JPEG stands for Joint Photographic Experts Group, which compresses color images to smaller files for ease of transport.

For more information on JPEG and GIF files, go to one of these sites: Wide Area Communications at http://www.widearea.co.uk/designer/compress.html Graphics 101 at About.com, at http://graphicdesign.about.com/.

In general, JPEGs work best for photographs and GIFs work best for line drawings. To save a file as a GIF or JPEG, open it in an image-editing program like Adobe Photoshop and save the file as one of the two types (for example, thardy.jpg or thardy.gif).

For more information on securing permission for borrowed material on your Web site, see Chapter 7, pages 104–105.

When the graphic is ready, you can insert it into your electronic research paper. Programs usually have specific menu commands for inserting graphics; refer to your user documentation to find out how to do so.

You can also borrow images from clip art or other Web sites (with proper documentation, of course). To borrow an image, go to the site with your Web browser, right-click on the image that you want, and left-click on "Save image as …" to put it on your hard drive or a portable storage device. You can then insert the image into your research paper.

Creating Your Own Digital Graphics

Making your own graphics file is complex but rewarding. It adds a personal creativity to your research paper. Use one of the following techniques:

- **Use a graphics program,** such as Macromedia Freehand or Adobe Illustrator. With such software you can create a graphic file and save it as a JPEG or GIF file.
- **Use a scanner** to copy your drawings, graphs, photographs, and other matter. Programs such as Adobe Photoshop and JASC Paintshop Pro are useful for modifying scanned photographs.
- **Create original photographs with a digital camera.** Digital cameras usually save images as JPEGs, so you will not need to convert the files into a usable format.

As long as you create JPEG files or GIF files for your graphics, you can transport the entire research paper to a Web site.

18g Using Sound and Video in Your Electronic Research Paper

Because it usually requires additional hardware and software, working with sound and video can be complicated. It also makes your research paper large and difficult to compress and transfer. Before attempting to use digital audio or video, check into your own resources as well as those of your instructor and school. Many institutions have invested heavily in multimedia technology, while others have not.

For information on digital audio and video, consult the following Web site: Webmonkey's multimedia tutorial for audio and video resources, at http: // www.webmonkey.com/multimedia/.

A detailed discussion of digital audio and video is beyond the scope of this chapter, but the Web holds a wealth of information on the subject.

18h Delivering Your Electronic Research Paper to Readers

Follow your instructor's requirements for delivering your electronic research paper or use one of the techniques in the following checklist.

Delivering Your Electronic Research Paper

- **Zip disk.** A Zip disk or other proprietary format will hold much larger files, but your reader/professor must own a drive that can read it.

- **CD-ROM discs.** These discs hold large amounts of data and thus work well for transmitting graphics, sound, or video files. However, you must own or have access to a CD-R (Compact Disk Recordable) or CD-RW (Compact Disk Recordable/Writeable) drive. Most readers will have regular CD-ROM drives that can read your discs, but you might want to confirm this beforehand.

- **High-Speed USB Flash Drive.** These devices hold large amounts of data, so they work well for transmitting graphics, sound, or video files. Their compact size and plug-and-play operation allow easy access to your instructor's laptop or desktop computer with a USB port.

- **E-mail.** E-mailing your file as an attachment is the fastest way to deliver your electronic research paper; however, it works best if you have a single file, like a word-processed research paper, rather than a collection of related files, like a Web site.

- **Web site.** If you have created a Web site or Web page, you can upload your work to a Web server, and readers can access your work on the Internet. Procedures for uploading Web sites vary from school to school and server to server; work closely with your instructor and Webmaster to perform this process successfully. Regardless of what method you choose, be sure to follow your instructor's directions and requirements.

18i Preparing a Writing Portfolio

Writing is a form of art, but unlike other art forms such as dance or sculpture, writers usually do not invite others to watch them perform. Instead, it is the finished product that can have the most influence on others and also demonstrate a writer's abilities. But how can a writer, especially a student writer, demonstrate his or her writing ability to their peers, professors, the public, or more importantly, to a potential employer? The answer is a Writing Portfolio.

Over the past decade, writing portfolios have become a choice assessment tool for many instructors. As a result, most students who have participated in writing projects, from high school to PhD programs, have assembled portfolios of some kind. Writing Portfolios provide a tangible demonstration of talent and experience. Your portfolio will include selected previous written works in a class, plus any additional assignments that the instructor requests. The Writing Portfolio has several benefits:

- It provides clear objectives and evaluative criteria for writing assignments.
- It provides a real audience as you learn to direct your writing to an unknown reader.
- It provides informed feedback from your instructor, peers, and writing associates.

Specifically, the Writing Portfolio is a purposeful collection of writing assembled to demonstrate specified writing capabilities to an audience. Usually, a portfolio is used to demonstrate writing skills and talents, but it can also be used for obtaining a job, documenting job performance, or gaining entrance into an educational institution. In some respects, the Writing Portfolio is an individual's creative resume. Although it is not an actual resume, the Writing Portfolio displays the works and documents that a resume mentions. In that sense, the collection of writings gives a three-dimensional or amplified view of a learner's abilities.

At first, selecting folio material may seem like an overwhelming task, especially if you are starting from scratch. The truth is that most writers have many writing samples available, however. Listed here are some potential places to begin looking for folio material:

- Coursework from your classes, not just writing courses. Hanging on to class notebooks and assignments is beneficial and provides writing examples from a number of subject areas.
- Previous essays and research projects. These are great because they usually contain the writer's "best" work and include self-analysis essays regarding strengths and weaknesses as a writer.
- Journals and personal writing. Unconstrained writing reveals a lot about a writer's style and preferred voice.

Although the portfolio philosophy is to save everything, you need not feel pressured to hoard every scrap of writing. Instead, a light screening of portfolio materials should be conducted to prevent an unmanageable collection of samples from forming. Use the following criteria to help select folio material:

- Select materials that clearly demonstrate your abilities.
- Select materials based on quality. Choose documents that demonstrate audience analysis, grammar, clarity, conciseness, technical information, instructions, page layout and design, organization, group or independent work, diversity, and variety.
- Select materials that demonstrate learning. For instance, if a particular piece demonstrates your understanding of persuasive methods, include it.
- Select materials that will have long-term value and usefulness.

Storing and organizing the portfolio material can be chaotic. There are many storage/organizing products available. For example, expandable folders work nicely for grouping material because they come in varying sizes and can accommodate odd-sized documents. Another organizing option is a three-ring binder. If you use a three-ring binder, consider using plastic sheet protectors to store pages; it is better to avoid punching holes in your work if possible. Some people keep folio materials in a file drawer and organize the materials in files. You could also use a plastic storage container. Keeping your work on USB flash drive is another option. Choose whatever works best for you, but be sure to put the folio collection somewhere where it will be safe from damage or loss.

NOTE: The safest and most dependable way to store your materials is both on hard copy and on a flash drive.

Begin creating a collection of any and all materials that you might want to place in your Writing Portfolio. Remember, the portfolio philosophy is SAVE EVERYTHING! The more material you collect in your portfolio, the broader the selection and greater the flexibility you will have when pulling together a presentation of your writing talents.

For information on preparing a Writing Portfolio, consult the following Web site: http://writing.colostate.edu/guides /teaching/co301aman/pop5a.cfm.

18j Presenting Research in Alternative Formats

Current technology provides various options for presenting your research project. Desktop publishing programs such as Microsoft Publisher, Adobe PageMaker, or Broderbund Print Shop provide templates for the effective design of newsletters and brochures. Consider an alternative format for your findings when it includes information that can inform or assist a broad array of readers.

Often printed on both sides of a sheet of paper, **newsletters** usually contain multiple pages. **Brochures** are formatted with columns or "panels" that are designed to fit on the front and back of one single sheet of paper so that it can easily be folded. Both newsletters and brochures follow certain conventions of style:

- Place your information in a logical order.
- Use a type size, font style, and color of text that is easy to read.
- Use left-justified formatting that leaves a "ragged" right-hand margin. This is a style that is easier for readers to follow.
- Avoid distracting gaps between words and awkward hyphens dividing words at the end of lines.
- Keep paragraphs short when information is presented in columns.

For most class projects, newsletters and brochures can be printed from your personal computer. For documents in the workplace or for a social group, you may choose to consider using a professional printer; however, remember that a print agency will charge for its services.

Alternative formats for the presentation of your research, such as newsletters and brochures, should stimulate interest and highlight the key components of the project.

CHECKLIST

Publishing Alternative Documents

- Decide on the purpose of the document and the response that your want the audience to have about the information.
- Sketch out or visualize how each section or panel will look.
- Select a paper size, binding, or folding that presents your research in a straightforward, clear method.
- Consider graphics, colors, and formatting that add to the clarity of your document.
- Use a distinctive font in the masthead or title as well as headlines for the sections of the document that emphasize their importance.
- Make each section or panel an independent item that can be understood if the brochure is folded or turned to a secondary page.
- Limit information to what readers can comprehend in a brief reading, while informing them where more information can be found.

YOUR RESEARCH PROJECT

1. If you are interested in producing an electronic research paper, consult with your instructor for advice and to learn about institutional support.

2. Begin by building a basic model with word processing, one that might include graphics and other elements as described in section 18f.

3. If the assignment includes an oral presentation, consider building a slide show as described in section 18c.

4. Try building a Web page and then a Web site. Consult with your instructor before uploading it to the Web.

5. Make yourself comfortable about your knowledge of technical terms such as Zip disk, CD-ROM, USB flash drive, e-mail, and Web site.

Glossary
Rules and Techniques for Preparing the Manuscript in MLA Style

The alphabetical glossary that follows will answer most of your questions about matters of form, such as margins, pagination, dates, and numbers. For matters not addressed here, consult the index, which will direct you to appropriate pages elsewhere in this text.

Abbreviations

Employ abbreviations often and consistently in notes and citations, but avoid them in the text. In your citations, but not in your text, always abbreviate these items:

- technical terms and reference words (anon., e.g., diss.).
- institutions (acad., assn., Cong.).
- dates (Jan., Feb.).
- states and countries (OH, CA, U.S.A.).
- names of publishers (McGraw, UP of Florida).
- titles of well-known religious and literary works.

See also "Names of Persons," page 373, for comments on abbreviations of honorary titles.

A few general rules apply:

1. With abbreviations made up of capital letters, use neither periods nor spaces:
   MS JD CD-ROM AD
2. Do use periods and a space with initials used with personal names:
   J. K. Rowling T. S. Eliot

Abbreviations Commonly Used for Technical Terms and Institutions

abr.	abridged
anon.	anonymous
art., arts.	article(s)
bibliog.	bibliography, bibliographer, bibliographic
bk. bks.	book(s)
ca., c.	*circa* 'about'; used to indicate an approximate date, as in "ca. 1812"
cf.	*confer* 'compare' (one source with another); not, however, to be used in place of "see" or "see also"
ch., chs.	chapter(s), also shown as chap., chaps.
col., cols.	column(s)
doc.	document
ed., eds.	editor(s), edition, or edited by
et al.	*et alii* 'and others'; "John Smith et al." means John Smith and other authors
f., ff.	page or pages following a given page
ibid.	*ibidem* 'in the same place,' i.e., in the immediately preceding title, normally capitalized as in "Ibid., p. 34"
i.e.	*id est* 'that is'; preceded and followed by a comma
loc. cit.	*loco citato* 'in the place (passage) cited'

ms., mss.	manuscript(s) as in "(Cf. the mss. of Glass and Ford)"
narr.	narrated by
n.d.	no date (in a book's title or copyright pages)
n.p.	no place (of publication)
n. pag.	no page
ns	new series
op. cit.	*opere citato* 'in the work cited'
p., pp.	page(s); do not use "ps." for "pages"
proc.	proceedings
qtd.	quoted
rev.	revised, revised by, revision, review, or reviewed by
rpt.	reprint, reprinted
ser.	series
sic	'thus'; placed in brackets to indicate an error has been made in the quoted passage and the writer is quoting accurately.
supp.	supplement(s)
trans., (tr.)	translator, translated, translated by, or translation
vol., vols.	volume(s) (e.g., vol. 3)

Abbreviations of Publishers' Names

Use the shortened forms below as guidelines for shortening all publishers names for MLA citations (but *not* for APA, CMS, or CSE styles).

Abrams	Harry N. Abrams, Inc.
Barnes	Barnes and Noble Books
Farrar	Farrar, Straus and Giroux
MIT P	The MIT Press
U of Chicago P	University of Chicago Press

Abbreviations of Biblical Works

Use parenthetical documentation for biblical references in the text—that is, place the entry within parentheses immediately after the quotation. For example:

> He hath shewed thee, O man, what is good; and what doth the LORD
> require of thee, but to do justly, and to love mercy, and to walk humbly with thy
> God? (Mic. 6:8).

Do not italicize titles of books of the Bible. Abbreviate books of the Bible, except some very short titles, such as Ezra and Mark, as shown in these examples.

Acts	Acts of the Apostles	Matt.	Matthew
1 and 2 Chron.	1 and 2 Chronicles	Num.	Numbers
1 and 2 Cor.	1 and 2 Corinthians	Obad.	Obadiah
Deut.	Deuteronomy	Ps. (Pss.)	Psalm(s)

Abbreviations for Literary Works

Shakespeare

In parenthetical documentation, use italicized abbreviations for titles of Shakespearean plays, as shown in this example:

> MIRANDA O, wonder!
> How many goodly creatures are there here!
> How beauteous mankind is! O brave new world,
> That has such people in't! (*Tmp.* 5.1.181–184).

Abbreviate as shown by these examples:

Ant.	*Antony and Cleopatra*	*JC*	*Julius Caesar*
AWW	*All's Well That Ends Well*	*Lr.*	*Lear*
F1	*First Folio Edition (1623)*	*Mac*	*Macbeth*
H5	*Henry V*	*MND*	*A Midsummer's Night Dream*

Chaucer

Abbreviate in parenthetical documentation as shown by these examples. Italicize the book but not the individual tales:

CkT	The Cook's Tale	NPT	The Nun's Priest's Tale
CT	*The Canterbury Tales*	PardT	The Pardoner's Tale

Other Literary Works

Wherever possible in your in-text citations, use the initial letters of the title. A reference to page 18 of Melville's *Moby-Dick: The White Whale* could appear as: (*MD* 18). Use the following italicized abbreviations as guidelines:

Aen.	*Aeneid* by Vergil	*Lys.*	*Lysistrata* by Aristophanes
Beo.	*Beowulf*	*Med.*	*Medea* by Euripides

Accent Marks

When you quote, reproduce accents exactly as they appear in the original. You may need to use the character sets embedded within the computer software. Write the mark in ink on the printout if your typewriter or word processor does not support the mark.

> "La tradición clásica en españa," according to Romana, remains strong and vibrant in public school instruction (16).

Acknowledgments

Generally, acknowledgments are unnecessary. Nor is a preface required. Use a superscript reference numeral to your first sentence and then place any obligatory acknowledgments or explanations in a content endnote (see pages 319-322). Acknowledge neither your instructor nor typist for help with your research paper, though such acknowledgments are standard with graduate theses and dissertations.

Ampersand

MLA Style

Avoid using the ampersand symbol "&" unless custom demands it (e.g., "A&P"). Use *and* for in-text citations in MLA style (e.g., Smith and Jones 213-14).

APA Style

Use "&" within citations (e.g., Spenser & Wilson, 2009, p. 73) but not in the text (Spenser and Wilson found the results in error.)

Annotated Bibliography

An annotation describes the essential details of a book or article. Place it just after the facts of publication. Provide enough information in about three sentences for a reader to have a fairly clear image of the work's purpose, contents, and special value. See pages 122-124 for a complete annotated bibliography.

Arabic Numerals

Both the MLA style and the APA style require Arabic numerals whenever possible: for volumes, books, parts, and chapters of works; acts, scenes, and lines of plays; cantos, stanzas, and lines of poetry.

Bible

Use parenthetical documentation for biblical references in the text (e.g., 2 Chron. 18.13). Do not italicize the books of the Bible. For abbreviations, see page 369.

Clip Art

Pictures, figures, and drawings are available on many computers, but avoid the temptation to embed them in your document. Clip art, in general, conveys an informal, sometimes comic effect, one that is inappropriate to the serious nature of most research papers.

Copyright Law

"Fair use" of the materials of others is permitted without the need for specific permission as long as your purpose is noncommercial for purposes of criticism, scholarship, or research. Under those circumstances, you can quote from sources and reproduce artistic works within reasonable limits. The law is vague on specific amounts that can be borrowed, suggesting only the "substantiality of the portion used in relation to the copyrighted work as a whole." In other words, you should be safe in reproducing the work of another as long as the portion is not substantial.

To protect your own work, keyboard in the upper right corner of your manuscript, "Copyright © 20___ by ___." (Fill the blanks with the proper year and your name.) Then, to register a work, order a form from the U.S. Copyright Office, Library of Congress, Washington, D.C. 20559.

Covers and Binders

Most instructors prefer that you submit manuscript pages with one staple in the upper left corner. Unless required, do not use a cover or binder.

Definitions

For definitions and translations within your text, use single quotation marks without intervening punctuation. For example:

The use of *et alii* 'and others' has diminished in scholarly writing.

Electronic Presentations

If you have the expertise, many instructors will allow you to submit the research paper in electronic form. See Chapter 18 for more information.

Endnotes for Documentation of Sources

An instructor or supervisor may prefer traditional superscript numerals within the text and documentation notes at the end of paper. If so, see Chapter 16, pages 318–322.

Footnotes for Documentation

If your instructor requires you to use footnotes, see Chapter 16, pages 312–318, for discussion and examples.

Fonts

Most computers offer a variety of typefaces. Use a nonserif typeface like Arial (**Arial**) or a serif typeface like Times Roman (**Times Roman**). Use the same font consistently throughout for your text. Use 12-point type size.

Foreign Cities

In general, spell the names of foreign cities as they are written in original sources. However, for purposes of clarity, you may substitute an English name or provide both with one in parentheses:

Köln (Cologne)   Braunschweig (Brunswick)
München (Munich)   Praha (Prague)

Foreign Languages

Italicize foreign words used in an English text:

> Like his friend Olaf, he is *aut Caesar, aut nihil,* either overpowering perfection or ruin and destruction.

Do not italicize quotations of a foreign language:

> Obviously, he uses it to exploit, in the words of Jean Laumon, "une admirable mine de themes poetiques."

Do not italicize foreign titles of magazine or journal articles, but *do* underline the names of the magazines or journals themselves:

> Arrigoitia, Luis de. "Machismo, folklore y creación en Mario Vargas Llosa." *Sin nombre* 13.4 (1983): 19–25.

Headings

Begin every major heading on a new page (title page, opening page, notes, appendix, Works Cited or references). Center the heading in capital and lowercase letters one inch from the top of the sheet. Use a doublespace between the heading and your first line of text. Number *all* text pages, including those with major headings.

Indention

Indent paragraphs five spaces or a half-inch. Indent long quotations (four lines or more) ten spaces or one inch from the left margin.

Italics

If your word-processing system and your printer can reproduce italic lettering, use it in place of *underscoring* if you prefer that style.

Margins

A one-inch margin on all sides of each page is recommended. Place your page number one-half inch down from the top edge of the paper and one inch from the right edge. Your software will provide a ruler, menu, or style palette that allows you to set the margins. *Tip*: If you develop a header, the running head may appear one inch from the top, in which case your first line of text will begin 1 1/2 inches from the top.

Names of Persons

As a general rule, the first mention of a person requires the full name (e.g., Ernest Hemingway, Margaret Mead) and thereafter requires only usage of the surname (e.g., Hemingway, Mead). *Note*: APA style uses last name only in the text. Omit formal titles (Mr., Mrs., Dr., Hon.) in textual and note references to distinguished persons, living or dead.

Numbering

Pagination

Use a header to number your pages in the upper right corner of the page. Depending on the software, you can create the head with the Numbering or Header feature. It may appear one-half inch or a full inch down from the top edge of the paper and one inch from the right edge. Precede the number with your last name unless anonymity is required, in which case you may use a shortened version of your title rather than your name, as in APA style (see page 302). Otherwise, type the heading and then double-space to your text.

Use lowercase Roman numerals (ii, iii, iv) on any pages that precede the main portion of your text. If you have a separate title page, count it as page i, but do not type it on the page. You *should* put a page number on your opening page of text, even if you include course identification (see page 222).

Paper

Print on one side of white bond paper, sixteen- or twenty-pound weight, 8 1/2 by 11 inches. Use the best-quality paper available; avoid erasable paper. Staple the pages of your manuscript together with one staple in the upper left corner. Do not enclose the manuscript within a cover or binder unless your instructor asks you to do so.

Proofreader Marks

Be familiar with the most common proofreading symbols so you can correct your own copy or mark your copy for a typist or keyboarder. Some of the most common proofreading symbols are shown next.

Common Proofreading Symbols

ι	error in spelling (m/stake) with correction in margin
lc	lowercase (mis Take)
⌒	close up (mis take)
ℐ	delete and close up (mis take)
⊢⊣	delete and close up more than one letter (the ~~mistakes and~~ errors continue)
∧	insert (mi^s take)
∽ (tr)	transpose elements (the if)
⟝⟞	material to be corrected or moved, with instructions in the margin, or material to be spelled out, (corp.)
caps or ≡	capitalize (Huck finn and Tom Sawyer)
¶	begin a paragraph
No¶	do not begin a paragraph
∧	insert
ℓ	delete (a mistakes)
#	add space
⊙	add a period
⌃	add a comma
⌃	add a semicolon
∨	add an apostrophe or single closing quotation mark
∨	add a single opening quotation mark
∨ ∨	add double quotation marks
(bf)	change to boldface
stet	let stand as it is; ignore marks

Roman Numerals

Use capital Roman numerals in titles of persons as appropriate (Elizabeth II) and major sections of an outline (see pages 146–151). Use lowercase Roman numerals to number the preliminary pages of a text or paper, as for a preface or introduction (iii, iv, v). Otherwise, use Arabic numerals (e.g., Vol. 5, Act 2, Ch. 17, Plate 21, 2 Sam. 2.1–8, or *Iliad* 2.121–30), *except* when writing for some instructors in history, philosophy, religion, music, art, and theater, in which case you may need to use Roman numerals (e.g., III, Act II, I Sam. ii.1–8, *Hamlet* I.ii.5–6).

Running Heads

Repeat your last name in the upper right corner of every page just in front of the page number (see the sample paper, pages 226–238). APA style differs, see page 302.

Short Titles in the Text

Use abbreviated titles of books and articles mentioned often in the text after a first full reference. For example, after initially citing *Backgrounds to English as Language*, shorten the title to *Backgrounds* in the text, notes, and in-text citations (see also pages 184–185), but not in the bibliography entry. Mention *The Epic of Gilgamesh* and thereafter use *Gilgamesh*. (*Note*: Be certain to italicize it when referring to the work.)

Slang

Avoid the use of slang. When using it in a language study, enclose in double quotation marks any words to which you direct attention. Words used as words, however, require italics.

Spacing

As a general rule, double-space the body of the paper, all indented quotations, and all reference entries. Footnotes, if used, should be single-spaced, but endnotes should be double-spaced (see pages 318–319). APA style (see Chapter 15) requires double-spacing after all headings and before and after indented quotes and figures.

Spelling

Spell accurately. Always use the computer to check spelling if the software is available. When in doubt, consult a dictionary. If the dictionary says a word may be spelled two ways, employ one way consistently (e.g., accessory *or* accessary).

Statistical and Mathematical Copy

Use the simplest form of equation that can be made by ordinary mathematical calculation. If an equation cannot be reproduced entirely by keyboard, type what you can and fill in the rest with ink on the printout. As a general rule, keep equations on one line rather than two:

$(a + b)/(x + y)$

APA style requires quadruple line spacing above and below an equation.

Theses and Dissertations

The author of a thesis or dissertation must satisfy the requirements of the college's graduate program. Therefore, even though you may use MLA style or APA style, you must abide by certain additional rules with regard to paper, typing, margins, and introductory matter such as title page, approval page, acknowledgment page, table of contents, abstract, and other matters. Use both the graduate school guidelines and this book to maintain the appropriate style and format.

Titles within Titles

For an article title within quotation marks that includes a book title, as indicated by italics, retain the italic lettering.

"*Great Expectations* as a Novel of Initiation"

For an article title within quotation marks that includes another title indicated by quotation marks, enclose the internal title within single quotation marks.

"A Reading of O. Henry's 'The Gift of the Magi' "

For an italicized book title that incorporates another title that is normally italicized, do not italicize the internal title nor place it within quotation marks.

Interpretations of Great Expectations

Using Shakespeare's Romeo and Juliet *in the Classroom*

Typing

Submit the paper in typed 12-point form. Use no hyphens at the ends of lines. Avoid widows and orphans, which are single lines at the top of a page and single words at the bottom of a paragraph, respectively; some computers will help you correct this problem. Use special features—boldface, italics, graphs, color—with discretion. Your writing, not your graphics, will earn the credits and the better grades. You are ultimately responsible for correct pagination and accuracy of the manuscript. See also Chapter 13, "Revising, Proofreading, and Formatting the Rough Draft," pages 213–221.

Underscoring (Italicizing)

Do not italicize sacred writings (Genesis, Old Testament); series (The New American Nation Series); editions (Variorum Edition of W. B. Yeats); societies (Victorian Society); courses (Greek Mythology); divisions of a work (preface, appendix, canto 3, scene 2); or descriptive phrases (Nixon's farewell address or Reagan's White House years).

Underscoring Individual Words for Emphasis

Italicizing words for emphasis is discouraged. A better alternative is to position the word in such a way as to accomplish the same purpose. For example:

Graphical emphasis: Perhaps an answer lies in *preventing* abuse, not in makeshift remedies after the fact.

Linguistic emphasis: Prevention of abuse is a better answer than makeshift remedies after the fact.

Some special words and symbols require italicizing.

- Species, genera, and varieties:

  Penstemon caespitosus subsp. *thompsoniae*

- Letters, words, and phrases cited as a linguistic sample:

  the letter *e* in the word *let*

- Letters used as statistical symbols and algebraic variables:

  trial n of the t test or $C(3, 14) = 9.432$

Word Division

Avoid dividing any word at the end of a line. Leave the line short rather than divide a word.

Finding Reference Works for Your General Topic

We have tried to make this list as user-friendly as possible, which will enable you to select rather quickly a few basic references from one of ten general categories. Three or four items from a list will be more than sufficient to launch your investigation. Each category has two lists:

1. *Library reference books and electronic databases.* The books will require you to make a trip to the library, but the academic databases can be accessed anywhere by logging into your library's network—from your dorm room, computer lab, or at the library itself.
2. *Reputable Internet sources accessed by a browser,* such as Google, Lycos, AltaVista, and others, as listed on pages 40–43.

Remember, too, that the library gives you an electronic catalog to all books in the library as well as access to general-interest databases, such as:

InfoTrac
FirstSearch
NewsBank
Lexis-Nexis Academic
netLibrary
Online Books Page
Oxford Reference Online

Here are the ten sections and the page number that begins each:

1. Historic Issues of Events, People, and Artifacts, page 377
2. Scientific Issues in Physics, Astronomy, and Engineering, page 378
3. Issues of Health, Fitness, and Athletics, page 379
4. Social and Political Issues, page 379
5. Issues in the Arts, Literature, Music, and Language, page 380
6. Environmental Issues, Genetics, and the Earth Sciences, page 380
7. Issues in Communication and Information Technology, page 381
8. Issues in Religion, Philosophy, and Psychology, page 382
9. Issues in Business and Economics, page 382
10. Popular Culture, Current Events, and Modern Trends, page 383

By no means are the ten lists definitive, but one of them should serve as your launching pad at the beginning of the project. These works will carry you deeper and deeper toward specific material for collecting your summaries, paraphrases, and quotations.

Historic Issues of Events, People, and Artifacts

If you are interested in events of the past, classical architecture, famous people, and ancient artifacts, you need sources in history, biography, art history, architecture, anthropology, and similar sources. Listed here are important reference works in the library and on the Internet that can launch your investigation.

At the library, investigate these books and academic databases:

Abstracts in Anthropology. Farmingdale: Baywood, 1970–date. This reference book gives brief descriptions of thousands of articles on the cultural development of human history.

American National Biography. 24 vols. New York: Oxford, 2002. This set of books is the place to start for a study of most historical figures in American history.

Dictionary of American History. 3rd ed. 10 vols. New York: Scribner's, 2003. This set of books offers a well-documented, scholarly source on the people, places, and events in U.S. history and includes brief bibliographies to recommended sources.

Historical Abstracts. Santa Barbara, CA: ABC-CLIO, 1955–date. This set of printed abstracts provides a quick overview of historical issues and events worldwide.

Illustrated Encyclopedia of Mankind. 22 vols. Freeport, NY: Marshall Cavendish, 2006. This massive work has been a standard in the field for some time.

Lexis-Nexis Primary Sources in U.S. History. This academic database is wide-ranging and gives, for example, excellent sources on American women's studies.

Recently Published Articles. Washington: American Historical Association, 1976–date. These printed volumes provide an effective index to articles in *American Historical Review, Journal of American History, Journal of the West,* and many others.

On the Internet, investigate these sites:

Annual Reviews: Anthropology, at http://arjournals.annualreviews.org/loi/anthro?cookieSet=1

Anthropology Internet Resources, at http://www.uflib.ufl.edu/cm/anthropology/internet.htm

Archiving Early America, at http://earlyamerica.com

History Best Information on the Net (BIOTN), at http://library.sau.edu/bestinfo/Majors/History/hisindex.htm

Scientific Issues in Physics, Astronomy, and Engineering

If you are interested in the heavens (the stars, moon, and planets), the laws of supersonic flight, nuclear energy, plasma television screens, and similar topics, you need to begin your investigation with some of the reference works listed here, which you will find in the library and on the Internet.

At the library, investigate these books and academic databases:

American Chemical Society Publications (ACS). This database offers searchable access to online archives of chemistry journals dating back to 1879.

Astronomy Encyclopedia. Ed. Patrick Moore. New York: Oxford UP, 2002. This source suggests possible topic ideas for research in the field; good starting point for students.

Applied Science and Technology Index. New York: Wilson, 1958–date. This major reference work indexes recent articles in all areas of the applied sciences, engineering, and technology.

Current Physics Index. New York: American Institute of Physics, 1975–date. This book indexes most articles in physics journals such as *Applied Physics, Journal of Chemical Physics, Nuclear Physics,* and *Physical Review.*

Engineering Index. New York: Engineering Index Inc., 1884–date. This work is available in versions ranging from books to electronic databases; check the academic library to locate which version is available locally.

General Science Index. New York: Wilson, 1978–date. This index covers about 100 science periodicals, including many in the applied sciences.

Physics Abstracts. Surrey, England: Institute of Electrical Engineers, 1898–date. Using keywords, this reference helps you choose a topic and find abstracts to articles on that topic.

On the Internet, investigate these sites:

American Astronomical Society, at http://www.aas.org

Planet Quest, at http://planetquest.jpl
.nasa.gov/

Mount Wilson Observatory, at http://www
.mtwilson.edu

National Academy of Sciences, at http:
//www.nas.edu

Physics World, at http://physicsworld
.com/cws/home

Issues of Health, Fitness, and Athletics

If you have an interest in sports medicine, jogging, dieting, good health, nutrition, and similar topics, you should begin your investigation with some of the reference works listed here, which you will find in the library and on the Internet.

At the library, investigate these books and academic databases:

Atlas of Human Anatomy. 4th ed. Frank H. Netter. Teterboro, NJ: ICON, 2006. This reference work contains wonderful illustrations of the human body, extensively labeled.

Consumer Health and Nutrition Index. Phoenix: Oryx, 1985–date. This reference work contains an index, published quarterly, to sources for consumers and scholars.

Cumulated Index Medicus. Bethesda, MD: U.S. Department of Health and Human Services, 1959–date. This reference work is an essential starting point for most papers in medical science.

Cumulated Index to Nursing and Allied Health Literature. Glendale, CA: CINAHL, 1956–date. This reference work offers nursing students an index to *Cancer Nurse, Journal of Practical Nursing, Journal of Nursing Education*, and many more journals; may be listed as *CINAHL*.

Encyclopedia of Human Nutrition. 4 vols. San Diego, CA: Academic, 2005. This reference

work offers a good starting point for a paper on nutrition.

Miller-Keane Encyclopedia and Dictionary of Medicine, Nursing, and Allied Health. 7th ed. Philadelphia: Saunders, 2005. This reference work offers practical applications as well as explanations of concepts and terminology. The reference is now offered in an electronic version also.

Physical Education Index. Cape Giradeau, MO: BenOak, 1978–date. This reference work indexes most topics in athletics, sports medicine, and athletics.

On the Internet, investigate these sites:

Healthfinder, at http://www.healthfinder
.gov

MedWeb Community Medical Libraries, at http://www.medweb.emory.edu/SPT--Home.php

National Institutes of Health, at http:
//www.nih.gov

PubMed, at http://www.ncbi.nlm.nih.gov
/PubMed

SIRC ~ Sports Information Research Centre, at http://www.sirc.ca/

Social and Political Issues

If you have an interest in social work at nursing homes, current events such as rap music or rave parties, congressional legislation on student loans, education, and the SAT examinations, gender issues, and similar topics, you should begin your investigation with some of the reference works listed here, which you will find in the library and on the Internet.

At the library, investigate these books and academic databases:

ABC: Pol Sci. Santa Barbara: ABC-CLIO, 1969–date. This reference work indexes the tables of contents of about 300 international journals in the original language.

CQ Researcher. This reference work provides access to a database containing documents covering hundreds of hot-topic issues such as abortion, child abuse, election reform, and civil liberties.

Education Index. New York: Wilson, 1929–date. This reference work indexes articles in such journals as *Childhood Education, Comparative Education, Education*

Digest, and *Journal of Educational Psychology*.

Encyclopedia of Sociology. Ed. Edgar F. Borgatta et al. 2nd ed. 5 vols. Detroit: Macmillan, 2000. This encyclopedia offers a starting point for research, giving you terms, issues, and theories to motivate your own ideas.

Social Sciences Index. New York: Wilson, 1974–date. This reference work provides a vital index to all aspects of topics in sociology, social work, education, political science, geography, and other fields.

Westlaw. This database contains federal and all state court cases and statutes (laws).

Women's Studies Index. Boston: Hall, 1989–date. This reference work offers an annual index considered by many librarians the best source for immediate information on women's issues.

On the Internet, investigate these sites:

Internet Legal Resources Guide, at http://www.ilrg.com/

Online Educational Resources, at http://quest.arc.nasa.gov/

Political Science Resources on the Web, at http://www.lib.umich.edu/govdocs/polisci.html

Thomas, at http://thomas.loc.gov

Issues in the Arts, Literature, Music, and Language

If you have an interest in Greek drama, the films of Mel Gibson, the postcolonial effects on languages in the Caribbean, the music of Andrew Lloyd Webber, the poetry of Dylan Thomas, and similar topics, you should begin your investigation with some of the reference works listed here, which you will find in the library and on the Internet.

At the library, investigate these books and academic databases:

Art Index. New York: Wilson, 1929–date. This reference work indexes most art journals, including *American Art Journal, Art Bulletin*, and *Artforum*.

Avery Index to Architectural Periodicals. Boston: Hall, 1973–date. This reference work is a good source for periodical articles on ancient and modern edifices.

Bibliographic Guide to Art and Architecture. Boston: Hall, 1977–date. Published annually, this reference work provides bibliographies on most topics in art and architecture—an excellent place to begin research in this area.

Bibliographic Guide to Music. Boston: Hall, 1976–date. This reference work provides an excellent subject index to almost every topic in the field of music and gives the bibliographic data for several articles on most topics in the field.

Contemporary Literary Criticism (CLC). This database provides an extensive collection of full-text critical essays about novelists, poets, playwrights, short story writers, and other creative writers who are now living or who died after December 31, 1959.

Humanities Index. New York: Wilson, 1974–date. This reference work indexes all of the major literary magazines and journals; it may be listed as *Wilson Humanities Index*.

Music Index. Warren, MI: Information Coordinators, 1949–date. This reference work indexes music journals such as *American Music Teacher, Choral Journal, Journal of Band Research*, and *Journal of Music Therapy*.

On the Internet, investigate these sites:

The English Server, at http://eserver.org/

Project Gutenberg, at http://promo.net/pg

Voice of the Shuttle: Art and Art History, at http://vos.ucsb.edu/

World Wide Arts Resources, at http://wwar.com

Worldwide Internet Music Resources, at http://library.music.indiana.edu/music_resources/

Environmental Issues, Genetics, and the Earth Sciences

If you have an interest in cloning, abortion, the shrinking rain forest in Brazil, sinkholes in Florida, the Flint Hills grassland of Kansas, underground water tables in Texas, and similar topics, you should begin your investigation with some of the reference works listed here, which you will find in the library and on the Internet.

At the library, investigate these books and academic databases:

AGRICOLA. This database, produced by the National Agricultural Library, provides access to articles, books, and Web sites in agriculture, animal and plant sciences, forestry, and soil and water resources.

Bibliography and Index of Geology. Alexandria, VA: American Geological Institute, 1933–date. Organized monthly, with annual indexes, this reference work indexes excellent scholarly articles.

Biological and Agricultural Index. New York: H.W. Wilson. 1916–date. This reference work is a standard index to periodicals in the field.

Biological Abstracts. Philadelphia: Biosis, 1926–date. This reference work contains abstracts useful to review before locating the full articles at the library's computer.

Ecological Abstracts. Norwich, UK: Geo Abstracts, 1974–date. This reference work offers a chance to examine the brief abstract before finding and reading the complete article.

The Environmental Index. Ann Arbor, MI: UMI, 1992–date. This reference work indexes numerous journals in the field, including *Environment, Environmental Ethics*, and *Journal of Applied Ecology.*

Geographical Abstracts. Norwich, UK: Geo Abstracts, 1972–date. This reference work provides a quick overview of articles that can be searched for full text later.

On the Internet, investigate these sites:

The Academy of Natural Sciences, at http://www.ansp.org

AGRICOLA, at http://agricola.nal.usda.gov

Biology Online, at http://www.biology-online.org/

BIOSIS, at http://www.biosis.org/

Envirolink, at http://envirolink.org

Issues in Communication and Information Technology

If you have an interest in talk radio, television programming for children, bias in print journalism, developing computer software, the glut of cell phones, and similar topics, you should begin your investigation with some of the reference works listed here, which you will find in the library and on the Internet.

At the library, investigate these books and academic databases:

Computer Abstracts. London: Technical Information, 1957–date. This work provides short descriptions of important articles in the field.

Computer Literature Index. Phoenix: ACR, 1971–date. This index identifies articles on computer science in a timely fashion, with periodic updates.

Encyclopedia of Computer Science and Technology. Ed. J. Belzer. 22 vols. New York: Dekker, 1975–91. Supplement 1991–date. This reference work provides a comprehensive source for launching computer investigations.

Information Technology Research, Innovation, and E-Government. Washington, DC: National Press Academy, 2002. This site focuses on the use of the Internet in government administration.

The Elements of Style. William Strunk, Jr., and E. B. White. Boston: Allyn and Bacon, 1999. A classic book that teaches and exhorts writers to avoid needless words, urges them to use the active voice, and calls for simplicity in style.

On Writing Well. 25th anniversary ed. William K. Zinsser. New York: HarperResource, 2001. This book is a well-written text on the art of writing, especially on the best elements of nonfiction prose.

Style: Ten Lessons in Clarity and Grace. 8th ed. Joseph M. Williams. New York: Longman, 2004. This book provides an excellent discussion of writing style and the means to attain it.

On the Internet, investigate these sites:

Computer Science, at http://library.albany.edu/subject/csci.htm

Information Technology Association of America, at http://www.itaa.org/index.cfm

Journalism and Mass Communication Resources on the Web, at http://www.lib.iastate.edu/collections/eresourc/journalism.html

Society for Technical Communication, http://www.stc.org/pubs/techcomm General01.asp

Virtual Computer Library, at http://www.utexas.edu/computer/vcl/

Issues in Religion, Philosophy, and Psychology

If you have an interest in human values, moral self-discipline, the ethics of religious wars, the power of religious cults, the behavior of children with single parents, the effect of the environment on personality, and similar topics, you should begin your investigation with some of the reference works listed here, which you will find in the library and on the Internet.

At the library, investigate these books and academic databases:

Cambridge Dictionary of Philosophy. 2nd ed. Ed. R. Audi. New York: Cambridge, 1999. This reference work provides an excellent base for launching your investigation into philosophical issues.

Encyclopedia of Psychology. Ed. Alan E. Kazdin. 8 vols. New York: Oxford, 2000. This reference work contains the most comprehensive basic reference work in the field; published under the auspices of the American Psychological Association.

Humanities Index. New York: Wilson, 1974–date. This reference work indexes religious journals such as *Church History, Harvard Theological Review,* and *Muslim World*.

Philosopher's Index: A Retrospective Index. Bowling Green, OH: Bowling Green U, 1967–date. This reference work indexes philosophy articles in journals such as *American Philosophical Quarterly, Humanist, Journal of the History of Ideas,* and *Journal of Philosophy*.

Psychological Abstracts. Washington, DC: APA, 1927–date. This reference work provides brief abstracts to articles in such psychology journals as *American Journal of Psychology, Behavioral Science,* and *Psychological Review*. On the library's network, look for *PsycINFO*.

Religion: Index One: Periodicals, Religion and Theological Abstracts. Chicago: ATLA, 1949–date. This reference work indexes religious articles in such journals as *Biblical Research, Christian Scholar, Commonweal,* and *Harvard Theological Review*.

Routledge Encyclopedia of Philosophy. 10 vols. Ed. E. Craig. New York: Routledge, 1999. This work is the most comprehensive, authoritative, and up-to-date reference work in the field. A condensed version is available in some libraries.

On the Internet, investigate these sites:

The American Philosophical Association, at http://www.amphilsoc.org/

Episteme Links: Philosophy Resources on the Internet, at http://www.epistemelinks.com/

Humanities: Religion Gateway, at http://www.academicinfo.net/religindex.html

Subject Resources for Psychology, at http://www.libraries.psu.edu/ebsl/std/stdpsych.htm

Vanderbilt Divinity School, at http://divinity.library.vanderbilt.edu/

Issues in Business and Economics

If you wish to write about the impact of rising tuition costs, the effect of credit cards for college students, the marketing success of Wal-Mart stores, the economic impact of federal tax cuts, the stock market's effect on accounting practices, and similar topics, you should begin your investigation with some of the reference works listed here, which you will find in the library and on the Internet.

At the library, investigate these books and academic databases:

Business Abstracts. New York: Wilson, 1995-date. This reference work provides short descriptions of business, economic, and marketing articles.

Business Periodicals Index. New York: Wilson, 1958-date. This reference work indexes most journals in the field, such as *Business Quarterly, Business Week, Fortune*, and *Journal of Business*. See also on the library's network *Reference USA, Business Dateline*, and *Business and Company*.

Business Publications Index and Abstracts. Detroit: Gale, 1983-date. This reference work provides a place to launch searches on almost any topic related to business.

General Business File. This database lists citations and summaries of articles and the entire text of some articles in business, management, and economic periodicals.

Index of Economic Articles. Nashville: American Economic Association, 1886-date.

This reference work, arranged as both a topic and an author index, provides a good start for the student and professional alike.

Journal of Economic Literature. Nashville: American Economic Association, 1886-date. This reference work offers articles followed by bibliographies for further research.

World Economic Survey. 1945-date. An annual publication originally from the League of Nations and currently from the United Nations, this reference work offers varying topics each year to researchers.

On the Internet, investigate these sites:

All Business Network, at http://www.allbiz.com

Finance: The World Wide Web Virtual Library, at http://fisher.osu.edu/fin/overvw.htm

FinWeb, at http://www.finweb.com

International Resources in Business Economics, at http://www.lib.berkeley.edu/BUSI/bbg18.html

Popular Culture, Current Events, and Modern Trends

If you are interested in current events and popular culture as well as modern trends, consult sources that provide recent facts and details about famous people, developments in society, and changes in human customs. Listed here are important reference works in the library and on the Internet that can launch your investigation.

At the library, investigate these books and academic databases:

American National Biography. 24 vols. New York: Oxford, 1999. This set of books provides the place to start for a study of most historical figures in American history.

CQ Researcher. This reference works provides access to a database containing documents covering hundreds of "hot topic" issues such as abortion, child abuse, election reform, or civil liberties.

Illustrated Encyclopedia of Mankind. 22 vols. Freeport, NY: Marshall Cavendish, 1989. This massive work has been a standard in the field for some time.

NewsBank. NewsBank provides searchable full text articles appearing in local publications.

Recently Published Articles. Washington: American Historical Association, 1976-

date. These printed volumes provide an effective index to articles in *American Historical Review, Journal of American History, Journal of the West*, and many others.

On the Internet, investigate these sites:

Freedom Center, at http://www.horowitzfreedomcenter.org/

Gallup Organization, at http://www.gallup.com

The Internet Movie Database, at http://www.imdb.com

Multi-Channel News, at http://www.multichannel.com

Popular Culture: Resources for Critical Analysis, at http://www.wsu.edu/~amerstu/pop/

Credits

Ch. 4, page 49 From "Drug Education," an article on the United States Olympic Committee Web site, www.usoc.org. Reprinted by permission. Ch. 4, Figure 4.5, page 53 Home page of *Larchmont Chronicle*, www.larchmontchronicle.com. Used by permission. Ch. 4, Figure 4.6, page 57 Book search results for "Fad Dieting" from Barnes & Noble.com. Reprinted by permission of Barnes & Noble (www.bn.com). Jacket cover, from *The South Beach Diet* by Arthur Agatston used courtesy of St. Martin's Press. Jacket cover, from *No-Fad Diet: A Personal Plan for Healthy Weight Loss* by American Heart Association, used by permission of Clarkson Potter/Publishers, a division of Random House, Inc. Ch. 4, Figure 4.7, page 59 Red Earth museum page from www.redearth.org/museum.htm. © 2006. Reprinted by permission. Ch. 5, Figure 5.1, page 65 Entry "Prehistoric War, Le Blanc, Steven, Constant Battles" from *Bibliographic Index*. Copyright © 2003 by H. W. Wilson Company. Reproduced by permission of the publisher. Ch. 5, Figure 5.2, page 66 From *Subject Guide to Books In Print 2005*. Copyright © 2005 by R. R. Bowker, LLC. Ch. 5, Figure 5.3, page 68 Sample bibliography from the end of an article in *Encyclopedia of Psychology*, Second Edition, Vol. 1, p.287, edited by Raymond J. Corsini, John Wiley & Sons. Ch. 5, Figure 5.4, page 68 From *Out of the Storm: The End of the Civil War* by Noah Andre Trudeau. Copyright © 1994 by Noah Andre Trudeau. Reprinted with permission of Little, Brown and Company. Ch. 5, Figure 5.5, page 69 From abstract in *The Journal of Nutrition*, January 2006, 136:277S-280S. As seen on InfoTrac, Farmington Hills, Michigan: Gale Group, 2002. Ch. 5, page 70 Bakersfield College Library home page used by permission. Ch. 5, page 71 Search results for keywords "gender and communication" on EBSCO Host. Used by permission. Ch. 5, page 71 From "Why Are Women So Strange and Men So Weird?" by Christopher Bruce from *Business Credit*, February 2008, Vol. 110, Issue 2. Used by permission. Ch. 5, Figure 5.6, page 74 "Vehicles of desistance?" a sample entry on EBSCO Host. Used by permission. Ch. 5, Figure 5.7, page 75 ProQuest Basic Search Interface and ProQuest Advanced Interface is produced by ProQuest LLC. Inquiries may be made to ProQuest LLC, 789 Eisenhower Parkway, Ann Arbor, MI 48108. Telephone (734) 761-4700; E-mail: info@proquest.com; Web page: www.proquest.com. Ch. 5, Figure 5.8, page 76 ProQuest Basic Search Interface and ProQuest Advanced Interface is produced by ProQuest LLC. Inquiries may be made to ProQuest LLC, 789 Eisenhower Parkway, Ann Arbor, MI 48108. Telephone (734) 761-4700; E-mail: info@proquest.com; Web page: www.proquest.com. Ch. 5, Figure 5.9, page 77 "Clinton, Hillary Rodham" from *Biography Index*. Copyright © 2008 by The W. H. Wilson Company. Reproduced with permission of the publisher. Ch. 5, Figure 5.10, page 79 "The Irony of Climate" by Brian Halweil, from *World Watch Magazine*, March/April 2005, www.worldwatch.org. Used by permission of the Worldwatch Institute. Ch. 8, page 109 From *Journal of World History*, Vol. 18, No. 4, December 2007. Used by permission of the University of Hawaii Press. Ch. 8, Figure 8.1, page 117 From "The Classroom Outside" by Jason Mark in *Earth Island Journal*, Vol. 22, No. 4, 2008. Used by permission. Ch. 8, page 118 Excerpts from *Oscar Wilde* by Richard Ellman. Vintage Books, 1988. Reprinted by permission of Alfred A. Knopf, a division of Random House, Inc. Ch. 8, Figure 8.2, page 119 Reprinted with permission from *Issues in Science and Technology*, Workman "How to Fix Our Dam Problems," Fall 2007, pp. 31–42, Copyright © 2007 by the University of Texas at Dallas, Richardson, TX. Ch. 9, page 137 From "The Love Song of J. Alfred Prufrock" in *Collected Shorter Poems 1909-1962* by T. S. Eliot. Reprinted by permission of Faber and Faber Ltd. Ch. 10, Figure 10.3, page 165 Line graph from "Cognitive Aspects of Psychomotor Performance" by Edwin A. Locke and Judith F. Bryan from *Journal of Applied Psychology*, Vol. 50, 1966. Copyright © 1966 by the American Psychological Association. Reprinted by permission of the author. Ch. 11, page 174 From "Parenthood" by Karen S. Peterson, *USA Today*, September 19, 1990. Ch. 11, Figure 11.1, page 175 Sample pages from JSTOR database, "Shakespeare's Conception of Hamlet" from *PMLA*, Vol. 48, No. 3, pp. 777-8. Reprinted by permission of the Modern Language Association. Ch. 11, page 177 "The Red Wheelbarrow" by William Carlos Williams from *Collected Poems: 1909-1939, Volume 1*. Copyright 1938 by New Directions Publishing Corp. Reprinted by permission of New Directions Publishing Corporation and Carcanet Press Limited. Ch. 11, page 186 First three lines from "Morning Song" from *Ariel* by Sylvia Plath. Copyright © 1961 by Ted Hughes. Reprinted by permission of HarperCollins Publishers Inc. and by Faber and Faber Ltd. Ch. 13, page 228 "Rules for Fantastic Communication" adapted from *What Every Family Needs* by Carl Brecheen and Paul Faulkner, Gospel Advocate, 1994. Used by permission.

384

Index

Note: Page number followed by the letter *f* indicates figures.

385